HOW IT ALL STARTED

HOW STA

THE HISTORY BEHIND THI

FOREWORD BY ASA BRIGGS

IT ALL

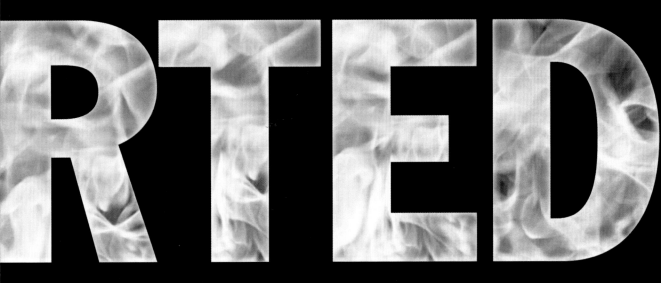

RTED

WAY OUR WORLD WORKS TODAY

Published by The Reader's Digest Association Limited
London • New York • Sydney • Montreal

1 NATIONS AND CITIES

The boundaries of countries and the locations of cities seem permanent and immovable. But in fact they are anything but. A series of quirks and accidents have often dictated the shape of our nations and forged their political complexion.

8-51

2 EATING AND DRINKING

Where do some of our most popular foods and drinks come from and why do we prepare and cook them in the way we do? What determined the order that we eat different courses and when did people first start eating outside the home and on the move?

52-81

3 GREATEST SHOW ON EARTH

Humans have played at sport, music and drama since ancient times. But how did the rules of those sports come to be and how were the number of players decided? What set of circumstances dictated the acts in a circus or the instruments in an orchestra?

82-125

4 RELIGION AND IDEAS

How did the world's major religions come to be organised in the way that they are? Why does faith seem to be allied to geography? How did some of the modern era's core beliefs, such as democracy, psychology and political correctness, originate?

126-171

5 DISCOVERY AND CHANGE

When and how did humans move from Africa to dominate the globe? Why have we conquered some diseases while others have spread? When did technology first allow information to be sent through cyberspace and how has it changed our world?

172-207

6 LIVING AND WORKING

People didn't always work a full day, use timetables, adhere to traffic systems and exchange money rather than goods. But they do now. When did it start? And why do we plant gardens for pleasure and build ever higher into the sky?

208-241

7 WHY DO THEY DO IT LIKE THAT?

Why do we wear our clothes and hair as we do? Why do we eat certain animals and not others? Why do we have such strange rules of etiquette? And why are do we still subscribe to beliefs that have no basis in fact, such as horoscopes and superstitions?

242-277

8 WAR AND PEACE

How did the era of the nuclear superpowers arise? Who invented the submarine? Why does the military wear uniforms? What has allowed western Europe an unprecedented 60 years of peace? When was propaganda first used to control the flow of information?

278-313

'LIBERTY LEADING THE PEOPLE' BY EUGÈNE DELACROIX (1830) CELEBRATES PARISIANS TAKING ARMS UNDER THE REVOLUTIONARY TRICOLOR.

Foreword by Asa Briggs

The distinguished historian Asa Briggs has written widely about Victorian society and 20th-century broadcasting, among other topics. He has been consultant editor on many successful Reader's Digest books over the years. Lord Briggs was made a life member of the House of Lords in 1976.

It is always interesting to look back to the beginning of things. As this beautifully illustrated book reveals, they often take us back far across the centuries, to what we call the ancient world. The endings of things are more complicated. History goes on. As we look ahead we know that, as in the past, there are surprises to come.

The book is divided into eight chapters. They do not aim to be comprehensive. The subjects covered in them were chosen because there is no immediately obvious explanation as to why we have ended up in the present with the particular situation and circumstances that we find ourselves in today. Each section in each chapter asks at least one central question. The fascination of history is that usually there is more than one answer.

We begin not with words but with lines on the world's map. We end with 'everything but the truth'. Why do so many answers mislead us? Having finished the book we should by then be in a position to judge.

Deliberately the book deals with little things as well as with big things. Chapter 7, 'Why do they do it like that?', which deals with customs and conventions, is followed by the last chapter, 'War and peace'. War or peace is perhaps the biggest question that we all ask, but now the fate of the planet raises questions of environmental control by human beings which may be even bigger.

Throughout the book the illustrations, as carefully chosen as the themes they illustrate, are an integral part of the text. So, too, are the inset boxes which explore in detail aspects of the general text. The book as a whole sets out to entertain as well as to inform, and entertainment, which now can be big business, is the theme of Chapter 3, which has been given the evocative title of 'The greatest show on Earth'.

What happens both to information and entertainment in the digital age of the internet? Does its arrival mark a major break in human history? We will live through the answers to these questions, 'eating and drinking' as we must (the theme of Chapter 2) but (maybe) watching more carefully just what we are eating and drinking. What are the restraints on human choice? What are our expectations and opportunities? *How It All Started* takes us to the heart of the matter.

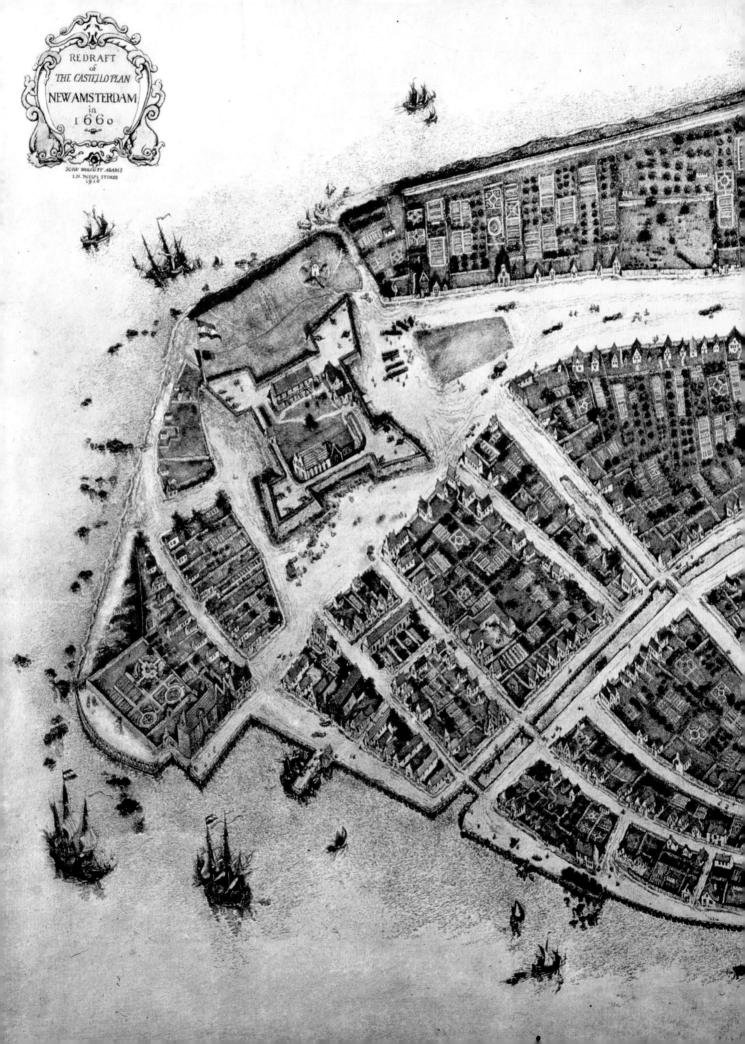

REDRAFT
of
THE CASTELLO PLAN
NEW AMSTERDAM
in
1660

JOHN WOLCOTT ADAMS
I.N. PHELPS STOKES
1916

NATIONS AND CITIES 1

Lines on the map Often national boundaries take no account of natural barriers or ethnic divisions. So who decides where the borders between countries are drawn?

On 6 May 1998, a group of Eritrean soldiers approached the town of Badame, located on an arid plain on the nation's disputed border with Ethiopia. Local police and militia defending the outskirts were quickly routed, and the Eritreans duly took possession of the settlement, whose 1,500 inhabitants scratched a living from growing sorghum and raising livestock. Following the takeover, Ethiopia responded by mobilising its armed forces, and soon the two nations were at war. By the time the conflict ended two years later, 70,000 people were dead and the economies of both countries were in ruins.

The Ethiopian-Eritrean War graphically demonstrates the importance of well-defined borders. The American poet Robert Frost once wrote that 'Good fences make good neighbours', and the principle holds true on a magnified scale for the frontiers between nations. But what exactly makes a border, and who decides where they should go?

Creating barriers

Some borders are unmissable. Fortified examples, some of them dating back to early in recorded history, are among the world's most prominent man-made features. The Great Wall of China was built to defend the emperor's lands from the mounted tribesmen – regarded as barbarians by the Chinese – who roamed the territory to the north of the Middle Kingdom. Constructed over more than two millennia, the barrier eventually stretched for around 6,500km (4,000 miles) from the Yellow Sea east of Beijing to Lop Nur in the Xinjiang region of central Asia.

When originally built, it was guarded by watchtowers 12m (40ft) high, erected every few hundred metres along its length. Barracks for the troops who garrisoned the wall were located at greater intervals. The guardhouses were positioned two

arrow-lengths apart, so that no point on the wall was beyond the range of a sentry with a crossbow.

Later rulers constructed fortified boundaries in far-flung lands. Britain has two examples: the wall that Emperor Hadrian had built to defend the northern reaches of the Roman Empire, and the earthen dyke constructed for Mercia's King Offa in the 8th century AD to keep Welsh tribesmen out of his Anglo-Saxon realm. In the modern era, the Berlin Wall separated Soviet and Western sections of the divided German capital; fortifications likewise ran along the entire frontier between East and West Germany during the Cold War, stretching for almost 1,400km (865 miles) from the Baltic Sea to the Czech frontier. A similar arrangement has long divided Communist North Korea from democratic South Korea, while the US government is considering the erection of a separation barrier along much of the nation's 3,200-km (2,000-mile) border with Mexico.

Fortified borders

The longest manned fortified border is the berm (sand wall) built in the 1980s, stretching for roughly 2,000km (1,240 miles) down the length of Western Sahara, a sparsely populated land on Africa's west coast. It protects territory claimed by Morocco as their Southern Provinces from the desert regions roamed by the camel-borne guerrillas of the Polisario Liberation Front.

For all their brutal obtrusiveness, fortified borders have the advantage of being unambiguous. In early times the boundaries between tribal areas were often unmarked, and the outcome was frequently war. Eventually, one group would establish the right to claim possession of a specific territory, whose boundaries would be defined by easily recognised landmarks – either natural features like rivers or mountain ranges or, if necessary, man-made markers such as pillars or boundary stones. Borders that were not clearly marked had a tendency to develop into dangerous no-man's-lands. One such was the

IMPERIAL BARRIER China's Great Wall began as separate barriers, built by individual states. When, in 221 BC, the states were unified under one emperor, he ordered the walls to be joined up and additional sections built.

WALL OF SAND The barrier that divides Western Sahara (seen left on a satellite image within the dotted lines) is just 3m (10ft) high and built of sand and stone. It is heavily defended with bunkers, fences and landmines.

chiefs, sometimes extorted under duress. The Congo Pedicle, a narrow neck of land extending southwards from the Democratic Republic of the Congo that cuts deep into central Zambia, was a case in point. It was created after mercenaries in the service of King Leopold II of Belgium seized the mineral-rich province of Katanga, killing and then decapitating its former African ruler Msiri in 1891. By this act of violence the Congo Free State, ruled

frontier between England and Scotland, a disputed region fought over for centuries by rival bands of *reivers* (local dialect for 'raiders'), also known from their armoured headgear as 'steel bonnets'. There was a word for such disputed territories – marches – and the first marquises were noblemen appointed by kings to keep order within them. The appointees were not always loyal to their feudal seigneurs; one lord of the Welsh marches, when asked if the king's writ ran in his lands, supposedly replied, 'It runs as fast as any hare if my men are after it.'

Border conflicts between neighbouring states have been the single most common cause of wars in world history. From early times, the terms on which the contenders settled their differences were spelled out in treaties. These documents had vital importance as reference points in case of future disputes, so great care was taken to preserve them. One of the earliest to have survived was negotiated between Egypt's Pharaoh Ramses II and the Hittite King Hattusilis III around 1280 BC. The

two rulers not only had the terms recorded on papyrus and clay tablets but inscribed on a sheet of silver. Ramses also had the clauses engraved on the wall of the great temple he was building at Karnak on the Nile, where they can still be seen today.

Imposed borders

In more recent times, borders have sometimes been imposed by external powers on foreign lands, often with scant regard for local ethnic and linguistic boundaries. Much of Africa still suffers from the opening up of the continent from the 1870s by rival imperialist countries engaged in the 'Scramble for Africa'. Imperial administrators divided the continent into largely synthetic 'nations', often cutting across tribal and cultural boundaries as they did so.

The colonial borders were generally marked out by boundary commissioners who took their remit from diplomats and bureaucrats with little or no knowledge of local conditions. They in turn negotiated settlements on the basis of dubious treaties with local

The Congo Pedicle

Just 100km wide and 200km long (60x120 miles), the Congo Pedicle (circled) was created in 1894 by Belgian and British signatories to the Anglo-Congolese Treaty. Africans were not consulted during the imperialist squabble for ownership of the mineral-rich land.

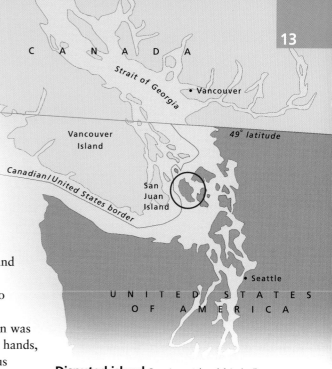

at the time as a Belgian protectorate, found itself in a position to assert sovereignty over the Pedicle in face of counter-claims by Cecil Rhodes' British South Africa Company, which at the time was extending its grip northwards into the land that would eventually become Zambia. The Pedicle survives to this day as a reminder of the illogicality of frontiers shaped by imperial ambition and chance.

Borders of convenience

Sometimes borders were adjusted by the colonial powers for simple administrative convenience. In 1902 the British government, which controlled both Egypt and the Sudan at the time, chose to switch a wedge of land on the Red Sea coast that had previously been considered a part of Egypt to the jurisdiction of the Sudanese capital, Khartoum, which was geographically closer. With the coming of independence both nations laid claim to the area, known as the Hala'ib Triangle. The discovery of potential oil reserves in the territory, which is over 20,000km² (7,700sq miles), has meant that the issue currently remains unresolved.

South America suffered similar treatment under Spanish rule from the early 16th century. Lingering uncertainties over borderlines in the coastal Atacama Desert sparked the four-year War of the Pacific between Chile, Peru and Bolivia in 1879. At the end of the conflict Bolivia found itself landlocked, having lost the war and with it its access to the sea.

For the most part, happier results were achieved when international borders were settled by negotiation. One such case occurred in the early 19th century, when the recently independent USA set out to define its frontier with the Canadian lands to the north that had remained loyal to Britain in the course of the Revolutionary War. In 1818, the two

powers signed a convention establishing the demarcation line between their respective territories westwards from the Lake of the Woods, today on the Ontario-Minnesota border, along the 49th parallel. Initially, the agreement only stretched as far as the Rocky Mountains; the land beyond, little explored at the time, was jointly assigned to both nations.

At the time the affected region was still largely in Native American hands, and the wishes of the indigenous inhabitants were not taken into account. By 1844, settlers on both sides of the line had driven westwards, and the issue of sovereignty over the lands beyond the Rockies, known at the time as the Oregon Territory, suddenly became a hot issue. US expansionists coined the slogan 'Fifty Four Forty or Fight!' to express their demand for all the land north to that degree of latitude – a claim that, if successful, would have given the USA roughly half of the present-day Canadian province of British Columbia. In fact, the dispute was settled diplomatically when both parties agreed to extend the 49th parallel borderline all the way to the Pacific coast. Offshore Vancouver Island, whose southern-most tip extended south of the parallel, was awarded in its entirety to the British sphere. One strange anomaly of the decision was the inclusion of Point Roberts, lying at the tip of a mainland peninsula south of what was to become the Canadian city of Vancouver, within US territory. Today this exclave, barely 12km² (5 sq miles) in extent and with no land link to the rest of the USA, is administratively part of the US state of Washington. Although war was averted by the

> **US expansionists coined the slogan 'Fifty Four Forty or Fight!'**

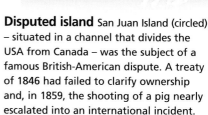

Disputed island San Juan Island (circled) – situated in a channel that divides the USA from Canada – was the subject of a famous British-American dispute. A treaty of 1846 had failed to clarify ownership and, in 1859, the shooting of a pig nearly escalated into an international incident.

compromise, disputes continued to arise, encouraged by the ambiguities that plague all but the most precise border agreements.

The Pig War

One such ambiguity, in 1859, led to a confrontation between the USA and Britain that has gone down in history as the Pig War. The cause was an incident involving two settlers on San Juan Island, one of a group in the middle of the strait separating British-owned Vancouver Island from the US mainland. Questions over whose jurisdiction ran on the island came to a head when a US resident shot a pig that was rooting in his garden. The animal, it turned out, belonged to a British employee of the Hudson's Bay Company, and nationals on both sides looked for protection to their respective governments. Before long the US authorities had dispatched 460 troops to the island to protect their citizens' rights, and the British had responded by sending a fleet of five warships to uphold the imperial cause. Fortunately, wise counsel prevailed

CUT OFF FROM THE CITY Israel's concrete Separation Wall, built to provide security against terror attacks, divides the Palestinian village of Abu Dis on the West Bank from East Jerusalem.

and the guns remained silent. After negotiations, the island was temporarily placed under joint military occupation. The issue of sovereignty over the island was referred for arbitration to Kaiser Wilhelm I of Germany, a neutral observer. In 1872 he decided in favour of the USA, and the question was settled peacefully with no casualties other than the pig.

A more significant example of third-party arbitration occurred following Christopher Columbus's first voyage to America in 1492. Columbus sailed under the Spanish flag, although most of the earlier exploratory voyages had been commissioned by the Portuguese crown. His discoveries raised the question of suzerainty over the new-found lands. To legitimise their claims,

Spain's rulers looked to the Pope, Alexander VI, who duly granted them exclusive possession of all non-Christian lands west of a line drawn 100 leagues (*c.*300 miles) beyond the Azores and Cape Verde Islands. The Portuguese contested the decision, and the matter went to negotiation. The 1494 Treaty of Tordesillas, moved the line 270 leagues further west. The adjustment proved crucially important when mariners charted the South American coast in the next decade, for the region that was to become Brazil

extended east of the new line. As a result, Brazil became a Portuguese colony for more than three centuries, and its people still speak Portuguese rather than Spanish.

Ongoing disputes

In the 21st century, the United Nations seeks to offer options for peacefully negotiated settlements for areas in dispute. There are currently almost 200 disputed territories around the world, from flashpoints like the Golan Heights (claimed by both Syria and Israel) to remote desert regions and islands. A recent estimate is that 100 million people live in areas claimed by more than one country.

The epilogue to the Ethiopian-Eritrean War suggests just how hard border conflicts can be to resolve. Once a ceasefire was arranged, a UN peacekeeping force was sent to monitor it. The dispute that caused the conflict was referred to the Permanent Court of Arbitration in the Dutch city of The Hague. The court established a boundary commission to look into the problem, and both sides promised to accept its verdict. Yet when the commissioners presented their findings in 2002, Ethiopia quickly expressed a number of reservations. Today, both countries have remobilised their forces along the frontier and the UN force is still in place to keep them apart. Although the guns may no longer be firing, permanent peace between the two nations still seems a long way off.

The man who partitioned India

In the aftermath of the Second World War, it became clear that the British Government would have to grant India its independence. In 1947, the new Viceroy, Lord Louis Mountbatten, concluded that it would be impossible to find an agreement between the various parties, in particular the Hindu-dominated Indian National Congress and the Muslim League. In July 1947, he set a deadline of 15 August for the completion of the decolonisation process. The man appointed to decide where the border between the two new states of India and Pakistan would run was a distinguished London barrister named Cyril Radcliffe.

Radcliffe's task was daunting. The boundary question had scarcely been addressed. He had just six weeks to

settle it. Two commissions were set up: one for Bengal, in the northeast, and one for Punjab in the northwest. Each had four South Asian judges, two each chosen respectively by the Congress and the Muslim League. Their political bias produced deadlock and Radcliffe had to make the most difficult decisions himself. The maps and censuses he was given to work from were out of date and the brevity of the timescale meant he could not visit any of the disputed areas. Many communities were fractured from their industries and infrastructure, but Radcliffe did what he was asked. He dissected the sub-continent as best he could. But though he created two new nations, tens of millions of people became foreigners in their own land.

Antarctica – everyman's and no man's land

The world's most southerly continent is claimed in part by many nations and settled by none except the odd hardy scientist. The pristine icy wilderness is governed by a brief, but effective treaty that commits its signatories to an agreement that Antarctica will never become the scene or object of international conflict.

Antarctica's extreme isolation and climate kept humans at bay until the early 20th century. When improved technology allowed greater access in the mid-20th century, there was a gradual influx of scientific researchers and a number of permanent stations were established. In 1957-58, 12 nations (Argentina, Australia, Belgium, Chile, France, Japan, New Zealand, Norway, South Africa, the UK, USA and the then USSR) took part in an international research programme, the International Geophysical Year (IGY). But by this point, several countries had started to assert territorial claims that threatened the future of peaceful scientific cooperation.

Although nine of the countries involved had made or reserved the right to make territorial claims in Antarctica, the success of the IGY led those who had taken part to agree that their political differences should not be allowed to affect future research. The result was the Antarctic Treaty, signed by the IGY countries on 1 December 1959, a wholehearted commitment to peaceful scientific cooperation and consultation on the uses of the continent. The 14 articles of the Treaty bind its signatories to a number of important promises, such as the prohibition of military activities, including nuclear testing; the assertion that no activities will be allowed to challenge previously held territorial positions; provision to allow inspection by observers to check compliance with the Treaty; and an undertaking to give advance notice of any expeditions.

The Antarctic Treaty is open to any member of the UN and the list of signatories has grown from the original 12 nations to 46 today.

INTERNATIONAL COOPERATION
American scientists outside the Polish Henryk Arctowski Research Station, an Earth sciences and ecological base on King George Island. Poland is one of the 46 signatories to the Antarctic Treaty, acquiring the status of Consultative Party in 1977 for active scientific research. Below: flags of the original 12 signatory nations fly at McMurdo Station, Ross Island.

FRENCH TRADITIONS Street markets for local produce are as much a feature of French-Canadian life as they are in France itself; bilingual signs and labels reflect the produce's dual heritage.

Je suis Canadien Why is it that some Canadian people speak French? Why weren't they assimilated like the Italian, German, Yiddish and Polish-speaking minorities of the USA?

Canada has ten provinces and three territories. One of the provinces, Quebec, has a largely French-speaking population and French is its only official language, with 79 per cent of people speaking French as their first language compared to 17 per cent in the rest of Canada. The difference has often been controversial, with a number of attempts to create a separate Quebecois nation as well as the introduction of educational 'bilingualism' to ensure that both languages retained their importance within an integrated nation. Former Prime Minister Pierre Trudeau reflected that Canadians 'peer so suspiciously at each other that we cannot see that we Canadians are standing on the mountaintop of human wealth, freedom and privilege'. But how did the dual-language system arise and why has it endured?

In the early years of its colonial history, Canada's new European population was largely French.

EARLY ADVENTURERS 18th- and 19th-century hunters blazed new trails, travelling from Quebec deep into the North American interior to trap and trade furs for the European market.

French settlers established the first continuously occupied European settlement on the North American continent in 1605, when Pierre du Gua de Monts founded Port-Royal, a small colony of trappers and traders at the mouth of the Bay of Fundy. Three years later de Monts' fellow-adventurer Samuel de Champlain sailed up the St Lawrence River to build a fort and trading post at a location that local tribes knew as Quebec – translated literally as 'where the river narrows'. Quebec City remains the capital of the province of that name to this day.

Quebec flourished over the next 150 years as a centre of fur trading. Its prosperity was built on the European fashion for beaver hats, made from the soft underfur of the mammal, which flourished in Canada's myriad rivers. Known as *coureurs de bois* ('wood-runners'), the canoe-borne trappers who hunted the animals were the first Europeans to venture into the unknown western lands, exploring and exploiting the great American wilderness with the aid of the indigenous tribes with whom they did business.

A clash of ambitions

The British presence in the northern lands was by then also growing. Adventurers established settlements in Newfoundland in 1610 and Nova Scotia 19 years later. Commercial interest in the region intensified with the founding of the Hudson's Bay Company, grandly granted monopoly rights over the bay and its huge catchment area by King Charles II in 1670. Soon British and French ambitions clashed. When a series of European wars broke out between the mother countries from 1689 on, the fighting quickly spread across the Atlantic to the New World.

The first encounters were indecisive. It was only with the Seven Years' War of the mid-18th century that the British gained a lasting advantage. Major-General James Wolfe won the decisive victory at the Battle of the Plains of Abraham (at Quebec City) in 1759. The Treaty of Paris, which brought the conflict to an end in 1763, made colonial North America in effect British.

Victory provided Britain with a dilemma. In Canada, unlike the colonies to the south, the bulk of the population was French. The British military had already had to confront French civilians in the course of the war, and had taken desperate measures to overcome them: in 1754, when fighting first broke out, they had forcibly expelled some 14,000 people from the Maritime Provinces on the Atlantic coast, known at the time as Acadia. Some of those forced out eventually found their way south to the French-owned state of Louisiana, where they established the distinctive Cajun (short for 'Acadian') culture. Inland Canada had a much larger French-speaking population, numbering over 50,000 people. Only the most hawkish British leaders relished the prospect of repeating this early exercise in ethnic cleansing on a larger scale. Their reluctance was the greater for the lack of substantial numbers of British settlers to replace the evicted French.

Together but apart

Instead, the sheer size of the country – today Canada is the world's second largest after Russia, occupying one-fifteenth of the world's total land area – helped ensure that the colonial government adopted a federal structure. Quebec, where the vast majority of the French-speakers lived, was officially renamed Lower Canada (the modern province of Ontario was then known as Upper Canada). Its inhabitants usually adopted a low profile, putting their hopes simply in *La Survivance*, the survival of their distinctive way of life.

For the most part their colonial rulers were happy to accommodate them, the more so after 1776 when the American War of Independence was raging south of the border. The Quebecois remained loyal at that time, possibly having come to the pragmatic conclusion that they had a better chance of retaining their separate identity as a large minority in a British-ruled enclave than as a small minority in an independent English-speaking nation.

There was never much love lost between Canada's twin communities. Lord Durham, author of a famous 1839 report on the future of the nation, called the French Canadians 'a people with no history and no literature' and opined that 'there can hardly be conceived a nationality more destitute of all that can invigorate and

There was never much love lost between Canada's twin communities

BATTLE FOR A NATION The British took Quebec in 1759 after outflanking the French garrison by boat and climbing the steep cliffs to the French camp, surprising the outnumbered soldiers.

VIVE LE QUÉBEC LIBRE 'Long live free Quebec!' French president Charles de Gaulle gave a controversial speech in favour of separatism during a 1967 visit.

that made French the nation's second official language. In future all Canadians had the right to receive government services in either English or French and could choose either language to be heard in federal courts.

Trudeau's gesture was not enough to appease the separatists, who came to power in the Quebec provincial legislature in 1976. In the following year they passed a measure that recognised French as the sole official language of the province, making its use compulsory in state schools and workplaces. Despite riders protecting other languages, this was enough to persuade many Anglophones to leave.

For a time there seemed a real danger of breakdown between the two communities. Matters came to a head in 1980, when Quebec's PQ administration finally held a long-threatened referendum to decide whether the province should seek independence. The Quebecois voted 60:40 against the proposal, and subsequent attempts to revive the issue in modified form have also failed.

Quebec today

In recent years Quebec has flourished and its largest city, Montreal, has become a showpiece of sophisticated urban living. Ironically, its material success has been at the expense of the community's birth rate. This, which once outpaced all others in North America, has recently fallen to just 1.5 children per couple, below the 2.1 mark needed to replace the existing population – and a possible threat to the future of French Canada.

Today's French-speakers are not just a minority in a largely English-speaking continent, but also one that is shrinking and ageing. Most of the 250,000 or so new immigrants arriving in Canada each year choose English, not French, as their adopted language, further threatening their position. French Canadians may no longer seriously fear oppression, but atrophy has become a real concern.

elevate a people'. The relationship between French- and English-speakers was at best a marriage of convenience. Yet both sides got something out of it. British – especially Scottish – businessmen took the opportunity to seize the commanding heights of the Quebecois economy, growing rich through the exploitation of their Francophone labour force. French Canadians took consolation in the *revanche du berceau* ('revenge of the cradle') – one of the highest birth rates in the developed world, which saw the French-speaking proportion of the population increase.

But by the mid-20th century, the economy of Quebec was in decline. The French-Canadian population, which made up more than 90 per cent of the province's total, had become largely rural and inward looking, dominated by the Roman Catholic establishment. That situation changed with the so-called 'Quiet Revolution' of the 1960s. A new generation of leaders prised loose the Church's grip on education and showed a new assertiveness in promoting equality with Anglophones in the workplace.

The separatist movement

The scene was set for the rise of the Parti Québécois (PQ), militant separatists demanding Quebec's independence from the rest of Canada. At the same time, moderate French Canadians, led by the charismatic Pierre Trudeau, threw themselves into the task of attaining their goals using the existing federal structure. As head of Canada's ruling Liberal Party, Trudeau in 1969 pushed through an act of parliament

> A 1969 act of parliament made French the second official language

Why are there virtually no Caribs in the Caribbean? The first European visitors to the New World made landfall on islands they named after the local peoples who greeted them. But whatever happened to the Caribs?

Reporting on the status of the Caribs on Dominica in 1902, the governor, Henry Hesketh Bell, gave a brief account of their former reputation: 'The smaller islands, stretching from St Thomas to Tobago, seem ... to have been peopled ... by a warlike and indomitable race of savages, collectively known as "Charaibes" or "Caribs", who heroically resisted every attempt at colonisation on the part of European intruders, and preferred death to the withering slavery that became the fate of the natives of the larger islands. So stubborn was the resistance offered by these dauntless savages that settlements in the places held by them were not effected until long after the other islands had become flourishing plantation and civilised communities.'

When Christopher Columbus sailed to the Americas in 1492, he was seeking a sea route to the spice islands of the Indies. Discovering inhabited lands in the Caribbean, he called the tribes who peopled them 'Indians', a term perpetuated to this day in the name 'West Indies'.

Two main native groups lived on the islands at the time: Arawaks and Caribs. Both had found their way there from the South American mainland, island-hopping up the Lesser Antilles chain from homelands in the Orinoco rainforests of Venezuela. As first comers, the Arawak tribes had travelled farthest, reaching Cuba and Hispaniola in the Greater Antilles group, and it was

they who met the Spaniards when they made their first landfalls. They regaled the newcomers with tales of the fierce Caribs, mortal enemies who had in fact displaced them from many of the islands they had once inhabited.

Later Spanish settlers repaid the Arawaks for their hospitality by enslaving them under the *encomienda* system, which purportedly provided the native peoples with protection and the benefits of the Christian religion in return for unpaid labour. The warlike Caribs proved an altogether more daunting proposition to overcome and they managed to fend off the European colonisation of several of the islands they controlled until well into the 17th and 18th centuries.

Resistance overcome

Eventually, European weaponry proved too much for the Caribs, and British and French settlers established a presence even on Dominica and St Vincent in the Leeward group, the islands where the Caribs had been most firmly entrenched. Thereafter, like the Arawaks, they

fell victim to imported diseases or were killed in one-sided wars against the colonisers. One group on St Vincent – known as 'Black Caribs' because their ancestors had interbred with marooned African slaves – were deported en masse to Roatan Island off the coast of Honduras following a 1795 rebellion. Their descendants, the Garifuna, still live there today.

Assimilation also took its toll on Carib identity and by the 20th century the population had been reduced almost to nothing even on islands they once dominated. But they have not completely disappeared. Today, they remain a residual presence, notably on Dominica where a population 3,000-strong still inhabits the Carib Reserve, a 1,500-hectare (3,700-acre) territory set up by the British Crown in 1903. In addition, almost half a million Garifuna living on the mainland coast of Central America claim descent at least in part from the Black Caribs.

RESERVATION LIFE Members of a Carib family on their Dominican reserve, holding traditional works of art and a live snake.

Why did France and Germany develop so differently?

Europe's two biggest countries, neighbours and partners in the European Union, France and Germany should have much in common. Both have roots in the Holy Roman Empire, yet they are politically, culturally and institutionally distinct. Why?

'As happy as God in France,' Germans used to say, borrowing a Yiddish phrase to describe contentment. Yet relations between the twin great powers of the European mainland have often been less than happy. Geographical proximity may go some way to explain the rivalry that has traditionally divided the two, but it can hardly account for the gap in national temperament and language that still separates them. French individualism and the German love of order still seem poles apart, as different as chalk and cheese.

But both peoples originally came from similar ethnic stock. The Franks, who lent their name to France, were themselves a Germanic tribe, one of many that confronted the might of Rome in the latter days of the empire. Little distinguished them from their neighbours, other than their taste for fighting bare-chested and their use of double-bladed throwing axes in battle.

The Franks move into France

Having initially struggled against the Roman legions intruding into their lands, the Franks eventually reached an understanding with the imperial power, and their old enemies apparently raised few objections when they moved across the Rhine, first into the Low Countries and then on into what was to become France.

That nation first took recognisable shape under the warrior leader Clovis. He not only extended the borders of his kingdom south to the Mediterranean and the Pyrenees but also converted his people to Christianity. Clovis chose a small town on the River Seine as his capital – the future Paris.

In the 8th century AD, one of Clovis's successors extended Frankish power to the Baltic Sea and eastwards to the Danube Basin. This was Charlemagne – Charles the Great – who, on Christmas Day 800, was proclaimed the first Holy Roman Emperor by Pope Leo III in Rome. By the time of his death in 814, Charlemagne – who chose to rule from Aachen, near Germany's border with Belgium – ruled an empire that

included most of France, Germany and Austria but also much of Italy. Charlemagne's empire did not long survive his death. His heirs squabbled among themselves, and in 843 three of his grandsons agreed to divide the realm between them, one taking the bulk of the French lands, another the German realms, and the third a central tranche that lay between them. The title of Holy Roman Emperor,

which originally fell to the ruler of the middle kingdom, moved around between the heirs of Charlemagne's Carolingian dynasty until 962, when it settled on the Saxon king Otto the Great, heir to the German lands. From that time, on the title passed in an unbroken line of descent for more than eight centuries until the empire was finally abolished by Napoleon in 1806.

In the centuries between, fealty to the Holy Roman Empire was the cement that bound the German people. The emperors commanded loyalty over a patchwork of more than 1,800 separate political units – kingdoms, principalities, bishoprics, free cities and the like. In contrast, the French kings at times ruled little more than the Île- de-France area around their capital. But when,

from the 12th century on, they rebuilt their realm, they did so as a unified entity. As a result, Germany emerged from the Middle Ages still medieval in its fragmentary structure, while France was on the way to becoming a modern state.

From the 1500s, the Reformation amplified the differences between the two nations. Both were torn apart by religious wars between Catholics and Protestants. The outcome in each case was very different. In France, the Protestant king, Henry IV, also known as Henry of Navarre, gave up his faith to preserve national unity, accepting the majority Catholic persuasion

Family split

In AD 843, the Holy Roman Empire was divided between Charlemagne's three grandsons and heirs.

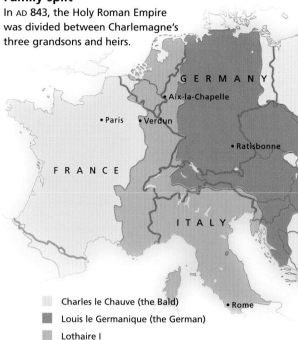

- Charles le Chauve (the Bald)
- Louis le Germanique (the German)
- Lothaire I
- Present-day borders

and famously declaring that 'Paris is well worth a Mass'. In Germany, the two factions fought one another to a standstill, and the resulting Peace of Augsburg enshrined the principle of '*Cuius regio, eius religio*' ('Whoever rules a region decides its religion'). Parts of the German patchwork, above all in the north, accepted Protestantism while much of the south remained Catholic – a recipe for national disunity.

A unified modern nation

Religious divisions brought on by Gregorian reformers, who sought to restore power to the Church, hobbled the control of the Holy Roman emperors. They never again dominated European politics as they had in their medieval heyday. Germany fractured into a multiplicity

GREAT DIVIDE A 16th-century illustration by German artist Lucas Cranach the Elder depicts the harmony of the 'true religion' of Catholicism (left), compared with the austerity of Lutheranism.

of little courts owing only nominal allegiance to the imperial overlord. In contrast to this, government in France became increasingly centralised. Throughout the 17th century, a succession of royal ministers tamed the independent-minded French nobles and built an efficient administration. France became Europe's superpower, reaching its culmination in the 72-year reign of the Sun King, Louis XIV.

The European trendsetter

At the same time the nation became the cynosure of good taste. French architecture, furniture and fashions were *à la mode* from London to St Petersburg and the continent's rulers modelled their courts on Louis' sumptuous Palace of Versailles. France became an world leader in the luxury industries. Gobelins tapestries, Aubusson carpets and Sèvres porcelain were sought after internationally,

while the Benedictine monk Dom Pérignon learned, with others, how to put the fizz into champagne.

Another element in France's cultural dominance was the spread of the French language, which emerged as the medium of civilised discourse across Europe. Well-brought-up children in Germany, Spain and Russia had French tutors, and major German writers like Johann Wolfgang von Goethe and the philosopher Gottfried Wilhelm von Leibnitz wrote fluently in the borrowed tongue. Before long French was the chosen language of international diplomacy, as Latin had once been. Ironically, when Germany, Austria-Hungary and Italy combined against France in 1882 in the Triple Alliance, the language of the treaty was French.

By the early 18th century, the identification of France with style and culture was almost complete. Paris set

COURT OF THE SUN KING Louis XIV of France receives a Persian ambassador in the magnificent setting of his Palace of Versailles.

the fashion for elegant living across Europe. By comparison, German court life seemed provincial and dowdy.

The great change came with the French Revolution of 1789 and its aftermath. Almost overnight France became the champion of the Rights of Man, while losing none of its ambition for political power. For a brief period under Napoleon Bonaparte, France held sway over almost all of Germany and much of the rest of Europe.

Napoleon's defeat in 1815 heralded the start of a long period that reversed the trends of earlier times. In the 19th century, fragmented Germany came together to form a united nation. The man who did more than any other to forge the new state was Prince Otto von Bismarck, who believed that the great questions of the day would be decided 'not by speeches and majorities ... but by iron and blood'. The newly unified German confederation was able to test its mettle against its old rival in the Franco-Prussian War of 1870-1, which it easily won, to the humiliation of France. When the French Emperor Napoleon III surrendered to his cousin, Prussia's Wilhelm I, Germany became the dominant power in Europe. In the years up to the First World War, France fell further behind its rapidly industrialising neighbour. Even its population stagnated: in 1870 the two countries had roughly the same number of people, but by 1914 France had only 38 million to Germany's 65 million.

The era of war

The period between 1870 and 1945 saw Franco-German enmity at a peak. In 75 years the two nations fought three wars and between them suffered almost 10 million dead as a result. Most of the negative stereotypes that nationals of one country had of the other date from that unhappy era. France, which had lived through the royal absolutism of the *ancien régime* in the 17th and 18th centuries, now experienced a sequence of short-lived governments under the democratic Third Republic.

Germany, having had no effective overall leader for centuries before 1871, found itself first under the control of the erratic and insecure Kaiser Wilhelm II and then, in the 1930s, in the clutches of Adolf Hitler's democratically elected National Socialist or Nazi Party.

It took German military defeat in two world wars to level the playing field once more. In the years after 1945, the victorious Allies pursued a policy of reconciliation that turned the previous hostility into friendship and cooperation (page 306). Soon the old enemies were working together in the European Economic Community, the predecessor of today's European Union.

Into the new century

Germany and France both entered the 21st century as prosperous democracies committed to similar social welfare policies and concepts of citizens' rights. Yet the long shadow of history continued to fall between them. Today's French citizens have inherited from their predecessors an abiding sense of style and a concern for the quality of life, along with an individualism that harks back to the revolution of 1789. French leaders never forget the fate of the rulers of the *ancien régime* and even now tend to back off from unpopular policies when faced with mass protests.

At first sight, Germany's history of disunity in the pre-Bismarck era might have been expected to produce similarly anarchic tendencies. In practice, many of the small states of the Holy Roman Empire were themselves absolutist, made the more so by the insecurities inherent in the nation's geographical position: lying in the flat lands of north-central Europe, it has always been open to attack from all sides. And while the French Revolution encouraged individualism, Germany's greatest social and spiritual upheaval had the opposite effect. The Protestant reformer Martin Luther preached obedience to the secular authorities, whoever they might be, and the religion named after him quickly became a conservative force. As a result, the German people had no experience of successful rebellion against the ruling powers.

Educationalists passed on the lessons of history to new generations. The German philosopher Immanuel Kant opined that, 'The characteristics of a child must include, above all, obedience ... [which] is an absolute necessity because it prepares the child for adherence to the laws he will have to obey as a future citizen, whether he likes them or not.' To this day Germany remains an unusually law-abiding society.

Long live difference

And so the modern France and Germany maintain *la différence*, even though they are now good neighbours. In the words of one wit, seeking to sum up the contrast in a single sentence: 'In Germany everything is forbidden except what is specifically allowed; in France everything is allowed, even what is forbidden.'

GERMAN INDUSTRIAL POWER The Krupp arms factory at Essen was the powerhouse of German militarism in the early 1900s.

Main ethnic groups

- Slovene
- Croat
- Bosniak
- Serb
- Hungarian
- Montenegrin
- Macedonian
- Albanian
- Valach
- Turk

The Balkan Peninsula
The former Yugoslavia, its 1945-92 borders seen in outline, now comprises seven countries including Kosovo, which declared independence in 2008.

The unmaking of a nation
Why did the unified and relatively prosperous federation of Yugoslavia tear itself apart so violently? What makes the Balkans a byword for political instability?

In the grounds of the military hospital in the Bosnian town of Niš is a strange and ghoulish edifice. It was built in 1809 by Hursid Pasha, a Turkish Ottoman general, to mark his victory over a Serbian army at the Battle of Cegar Hill. The monument was originally adorned with the bleached skulls of 952 Serbian soldiers, arranged in 14 neat rows on all four sides. Only 50 or so skulls are left in place today, but they are still an unnerving sight, a reminder that the fierce Balkan wars of the 1990s have many precedents.

The Balkans are Europe's borderlands. They form a wedge-shaped peninsula that touches Turkey at its eastern end and in the west falls just short of the Danube. The long edges of the wedge are bounded by the Adriatic Sea on one side and the Black Sea on the other. The Balkan states are Albania, Bulgaria, the countries that until recently constituted Yugoslavia, Romania, and the part of Turkey west of the Bosphorus. The east of the region was once part of the Byzantine Empire, while the west was oriented towards Catholic Europe. After Byzantium fell to the Turks, the Balkans were divided between the Christian Hapsburg Empire to the west and the Ottoman Muslims to the east. The frontier ran through the territory that was later to become Yugoslavia. It is said that Yugoslavia sat on a 'cultural fault line'.

Cultural differences
If the fault-line theory is too fatalistic, the centuries of imperialism and foreign rule undoubtedly led to extreme cultural differences between the peoples of the future Yugoslavia. The Slovenes and Croats in the north and west were Roman Catholic and used the Latin alphabet for writing. The easterly Serbs and Macedonians, who were in the Byzantine sphere of influence, were Orthodox Christians – and although they spoke the same language as the Croats they wrote it in the Cyrillic script used by the Russians. Under Ottoman rule, a significant proportion of Slavs in the provinces of Bosnia and Herzegovina adopted Islam. Yet, though their religions differed, the Slavonic people of the west Balkans were of the same ethnic stock. Serbs, Croats, Bosnians, Slovenes and Macedonians (and Bulgarians) all belong to the southern branch of the Slav people. They are distant cousins of the eastern Slavs (the Russians, Belorussians and Ukrainians) and of the western Slavs (the Poles, Czechs and Slovaks).

The southern Slavs were swept along by the general surge of nationalist feeling that welled up in many European peoples in the late 19th century. Serbs, Croats and Slovenes rediscovered their cultural roots, created national myths and occasionally rose in rebellion against Austria-Hungary and the Ottomans –

SKULL TOWER The monument at Niš was built to mark a Turkish victory but remains as a memorial to the defeated Serbs.

Alexander I, a Serb, renamed his kingdom Yugoslavia, imposing through personal rule a Yugoslav identity on his subjects. He was assassinated in 1934 in a Croat plot backed by Italy and Hungary. His successor, Peter II, reigned as a minor until 1941 when his uncle, the regent Paul, was deposed in a *coup d'état* followed by a German and Italian invasion. The Nazis exploited Croat ill-feeling towards their neighbours by creating a puppet Croat state. Croatian fascists took the opportunity to wreak horrifying violence on the Serbs. Meanwhile, the Chetniks, a group of Serb monarchist guerrillas, organised resistance to the Nazis. Ultimately, though, it was not the Chetniks but

communist guerrillas who played the greatest role in defeating the Germans. Their leader, Josip Broz, was of Croat-Slovene parentage – a fact acknowledged in his *nom de guerre*, which was 'This-That': Tito.

Tito and the 'second Yugoslavia'

Marshal Tito's forceful wartime leadership of a well-organised partisan force ensured that he would become peacetime premier and later President of the new Communist Federation of Yugoslavia, formally set up in 1946. It was made up of six constituent republics, all formed on the basis of the ethnic and cultural entities of the southern Slavs. They were Serbia, Croatia, Montenegro, Bosnia and Herzegovina, Slovenia and Macedonia. This neat arrangement ignored the fact that many Croats had for generations lived in Serbia,

RESISTANCE RIVALS Tito (far right) and Chetnik leader Draža Mihailović (fourth from right) were initially allies against the Nazis but ended up, in effect, fighting a civil war, a foretaste of troubles to come.

the two empires between which their lands were divided. Although Serbia achieved independence from the Ottomans, this was not enough for many nationalists. They dreamed of a political union of all the southern Slavs. *Yug* means 'south' in the Slavic tongue, and the term *Yugoslav* – 'south Slav' – was coined to express their aspiration for a country of their own. In June 1914, a terrorist named Gavrilo Princip struck a blow for Yugoslav nationalism when he assassinated the Archduke Franz Ferdinand, heir to the throne of Austria-Hungary. This act set in train the series of diplomatic and military manoeuvres that quickly led to the First World War. The war ended in 1918 with the collapse of both Austria-Hungary and the Ottoman Empire. The same year a 'Kingdom of Serbs, Croats and Slovenes' was created from the wreckage.

The new country was unstable from the start, and its unity was constantly threatened by resentment, particularly among Croats, of the political dominance of the Serbs. In 1929 King

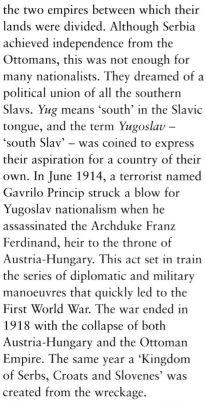

and vice versa. There was also a large majority of Albanians (who are not Slavs) in the Serbian region of Kosovo. And in Bosnia less than half the population were Bosnians – that is to say, Muslim Slavs.

Unity for a disparate people

Under Tito's firm rule, which lasted until his death in 1980, none of this seemed to matter. Socialist ideals appeared to have displaced old enmities and many citizens thought of themselves simply as Yugoslavs. They were proud that they lived as one people with two alphabets, three languages, four faiths, five nationalities and six republics. Yugoslavia looked

like the very model of a multi-ethnic, multi-cultural country. Moreover Yugoslavia, though it was Communist, asserted its independence from the Soviet Union in 1948 and followed its own policies. Yugoslav society was unusually open and prosperous by Communist standards: there was plenty of food in the shops, the press was relatively free, and citizens were allowed to travel abroad. There were serious shortcomings in the economy but, for most Yugoslavs, life improved in the post-war decades. So what went wrong?

The starting point of Yugoslavia's descent into anarchy is often said to be the death of Tito, as if his passing lifted the lid on a cauldron of ethnic mistrust that had simmered unseen for a generation. It is truer to say that Tito's death was a pre-condition for all that followed. No leader emerged with the authority to guide the Yugoslav people through the turbulent

DESTRUCTION AND RESTORATION
Dubrovnik (below) under fire
in 1991 and the reconstructed
bridge at Mostar (left),
a sign of hope for
the future.

decade that lay ahead. In the 1980s, other Communist regimes in Europe began to collapse. Socialism was abandoned in the USSR and the Soviet satellites. It was replaced everywhere with a brand of nationalism that saw independent statehood as an absolute right and a democratic necessity.

This view was understandable in countries such as Lithuania and Armenia, which had been forcibly incorporated into the Soviet Union. It was more surprising in Czechoslovakia where – though Czechs and Slovaks shared ethnicity, history and culture – the country nevertheless split in two.

The cauldron boils over

All the upheaval taking place inside the eastern bloc was mirrored within the Yugoslav Federation. National independence movements sprang up in Slovenia and Croatia – and in the Albanian enclave of Kosovo inside Serbia. Most Serbs wanted to continue the federation which they had always dominated. The political instability was worsened by economic troubles. There was no need for the west to shore up non-aligned Yugoslavia now that the Soviet Union was no longer a threat. But without this help, Yugoslavia spiralled into crisis.

In June 1991, Slovenia seceded from the Yugoslav Federation. It was a more or less clean break, since most Slovenians lived in Slovenia and there were practically no ethnic minorities within the republic. Croatia declared independence the same day – but here there was to be no easy parting of the ways. The Serb minority in Croatia, mainly in the region of Krajina close to Bosnia and Herzegovina, responded to Croatia's move by declaring its independence from independent Croatia. The Yugoslav Army, which was mostly Serb, advanced into Croatia to protect the perceived rights of the Serbian minority. That was the trigger for a full-scale war between Croatia and Yugoslavia's national army – the first armed conflict in Europe since the defeat of Hitler.

A three-sided war

This initial phase of the Yugoslav wars was medieval in its ferocity and methods and set the pattern for years to come. A distinctly old-fashioned feature of the war was the use of siege tactics. At the outset of the war, Croatian forces besieged Yugoslav Army units in their barracks. The army, meanwhile, laid siege to the Croatian border town of Vukovar and to the ancient and beautiful coastal city of Dubrovnik. During this time,

> This initial phase of the Yugoslav wars was medieval in its ferocity

the chilling euphemism 'ethnic cleansing' became widely known. The phrase referred to the practice of removing from the land all civilians belonging to the enemy's ethnic group, making it available for colonisation. All sides in the conflict practised ethnic cleansing at one time or another, using methods that ranged from intimidation and forced migration to mass murder.

In March 1992, the Croats and Muslims of Bosnia voted for independence from Yugoslavia. The immediate result was a three-sided war between Bosnian Serbs, Bosnian Croats and the Muslim Bosnians (who called themselves 'Bosniaks').

At first the Serbs had the upper hand. The Serb Army, fighting alongside outlandish groups of paramilitary gangsters, such as 'The Tigers', overran large parts of the republic. Serb forces laid siege to Sarajevo and to the Muslim city of Srebrenica and once again drew the condemnation of the global community. The Croats, who were at

first allied with the Bosniaks against the Serbs, fell to fighting the Bosniaks for territory in the latter part of the war. When Croat artillery destroyed the ancient bridge at Mostar, it provided the Yugoslav people with a most poignant symbol of the destruction and disunity that had been visited upon their country.

The third and so far final war was fought between Serbs and Albanian Muslims in the Serbian province of Kosovo. The new feature was the involvement of NATO, which bombed Serb targets throughout Yugoslavia. Under pressure, the Serbs withdrew from Kosovo. In 2006, Montenegro declared independence from Serbia, but when, in 2008, Kosovo declared its wish for independence, the plan was challenged by Russia.

It may be that the Yugoslav wars have not come to an end. Their current legacy is a death toll running into hundreds of thousands, a huge catalogue of grievances on all sides, and splintered countries that are more or less hostile to each other. There is a neat word for this kind of geopolitical fragmentation, wherever in the world it occurs: it is called *Balkanisation*.

INDEPENDENT KOSOVO Ethnic Albanians in the province of Kosovo welcome the proposed declaration of independence in February 2008.

The division of Ireland

Why is Ireland divided into two countries? When was it decided that the northern counties should belong to Great Britain?

Population shifts
Ireland's population doubled to two million by 1700, partly through 'plantation' (settlement).

Plantations in Ireland 1550-1625

- The Pale in 1537, at its smallest size
- Extent of The Pale in 1596
- Plantations under Mary Tudor and Elizabeth I
- The Ulster plantation under James I
- Other plantations under James I
- Unplanted areas
- Modern border of Northern Ireland

Ireland's divisions have been passionately disputed for centuries. In the late 19th century, the nationalist leader, Charles Stewart Parnell asked, 'Why should Ireland be treated as a geographical fragment of England ... Ireland is not a geographical fragment, but a nation.'

Patrick Henry Pearse, a leader of the 1916 Easter Rising, put it even more strongly: 'Life springs from death and from the graves of patriot men and women spring living nations ... They think that they have pacified Ireland. They think that they have purchased half of us and intimidated the other half. They think that they have foreseen everything, think they have provided against everything; but the fools, the fools, the fools, they have left us our Fenian dead, and while Ireland holds these graves Ireland unfree shall never be at peace.'

More recently, as diverse parties sought to find a solution to the years of violence in Northern Ireland, the Democratic Unionist MP, Ian Paisley expressed the suspicion of many of his fellows: 'The world will see what the Protestant people really think of this so-called peace process, which is really a surrender process.'

Even in medieval times the island was split between numerous rival kingdoms and smaller tribes at war with one another. In 1167 an exiled Irish king arrived in Leinster with a party of Anglo-Norman lords to regain his throne. Four years later

THE TROUBLES A British Army soldier prepares to fire a rubber bullet against demonstrators in Londonderry in 1970.

Henry II came to his aid with an army, and from that time the English never left. At first, English settlement was limited to a narrow strip of land centred on Dublin and known as 'The Pale'. Within it, English was the language spoken and English law applied. The Gaelic-speaking Irish were literally kept 'beyond the Pale'.

Tensions between the British and Irish ratcheted up several notches in the 16th century when, following Henry VIII's severing of religious ties with Rome, much of England, Scotland and Wales converted to Protestantism, while Ireland remained loyal to the Roman Catholic Church. A religious divide was now added to the differences in language and culture that separated the communities.

The arrival of Protestantism

The Reformation coincided with the adoption of a new policy by England's kings. From the reign of Henry VIII, Protestant communities imported from Britain were 'planted' on Irish soil. The first plantations were small-scale, model farming settlements intended to provide an example for the native Irish to emulate. In the face of continuing uprisings against the king's government in Dublin, the policy took on a punitive turn. Rebels' lands were seized and handed over to British colonists in the hope of permanently changing the inhabitants' mindset.

The movement gathered momentum at the turn of the 17th century. In 1607, following nine years of war in Ulster, the most Gaelic of all the Irish provinces, the region's ruling earls set sail for Spain, seeking to raise troops against the British. King James I saw the earls' flight as a golden opportunity to break Ulster's resistance for good. He declared their lands forfeit and offered them to wealthy British landowners with the proviso that each one had to people their holdings with English-speaking Protestants. Soldiers who had fought against the Irish were also rewarded with land grants, subsidised by City of London merchants. By 1622, the Plantation of Ulster, as the population shift was called, had transferred some 13,000 adults of English stock to the province. About 7,500 English and Scots were living in Down and Antrim, and some 12,000 settlers in Munster – and the process continued. With the Irish marginalised, the colonists provided the demographic foundation from which modern Northern Ireland would grow.

The 17th century was a time of religious wars between Protestants and Catholics across much of Europe. In Ireland the conflicts were

Divided islands

Ireland is not the only large island to be split politically into two or more parts. Hispaniola in the Caribbean has been divided since 1697, when its western portion, long the haunt of buccaneers, was ceded by Spain to France as a spoil of war. The French section rose in revolt at the end of the 18th century, when a slave army inspired by the ideals of the French Revolution temporarily reunited the island, renaming it Haiti from the Arawak word *Ayti*, meaning 'Mountainous Land'. The uprising's leader, Toussaint L'Ouverture (right), was later betrayed and shipped off to prison and death in France, but his successors succeeded in keeping Haiti independent. The Spanish-speaking eastern part of the island eventually broke free once more, winning independence itself in 1844 as the Dominican Republic.

On the other side of the globe, New Guinea was split into three parts by colonial powers. The Dutch claimed the western half, while the east was split between German New Guinea in the north and British Papua in the south. In 1963 the former Dutch lands became a province of Indonesia, formerly called Irian Jaya, but since 2002 officially retitled Papua. The reunited eastern half now forms Papua New Guinea.

Other islands have been divided by ethnic conflict. Greece and Turkey have long contested Cyprus, currently divided between the Turkish north and the Greek south. In Sri Lanka, Tamil insurgents have been fighting since the 1970s to set up a separate state, but have so far failed to impose their will on the Sinhalese majority.

EASTER RISING The ruins of Dublin's General Post Office after its recapture by British troops during the Republican rebellion of 1916.

particularly bitter, compounded by divisions of language and nationality.

Both sides committed atrocities in the course of the struggle, which ended in 1690 with decisive victory for the Protestant cause at the Battle of the Boyne. The former Catholic king, James II, was defeated by the new monarch, William of Orange. Fervent Ulster Protestants today are still known as Orangemen, after the Orange Order set up in the following century to celebrate the triumph of 'King Billy'.

Protestant ascendancy

For Ireland's Catholics the results of defeat were the escalation of the Penal Laws, a series of measures that effectively made them second-class citizens in their own country. Catholics were forbidden to vote in elections, sit in Parliament, go to university, teach in schools, own firearms, enter the army, marry Protestants or serve as lawyers or

judges. More seriously still, they were largely prevented from buying property, so that by the end of the 18th century, 95 per cent of the land was in the hands of the minority community.

It was gradually recognised that the conditions of life for Ireland's Catholics had become intolerable and over the next 100 years the Penal Laws were very slowly dismantled. But they left behind a legacy of bitterness and enduring poverty. Frustration turned to fury after the Great Famine of the 1840s killed almost a million people and forced one-and-a-half million out of a total population of eight million to emigrate. Although the potato blight that caused the disaster was unavoidable and no one's fault, the British Government was blamed for not doing enough to soften its

calamitous effects. Starvation and repression gave rise to the Fenian Brotherhood, born in the wake of the Great Hunger. This was the first ancestor of the Irish Republican Army (IRA) in its willingness to use terror to drive out the British.

More moderate Irish opinion sought redress in the compromise of Home Rule, by which the nation would have had its own parliament in Dublin to manage Irish affairs while remaining part of the United Kingdom. Home Rule was one of the hotly debated political topics in the decades around 1900, and attempts to enact the measure were twice defeated in the British Parliament.

Opposition came from mainland Britons opposed to the break-up of the Union, and also from Ulster's Protestant community, which was horrified at the prospect of becoming a minority in a Catholic-run Ireland. The Protestants found a spokesman in Sir Edward Carson, a lawyer and Conservative MP who raised a volunteer force, 100,000 strong, to resist Home Rule. The slogan of the Ulster Volunteer Force (UVF) was 'Ulster will fight, and Ulster will be right', and its leaders made it clear that they were prepared to use armed force to achieve their ends. However, in spite of such opposition, a third bill was passed in 1914, although its implementation was delayed by the outbreak of the First World War.

The war split Irish opinion. Many Irishmen, Catholic and Protestant alike, went off to fight in the British Army, but a minority saw a chance to benefit from Britain's distraction and strike out for total independence.

> The Great Famine of the 1840s killed almost a million people and forced one-and-a-half million to emigrate

The result was the Easter Rising of 1916, when around 1,760 Republicans seized the centre of Dublin, holding out against British troops for five days. The rising itself was quickly crushed, but its aftermath had lasting significance. Seeing the rebels simply as traitors in time of war, the British authorities had 15 of the leaders shot.

A wave of revulsion swept across Ireland, uniting moderate and hard-line Catholic opinion against the sentences. By the end of the war, Home Rule was no longer enough for public opinion in southern Ireland – complete independence was now the demand. In Ulster, by contrast, the events of 1916 only hardened support for the UVF and for the continuation of the union with mainland Britain.

Ireland split in two

Two years of bitter fighting convinced the British Government to accept the Republicans' demands. When the Anglo-Irish Treaty was signed in 1921, most of southern Ireland became the Irish Free State, with only residual British ties. But the treaty did not apply to the area of Ulster that had a majority of Protestants. As Northern Ireland they remained an integral part of the United Kingdom, although they now had a parliament of their own at Stormont, while also sending MPs to Westminster to maintain a voice in matters affecting the entire realm. The partition of the island established in

1921 is still effectively in place today. The Irish Free State has evolved into the modern Republic of Ireland, having cut its remaining links with mainland Britain. Since 1973 the United Kingdom and Ireland have been members of the European Community (now the European Union), and Ireland has found an unprecedented level of prosperity thanks to an economic surge – the so-called Celtic Tiger effect – of the past two decades.

Peace at last

Northern Ireland's recent history has been violent and difficult. It was something of a backwater until the 1960s, when 'the Troubles' threw it firmly into the political spotlight. The large Catholic minority, about 40 per cent of the population, demanded a greater share of political and economic power, with a hard core of Republicans holding out for union with the Republic of Ireland. Terrorist attacks on military and civilian targets occurred in Northern Ireland itself and on the British mainland.

Today, the country is seeking to put the past behind it and the two communities are struggling to find a satisfactory form of power-sharing. Peace has returned to the Six Counties, but the division of Ireland between Catholics and Protestants remains as much a reality as it has been since the Plantation of Ulster four centuries ago.

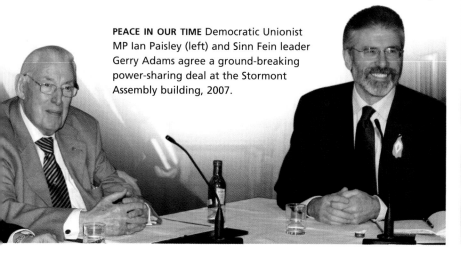

PEACE IN OUR TIME Democratic Unionist MP Ian Paisley (left) and Sinn Fein leader Gerry Adams agree a ground-breaking power-sharing deal at the Stormont Assembly building, 2007.

Going their separate ways

Czechoslovakia ceased to exist on 1 January 1993. The nation, created after the First World War split into its two constituent parts: the Czech Republic in the west and Slovakia to the east (which existed as a separate state in the Second World War). Speaking different languages, Czechs and Slovaks had concluded that they could best pursue their respective national ambitions separately. Both nations are now partners within the European Union.

The peaceful 'velvet divorce' that separated them has few parallels in world history. A rare European precedent was set in 1905, when Norway opted out of the union that had joined it with Sweden since 1814. The Swedes at first threatened to go to war, but when Norwegians voted by an overwhelming majority in favour of the dissolution, they swallowed their pride and reluctantly agreed to accept the people's will.

Bloody beginnings

More typically, new nations are born in bloodshed. The partition of India in 1947 was accompanied by horrific violence and a heavy death toll (page 41). East Timor achieved independence from Indonesia in 2002 after a prolonged struggle that left more than 100,000 people dead. Like Czechoslovakia, Yugoslavia was created at the end of the First World War. The eventual break-up of the country in the 1990s led to the creation of half a dozen new states, but, unlike Czechoslovakia, only after the most savage fighting seen in Europe since the end of the Second World War.

Winning words Why have some of the world's languages survived and others disappeared?

The ancient tongue known as Frisian has been spoken on the North Sea coast since *c.*1200. Once this Germanic language was widespread; now it survives in a few pockets of land in the Netherlands, Germany and Denmark. It is an endangered linguistic species and seems certain to become extinct within the next hundred years or so.

Yet while Frisian seems doomed, it has a close relative for which the prospects are very different. This language is spoken by descendants of those who migrated from the ancestral Frisian coastline 1,500 years ago and established a colony on an offshore island. The settlers flourished there, and took their way of speaking to other parts of the world, where it often took root and adapted to local linguistic conditions. The name of this luckier cousin of the moribund Frisian tongue: English.

The death of languages

By a series of geopolitical accidents, English has become the world's most dominant language. But its success is atypical. The Frisian model is the more common and the history of human speech is littered with the bones of extinct tongues. More than 3,000 languages are known to have vanished forever. They include Norn, a variety of Old Norse spoken in Orkney and Shetland until the 18th century; Dalmatian, which was similar to Romanian and spoken on the Croatian coast until the end of the 19th century; Knaanic, a Slavic tongue spoken by Czech Jews well into the Middle Ages; and Bungee, a mixture of

Scots Gaelic and Cree spoken in western Canada until 60 years ago.

Why did these languages not survive? Linguists like to joke that 'a language is a dialect with an army' – and, indeed, languages tend to prosper when their speakers are a political force in the world. This is part of the historical explanation for the spread of English, and for the present hegemony of its offspring, Standard American. But armies are usually better at destroying languages than preserving them: the conquistadors in South America wiped out the languages of the indigenous peoples along with the people themselves. During the Third Reich, the Yiddish language of the Jewish people was made the victim of virtual 'linguicide' across Europe.

It is not so much an army that a language needs in order to endure, but a government. A language will prosper if the area in which it is spoken corresponds to national borders; if it has a standard form that all speakers look up to (usually the dialect of the capital city); if it has a written form used for national purposes, such as taxation and law; if it has a body of literature – written or spoken – that unites the speakers in a common culture. This is the case with most of the major languages of Europe – from Danish to Georgian, and from Portuguese to Finnish.

The losers are the languages of ethnic minorities. Small language communities

LANGUAGE REVIVAL In Wales, signs display both languages. Depending on the area, either English or Welsh may be shown first.

Watch your tongue

Languages are dying out globally, but some language communities have managed to buck the trend. Among the success stories is Welsh, a descendant of the Celtic tongue spoken by the Britons before the Roman invasion. Wales was entirely Welsh-speaking until unification with England in 1536. But only half the population spoke the language in 1900 – and less than one-fifth by 1981. The language benefited from a revival of Welsh nationalism in the 1970s, and has been further boosted by political devolution in the 1990s: a language with state support is one with a lifeline.

Catalan under siege

Spoken in Valencia, Andorra and the Balearic Islands, Catalan is in a similar position to Spanish: it is officially recognised, but socio-linguistically pressured by the language of the nation-state. Basque is spoken by the people who live on both sides of the Pyrenees, in northern Spain and southwest France. Of a total of three million Basques, about 600,000 are language speakers, most of them on the Spanish side. Basque nationalism and Basque-language schools have taken it to places where it may not have been historically spoken.

At the same time, the cultural necessity for Welsh people to speak English, and for Catalan and Basque speakers to know Spanish and French, has not gone away. So it remains to be seen if these tongues will survive in the long term.

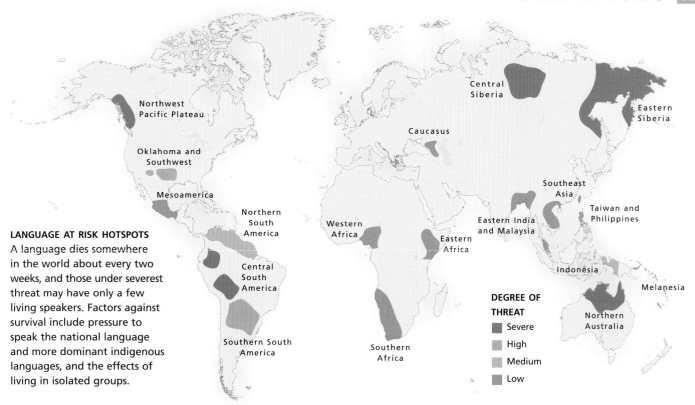

LANGUAGE AT RISK HOTSPOTS
A language dies somewhere in the world about every two weeks, and those under severest threat may have only a few living speakers. Factors against survival include pressure to speak the national language and more dominant indigenous languages, and the effects of living in isolated groups.

tend to diminish when they are inside a state that speaks a different language. Young people within a minority community know that to get on they must speak the majority language and become disenfranchised or move away. So a situation arises where the older people know the ancestral tongue better than the young. Once that happens, a language may be on the road to oblivion. Sometimes governments have discouraged or even outlawed minority languages in order to foster cultural cohesion: Welsh, Scots Gaelic and Catalan have all been victims of 'coercive assimilation'.

Disruptive technology
All the factors that militate against the survival of a language are magnified by the technology of the information age. Languages that once competed only with a more powerful or prestigious neighbour are now up against the global giants. In the present world, it seems that there is almost no hope for a language that has no digital resources. Whatever their native tongue, people around the world feel obliged to learn English or Spanish if they want access

to the riches of the internet. The first generation to do so struggles with the task and uses the international language of the net only when it is interacting with the wider world; these people will continue to speak the language of their birth at home. The second generation will be equally at ease with both languages. The third may drop their grandparents' native language entirely, because it is no longer useful to them.

Business is another factor. China's increasing economic importance could see Chinese take over from English and Spanish over the next century. Mandarin Chinese is currently the most widely spoken first language and more than one-sixth of the global population speaks some form of the language. As a result of such international sociological pressures, our global linguistic heritage is shrinking.

Languages are dying at a startling rate. It has been predicted that roughly 3,000 of the 6,500 languages spoken today will be gone by the end of this century. Some linguists believe as many as 5,900 will disappear in the course

of our grandchildren's lifetimes. And once a language is gone, it is as extinct as a triceratops.

Last speakers
The collapse of the linguistic ecosystem is clear. The last speaker of the Caucasian language Ubykh, for example, died in 1992. Cameroon's Kasabe became extinct in 1996. And when Marie Smith Jones died on 24 January 2008, so did the Alaskan language Eyak. In her last years, the only people she ever spoke to in her native tongue were field researchers, who came to record her speech while they still could. At the time *The Guardian* newspaper noted, 'Her passing means that nobody in the world can effortlessly distinguish a *demex'ch* (a soft, rotten spot in the ice) from a *demex'ch'lda'luu* (a large, treacherous hole in the ice). It means that *siniik'adach'uuch'* – the vertical groove between the nose and upper lip, literally a 'nose crumple' – has fled the minds of the living.'

> More than 3,000 languages are known to have vanished forever

A land of milk and honey Never a day goes by when there isn't conflict in the Middle East. Why?

The book of Exodus tells how God spoke to Moses from a burning bush. During the encounter, God revealed his plan for bringing the Israelites out of captivity in Egypt and leading them 'to a good and broad land, a land flowing with milk and honey, to the country of the Canaanites, the Hittites, the Amorites, the Perizzites, the Hivites and the Jebusites.' Here is the root of the troubles that blight this area of the Middle East: successive peoples, often with a common Semitic origin, sought possession of a country that was inhabited by someone else. The scenario adds up to a lengthy chronicle of conquest and re-conquest, claim and counter-claim, exile and return.

The Promised Land

The arrival of the people of Moses in their promised land was one of the earliest chapters in the chronicle. The Israelites destroyed or dispersed the inhabitants of Canaan – all the peoples that God listed to Moses –

and settled in the uplands west of the River Jordan. The coast at that time was under attack from the 'sea peoples', among whom were the Philistines (their name, in its Greek form, is the root of the word Palestine). To counter this menace, the Israelites united under Saul, the first king. He was succeeded by David, who made his capital at Jerusalem. After the death of David's son Solomon, the Israelite kingdom split into two warring states: Israel to the north and Judah to the south. Both were eventually conquered by the Babylonian Empire and many Jews (the people of Judah) were deported to Babylon. When the Assyrian Empire was conquered by the Persians, the Jews could return to the land they believed had been given to them by God, though some stayed on. But they had no political control over it: the Israelite state was gone.

This much is part of the Bible account. The next phase in the history

of Judaea (as it became known) is part of the wider story of the ancient world. For the first time it involved a European power: the Greek Empire of Alexander the Great, who took Judaea in the course of his conquest of the Persian Empire. After his death, the Greek-speaking Seleucids won control of Judaea. But their rule was ineffective and the high levels of taxation imposed upon the people led to an uprising. The Seleucid regime was overthrown and a new, independent Jewish kingdom was established in Judaea. There were also Jewish communities in north Africa and as far south as Yemen.

The independent kingdom of Judaea lasted for a century, until it was overrun by the Romans in the 1st century BC. The coming of the Romans was a disaster for the Jews,

HEAVY CLASHES A visit to Jerusalem's Temple Mount by Ariel Sharon in September 2000 sparked fighting between Israeli security forces and Palestinian *intifadas*.

whose way of life was founded on uncompromising and precise observance of a multitude of tiny rituals. To the Romans the Jewish obsession with their religious rites was pernickety nonsense, and they trampled all over it. The Jews tried on numerous occasions to rise up against their new rulers, but the extensive and long-lasting Roman Empire was a formidable force. They put down revolt after revolt, until at last they lost patience altogether with what they saw as the fastidious, cantankerous Jews.

A precious symbol destroyed

In AD 70, the Romans obliterated the Jewish Temple in Jerusalem and built a Roman one on the site. The Jews were dispersed throughout the Roman Empire so that they could not organise themselves into a resistance movement. Jews were banned from their beloved Jerusalem, which in AD 135 was given the new Latin name, Aelia Capitolina, by Emperor Hadrian. At the same time, Judaea itself was re-named Syria Palaestina, to rid it of any association with the Jews. The Romans clearly recognised that the land perceived as sacred was at the root of the political unrest in Judaea, and the Romanising measures were an attempt to desanctify it. They failed in that aim: in the centuries that followed the scattered Jews never forgot Zion, their sacred homeland. On the contrary, sorrow

over the destruction of the temple became a profound and intense element in Jewish identity. It has remained one of the memories that connects all Jews, however divergent their cultural backgrounds may be.

The Romans not only failed to destroy the ancient Jewish tradition; they even saw a new religion, based on the teachings of Jesus of Nazareth, take root in the same parched Judaean soil. Christianity, which arose shortly before the destruction of the temple, proved far more subversive than mainstream Judaism. It carried a gospel that won adherents at every level of Roman society – up to and including the emperor. It became strong enough to survive in Roman provinces and colonies even after the Roman Empire collapsed. Christianity effectively conquered Europe, and as a

result, generations of European kings, though far removed from the Middle East, came to feel that they had a stake in the region because the founding events of their faith took place there. Their interest in the sites connected with the life of Jesus was both religious and territorial. They wanted both to venerate them and own them, an attitude neatly conflated in the medieval term for Palestine – the 'Holy Land'.

The third religion

But the holy places of Christianity were not accessible to Christians. They now belonged to adherents of an even newer religion, the third to spring from the Middle East. The dynamic new faith was Islam, which acknowledged its Abrahamic roots through Hagar and Ishmael. It had incorporated all the Bible lands into its growing empire within a few years of the Prophet Mohammad's death. The Crusades of the Middle Ages were an attempt by the Christian states of Europe to take back control of the Holy Land and

What is meant by the term 'Middle East'?

Most people could probably name some countries of the Middle East, but they might find it harder, even with the help of a map, to say which countries make up the whole of the region. This is not surprising, since geopolitical terminology can shift and change like the sands of the desert.

The precise definition of the Middle East has changed many times since the term was coined at the beginning of the 20th century. According to the current definition, the Middle East comprises all the states on the eastern edge of the Mediterranean (Syria, Jordan, Lebanon and Israel), as well as Iran and Iraq further to the east, the entire Arabian peninsula to the south and Egypt to the west. Much of this arid landscape is the heartland of the Arabs and of Islam itself. But within the Middle East there are Muslims who are not ethnic Arabs (the Iranians) and ethnic Arabs who are not Muslims (a large proportion of Lebanese, for example). There are peoples who have no recognised country (such as the Palestinians and the Kurds), and there is a country that has gathered in its people from many other states (namely, Israel).

MODERN CONSENSUS The countries generally grouped under the title 'Middle East' today.

of Jerusalem above all. Only the First Crusade achieved that aim: a Crusader-backed kingdom of Jerusalem was established in 1099 and lasted for 192 years. But the slaughter committed by Christian armies was so dreadful that it has never been forgotten. The word 'crusade' has today become part of the terminology of Islamist extremism, where it is shorthand for what is seen as the imperialistic, self-serving involvement of the western powers in Middle East affairs.

The short-lived, blood-soaked Crusader kingdom was the only pause in almost 1,300 years of Muslim rule over Palestine. This long term of control is one of the factors that led modern Palestinians to believe that they had more right to the country than the Jews, who claim that the land is theirs by tradition even though they were absent from it for almost 2,000 years. In the event, it was a Christian nation that next took control of Palestine. In the First World War, as the Ottoman Empire, which had ruled the region since the 16th century, collapsed, British troops occupied Jerusalem. Soon after, the League of Nations granted Britain a mandate to govern Palestine, with the proviso that a 'homeland' for the Jews should be established there without prejudice to the rights of the existing population.

Two connected events in the years between the two world wars sowed the seeds of a new round of strife. The first was the illegal immigration of more than a third of a million Jews to Palestine, which caused huge

resentment among Palestinian Arabs and led to violent attacks on the settlers. The second was the onset of the persecution of Jews in Germany in the 1930s. The awful culmination of this was the genocide of six million people, in some cases nearly 90 per cent of the Jewish population of the countries that the Nazis occupied.

After the Holocaust

The enormity of the Holocaust reinforced international opinion that the Jews should be granted a national home, and that it should be in Palestine. A series of partition plans were worked out whereby the Holy Land would be divided into two states – one for Jews and one for Arabs. In 1948, in the face of bitter conflict, British forces withdrew, the mandate came to an end, and the new nation of Israel came into being. But Palestinian Arabs and the Arab nations in the Middle East would not favour a Jewish state in their midst. When Israel declared independence, the new country was attacked by a coalition of

Arab countries. That war ended in total and unexpected defeat for the Arab armies. Worse than that, it left Israel in control of large sections of Arab territory that it was now loth to give up. Arabs who had lived in Palestine for generations were forcibly expelled by the Israeli government, which feared that their possibly hostile presence constituted a security risk to Israel. They have formed an embittered refugee population ever since.

Both sides believed that they were the injured party: Israel because the attack was felt to be unprovoked; the Arabs of Palestine because they felt that they had lost their land without being given compensation. All the subsequent bad blood – culminating in the Six-Day War of 1967, the Yom Kippur War of 1973, the two *intifadas* (Palestinian

uprisings) of 1987 and 2000, the many acts of terrorism on one side and military repression on the other – is rooted in this first war between Israel and her Arab neighbours. Arab hostility grew after 1967, when Israel occupied the West Bank of the Jordan and Gaza, creating Jewish settlements.

All but the most hard-line elements on both sides are agreed that a resolution must involve an independent Palestinian state – that is, an exchange of land for peace. But questions arise as to how much land, on what terms, and with what guarantees – and these have proved intractable. These are minor details compared to the issue of Jerusalem, the fulcrum on which the politics of the region turn. So far neither side is ready to cede any part of the Holy City to the other, or even to have it administered by a neutral authority. The day is still far off when Jews and Arabs will see the fulfilment of another of God's promises to Moses: 'And I will give peace in the land, and you shall lie down, and none shall make you afraid.'

LASTING EVENT The Six-Day War between Israel and its Arab neighbours resulted in the capture of the Gaza Strip and the West Bank – the repercussions of which are still being felt today.

India's clash of faiths
Why is the Indian subcontinent divided between Hindus and Muslims?

Both the Hindu and Muslim faiths came to India by conquest, but almost 3,000 years apart. Hinduism traces its origins to Aryan invaders who descended from the Hindu Kush mountains of Afghanistan onto the North Indian Plain from about 1700 BC. Armed with bronze weapons, the warriors and horsemen had migrated from a homeland on the Eurasian steppes to settle in Iran by the start of the 2nd millennium BC.

The lands where they arrived already had an urban civilisation, one of the world's earliest. The Indus Valley culture is known principally from sites at Harappa and Mohenjo Daro in present-day Pakistan. The citizens enjoyed sophisticated amenities, including the earliest known covered drains, but they left little record of their religion owing to a lack of decipherable written texts. Seals showing figures in the lotus position indicate that they were already familiar with the traditional yogic posture, while a large communal bathhouse at Mohenjo Daro suggests that ritual bathing may have been an established custom, as it is for many Hindus in the sacred waters of the River Ganges today.

Early development of Hinduism
Although Indus Valley beliefs and those of India's aboriginal Dravidian peoples probably mingled with Aryan custom to shape the development of Hinduism, it was the invaders who introduced the first sacred texts. These were the *Vedas*, religious poems that were passed down orally before being committed to writing from about 1400 BC. The *Vedas* reveal that the Aryans worshipped 33 separate gods, each one representing some part of the cosmos or a natural force. The most frequently invoked was the thunderbolt-wielding Indra.

The Aryan incomers paid homage to their gods through an intricate system of animal sacrifices. Over the centuries the rituals grew increasingly complex, encouraging the priests who alone understood them to assume ever-greater powers. The Brahmans, as they were known, occupied the top rung of the ladder of caste, with warriors and aristocrats in second place, above traders and, at the bottom, agricultural labourers.

As the system became more rigid, individuals in search of a more personal faith went to the countryside to seek spiritual truth. Their thoughts were collected in the *Upanishads*, a collection of discussions on philosophy, meditation and the nature of God, which were written down from about the 8th century BC. They articulated the idea of a single universal spirit, ubiquitous and animating all life. Other important

RAISING CAPITAL Builders and elephants at work on the Fatehpur Sikri palace, the Mughal Emperor Akbar's capital in the late 1500s.

Hindu notions that developed at the time included the idea of the transmigration of souls through the endless reincarnation cycle of *samsara* and the belief that an individual's collective actions, or *karma*, decided his or her fate in the next life.

For almost two millennia, the interweaving strains of Hinduism dominated the religious life of the

subcontinent. Other faiths arose, but none threatened to supplant its complex and disparate beliefs. The situation only started to change about AD 1000, when foreign raiders brought with them a proselytising faith that sought to supplant Hinduism's multiple divinities with a single god.

Warriors for a new faith

The newly introduced religion was Islam, born 350 years earlier in Arabia. Desert warriors had spread the new faith's message – that there was one God, Allah, and that Mohammad was his prophet – across much of western Asia and North Africa. The eastward wave of military expansion reached Sind, in what is now southern Pakistan, in the 8th century, but there it stopped, halted by the Thar Desert and the might of the Hindu dynasties that ruled the Indian lands beyond.

A fresh Muslim onslaught got under way in the 11th century, this time coming from further north. Mahmud of Ghazni, ruler of the Afghan province of that name, started raiding North India, and was soon nicknamed 'the Idol Breaker' for his looting of Hindu temples. Mahmud made at least 17 incursions between 1000 and his death in 1030. The greatest of these was the sacking of the temple of Somnath, dedicated to the god Shiva, an expedition that netted treasure equivalent to 1.3 tonnes of gold.

Mahmud's goal was always to strike swiftly in the dry season, returning home before the monsoon rains made the rivers impassable. His rich pickings

India's other faiths

Throughout its history India has been an incubator of religions. Besides Hinduism, Buddhism was born there in the 5th century BC when the young prince Siddartha Gautama discovered enlightenment at the age of 35 and became known as the Buddha.

The Jain faith, with some 4 million adherents, is older, dating from at least the 6th century BC. Reacting against Hinduism's caste elitism and the tradition of animal sacrifice, it opened its ranks to all classes and preached the sanctity of all life.

Sikhism is a more recent creation, founded by Guru Nanak in the early 16th century. It is a monotheistic religion that combines elements of both the Hindu and Muslim traditions. In the face of persecution by the Mughal Emperor Aurangzeb, Sikhism took on a military complexion with the founding of the Khalsa Order by Nanak's 17th-century successor, Guru Gobind Singh.

The Parsis, who have a presence around the city of Mumbai, are an exception in that their Zoroastrian faith originated in Persia. The name itself is Gujarati for 'Persian', reflecting the fact that their ancestors migrated to the subcontinent to escape persecution after the Muslim conquest of Iran in the 7th century.

encouraged later raiders to envisage a more permanent presence in India, but for the next 150 years political infighting prevented his successors from putting such plans into action.

Eventually, Mahmud's Ghaznavid heirs came under pressure from the Ghurids, a mountain people from western Afghanistan. Ghazni fell to the invaders in 1150 and from 1173 a Ghurid sultan, Ghiyas al-Din, ruled from a new capital, Firozkoh. Ghiyas concentrated on defending the western approaches of his kingdom while entrusting the eastern front to his brother Muizz al-Din, known in Europe as Mohammad of Ghur. By 1186, Mohammad had overcome the remaining Ghaznavid princelings in the area, opening the path to India.

Power in India had meanwhile become fractured among a multitude of small states ruled by members of a Hindu warrior aristocracy, known as the Rajputs. Their combined military strength repelled Mohammad's first assault on the North Indian Plain in 1191. Undeterred, he returned the following year with a larger force. This time the Hindu infantry were systematically picked off by 12,000 mounted archers in a battle of attrition that lasted most of a day.

VIOLENT PARTITION Rioters outside Rawalpindi in 1947 in the run-up to independence. The city, in the western half of the province of Punjab, ended up in Pakistan following Partition.

The victory at Tarain (modern Taraori) broke Rajput power and opened the road to Delhi.

When Mohammad returned to Ghazni to cope with a rebellion, he left the newly conquered lands in the hands of a trusted lieutenant – a Turkic officer named Qutb al-Din Aybak who had entered his service as a slave. Qutb occupied Delhi in the months after the battle, demolishing its Hindu temples and using the stone to construct the Quwwat al-Islam Mosque (the name means 'Might of Islam'). Over the next 10 years he fought a series of campaigns that brought all of northern India under Muslim control.

With the Ghurid conquests Islam had made an indelible and permanent impact on India. Qutb's successors established the Delhi Sultanate, which endured for over 650 years; the last sultan was deposed by the British after the Indian Rebellion of 1857. At first the Muslim religion was a foreign imposition, but it quickly established Indian roots. In the course of the 13th century, Islam largely supplanted Buddhism, which had previously flourished in Bengal under the patronage of local rulers. Many Hindus also converted to the new faith, which attracted people from the disadvantaged lower castes with its egalitarianism.

The era of the Mughals

In the early 16th century, the Muslim presence was rejuvenated by the arrival of a vigorous new dynasty, the Mughals. Their founder, Babur, first came to northern India in time-honoured fashion as a raider descending from the mountains of the Hindu Kush. After years of armed incursions, he defeated the reigning sultan of Delhi, Ibrahim, the last of the Afghan Lodi dynasty, at the Battle of Panipat in 1526 and replaced him on the throne.

Babur's empire was almost lost under his heir Humayun, but revived under Humayun's son Akbar. Akbar proved a wise ruler, who learned from a Persian tutor the principle of *sulh-i kull*, or 'universal toleration', applying it throughout his long reign. He forged an alliance with India's Hindu ruling class by marrying a Rajput princess and entrusted much of the defence of his realm to Rajput generals. He also sought to conciliate Hindu opinion by abolishing pilgrim taxes on the faith's holy places and by dispensing with the hated poll tax paid by non-Muslims. Akbar encouraged dialogue between proponents of all the religious traditions in his realm, and in his later years he even

MUGHAL MAUSOLEUM Indian Muslims pray next to the Taj Mahal, which enshrines the sarcophagi of the Mughal Emperor Shah Jahan and his wife Mumtaz.

devised a belief system of his own, the Divine Faith, that sought to combine the best elements of all the different traditions.

From tolerance to division

Akbar's legacy of tolerance was lost in the long reign of his great-grandson Aurangzeb, a mighty conqueror who was also an Islamic zealot. The Rajputs, who had been close allies of the Delhi sultans in Akbar's day, rebelled against his successor's bigotry, reopening divisions between Hindus and Muslims that ultimately helped British colonialists to take power.

During the 19th and early 20th centuries, the British Raj controlled Hindus and Muslims alike. In the latter days of imperial rule, colonial governors pursued a conscious policy of 'divide and rule'. By seeking to exploit differences between the two communities, they hoped to lessen the appeal of the National Congress,

a predominantly Hindu organisation that was the main force agitating for India's independence from Britain.

The large Islamic minority found a mouthpiece of its own in the Muslim League, which from 1940 was committed to the creation of an independent state. The name chosen for the proposed nation was Pakistan, an Urdu word meaning 'Land of the Pure', which also served as an acronym for the provinces and communities the new land was intended to comprise – P for the Punjab, A for Afghans, K for Kashmir and S for Sind, combined with the last syllables of Baluchistan.

The new state of Pakistan and the newly independent India were born in bloodshed. When the British withdrew from the subcontinent in 1947, brutal and widespread inter-ethnic violence broke out between Hindus and Muslims. In the process, an estimated 500,000 people were killed, although some have put the toll at a million. In

FAST FOOD The festival of Karwa Chauth is celebrated by married Hindu women to bring long life to their husbands. They fast for 24 hours, then eat a ritual meal.

all, over 14 million citizens crossed the borders dividing India from East and West Pakistan; the eastern lands were to split off in 1971 to form the separate nation of Bangladesh.

Even though partition was carried out on religious lines, both India and Pakistan today have sizeable minorities of the opposite faith. In 2007, India had around 150 million Muslim citizens, compared with 166 million in Pakistan. The Hindu minority in Pakistan was far smaller, less than 1.5 per cent of the total population, but still numbered well over two million people. Although both nations guarantee full civic rights to citizens of all faiths, tensions continue to exist and have led to occasional outbursts of violence.

Rising China Given its size and sophistication, why is China only now emerging as a world economic power?

The Pudong district of Shanghai is one of China's most spectacular sights. A Manhattan of the east, it is a forest of 100-plus futuristic glass-and-steel skyscrapers: from the opposite bank of the Huangpu River they look like a collection of gleaming Modernist vases. Most are the headquarters of trade organisations and banks, for Pudong is the beating heart of Chinese finance and money is its lifeblood. In 2005, the gross domestic product (GDP) of this one suburb was officially estimated at over $25 billion.

But the most astonishing thing about Pudong is that until recently there was nothing there. If you had come to Shanghai any time before 1990 and looked across the same stretch of water, you would have seen nothing more than a few dilapidated wharves with paddy fields beyond. The change is both an example and a symbol of the Chinese economic miracle. The People's Republic already has a national output that is larger than Britain's or Canada's. If it continues to grow, it will outstrip Japan's and America's. China will then be the largest trading nation globally.

A history of innovation

Chinese economic dominance might be expected. After all, China is the most populous nation on Earth, with 20 per cent of the planet's population. So the consumer needs and the wealth-generating activities of its people are major factors in the world economy. Historically, China invented many of the key technological advances that make long-distance trade and communication possible: paper money, moveable type, the modern abacus and the compass. Perhaps the most surprising thing about its emergence as an economic power is that it did not happen sooner. With its traditions of industriousness, innovation and vast human resources, why has China waited until now to join in the great global game of buy, sell and get rich?

The answer lies partly in the country's unhappy experience of economic interaction with the rest of the world. China first opened up to overseas trade with western nations in the 16th century. During the Ming dynasty, Portuguese traders established a foothold at Macau, which remained a Portuguese colony until 1999. Via the port of Guangzhou (Canton), China exported vast quantities of silk and porcelain (which at that time only China knew how to produce, therefore giving rise to the generic term 'china' for crockery). These goods were shipped off to markets in Europe, paid for in silver extracted from mines in South America.

The profits to be had in the Chinese market attracted other western nations. By the end of the 18th century Britain was not only the world's leading imperial power, it was also the foremost of the nations commercially involved with China. Tea was the main Chinese export to Britain, but it was no longer economically viable for British traders to pay for it in silver. There was another commodity, though, that Britain had in plentiful supply and for which a demand could easily be created: opium. In the first decades of the 19th century, opium was brought by the shipload to China from British India. But the new trade troubled the Qing authorities. They were alarmed both by the dwindling supply of European silver, and by the damaging effect of British opium on the millions of Chinese who became addicted to it. They tried to stop the influx of opium and ban its use, but the British East India Company had a trading monopoly, and was determined not to allow such a lucrative market to close.

Imperial exploitation

In 1839-42 and 1856-60, two Opium Wars were fought over the issue of British access to Chinese markets, and Britain won them both. A series of 'unequal treaties' was imposed on China. They granted Britain unfettered access to Chinese markets, created dozens of 'treaty ports' where foreigners could live and work without being subject to Chinese law or taxation, and gave western missionaries the right to proselytise in Chinese cities. These terms were deeply humiliating for China. In 1898, popular resentment of the European interlopers bubbled over into an uprising against foreign influence. It was spearheaded by a secret society called the 'Righteous and Harmonious Fists', a name that was crudely reduced to 'Boxers' by western interpreters. The Boxer Rebellion was suppressed by a military alliance of eight nations that had commercial interests in China: Italy, the USA, France, Austria-Hungary, Japan, Germany, Britain and Russia.

The rebellion was the start of a century of unremitting and debilitating turmoil for China. In 1911, there was another uprising – this time directed against the corrupt and subservient Qing dynasty itself. The revolt turned into a countrywide revolution. The Qing were overthrown and China became a republic. In the 1920s, the nationalist government became involved in a civil war with communists led by Mao Zedong. It rumbled on for 10 years, until the two sides suspended their conflict to fight jointly against Japan, which invaded China in 1937. But fighting

> In 1898, resentment of the European interlopers bubbled over

FINE CHINA Porcelain like this late 16th-century Ming ewer, created by skilled Chinese artisans, was a major luxury export. It was produced in factories by workers who specialised in different parts of the process.

between nationalists and communists resumed as soon as the Second World War ended. Mao's forces now had the upper hand. They defeated the nationalist armies, and the People's Republic of China – a communist state with Mao at its head – was declared in 1949.

The great leap backwards

The new regime swiftly erected barriers against other nations. The western powers were reviled on the grounds that their interest in China had always been imperialist. Mao's new China would have nothing to do with a world economy that was by definition capitalist, and that had always been used as a weapon against the Chinese people. The People's Republic of China turned in on itself and became isolated from the world beyond its borders. Behind this new Chinese wall, half a billion people followed Mao's revolutionary agenda without interference or distraction from outside nations.

The pursuit of socialism in China was even more destructive than the decades of civil war that preceded it.

Mao forced his people through some colossal upheavals – reforms that were intended to catapult China's largely rural people into the vanguard of the developed world. The most ambitious of these programmes was the 'Great Leap Forward'. Possibly no event in history has been endowed with such a grimly ironic name, because the Great Leap Forward achieved the exact opposite of its intended effect.

The plan involved massively increasing steel production while also creating immense agricultural communes. These twin aims conflicted with each other disastrously. Peasants were encouraged to set up 'backyard furnaces' in which to smelt iron. Under pressure to meet targets, and in the absence of any raw materials, millions of peasants melted down their hoes and ploughs. The resulting scrap was industrially useless and the peasants were now unequipped to work the fields. From 1959, severe floods and drought meant that the harvest failed several years in a row and widespread famine ensued. Estimates of the number of people who died as a result

of the Great Leap Forward (1958-60) vary from 20 million to 43 million.

The Great Leap Forward was followed in the 1960s by the Cultural Revolution. It was Mao's attempt to keep the revolutionary movement from becoming stagnant by enlisting the nation's youth in a campaign against the 'Four Olds': old ideas, old culture, old customs and old habits. Students organised themselves into units of 'Red Guards' and went on the hunt for 'bourgeois reactionaries'. Teachers, managers and technicians – anyone with a skill – were liable to be beaten and packed off to the countryside to work in a commune. China's skill base was destroyed and its factories, schools and universities ground to a halt.

The Cultural Revolution rumbled on until Mao died in 1976. He left behind him a country exhausted and demoralised by the years of artificially induced class war and misplaced effort. But he had not entirely succeeded in expunging the 'bourgeois' aspirations of the urban proletariat. Their yearning for a better life was summed up in the 'Four Musts', the must-have items for a Chinese worker: a bicycle, a radio, a watch and a sewing machine. These green shoots of ambition were the starting point for the economic revival that began under the man who emerged as leader two years after Mao's death: Deng Xiaoping.

A new Chinese era

Deng set about nurturing the entrepreneurial spirit of the Chinese people without for a moment loosening state control of the political process or undermining the communist ideology. He tentatively introduced market forces into the planned economy, allowing peasants to sell their excess for a profit. He gradually dismantled the fixed-price system whereby the state decided the price of all goods. Deng justified these changes by saying that they worked and they made life

PROPAGANDA KING A poster proclaims: 'Chairman Mao is the everlasting red sun in our hearts'.

毛主席是我们心中永远不落的红太阳

better for the people. 'Socialism does not mean shared poverty,' he said. 'Whether a cat is black or white makes no difference. As long as it catches mice, it is a good cat.' The Chinese agreed: their lives were improving year after year, and did not care whether the system that made it happen was called Maoism, anti-Maoism, market socialism or state capitalism.

These first reforms were internal. China still did not have the capability to compete in the international market. That came in the 1980s, when China began to set up joint ventures with western firms, to put a financial and banking system in place, and

to allow private citizens to set up in business. Western companies began to make use of China's enticing combination of cheap labour and excellent industrial discipline. China became the workshop of the world.

Economic success

At first Chinese production line workers concentrated on goods that required few skills on the part of the workers – toys and toasters. Later, China became the main manufacturer of complex articles, such as cameras and computers. Western companies, buoyed by the turn, once again queued up for a slice of China, but

this time the country was dictating the terms and making sure that it reaped the benefits as a result.

As a result of the reforms, the People's Republic – still nominally a Marxist state – now has 41 home-grown US dollar billionaires. The gap between rich and poor remains vast – it is perhaps wider than anywhere else in the world. But there has been a huge rise in the standard of living for most Chinese. The modest Four Musts of Mao's era have been superseded by the more upwardly mobile 'Eight Bigs': colour television, fridge, camera, stereo, motorcycle, suite of furniture, washing machine and electric fan.

The reins of political control are still tight, however, and many western observers are concerned by the widespread abuse of human rights in the new China. But it is undeniable that the economic potential of the Chinese people, which had been dammed up or depleted by 90 years of civil strife and uncompromising ideology, has now been released. When a dam breaks, and pent-up waters begin to flow, the entire landscape surrounding it changes. The present rise of China is just the beginning of that change. We are still in the first years of what many political economists are predicting will be 'the Chinese century'.

Venice – a city built on water Surely a marshy lagoon is the last place you would choose to build a city? So why is it there?

Venice, almost uniquely among the great Italian cities, is not a creation of the Roman Empire. The marshlands at the northern point of the Adriatic were a wet and useless wasteland as far as the Emperors were concerned. Though the legions did occupy the region inhabited by the Veneti tribe, they skirted round the soggy lagoon with its inhospitable mosquito-infested islands and marched on down the Dalmatian coast.

A refugee crisis

It was the fall of Rome that brought Venice into being. From the 4th century AD, waves of invaders came from the northern side of the Alps and crashed through the Brenner Pass. Huns, Germanic Ostrogoths and Visigoths, Lombards: one after the other they overwhelmed the rural population and spread down the Italian peninsula. The invasion created a huge refugee crisis within the Empire. Many countryfolk flooded into the cities, but in the Venetian region some fled away from centres

VENICE SUCCUMBS TO THE SEA
During seasonal floods, pedestrians by the San Marco Canal cross the city on makeshift walkways.

such as Padua and Aquilea to the unpopulated islands of the Venetian lagoon. The island we now know as the Rialto, the largest in the archipelago, was cut off from the mainland by three miles of clear water at high tide. The water was too shallow and treacherous for a ship-borne assault; the invading hordes usually went for easier targets. By the time the flood of intruders had receded, some of the refugees had found ways to make a home – and a living – in the brackish wetlands of the lagoon.

The beginnings of a settlement

It was a strange kind of existence, or so it seemed to Cassiodorus, secretary to the Ostrogothic king Theodoric, who passed that way in around 535 AD. 'The houses are like seabirds' nests', he wrote. 'Where first you saw land, you soon see islands, more numerous than the Cyclades. The reflections of their scattered houses stretch far on the flat sea. Nature provides a place that the care of man enriches. With slender branches tied in bundles, they consolidate the land and have no fear of facing the sea waves with such delicate defences. All their exertion is in the saltworks; in place of the plough and the scythe they rake the salt … They tie their boats to the walls of their houses, like domestic animals.' Cassiodorus' description touches on all the things that would preoccupy Venice for the next thousand years and make it rich. There is the endless fight against the sea; the clever commercial exploitation of its unique topographical circumstances; and the masterful use of ships and boats.

In the 7th century AD, the people of the scattered islands were settled

AN ISLAND CITY Venice has few physical links to the mainland, even today. Its unlikely position eventually proved its making as a centre of trade and seafaring.

enough to begin to organise themselves politically. In the same century, large buildings appeared. A cathedral was consecrated on the island of Torcello in 639; the name of its bishop is inscribed on the oldest known document of Venetian history. In 697, the Venetians elected a leader – *dux* in classical Latin, *doge* in the dialect of the Italian northeast. By the middle of the next century, Venice was sufficiently coherent as an entity – and perfectly sited geographically – to strike trade agreements with the Frankish Empire to the north, and with the Byzantine Empire across the sea to the east.

An instant empire

Venice's location also made it an important stopping-off point for Crusaders en route to the Holy Land. After the Fourth Crusade was proclaimed, the ruling doge, in 1201, agreed to supply the Christian armies with 4,500 knights and horses, 9,000 esquires and 20,000 foot soldiers, with provisions for them to last a year. His price was 85,000 silver marks up-front, and half of the territory conquered. This turned out to be a superb deal

for Venice: the city's share of the spoils included many of the Greek islands, the entire seaboard of the Eastern Adriatic (roughly the coastline of modern Croatia), and the islands of Crete and Cyprus. Venice also gained access to the ports of the Black Sea and consolidated its position in the Levant. The floating town at the head of the Adriatic was transformed from a rich city-state into the capital of a large Mediterranean Empire.

In the 13th century, Venetian armies fought long wars to acquire mainland territory in northern Italy – a western empire to mirror its acquisitions in the east. Venice needed control of the trade routes that were its lifeblood, but it also needed agricultural land on which to grow food. Padua, Verona, Ravenna and Trieste all came under Venetian control. So did the Brenner Pass, the main route through the Alps to the silver markets of Germany.

Ironically, it was the expansion of Venice that sowed the seeds of decline. Venice the city was compact and defensible; Venice the empire had long frontiers that were hard to defend. And it had many enemies, too. In the west, the Dukes of Milan chipped away at the brittle

borders of Venice's Italian territory. In the east, Venice came up against the growing power of the Ottoman Empire. In 1453, the Ottomans took Constantinople, thereby excluding Venetian traders from the Black Sea. A generation later, in 1488, the Portuguese explorer Bartolomeu Dias found a route round the tip of Africa to India. This broke Venice's monopolistic control of commercial traffic between east and west and spelled the end of the empire.

In the meantime, Venice the city had clothed itself in glorious architectural finery. San Marco – St Mark's Basilica – was built to house the bones of the apostle, which were stolen from Alexandria and brought to Venice in 829. Several churches have stood on the site: the present version was completed in 1071. The face of the city was transformed in the 1450s and 1460s as an unbroken row of magnificent palazzi were constructed side by side along the Grand Canal. The watery gaps between the many islands were filled, forcing the rivulets and channels of the lagoon into ever-tighter spaces (a process that continued well into the 20th century). On the reclaimed land

> **Venice was perfectly sited between the Frankish Empire to the north and the Byzantine Empire to the east**

were constructed the ministries, banks and shipyards that were the engine of Venetian wealth. At its height Venice waged war on the encroaching sea in the same way it quelled its other enemies. This victory was celebrated in the ceremony known as the Sposalizio del Mar, 'The Wedding of the Sea'. Each year, on Ascension Day, the doge sailed to the edge of the lagoon, threw a ring into the Adriatic and declared: 'We wed thee, O Sea, in token of our true and perpetual dominion over thee.'

Controlling the flood

But it was not entirely possible to subdue the shrewish waters – then or now. The weight of Venice presses down on the wet earth like a brick on a waterlogged cushion and it has been slowly sinking for centuries. At least five pavements have been laid on the Piazza San Marco, one on top of the other, as the square sinks a millimetre at a time. St Mark's Square is regularly awash in spring and autumn, and occasionally, as in 1966, catastrophic floods engulf the town centre.

The paraphernalia of the modern world is accelerating the damage, too. Underwater turbulence, caused by the outboard motors of the *vaporetti* (water taxis), is known to be eating away at the foundations of Venice's oldest buildings. And the whole city is at risk from rising water levels in the Adriatic – which are possibly a consequence of global warming.

One proposed solution to the structural disaster involves making use of the water that has always been its lifeblood, as well as its bane. The idea is to pump water into the earth beneath the city, causing the sands to expand like a sponge and physically lift the city by several metres. It is not certain that the scheme is technically possible and there are questions about the effect it would have on the historical integrity of the waterfronts. But if it could be made to work, 300 years of subsidence could be reversed at a stroke and Venice would rise again.

How was Venice built?

The marshy islands were a good place for the founders of Venice to hide, but they were a bad place for their descendants to build. It was not easy to construct a fisherman's shack, let alone a stone cathedral or a doge's palace, on the spongy, waterlogged earth.

A solid foundation

The technical problems involved in making the city were overcome over the course of centuries. At first the Venetians relied on the technique of driving piles into the earth in the hope of striking bedrock, and planting their buildings on top. It was a haphazard business: many a sturdy tree trunk would have been driven into the soft ground, and then have sunk without trace. Houses were roofed with thatch – not for warmth but because that was the lightest material available. Many homes toppled over after they had been finished.

But by the medieval era, sizeable stone buildings were being successfully set on foundations made from hundreds of pine or larch logs, pressed into the soft earth like so many matchsticks into butter. The stones themselves were recycled from the ruins of cities such as Aquilea and many of the oldest buildings in Venice have fragments of Roman inscription in the stonework. It was also in the

Middle Ages that Venetian engineers began to master the techniques of drainage, and so provide firmer ground to build on. The job fell to a state official called the *proto alle acque* – overseer of the waters – to coordinate canal digging and river diversion. (The water that was filtered down from the high-lying land, or carried away by watermills, was used to irrigate surrounding rice fields.)

Centuries of damage

The most gifted proto alle acque of the Renaissance was a man named Cristoforo Sabbadino. He was one of the first to see that human actions such as unauthorised building of channels and ill-conceived reclamation projects were the main cause of damage to Venice and its lagoon. He would have been horrified to know that nearly 500 years after his time Venice would still be sinking, and that mankind would still be to blame.

FIRM FOUNDATIONS
Logs – or piles – were hand-driven into the lagoon mud until they hit the rock beneath. Wood does not rot when waterlogged; it hardens, so the close-packed piles remain strong for centuries.

Making capital Why is the city of Moscow, not St Petersburg, the capital of Russia. Wasn't St Petersburg built specifically for that purpose?

Russia, it is sometimes said, has had two capitals. But the first capital of the Russian state was neither Moscow nor St Petersburg; it was Kiev. Though it is now the capital of the independent Ukraine, Kiev is still described in Russian history books as the 'mother of Russian cities'. The Kievan state was destroyed by the Mongol hordes that swept across the Slav lands in the 13th century. This had the effect of disrupting civil life and reducing Russia to a patchwork of states, each with its own capital. The princes who ruled these cities were little more than tax collectors for the Mongols.

During these years Moscow began to come to the fore. Then a small town centred on a wooden fortress, or *kremlin*, it was centrally placed within the Russian lands and so slightly less likely than other parts of Russia to be attacked by either the Mongols to the east or the large Polish-Lithuanian state to the west. And while most Russian princes bequeathed their lands to all their sons, in Moscow the inheritance was passed on intact to the eldest.

This gave Moscow an edge: it remained a coherent entity while all the states around became ever more fragmented. But Moscow's main advantage was the calibre of its princes. In the 1330s, when Mongol might was unassailable, Grand Prince Ivan of Moscow won the right to collect tribute on their behalf from the other states (earning himself the nickname *Kalita* – 'Moneybags'). His success at this dubious function made Ivan the chief of Russian princes and his citadel the richest of Russian cities. Ivan's grandson Dmitry reversed the collaborationist policy and raised an army to defy the Mongols. He smashed them utterly at the Battle of Kulikovo in 1380, an unexpected victory that united the people around its leader. Over the course of the next hundred years, as the Mongols faded away, more and more principalities were drawn into Moscow's orbit. A more or less unified Russian state was in place by the reign of Vassily III at the beginning of the 16th century. His son Ivan IV (later known as 'the terrible') was the first Muscovite prince to have himself crowned tsar 'of all the Russias' – meaning all the obsolescent little states that made up his kingdom.

A new capital for a new age

Moscow remained the capital until 1712 in the reign of Peter the Great. Peter hated Moscow. To him it was just a huge muddy village that epitomised the backwardness of his people and his country. He wanted a new capital that would be a 'window on the west' – a city to advertise and dramatise his efforts to drag Russia out of the Middle Ages and provide access to the Baltic Sea and European trade. So Peter's city, named St Petersburg in

FORMER GLORY Home to Russia's national icon, Our Lady of Vladimir, the eponymous church in St Petersburg has both Baroque and Classical features along with some peculiarly Russian ones like onion domes.

part after its dynamic founder, had to be everything Moscow was not: modern, western, light and airy – a capital fit for an up-to-date European monarch and his nation.

But by the time the Revolution came in 1917, the rich palaces of Peter's capital symbolised something else: the immense, immoral gulf between the tsar and the common people. In 1914, on the outbreak of the First World War, St Petersburg was renamed Petrograd as a patriotic gesture. Three years later, one of the first acts of the triumphant Bolshevik regime was to demote the city and to take away its crown as they had taken away the tsar's. Later, they took away its name altogether, rechristening it Leningrad. The Russian capital was moved back to Moscow, which (as of old) was far from potential foreign enemies and at the same time centrally located. In 1918 the Soviet government took up residence inside Moscow's Kremlin.

Since the break-up of the Soviet Union in 1991, Moscow has remained Russia's first city, but Peter the Great's capital has regained some of its old prestige. On 6 September 1991, the name St Petersburg was restored, while in 2008 Russia's Constitutional Court moved back, partly restoring the city's historic status.

Rivalry between the two cities persists. In 2000, President Vladimir Putin, a St Petersburg native, controversially entertained the British and Japanese heads of state in his home city, and there has been outrage in Moscow at proposals that the Russian parliament be relocated to St Petersburg.

Why do some states locate their capitals in places other than the country's main city?

There is no rule to say that a country's largest city has to be the capital, but in older nations that is often the case. Some nations deliberately create a capital from scratch. Washington, DC is the first and best-known case. It was founded in the 1790s for reasons of municipal egalitarianism – so that none of the existing cities in the United States could place itself above the others. The land on which it stands was ceded from Maryland and Virginia – so the American capital is not located in any US state but in its own statelet, the District of Columbia.

Canberra, the capital of Australia, is a 20th-century example of a similar phenomenon. Before the Commonwealth of Australia was established in 1901, there was a dispute between the cities of Sydney and Melbourne, still Australia's largest metropolises, as to which of them should be the capital. In the end it was decided that the capital should be founded at a site deliberately located halfway between the two. The name Canberra comes from the Aboriginal word for the chosen site, which fittingly enough, means 'meeting place'.

It is not only new nations that plant capital cities like saplings in the national backyard. At least 14 countries moved their capitals or built new ones in the second half of the 20th century (see table) despite the huge logistical, financial and political costs involved.

Brazil symbolically relocated its capital from the coast to the geographical heart of the country in the 1950s. The new capital, Brasilia, was the idea of the Rio-born architect, Oscar Niemeyer, who designed many of its great buildings, while its unique plan was conceived by his friend Lucio Costa. The city is itself a huge symbol: its built-up area takes the form of a great bird with outstretched wings – though this is a view of the city that can only be seen on maps or from a high-flying aircraft.

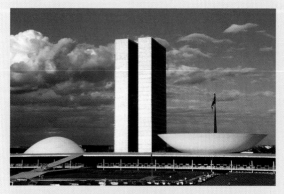

VISIONARY'S DREAM Thoroughly modern Brasilia stands within its own statelet. Its Palace of National Congress is a masterpiece of modern architecture.

Country	Year	New capital	Old capital
Pakistan	1959	Islamabad	Karachi
Brazil	1960	Brasilia	Rio de Janeiro
Mauritania	1960	Nouakchott	Saint Louis (Senegal)
Botswana	1965	Gaborone	Mafikeng
Belize	1970	Belmopan	Belize City
Libya	1972	Tripoli	Benghazi
Tanzania	1974	Dodoma	Dar es Salaam
Malawi	1975	Lilongwe	Zomba
Ivory Coast	1983	Yamoussoukro	Abidjan
Germany	1990	Berlin	Bonn
Nigeria	1991	Abuja	Lagos
Kazakhstan	1997	Astana	Almaty
Malaysia	1999	Putrajaya	Kuala Lumpur
Burma	2006	Naypyidaw*	Rangoon (Yangon)

also known as Pyinmana

EATING AND DRINKING 2

Food fact and fiction

There are many extraordinary stories about how particular foods and dishes came about. Some are true – and others are nonsense. So how do food myths arise?

It is an odd fact, but the most enduring myths about food are often the ones that are easiest to disprove. Among the most famous is the tale of how pasta came to be the national dish of Italy: it was brought back from China by the pioneering Venetian explorer Marco Polo. The Chinese, after all, are known to have enjoyed noodles for three thousand years – and what is pasta, if not the ancient Chinese noodle under another name?

The noodle story seems plausible because the Western world adopted so many ideas and innovations from China during the Middle Ages. But the tale of the Chinese origin of pasta is a complete fabrication. To prove it, we need only to show that pasta existed in Italy before 1295, the year Marco Polo returned from his 20-year voyage of discovery in the east. Sure enough, there is a legal document dating from 1279 that lists the possessions of a Genovese soldier named Ponzio Bastone. Among them are *una bariscella plena de macaronis* – 'a basketful of macaroni'. It seems that footsoldiers routinely carried pasta in their rations.

The Marco Polo anecdote seems to be a fairly recent invention. In 1929 an article entitled 'A Saga of Catai' was published in the *Macaroni Journal*, then the official trade magazine of the US National Pasta Association. It describes how an Italian sailor with Polo's expedition went ashore in China and met a beautiful girl who was making fine strings of noodles. He persuaded her to let him try this dish and to take some noodles back to his ship to show Marco Polo. The name of this intrepid sailor: Spaghetti.

Culinary creation myths

Why did such a fanciful tale catch on? It might have been the authoritative nature of the source – one would think the National Pasta Association would know where its product originated – but the appeal of the story is due mostly to its fairy-tale quality. The encounter between the humble sailor and the beautiful girl are straight out of Sinbad; the gift of noodles that turns out to be immensely valuable is like the seed from which Jack's beanstalk grew.

There is another kind of food myth that might be subtitled: 'How the

IN EVERYTHING GIVE THANKS

ANCIENT CUSTOM A 17th-century stained glass depiction of a picnic lunch featuring a sandwich. The rabbi, Hillel the Elder, is credited with its invention, beginning the custom of putting nuts, apples, spices and herbs inside two *matzohs* in the 1st century BC.

Why is it easier to get pizza in America than in Italy?

In Italy pizza was traditionally the food of the poor. In 19th-century Naples, a pizza was often no more than a flat disc of bread with salt and oil. Tomatoes were an occasional luxury and cheese did not feature until 1889, when a Neapolitan chef created a pizza in the colours of the Italian flag (with red tomatoes, white mozzarella and green basil) and named it in honour of the reigning queen, Margherita. This was the dish that Italian emigrants took to the USA at the turn of the century. The first American pizzeria opened in New York in 1905, but the dish did not catch on outside the Italian community.

A reinvented dish

Pizza only came to the attention of the broader American public after the Second World War. The late 1940s saw a

A SLICE OF HEAVEN Frank Pepe Pizzeria Napoletana in Connecticut is one of the oldest pizzerias in the USA. The New Haven restaurant, specialising in white clam pizza, is on *American Heritage* magazine's list of 'top ten' American pizza restaurants.

countrywide pizza boom. Entrepreneurs in Chicago reinvented the Neapolitan dish for American appetites by giving it a thicker base and creating all manner of varied toppings. The infinite adaptability of pizza made it almost impossible not to like: today, 93 per cent of Americans eat pizza at least once a month. However, back in Italy food is

still an intensely parochial affair. At the start of the 20th century, before the wave of Italian emigration to America, pizza was almost unknown in the northern cities of Milan or Florence. That is no longer the case, but real pizza is still considered the culinary property of Naples and so is easier to find in the region where it belongs.

Hasty Solution to a Pressing Culinary Problem Turned Out To Be a Great Dish'. The archetype in this category is the sandwich, which is named after the 4th Earl of Sandwich, who supposedly wanted to eat supper without having to abandon his card game. It is true that the sandwich bears the earl's title, but he certainly did not invent the dish – he merely provided a new name for what was previously known as 'bread and meat'. And it is likely that Sandwich, a hard-working First Lord of the Admiralty as well as a keen card-player, ate his at his office desk rather than at the gaming table. The detail about his love of gambling adds a spicy hint of scandal to the mix and makes it a better story.

The chop suey story

The story of the popular Chinese dish chop suey is another tale of improvised cuisine and it shows how, once the basic ingredients are in place,

the mythmakers can vary the recipe to suit their taste. The story goes something like this: during the California gold rush (or the building of the Grand Pacific railway) a Cantonese cook was importuned by some miners (or drunken railway workers, or a visiting Chinese delegation or a local political bigwig) who demanded to be fed right away. Put in a position where he could not refuse, the cook fried up all the kitchen leftovers with some bean sprouts and called it 'chop suey' – from the Cantonese *tsap sui*, meaning 'odds and ends'. The only true thing about this story is the etymology of the dish's name: tsap sui does translate as 'miscellaneous scraps'. But it is not an American invention; it is genuinely Chinese and hails from Taishan, near Guangzhou, the district to which many Chinese Americans trace their ancestry.

A legend similar to the chop suey tale is told in Britain about chicken

tikka masala, a dish unknown in India. Apparently, a late-night customer at an Indian restaurant – which may have been in Glasgow – wanted sauce with his chicken tikka, which is always served dry. The chef improvised a kind of gravy using a can of tomato soup and some spices and Britain's favourite food was born.

A satisfying myth

This chicken tikka tale is the chop suey myth transposed to another country, a different cuisine and a later century. The Indian chef of the story has never been identified because, like the Chinese cook who invented chop suey, he doesn't exist. In this case, the reworked myth serves to fill in a baffling gap in our knowledge: Britons eat 23 million portions of chicken tikka masala every year, which makes it hard to credit the truth that no one knows where the dish actually sprang from.

The archetypal tale of the harassed Indian cook provides a ready-made answer: it is a just-so story for people who love their food.

The tale of the croissant

Other food fables persist for similar reasons. Well into the 1960s the revered culinary encyclopedia *Larousse Gastronomique* stated as historical fact that the croissant dates back to the siege of Budapest – then in Turkish hands – of 1686. The story goes that the besieging Imperial forces were digging a tunnel beneath the city walls. Budapest's bakers, who were always at work in the small hours, heard these nocturnal excavations. They raised the alarm and the attack was defeated. As a reward the bakers were granted the right to make a special pastry in the shape of the Ottoman emblem, a crescent moon.

Other respectable sources place the same incident at the siege of Vienna in 1683. Some versions ascribe the heroic deed and its reward to a single person. In dramatic terms, this 'lone baker' scenario is more satisfying because it taps into another archetypal legend: the Small Man Who Becomes a Hero. The Viennese (or Hungarian) baker is like the little Dutch boy who stuck his finger in a dyke and prevented a flood. The point of both stories is not historical, but moral: the ingenuity and vigilance of a single individual can have far-reaching benefits; one person who does the right thing can save us all.

None of the stories about the origin of the croissant ever explains how it

FLAKY PASTRY The siege of Vienna by the Turks in 1683, painted by Flemish artist Frans de Geffels. Vienna held out against the Ottoman forces for two months before achieving victory and, according to some sources, granting their heroic bakers the right to make pastries shaped like the crescent moon on the Ottoman flag.

came to be associated with French patisserie. Surely, if the Vienna story were true, we would all know the croissant as a *halbmond*, the German word for a crescent. And if Budapest were its birthplace, then some link with Hungary would have remained. The truth is that there is no mention of the croissant in any dictionary before 1853. The first recipe that resembles the flaky pastry we know today was published in 1905 – not entirely unexpectedly – in Paris.

Strange brew Neither tea nor coffee can be grown in cold climates. So how and when did tea- and coffee-drinking become such an important part of everyday life in Europe?

Tea and coffee arrived in Europe more or less simultaneously in the middle years of the 17th century, both beverages liquid boons of an early bout of globalisation in world trade.

Coffee had a slight head start over tea. It was drunk widely in the Arab world during the Middle Ages, but came to the attention of Europeans much later, in 1573. That year a philosopher called Leonhard Rauwolf noted that in Aleppo in the Ottoman Empire, 'This liquor is very common among them, wherefore there are a great many of them that sell it.' He noted it was drunk communally 'but little at a time'.

The first batch of coffee to arrive in Europe was brought from Turkey to Marseilles around 1642. It was sold on by the commercial agents of the Ottoman Empire who kept a monopoly of the supply line. Around 1654 a coffee house called The Angel opened in Oxford and proved popular with scholars who wanted to stay awake and study into the night. A coffee-drinking craze hit London in the 1660s, where the bitter brew was advertised as a drink to 'prevent drowsiness, and make one fit for business'.

Chocolate had become known to Spanish conquistadors, such as Hernán Cortés, after their invasion of Central America, and it finally reached Europe in 1544. Beans were traded some 40 years later, with Spain controlling growth and production for nearly a century. By the 1600s cocoa exports began to spread through Europe. Beans were roasted, pounded with sugar and spices into little cakes, then shaken in water to make a frothy, invigorating drink. From the 1640s France, then England adopted the drink, and in 1657 the first chocolate house – run by a Frenchman – opened

in London. But it was chocolate's value as confectionery that won out; by the 19th century 'eating chocolate' was more popular than the drink.

The complete global cuppa

Tea was viewed initially as a medicinal tonic. The English diarist Samuel Pepys tried it once in 1660: 'I did send for a Cupp of Tee, a China drink of which I never had drank before'. At 40 shillings a pound it was hugely expensive, though more accessible in England than in other European countries because the London-based East India Company dominated the 18th-century tea trade. The price fell as the volume of traffic increased: England imported 100,000 pounds in 1700; by 1801 imports had reached 24 million pounds. Englishmen made it their own by adding milk and also sugar, bringing together two of the

most lucrative commodities of Empire – tea from the east and sugar from the west in one sweet, reviving brew.

So global trade brought tea-drinking and coffee-drinking to Europe, but colonialism fixed the habit forever. The British broke the Chinese monopoly on tea by planting bushes in their overseas territories, India and Ceylon. Similarly, Portuguese and Dutch entrepreneurs introduced the coffee bean to Brazil and Java. Tea and coffee had become the pre-eminent cash crops of the European powers – and the indispensable daytime tipples of European citizens.

TEA FOR THREE A family at tea in 1727. A luxury drink, tea was prepared exclusively by the lady of the house and served in porcelain bowls specially imported from China.

The queen of cuisine
Why is France considered the home of fine cooking and why is French the language of haute cuisine around the world?

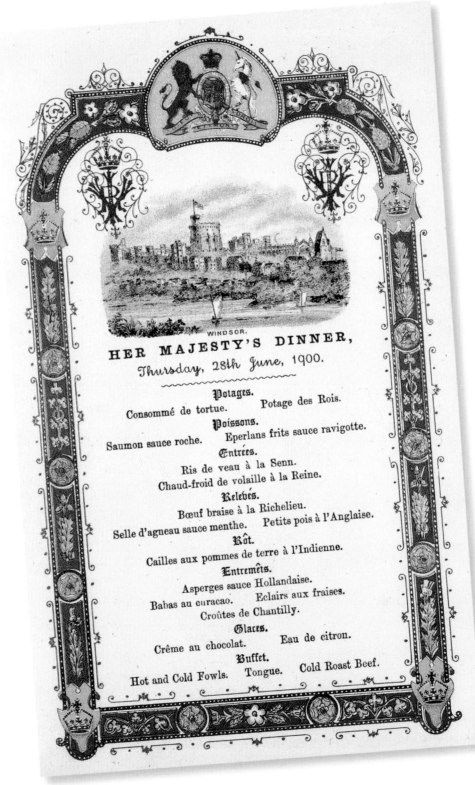

WINDSOR.

HER MAJESTY'S DINNER,
Thursday, 28th June, 1900.

Potages.
Consommé de tortue.   Potage des Rois.
Poissons.
Saumon sauce roche.   Eperlans frits sauce ravigotte.
Entrées.
Ris de veau à la Senn.
Chaud-froid de volaille à la Reine.
Relevés.
Bœuf braisé à la Richelieu.
Selle d'agneau sauce menthe.   Petits pois à l'Anglaise.
Rôt.
Cailles aux pommes de terre à l'Indienne.
Entremêts.
Asperges sauce Hollandaise.
Babas au curacao.   Eclairs aux fraises.
Croûtes de Chantilly.
Glaces.
Crême au chocolat.   Eau de citron.
Buffet.
Hot and Cold Fowls.   Tongue.   Cold Roast Beef.

Many peoples of the world have great culinary traditions and it is surely impossible to say which country has the best national cuisine – and even that would be a matter of opinion. But at the same time France seems to dominate the cooking culture. In the language of cookery, French ideas and terms pervade the professional kitchen: *à la carte*, *chef*, *sauté* and *cuisine* itself. French terminology is part of the eating out experience, too. You can't understand the menu in a fine-dining restaurant unless you know a *coulis* from a *velouté*.

French interest in cookery has a long history. One of the oldest cookery books in the world was written by a French chef, Guillaume Tirel, also known as Taillevent. Born in *c*.1312, he began his career as a kitchen boy, and from the age of 20 worked as head cook in several royal households, including that of Phillipe VI, the Dauphin, the Duke of Normandy, and Charles VI. His book, *Le Viandier*, written in the 1370s, is based – as was common at the time – on an earlier, anonymously authored work. Among the sweet and savoury recipes, Taillevant describes a range of highly spiced – almost curry-like – meat dishes, often flavoured with wine. The book remained in print for 200 years, by which time a culinary revolution in Paris changed the needs and desires of the populace.

A revolution in food
It is often said that the new ideas arrived with Catherine de Médicis, queen to Henry II of France. Catherine was from Florence, seat of the wider cultural renaissance

FASHIONABLE FRENCH A menu for Queen Victoria from Windsor Castle, 1900, written almost entirely in French. The word menu was first recorded in 1830. From Old French 'tiny', it came to mean 'detail', or 'detailed list', as it set out all the items of the meal.

then under way in Italy. She was fond of masques and courtly entertainments and her presence may have stimulated the appetite of the French aristocracy for showy cuisine. But in fact French cooks were scouring the works of Greek and Roman authors for ideas way before Catherine arrived from Florence in 1533.

At the same time the markets of the French capital drew traders from all over France: there was a wider range of ingredients to be found in the streets of Paris than in any other European city – even London. Over time, the kitchens of French noble houses became culinary laboratories and by the middle of the 17th century a distinct new style of cookery had emerged. It was *haute cuisine* – high

cookery – in the sense that it was developed for the pleasure of those at the top of the social scale and practised only by professionals.

Codifying the new cooking

French cooks in noble houses tended to guard their secrets, so while foreign visitors noted the emerging excellence of French cuisine, the new techniques and knowledge did not spread immediately. That changed in 1651, when a chef named La Varenne published a book entitled *Le Cuisinier Français*, 'The French Cook'. The book contained a set of recipes reflecting the new French cuisine and also a set of rules for fine cooking. La Varenne rejected most of the old foreign spices in favour of native herbs, such as

parsley, thyme, sage and tarragon. He introduced the term *bouquet garni* for a bundle of such herbs. He insisted that meat and vegetable flavours should not be masked, and recommended using flour and butter – *roux* – to thicken sauces and egg white to clarify them. He was the first to use in print such kitchen terms as *à la mode*, *au naturel* and *au bleu*.

La Varenne's book was an immense success and was soon translated into other languages. The preface to the English edition, published in 1653, states confidently that, 'of all Cookes in the World, the French are esteem'd the best'. It also gives a glossary of untranslatable French words, in effect elevating them to jargon terms for all English-speaking cooks: *fricassée*,

King in the kitchen

Most modern restaurants operate the 'brigade system', whereby the jobs of kitchen staff are assigned according to an army-style hierarchy. The *chef de cuisine* is the general, and each station within the kitchen – meat, fish or desserts – is run by *chefs de partie* who are akin to senior officers. *Commis chefs* and *cuisiniers* are the NCOs, responsible for producing specific dishes and maintaining the kitchen equipment. Below them are

the kitchen infantry: the *apprenti*, the *plongeur* (dishwasher) and the *marmiton* (potwasher).

The military hue of it all is no coincidence. The brigade system was devised by the great French chef Georges Auguste Escoffier, who had served in the Franco-Prussian war of 1870 and realised that the chaos and disorder of the kitchen was not far removed from the confusion of the battlefield. The best way to impose order on both was through a strict assignment of roles and a clear chain

of command. In Escoffier's huge kitchen at London's Ritz hotel – where the disciplined system was first implemented – there were a great many specialist cooks, including *frituriers* (fry cooks), *potagers* (soup cooks) and *confiseurs* (sweet makers). But many present-day chefs manage with a single assistant called a *sous-chef*. In Escoffier's scheme, the *sous-chef* was the powerful deputy of the chef de cuisine, but today he or she is the skilled but put-upon workhorse of the hot, hot stove.

Why can Arbroath smokies only come from Arbroath, but Cheddar cheese can come from anywhere?

Many foods have names that link them to their place of origin and Parma ham, from the Italian city of that name, is one of them. World-famous foods, such as Champagne and Camembert, proclaim where they come from, as does proud local produce such as the Arbroath smokie (below), a distinctively Scottish form of smoked haddock.

Protected by law

All of these foods are enshrined in EU law: they have 'Protected Geographical Indication' (PGI), meaning that, for example, the German delicacy Black Forest ham must hail from a location within the Black Forest.

The European Union grants PGI status on a case-by-case basis and tries to legally protect its PGIs elsewhere in the world. But sometimes long-standing usage and differences of linguistic interpretation make this impossible. The term Cheddar cheese is in America understood to be a generic description of a style of cheese, not an indication of its place of origin. And the USA (along with many countries outside the EU) does not recognise most European PGIs. In New York one can buy a cheese called Parmesan that is a pale imitation of the genuine article. But even if it were delicious it would be illegal to sell it in Britain or Poland under that name, because Parmesan means 'from Parma' and has the same PGI status as the ham that is made there.

PGI status can create absurdities. The name 'Newcastle Brown Ale' is protected but in 2005 the beer's manufacturer moved its factory to a new site on the opposite bank of the River Tyne. The brewery was now technically no longer in Newcastle but in the neighbouring municipality of Gateshead. The company was faced with the choice of moving back across the river or relinquishing its PGI status; it chose the latter.

lardon, hashis, cornet, ramequin, bisque. The genius of La Varenne was that he treated cooking as both an art and a science. At the same historical moment when the French Academy was prescribing the grammar of the French language and the French polymath Descartes was setting the parameters of philosophical enquiry, La Varenne began the process of codifying French cuisine.

Defining modern dining

In addition to new ways of preparing food, France introduced new ways of eating. Traditionally, *service à la française* presented the vast number of dishes from four distinct courses on one large table: diners could help themselves, pass platters to their neighbours and ask for others to be passed to them. Eating was never tranquil; at worst it was a free-for-all, with the shy diner left to eat what was closest or go hungry. In the 19th century, as middle class entertaining achieved the status of competitive sport, households switched to *service à la russe*. Dishes were displayed on a sideboard and served to the diners by household staff, or by a waiter at public functions. The system was not without its critics for the sometimes lengthy wait for courses, and for the diminished choice available within each course. Being served, however, generally made for a more pleasant dining experience – for one thing, the food was generally served hot. The system suited the new restaurants that were springing up across the capital.

French cuisine was never superseded because French chefs were always seeking to write new rules. Among them were Georges Escoffier, who laid down the rules of the professional restaurant kitchen, Marie-Antoine Carême, who defined French haute cuisine for the 20th century, and Paul Bocuse, credited with popularising nouvelle cuisine: essentially a simpler, more natural way of eating that has influenced cooking the world over.

Hot! hot! hot! The peppers that paprika is made from come from the Americas – so how did paprika develop into the defining ingredient of Hungarian cuisine?

PREPARED PAPRIKA on a Hungarian market stall. The powder and paste come in several strengths from pungent to sweet.

Paprika is made from *Capsicum annuum*, the sweet pepper that is native to the Caribbean and Central America. Christopher Columbus found it on the island he called Hispaniola (present-day Haiti) in 1493. He also came across *Capsicum frutescens*, the fiery shrub also known as chilli. One of the aims of Columbus's voyage was to find an alternative trade route for importing black pepper (*Piper nigrum*). The capsicums seemed like the next best thing: new varieties of peppery plant.

Three kinds of peppers

So grouping both varieties of capsicum together, Columbus gave them a name that was a masculine version of the feminine Spanish word for pepper: *pimienta* became *pimiento*. This is why three different foods – the tiny berries that are dried to make black pepper, bell peppers and the little witches' hats of the chilli shrub – are all called 'pepper'. Columbus's new-world peppers did not immediately appeal to European palates, but they continued to be exported to Europe, as there was a ready market for them further east in Arabia, Asia and Turkey.

The Turkish influence

In the middle of the 16th century the Ottoman Turks conquered Hungary and took possession of Budapest. It was during their occupation that paprika was introduced. The first mention of paprika in a Hungarian source comes in a dictionary published in 1604 where it is described as *török bors*, or 'Turkish pepper'. The Hungarians, whose ancestors were migrants from Central Asia, quickly developed an affinity for this novel spice. By the 19th century it had become the key ingredient of many national dishes. Hungarians liked the taste and the colour paprika lent to hearty fare such as *gulyás* (a beef soup), *halászlé* (fish soup) and *pörkölt* (a meat ragu that most closely resembles foreigners' idea of goulash). The peppers from which paprika is derived are now grown in two southern regions of Hungary: one near the city of Szeged, the other close to Kalocsa on the Danube, a subtropical plant now as firmly rooted in the Hungarian soil as a rhapsody by Liszt.

Food from afar

Another food that took root a long way from home and became a staple crop is the tomato. Spaniards first encountered the tomato in Mexico: the word *tomatl* was Aztec for ripe fruit. Tomatoes were brought to Seville in the 16th century, from where they were exported to Italy. Initially considered an ornamental fruit, the Italians got the idea that these new fruits were an aphrodisiac, and started to cook with them. but the Italian *pomodoro* does not, as is sometimes said, mean 'apple of love'. It means 'golden apple': the earliest variants to reach the west were yellow rather than red.

FORBIDDEN FRUIT Tomatoes, like this ornamental specimen drawn in 1613, were considered poisonous by most of Europe and America until the 1800s.

The land and the vine
French wines are defined by their region: Bordeaux, Champagne and Burgundy, but everywhere else in the world wines are described by their grape: Shiraz, Chardonnay and Cabernet Sauvignon. Why is that?

Wine, the fermented juice of grapes, has been drunk throughout human history and produced from grapes of many kinds. Some are known by their place of origin, others by the grape or grapes on which they are based.

Under the Roman Empire, Italy, following on from Greece, was the main wine-producing region. When Rome fell, France gradually became pre-eminent both in viticulture, the cultivation of vines, and in the operation of an increasingly important wine trade. Bordeaux, a city held by the English for much of the Middle Ages, was at the centre of the trade,

exporting many of its wines by sea to England, to the Low Countries and to northern France. The price of Gascon wines, as they were known, fluctuated sharply, partly because of the quality of the harvest, partly because of the impact of warfare, but at that time prices were always higher for new wine, *le vin de l'année*, than for old wine.

It was churchmen, who drank sacramental wine from chalices at Mass, who first drew distinctions by colour between kinds of wine. French churchmen led the way. *Vinum clavum* in Latin or *vin clair* in French,

a wine that would now be called rosé, was distinguished from red wine, *vinum rubrum* or *vin rouge*, which was thicker and with more tannin in it, and later from white wine. Bertrand de Goth, a Gascon archbishop of Bordeaux who in 1305 became Pope Clement V, a pope in exile, gave his name to a later wine of the Graves area near to Bordeaux: Château Pape-Clément. England, the best customer for the wines of Bordeaux, benefited

from the income from taxes imposed on wine imports. Gascon methods were specially favoured, and the scale of their trade was impressive even by 20th-century standards. In 1308-9 the huge figure of 850,000 hectolitres (104,895 *tonneaux*) of Gascon wines were exported to England, constituting one-third of English imports. Many of the wines came from the *haut-pays*, the upper country within the borders of Bordeaux. Bordeaux regulated their trade, laying down the rule that *haut-pays* wines could not be exported before St Martin's Day on 11 November.

St Martin, the 4th-century bishop of Tours and the main founder of monasticism in France, was a patron

UNIQUELY FRENCH Château de Monbazillac, Dordogne, with rolling vineyards that extend over 3,600 hectares. The French believe that wine is the product of its environment – the grape along with the soil, the rainfall, the sunshine and temperature combine to give each vintage its unique flavour.

saint of the wine trade. The Vintners' Company in London, a livery company that regulated the English end of the trade, was located in the parish known as St Martin in the Vintry. They drank not only Gascon wines but 'Rhenish' wines, some of them from Burgundy. As early as 1342 it was laid down in London that innkeepers could not keep Rhenish wines in the same cellars as Gascon wines.

The importance of place

Giving the place of origin of particular wines, the more specific the better, was a new feature in the 17th and 18th centuries. At that time there was a revolution in French wine-making, a *revolution viticole* which was part of a bigger revolution in drinks as a whole, which took in tea, coffee and chocolate (page 57). It long preceded the social and political revolution of 1789. It became practicable to 'age' wines and mature them in barrels and in bottles. *Grands vins* could be identified both by name and by year, with vintage years standing out. Such wines had a noble lineage with much importance being placed on *terroir*, a mysterious term that embodied far more than just the soil. Topography – in as much as it affected soil drainage on a given slope or the amount of sunshine the vines were exposed to – was as relevant to its definition as geology. Terroir determined the effect of a particular mix of vines in a French wine on the drinker's palate: connoisseurs maintained that it was impossible to replicate terroir in a different country – or even, for that matter, in the next valley. One such connoisseur, author Maurice Constantin-Weyer, has written that: 'The influences which rule the vine are so subtle that the slopes of Vosne-Romanée, Chambolle-Musigny and Clos Vougeot, planted with the same

Appellations were granted only after meticulous investigation at the points of origin

Pinot grape, produce wines of such distinct personality that no gourmet could mistake one for the other.'

Wine tasting became an art, and a number of national landmark dates affected all French wines. In 1865, the year of a great exhibition in Paris, the Chamber of Commerce in Bordeaux produced the first quasi-official listing of *crus classés* (or 'classed growth', meaning wines judged to be of exceptional quality). The best wines for ageing, the *grands crus*, were Lafite, Latour, Margaux and Haut-Brion, with Mouton-Rothschild being added, with some controversy, in the 20th century. In 1935 the Institut National des Appellations d'Origine des Vins et Eaux-de-Vies, was set up, which systematically documented the practices largely of Bordeaux wine production and merchants. Its seal of approval – or *Appellation* – was granted only after meticulous investigation at the points

of origin. There was also blind wine tasting to check for quality. No other country evolved such a careful and searching system.

In 1878 the French artist and caricaturist known as Bertall, produced *La Vigne: Voyage autour des Vins de France*, an entertaining atlas of wine that reached a wide audience. By this time the Bordeaux region was well-known for its wines, notably its *grands crus* – long-lasting red and white wines. But the region was also renowned for its cheaper wines and for its luscious sauternes, made from grapes which were overripe or even rotting at the time of gathering. One of these, Château d'Yquem, became an international symbol of luxury.

Another renowned luxury brand is Champagne, the most famous of all sparkling wines. All champagnes, taking their name from a French province of the *ancien régime* before the Revolution, were, and still are, made from only three grape varieties – Pinot, Meunier and Chardonnay. Land in areas producing Champagne, all by

CHATEAU
PERRON —— château

—— artwork

GRAND VIN DE BORDEAUX

LALANDE-DE-POMEROL —— appellation
APPELLATION LALANDE-DE-POMEROL CONTROLEE

2004 —— vintage

MICHEL-P. MASSONIE —— proprietor
PROPRIETAIRE A LALANDE-DE-POMEROL
GIRONDE - FRANCE

MIS EN BOUTEILLE AU CHATEAU —— bottler
PRODUIT DE FRANCE —— country of origin

maven

MARLBOROUGH 2007
SAUVIGNON BLANC

THE MARK OF TRADITION ...
French labels are rooted in the concept of *terroir*, naming – and often depicting – the château, geographic origin and more. The first paper labels were handwritten tags, but the advent of lithography in 1798 meant makers could add information, accolades and individual decorations.

... A BRAVE NEW WORLD
New World wines, named not after the region of production as in Europe, but after the variety of grape, are generally considered to be innovative, scientifically produced newcomers. Their labels often reflect their modern, spirited style, with a strong graphic or idiosyncratic design.

the same *méthode champenoise*, was carefully delimited in area. This area was only slightly increased – and then only following long discussion – in 2008 after world consumption in Japan, Australia and India increased dramatically during the last decades of the 20th century.

Wines around the world

Non-European countries are now producers as well as consumers of wines and spirits. Australia, together with New Zealand, Argentina, Chile and the USA, have extensive wine-growing areas and produce many fine wines and in India, Mumbai produces and markets its own sparkling wine. Perhaps the most famous wine producing area outside Europe is the Napa Valley in California. And some of the 'wineries', the US name for vineyards, now have French owners – just as Americans now own some of the oldest vineyards in France.

There was a dramatic 19th-century prelude to the 20th-century globalisation of a transformed wine trade. During the 1860s and '70s large areas of France were devastated by phylloxera, a disease carried by aphids which fed on the roots of vines. It started in the Rhône Valley in 1863 and was checked only after stocks of American vines, resistant to phylloxera, were imported from California and grafted on to local vines.

As in France, many European wines are known by the region in which they are produced, each with its own history like Rioja in Spain, Mosel in Germany and Barolo in Italy. But others are known by the names of the constituent grapes from which they are produced, as are most of the wines from outside Europe. Young wines are now favoured since wine buyers no longer have cellars in which they can store old wines. Although there are still connoisseurs who buy and hold their wines in bond, an increasing number of wine buyers purchase their wines not from specialised wine

merchants but from supermarkets (page 72). Most of the major stores have expert buyers who compare wines from differerent hemispheres to provide a varied selection to their customers at a range of prices.

In recent years, to differentiate their products from other New World wines, many producers have worked hard to endow their country's products with a sense of place and a geographical branding. Locations on the global wine map include Jacob's Creek in Australia and Cloudy Bay in New Zealand where the name of the place, not the grape, is the mark of quality. It is not so great a leap from there to a new world version of terroir.

What is the significance of the different shapes of wine bottles?

There are two predominant shapes for wine bottles, both French. Bordeaux bottles have rounded shoulders and a longish straight neck; Burgundy bottles sloping shoulders and a shorter neck. Corked cylindrical bottles first appeared in the 18th century to hold wines that would be aged. Square bottles would have been more economical, but were popular only in Holland where they held gin. It is said that the shoulders of the Bordeaux bottle are good for catching the sediment at the bottom of an aged bottle but that is an incidental benefit of the design, not its primary function.

With wines from other nations the bottle may indicate that the wine is similar in style to French Bordeaux or Burgundy. Californian, Australian and South American wines usually follow French wine-bottle shapes. Californian Cabernets are sold in Bordeaux bottles because Cabernet Sauvignon is the most common Bordeaux grape. But in some countries the shape of the bottle may be simply a whim of the vintner.

Even within Europe, there are other bottling traditions. German wine-makers often use tall, elongated Mosel bottles, while some Spanish and Portuguese wines that are drunk 'young' feature squat 'onion bottles', a throwback to the 18th century, when all wine was drunk young and did not need to be stored. From the onion, bottles developed into a 'mallet' shape with a squarer body.

Champagne was transported around the world in thick bottles crafted to withstand the pressure of the bubbles within. The deep 'punt' or indentation in the bottom adds tensile strength, which allows the bottles to be stacked upside down during the fermentation process.

ONION   MALLET   BORDEAUX   BURGUNDY   MOSEL   CHAMPAGNE

Say cheese Cheese is one of the most diverse foodstuffs in the world: every culture that herds animals consumes some form of cheese. But why not just drink the milk?

The biblical story of David and Goliath begins when the young shepherd-boy is told to take cheese to the Israelite army, where his brothers were fighting the Philistines: 'And Jesse said unto David his son, "Take now for thy brethren … these ten loaves, and run to the camp … And carry these ten cheeses unto the captain of their thousand …"' David lived around 3,000 years ago

A BOWL OF AYRAG Fermented mare's milk is a celebration drink for this Mongolian wrestler after a victorious fight. It is sour, sparkling and lightly alchoholic.

but there is evidence that cheese-making, as a culinary practice, existed for many millennia before that.

An ancient craft

The Vorderasiatisches Museum in Berlin holds the fiscal accounts of a Sumerian stock-breeder written on clay tablets during the 21st century BC. On them he records that his output of cheese increased from 8 litres a year to 63 litres over the course of five years. The physical evidence for cheese-mongering goes back further still. Throughout Europe and the Middle East, archaeologists have found

HOMER'S CHEESE A Bronze Age painted terracotta model from Ritsona in Greece shows a figure using a sharpened wedge to grate a block of hard cheese into a bowl.

fragments of pots pierced with small drainage holes: it is likely that these pots were used from at least 8,000 years ago to separate curds from whey, the essential first stage in any cheese-making process.

But why did prehistoric people bother to make cheese at all if the raw

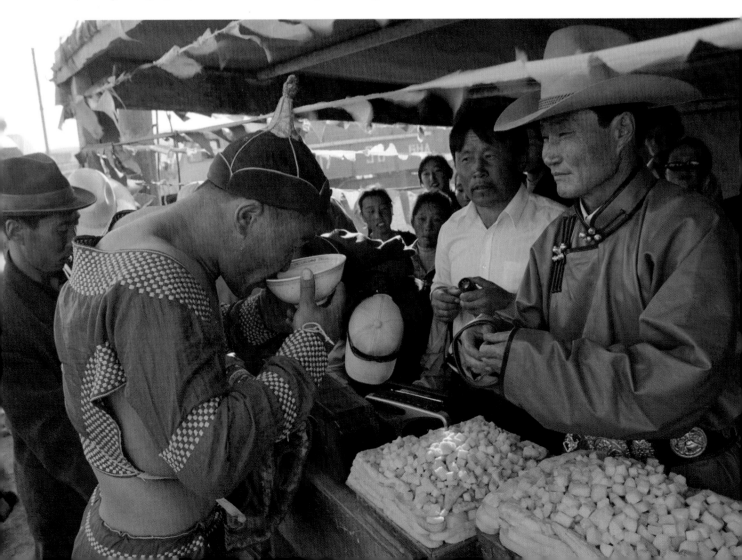

milk of a goat or cow is just as nutritious? The principal reason is humans' innate inability to digest milk. In its raw form, milk contains a sugar called lactose. The people of societies with no milking tradition (such as those in Asia) still lack the enzyme that would enable their bodies to digest the milk. The process of boiling, fermenting and cheese-making all destroy lactose, rendering the resource easy to eat, and it was these processed products that prehistoric pastoralists ate. Over time, their societies' diet enabled them to build up a tolerance for the raw product – a tolerance that exists in milk-using societies today.

Practical and portable

Cheese is essentially milk from which all the heavy and nutritionally superfluous water has been removed. It contains all the useful fats and proteins of milk, but is much denser and more portable; one might call it the first dehydrated food. But cheese has one other crucial property that makes it better than raw milk. Once it has been manufactured, cheese generally remains edible for a long time. In biblical times and earlier, animals such as goats and aurochs (ancestors of the domestic cow) would have borne their calves in season. The milk that nourished the calf would have been available to the earliest pastoralists for only a short time, from the birth of the calf until it was weaned. By harvesting the milk and turning it into cheese, the first herders were providing themselves with a renewable source of protein that they could consume over many months. It fulfilled the same function for milk as did jam-making for fruit, pickling for vegetables and smoking and salting for meat and fish.

Multiplicity of flavours

There have always been many ways of making cheese and there are countless variables involved in the process. These include the species of the animal that provides the milk: cow, ewe, goat, yak, horse or even reindeer; the method by which the milk is coagulated and the water extracted; the use of salt as a preservative and of bacteria to break down the proteins in the ripening cheese; the manner in which it is stored and the use of herbs or other foods to flavour it.

The result of this multiplicity of possibilities is a foodstuff that is more diverse than any other on the planet. The French president Charles de Gaulle once remarked: 'How do you govern a country with 246 different kinds of cheese?' He was understating the case: there are more like 400 known cheeses in France and the number of cheeses worldwide are too many to be counted. The soft, melting round ones of northern France, the dried Mongolian camel curd called *zookhii*, the venerable mould-ridden Stilton: each represents an adaptation of a universal principle to local circumstances. All cheese, just like all life, is a variation on the same single theme.

How did the idea that mouldy cheese was a delicacy arise?

Delicacies are not merely foods that taste exquisite: plenty of cheap and ordinary dishes are wonderful to eat. A delicacy is a food that requires a great investment of effort or expense to bring it to the table: truffles, for example, are extremely hard to find and so have rarity value for the gourmand.

The same applies to Roquefort, the most famous of the 'mouldy' cheeses and the so-called 'roi des fromages'. Its appeal lies in its unique nature. It is made from ewes' milk and the curds are stacked in layers with mouldy breadcrumbs to introduce the blue veining. After salting and pressing, it is matured extremely slowly in the natural caves of Roquefort, where the temperature is constant and the humidity high due to an underground lake. Only cheeses that emerge from these caves can be termed Roquefort.

A similar air of exclusivity is attached to Stilton – England's best-known 'mouldy' cheese. A Stilton cheese can be made only in one of the counties of Derbyshire, Nottinghamshire and Leicestershire. Oddly, this excludes the village of Stilton, which is in Cambridgeshire. The cheese that bears the village's name was never made there.

ROQUEFORT CHEESE

Dining out For centuries most people ate at home. Now city streets are lined with cafés, restaurants and snack bars. So when did eating out become the social event that it is today?

For as long as people have needed to spend time away from home, there have been institutions that would provide food in exchange for money. Wayside taverns have been a feature of every civilisation from the Romans to the Victorians. But in every age and every country, such inns did little more than satisfy hunger. For hundreds of years eating in public was not dining, it was merely feeding.

The coffee houses that flourished in Europe from the mid-17th century were principally meeting houses – forums for the intellectuals of the day. In England they earned the nickname 'penny universities' after the stimulating conversation and the coffee – which cost a penny a cup. Such establishments rarely offered any more than light snacks. Hungry patrons had to return home, or find a tavern that had the good sense to employ a cook. Coffee houses remained popular, evolving into cafés across Europe while in England they became gentlemen's clubs.

The restaurant revolution

The idea that cooking is an art, and that enjoying food is an aesthetic experience worth paying for, arose in France in the middle of the 18th century. The philosophical groundwork came from the French thinker Jean Brillat-Savarin, whose most famous aphorism is, 'Tell me what you eat and I will tell you what you are.' He noted the appearance in Paris of 'restaurants' – a word first recorded in its modern sense in 1765 – and defined them later as places where people could eat whenever they wanted, choosing from a list of dishes and knowing in advance how much they were going to pay.

The first luxury restaurants in Paris were hampered by the fact that in France the many guilds of caterers owned the exclusive right to prepare certain dishes: a *rôtisseur* was permitted to roast meat but not bake it in the oven; a *pâtisseur* could make and sell pastries, but not sell wine – which was the professional domain of the *aubergiste*. The 1789 Revolution abolished the guilds and swept away the legal obstacles to a varied menu. The Revolution also put many of the best chefs out of work, as they were generally employed by noble families, many of whom went to the guillotine. Deprived of patronage, France's chefs turned to commerce and opened food shops and restaurants.

After the Revolution a third gastronomical factor emerged: a burgeoning middle class ready to spend money on pleasures once enjoyed almost exclusively by the aristocracy. Dining out became democratised, reinvented as a leisure activity that a growing swathe of society could afford.

The experience provided by the classic Parisian restaurant would nowadays be described as 'fine dining' and is just one of many modes of 'eating out'. All the modern sub-species of restaurant have evolved over the past 150 years or so. The 'bistrot', a more informal, slightly rustic take on the restaurant, is first attested in the 1880s. It is sometimes said that the bistro was born when Russian soldiers found themselves in Paris at the end of the Napoleonic wars; they would sit in cafés and shout '*Bystro*!' – the Russian for 'quickly' – so a bistro came to mean a café where service was swift. This is a myth; the word probably comes from the French dialect term *bistraud*, meaning 'servant'.

Eating out – US style

Many modern ways of eating out were invented in America. The self-service cafeteria, for example, originated in California during the gold rush of 1849. And Prohibition led to the rise of luncheonettes and alcohol-free diners. Their limited menus were perfectly suited to urban office workers who wanted food that was cheap, consistent and speedy. As such, they paved the way for the 20th century's most radical change in eating out: the unstoppable fast-food revolution.

When did people start eating with a knife and fork?

Well into the 17th century, knives and spoons were the only utensils most diners in Europe ever used – and ever needed, as food was either dry or soupy, so could be cut or supped with a spoon. Large two-pronged forks were used in the kitchen for preparation purposes only, though refined diners in Greece and Italy had, for some time, used a smaller version at the table. An Englishman named Thomas Coryat observed them in action in 1608. 'The Italians doe alwaies, at their meales, use a little forke... The Italian cannot indure to have his dish touched with fingers, seeing all mens fingers are not alike cleane.' Though Coryat was ridiculed for effeminacy when he used a fork back home, the use of both knives and forks was becoming more common by the mid-17th century.

The modern curved, four-tined fork was invented in Germany in the 18th century. Around this time the dinner knife evolved a rounded end – its spearing function now obsolete. It was only in the 19th century that forks became prevalent in the USA, where they were often called 'split spoons'. The late adoption of the fork goes some way to explaining the modern American habit of cutting food, then transferring the fork to the other hand and using it as a spoon-like scoop.

Chopsticks and cuisine

Unlike those of the rest of the world, China's eating utensils evolved alongside its cuisine, which has always featured small morsels. In ancient China, the word for the art of cookery was *ko'peng*, which means 'cut and cook'. This mode of preparation meant that cooking could be swift, maintaining the texture and colour of the food. Spices and flavours could permeate all ingredients, too. Chopsticks are the perfect utensil for Chinese cuisine, because they practically guarantee that food can be savoured – a piece at a time. No prehistoric chopsticks survive: the earliest extant pair dates only to the Shang dynasty (c.1766-1122 BC).

NEWFANGLED FORKS Two gentlemen eating with the latest fashion in cutlery in an 11th-century Italian copy of the encyclopedic work, *De Universo*, written by the monk Raban Maur. It was at least five centuries before the fork found favour at the tables of northern Europe.

A place for pudding Why don't we start a meal with pudding? Is there any gastric or gastronomic reason that we tend to eat savoury foods to start a meal and sweet foods at the end?

People have always loved to eat sweet things. Indeed, babies are predisposed to prefer sweet flavours over sour or bitter ones. There is a 12,000-year-old rock painting at the Cueva de la Araña (Cave of the Spider) in Spain that shows a figure tentatively climbing a vine to raid a bees' nest. For millennia, hard-to-come-by honey was the only sweetener available to humankind. The ancient Greeks used it extensively. They had confections known as *melipekton* ('honey-curdled') and *melitoutta* ('honey-flavoured'). They also made *amphiphon*, a kind of sweet cheesecake, and they enjoyed a snack called *enkris*,

which was fried dough soaked in honey – the ancestor of that tooth-achingly sweet and sticky Greek dish, baklava.

But none of these sweetmeats were eaten for pudding. The amphiphon was baked once a year as a sacrificial offering to the goddess Artemis and offered at her shrine with lighted candles on it, the ancient precursor of today's birthday cake.

Honey, wine and meat

The Greeks and the Romans ate sweet, wine-infused bread at their meals (*mustaceus* in Latin), but its main function was to soak up meat

juices. The Roman writer Petronius, in a satirical account of a gluttonous feast, mentions a couple of dozen separate dishes, but only one of them appears to be sweet. It is a dish of 'cold tart and Spanish wine poured over warm honey'. It comes right in the middle of the meal: after the dormice with poppy seeds; the pig's liver and the beetroot; and before the

SWEET CENTREPIECE The 19th-century writer Mrs Beeton described about 170 puddings in her *Book of Household Management*. Presentation was key: even fruit was tastefully arranged.

Macédoine of Fruits.
Jelly with whipped Cream.
Pine Apple and Grapes.
Ice Pudding.
Lemon Jelly.
Charlotte of Pommes.
Mixed Fruits.
Strawberries.
Cherries.
Melon and Green figs.
Candied Oranges.
Apricots.
Plums.
Chantilly Basket.
Christmas Plum Pudding.
Ribbon Jelly.
Chocolate Cake.
Rice Croquettes.
Custards.
Ices.
Meringues.
Sponge Cake.
Tartlets.
Red and white Currants.
Greengages.
Open Tart.
Wedding Cake.
Compote of Pears.
Neapolitan Cake.
Tri le.
Plum Cake.
Compote of Apples.
Gâteau.

chickpeas and lupins, bear meat, tripe and cumin in vinegar.

As a rule, the Romans liked to end their meals with 'salads', which meant something salty and acidic such as oysters or sea urchins as well as leafy greenery. But during the reign of Trajan, at the end of the first century, salads had migrated to the beginning of a Roman feast. 'Tell me,' asked the poet Martial. 'Why is it that lettuce, which used to end our grandfathers' dinners, now ushers in our banquets?'

Changing tastes

The custom of eating courses in a fixed order died with the Roman Empire. At medieval European banquets, all dishes were served at once. Sweet things did play a part in medieval feasting: sugar was used in sauces for meat and to make frivolities such as crystallised fruit and sugared nuts. The sugar was imported from the east, the only source of cane sugar until the discovery of the West Indies. Arab traders kept a closely guarded sugar-cane refinery on the island of Crete – the Arabic name for which was *qandi*, or candy.

By the end of the 16th century, sweet tastes were beginning to find a place at the end of the meal. A 1582 account of Englishmen at table in Italy describes a five-course meal consisting of anchovies, followed by a vegetable 'mess of pottage', various boiled meats, then roasted meat and finally 'preserved conceits', sometimes figs, almonds and raisins, a lemon and sugar, a pomegranate, 'or some such sweet gear, for Englishmen loveth sweet meats.'

The gourmands of the Renaissance took the view that salty, savoury things were stimulating to the appetite and that sweet things killed it. This is why they relegated sweet things to the end of the meal, so as not to interfere with the long drawn-out enjoyment of a feast. The sweet course was not even considered part of dinner as such: it was served at the *voidée*, the close of the meal, after the table was cleared. In Italy, the most gastronomic country

CANDIED CONFECTION A popular French wedding cake, the *Croquembouche* is dessert of piled, cream-filled choux. Its name – 'crunch-in-the-mouth' – comes from its glossy, hardened sugar glaze.

of the Renaissance, even fruit was considered suspiciously sweet. It was still served at the start of a banquet, but always with preserved meat to counteract its appetite-suppressing effect. This is the origin of modern first-course pairings such as figs and prosciutto or sliced ham with melon.

A banquet of sweets

The sweet-toothed English also liked the idea of having meat and sweet things together, but they found a different way to do it. In the Stuart era there was a fashion, made possible by the growing trade in imported sugar, for spectacular confectionery made to look like savoury dishes: haunches of pork made from marzipan, fried eggs fashioned from sweet jellies and bacon slices crafted

from crystallised caramel. Sometimes these sweet banquets were social occasions in themselves. But more often they were an amusing diversion at the end of a meal – in which case they were known as 'desserts', from the French *desservir*, 'to clear away.' The word 'dessert', along with the practice of serving something sweet to end a meal, carried on after the fashion for sweet banquets died out.

The last course remained a piece of sugary virtuosity. In the 18th century, when all Europe was under the influence of the new French cuisine, desserts took an architectural turn. Marie-Antoine Carême, pâtissier and chef, popularised the *pièce montée*, a magnificent confection that was as much sculpture as pudding. Some resembled Greek ruins or fountains of spun sugar. These ensembles were sometimes populated with edible human figures. Today's intricate tiered and iced wedding cakes, topped with a model bride and groom, are perhaps the last vestige of this fashion.

The era of real puddings

Creams, jellies, syllabubs and fruit compôtes were often served alongside the creations of French confectioners, remaining popular once the fad for over-engineered desserts abated. The Victorians added 'puddings' to this more modest range of dishes. The word originally denoted a kind of boiled sausage like black pudding, but came to mean sweet dishes that were boiled in a similar way, such as the mixture of suet and dried fruit known in Britain as 'spotted dick'. In the course of the 19th century, the word pudding acquired its modern British sense: any sweet dish served as a last course. In the United States, that word did not catch on: Americans stuck with the older term 'dessert'. And it was America that popularised the appeal of sweet fare, such as pies, tarts and ice cream – all the toothsome dishes without which the main meal of the day seems somehow incomplete.

The rise of the supermarket

Supermarkets now account for more than 70 per cent of all grocery spending in the western world. How did one form of shopping come to dominate all the rest?

The modern supermarket is a machine for shopping in. It is a retail production line, carefully designed to draw people in at one end, to encourage them to buy, and to expel them quickly and efficiently at the other end. As is the case with any complex technological device, the elements of the supermarket appeared at different times in different places. But the key innovations came about in America in the first half of the 20th century and many of them were the brainwaves of inspired, driven pioneers.

One of these trailblazers was a businessman named Clarence Saunders and his contribution to the supermarket was to popularise the idea of self-service. Before the First World War, buying groceries was a matter of getting the storekeeper or an assistant to fetch items one at a time, weigh them out and pack them in bags. The arrangement was expensive, because a lot of time and trained manpower had to be invested in each customer. Saunders spotted that having the customer pick what they wanted off open shelves would reduce overheads, allowing shops to sell goods more cheaply and so undercut their rivals.

Piggly Wiggly pioneer

In 1916 Saunders opened a self-service grocery shop in Memphis, Tennessee. He called the store Piggly Wiggly – a deliberately facetious name that he believed would intrigue potential customers. On the day the store opened

SELF-SERVICE The first self-service grocery chain to open in America was the Piggly Wiggly group. It still operates across 17 states today.

he arranged for roses to be presented to all red-haired women who walked through the door. Bizarre showmanship of this sort was part of Saunders' method, but his inventive mind also came up with retailing ideas that are still part of the infrastructure of the supermarket. He stocked only prepackaged, branded goods and made sure that every item was individually priced. He dealt with shoplifting – a serious problem at first – by introducing separate points of entry and exit, along with turnstiles that made it difficult to leave through the in-door. Most recognisably of all, he installed individual tables for each cashier with a narrow gangway in between – the prototype of the modern checkout. Saunders' mix of attention-grabbing stunts and common-sense retail thinking created a new shopping phenomenon. By 1923, there were more than 2,500 Piggly Wiggly stores in the USA.

Improving the economics

The Piggly Wiggly empire was vast but the stores were quite small – like a neighbourhood shop. Michael Cullen, manager of an Illinois branch of a grocery chain named Krogers, was the first to realise that this was inefficient: large stores with a constant stream of customers and low profit margins would make more money than small stores with fewer customers and higher prices. This was just one of Cullen's

THE BIG SHOP By the 1960s supermarket shopping was a self-service experience. And the more work the customers put in – filling their own trolleys and loading their own cars – the more money the store owners saved.

How did chicken and smoked salmon lose their luxury status?

Before the Second World War, roast chicken and smoked salmon were rare treats. Chickens were farmed for their eggs and eaten when their laying days were over. Salmon was found only in the wild. In both cases, new intensive farming technology changed the status of these foods, shifting them from luxury to everyday purchases.

Chicken factories

From the 1950s, antibiotics introduced into animal feed have made it possible to keep tens of thousands of chickens in close proximity without running the risk of epidemics. And the creation of hatcheries have transformed chicken farming into an industrial process: artificially inseminated birds produce eggs that are cleaned, incubated and hatched thousands at a time. The resulting broiler chickens are plumped up and 'harvested' for the food industry on the same large, economical scale.

Salmon farms

The farming of salmon has come about as stocks of wild salmon dwindled to the point where it is unviable and ecologically unsound to fish them. Nearly all the salmon sold in shops comes from 'farms' where the fish are raised in pens suspended in the sea. Ideally, the fish occupy two per cent of the space inside the pens, the rest is fast-flowing seawater. The cages make it easy to net the fish ready for processing.

Such industrial methods have made chicken and salmon available for all. Whether food produced in this way tastes as good, or is an 'ethical' way to raise animals – is a matter of heated and continual debate.

many ideas. It also occurred to him that large food shops should have a car park. This could be marketed as a convenience for the shopper, but it was also a means by which the store could relinquish responsibility for delivering the goods to its customers' homes. Like self-service, it made the paying client do work that previously had to be done by a paid employee of the store. And if customers could be encouraged to shop in their cars, then their purchases were no longer limited to what they could carry: they would buy more. What is more, stores could be located conveniently away from busy city centres – which would benefit the store by keeping overheads low.

Cullen presented his ideas in a letter to the president of the company, William Albers. The letter ended with an impassioned exhortation: 'Nobody ever did this before,' wrote Cullen, 'But nobody ever flew the Atlantic either until Lindbergh did it … it would be a riot. I would have to call out the police and let the public in so many at a time. I would lead the public out of the high-priced houses of bondage into the low prices of the house of the promised land. What is your verdict?' Albers' verdict was 'No'. Perhaps he was put off by Cullen's overwrought tone. So in 1930 Cullen went it alone, opening his first 'King Kullen Market' in a disused garage in Queens, New York City, well away from Manhattan. He adopted a slogan – 'Pile it high, sell it low' – designed to appeal to shoppers in the hungry years of the Depression. That thought has since become a kind of unstated motto for supermarkets everywhere. Cullen, like Saunders

before him, soon had a chain of stores – all of them set up in cheaply acquired industrial buildings, such as warehouses and empty factories. His success was noticed by his former employer, William Albers, who paid Cullen the huge back-handed compliment of giving up his job as president of Krogers to found a self-service grocery chain of his own. Albers copied many of Cullen's techniques, but his main contribution to the evolution of the supermarket is the word itself: he called his chain Albers Super Markets. He meant the term descriptively – his markets were not just good, they were super – but the two words quickly fused into one and became the dictionary term for this new species of shop.

The birth of the shopping trolley

Meanwhile another essential feature of the supermarket – the supermarket trolley – was becoming a common sight. One early experiment in a Texas store involved baskets that were fixed to a tramline in the shelves. Customers were expected to push their basket along the rail, filling it as they went. But this system forced the shopper to follow the tramlines round every aisle in the store, whether they wanted to or not. And they made it impossible for faster shoppers to overtake. In the mid-1930s, many stores introduced 'folding basket carriers', X-shaped frames on wheels that could carry two standard baskets. These simple devices were described hyperbolically in trade journals as 'the greatest salesman ever put in a market'. They certainly removed one of the constraints on buying: the weight of the shopping before it was paid for.

The 'telescopic' trolley, where each carrier slots neatly and compactly into the one in front, was patented by an

> 'I would lead the public out of the high-priced houses of bondage into the low prices of the house of the promised land'
>
> Michael Cullen

engineer named Orla E. Watson in 1946. The Watson carts were first tried out at Milgram Food Store in Kansas City, from where they spread around the world. As sometimes happens with good engineering, the basic design has remained practically unchanged – except for the addition of accessories such as baby seats and the mysterious forward compartment.

Supermarkets come to Europe

The essential elements of the supermarket were in place by the mid-1930s. But they were still an exclusively American way of shopping. That changed after the Second World War, when two British businessmen independently visited the USA. One was Jack Cohen, owner of the growing Tesco chain of grocery shops. He was the son of East European Jewish immigrants and had started out as a stallholder in the East End of London. The other was Alan Sainsbury, grandson of John James Sainsbury, the wealthy Victorian founder of the family provisions business. Both men saw instantly that the American-style supermarket was the way forward for their firms and from the late 1940s they began to make over their stores to the self-service model.

The super supermarkets

In the early 1960s, an average supermarket had floor space of about 4,500sq ft (418m²). The 'footprint' of the supermarket grew steadily, but giant chains did not appear in Britain until the 1968, when a newcomer to the sector – ASDA – opened two vast purpose-built stores, each with 80,000sq ft (6,500m²) of space. They were a phenomenal success. On one occasion ASDA's founder, Peter Asquith, had to hold back the crowds at the door – fulfilling Michael Cullen's earlier prophecy about the irresistible attraction of large, out-of-town food stores. That magnetic effect was good for the supermarkets, but bad for small independents nearby.

Supermarkets tend to draw custom away from older retailers and may put them out of business. This is one of the long-standing criticisms of supermarkets and one of the main reasons for their dominance: the only kind of shop that can compete with a supermarket is another supermarket.

The biggest giant in this world of giants is Wal-Mart. It was founded in Arkansas in 1962 by Sam Walton, another of those energetic, eccentric moneymakers the supermarket industry seems to produce. He was personally very stingy, drove an old pick-up truck and once danced down 5th Avenue in a hula skirt as a forfeit when he was proved wrong about his company's profit forecasts. The company he built from a tiny chain of variety stores has become the largest private employer in the world, with almost two million members of staff. Walton himself was for several years the richest man on the planet.

Supermarkets have come a long way in the 90 or so years of their existence, but the business model has never really changed. Wal-Mart's slogan was for many years 'Always low prices, always', a business attitude and a sales pitch which Clarence Saunders and Michael Cullen would have understood and heartily approved.

How is it possible that we can now buy strawberries every day of the year?

The natural Northern European strawberry season lasts for about six weeks in the summer. Two things have allowed supermarkets to extend that season round the year. The first is the global supply chain, which makes it economical to fly strawberries into Europe from hot climates, such as California, parts of Japan and even the Gaza Strip. These foreign strawberries cover just part of the yearly cycle. The rest of the year, supermarkets sell strawberries artificially cultivated close to home. Growers in Europe – notably Spain and Poland – extend the season to six months by planting strawberries in sterilised soil inside vast heated polytunnels that protect the crop from rain. Only certain varieties can be grown this way so a consequence of the eternal summer for strawberry lovers is a narrower choice of fruit for everybody.

STRAWBERRIES FROM GAZA

Eating our way thin We in the west spend billions every year on trying to lose weight. How did dieting become such a massive and lucrative industry?

Dieting is big business. It has been estimated that two-thirds of Americans are overweight and in the USA alone the diet industry is worth over $30 billion annually. Every supermarket stocks hundreds of low-fat, 'lite' or 'sugar-free' food items; weight-loss manuals constitute an entire genre of the publishing industry; pharmacies sell diet shakes and slimming pills alongside toothbrushes and headache cures; boot camps for obese children and celebrity fat shows are a popular subset of reality TV. There are fat profits to be had from the global yearning to be thin.

All of this is a relatively new phenomenon. Our ancestors never dieted; most people were more worried about the prospect of starving than the perils of overeating. The idea that plumpness was unattractive did not exist in earlier centuries. A well-padded body was once seen as a sign of affluence and a large frame signified power: Louis XIV of France wore quilted clothes to bulk out his slight torso, making him look more impressive and powerful.

Linking diet to health

The first person to advocate the use of diet as a route to good health was an American minister named Sylvester Graham. He achieved a sizeable following in the 1830s and 1840s by advocating a vegetarian, teetotal regime that excluded spices and condiments of any kind. An important part of his dull but worthy diet was 'Graham bread', which prefigured modern nutritional thinking in that it was made from wholemeal flour. It was also baked without the use of industrial bleaching agents, such as chlorine, common in white bread at the time. Graham claimed his diet would help its adherents avoid gluttony. 'Excessive alimentation is the greatest dietetic error in the United States,' he wrote prophetically in 1838, 'And probably in the whole civilised world.'

An added benefit of the Graham diet, according to its author, was that it dampened carnal feelings. The sexual appetite and the appetite for food were, in Graham's philosophy, two heads of the same untamed beast. The link between food and sin,

BEFORE AND AFTER Diane Fing, 1979's Weight Watcher of the Year, sits next to her 'before' self. Weight Watchers believe that anyone can achieve long-term weight loss.

between fat and guilt, is one of Graham's enduring contributions to quasi-nutritional thought. His other legacy is the Graham cracker, though it is no longer the healthy rusk its inventor had in mind, but a kind of semi-sweet digestive biscuit.

A diet to lose weight

Graham's diet, though it railed against overeating, was not intended specifically to make people thinner. The idea of targeted weight loss through diet belongs to an upmarket undertaker from London named William Banting. He was so rotund that he could not tie his own shoelaces and had to walk downstairs backwards so as not to jar his overburdened knees. On the advice of his doctor he cut out 'starch and saccharine matter', and lost a great deal of weight. In 1863 he published a pamphlet – *Letter on Corpulence, Addressed to the Public* – in which he described his long quest to slim down. So Banting is not just the father of dieting; he is also the progenitor of the diet book.

The *Letter on Corpulence* employs some techniques that are still favoured by publishers of diet manuals today. They include the use of a spectacularly successful ex-fatty in the role of author; a confessional narrative documenting the failures and false trails while on the quest for slimness (which in Banting's case included living on sixpence a day, going to Turkish baths and horseback riding); and the eventual, triumphant discovery of an easy-to-grasp slimming formula – in this case, a century before Dr Robert Atkins, the low-carb approach. William Banting did not publish his diet for financial gain and made no money from his book. It became such a huge bestseller, however, that for decades after the author's name was used as a verb:

VICTORIAN VOLUME Diet writer William Banting as portrayed in the satirical magazine *Punch*, July 1895. Banting once quipped 'big ships are not built with scanty materials'.

'No cake for me, thank you, I am banting.' Both Graham's and Banting's diets were nutritionally sound, more or less. But by the end of the century an element of faddiness was creeping into the burgeoning diet business.

The first weight-loss guru

In 1895 a well-to-do and distinctly tubby American businessman hit upon a new and dubious route to thinness and in the process became the world's first champion of weight loss. His name was Horace Fletcher, and his method was called Fletcherism. The essence of the Fletcherist cult was that overeating could be avoided simply by chewing all food thoroughly. Fletcher recommended a minimum of 32 chews per mouthful – even for soup – and warned that 'nature will castigate those who do not masticate'. Eating in this manner, or 'fletcherising', he avowed, would turn 'a pitiable glutton into an intelligent Epicurean'. Fletcher backed

Horace Fletcher recommended a minimum of 32 chews per mouthful – even for soup

up his practices with a philosophy derived from the new mechanical age. The body was analogous to a motorcar and he exhorted his followers to be 'competent chauffeurs of our own corpoautomobiles'. He was obsessively interested in the machine's emissions: he regularly weighed his own faeces and made descriptive notes, such as 'No more odor than a hot biscuit'. It was the start of a preoccupation with the bowel that led ultimately to the late 20th-century craze for colonic irrigation.

Food alert

The merit of Fletcherism, if there were one, lay in the fact that it forced people to be mindful of what they were eating and to take their time over it – so Fletcher's disciples probably did end up eating less. As with Banting, his ideas gained currency because they had so obviously worked for him personally. Using his own methods, 'the Great Masticator' lost more than 40 pounds and remained slim for the rest of his life. He worked hard at publicising his ideas and as a result his 'industrious munching' caught on in fashionable circles. Ladies would sit and chew, thoughtfully and silently, for minutes at a time in voguish New York restaurants.

A different kind of thinking was brought to bear on the problem of 'reducing' in the 1920s, when a Yale economist named Irving Fisher drew an analogy between nutrition and economic theory. Fisher took the concept of market equilibrium – the idea that the influx of resources into the system should be equal to the outward flow – and suggested that in order to avoid a glut, the body should manage the intake of food as carefully and efficiently as a company manages its cash flow. So the value of food had to be totted up and accounted for like the pennies on a balance sheet. This idea seemed to make sense and there was a mania for calorie counting throughout the decade. Some restaurants printed calorie values alongside every dish on the menu and modish writers on diet advocated a lifetime of quantified frugality based on an intake of 1,200 calories a day. The analogy with sound business practice faded away after the Wall Street Crash of 1929 – but the obsession with calorie counting persisted for most of the century.

It worked for me!

In the 1930s, the diet world found a new set of champions: not the chubby male innovators of previous decades, but the svelte, beautiful female movie star who endorsed one regime or another. A ringing recommendation from Hollywood was what made a diet plan popular. Jean Harlow and Gloria Swanson sang the praises of a masseuse named Sylvia Ullbeck who could knead flesh until astonishingly, 'fat comes out through the pores like mashed potato through a colander'. Amelia Earhart, the first woman to fly solo across the Atlantic, appeared in adverts for Lucky Strike cigarettes and exhorted slimmers to 'reach for a Lucky instead of a sweet'. A generic 'Hollywood diet' tapped into the collective glamour of all the starlets of Tinseltown. It involved subsisting

SKINNY SNACKS Slimming biscuits, sometimes marketed as 'between-meal nibbles', provided 1960s' dieters with a flavoursome snack that didn't pile on the pounds.

mostly on grapefruit and boiled eggs – and gave followers a total energy intake of just 585 calories a day. Celebrity endorsement remains a key weapon in the armoury of the diet industry.

Pills and sweeteners

Chemical methods were first deployed against flab in the 1940s. It was known that amphetamines, widely used in the Second World War to keep fighter pilots alert, had the side effect of suppressing appetite. For the next 30 years they were prescribed by doctors and sold by pharmacists as slimming pills, alongside other drugs

that reduced weight, such as diuretics. In addition, synthetic sugar substitutes marketed under names such as NutraSweet and Sweet'N'Low were being popped into coffee cups by the billion in the 1960s and 1970s. The same substances were the miracle ingredients in 'lo-cal' soft drinks, such as Tab.

In the second half of the 20th century, the diet industry borrowed ever more widely from other spheres of knowledge. Weight Watchers, the brainchild of an overweight New York housewife named Jean Nidetch, was no more or less than the psychological practice of weekly group therapy applied to the mental challenges of losing weight.

Constant innovation

The concept of 'de-toxing' was adapted from pharmacology – as if food were a form of poison – and put forward as a way of kick-starting a diet program. The idea of the glycemic index as a kind of barometer of inner fatness was borrowed from medical research done to help diabetics manage their blood-sugar levels. All sorts of technological know-how has been devised for slimmers unwilling to do calorie-burning physical exercise, some of it effective, some not: vibrating belts that claimed to evaporate fat by jiggling it about; electric nodes that twitch the muscles to make them work while you rest; and liposuction, a surgical intervention to drain liquid blubber from various sites around the body – a procedure that is not without its risks, however. The strange paradox is

Diet of the day

Diets come and go like spring fashions. At any given time there will be a food regime that is trendy. One of the most popular programmes of recent times was the Atkins Diet, a low-carbohydrate, high-protein diet that reached a peak following in 2004. The diet challenged mainstream nutritional thinking, and provoked a controversy that served only to popularise the method more widely.

Many diets rely on an easily grasped core idea. This is the attraction of 'macrobiotics', a regime

in which grains are the staple, and all refined foods are avoided. Macrobiotic eating arrived in the west from Japan, and its exotic origin (underlined by its use of esoteric foodstuffs, such as 'bancha twig tea') reinforced its undeniable appeal.

The strangest latterday fad of all is 'breatharianism', proponents of which claim to be able to do without food altogether, or rather to extract all necessary nutrients from the air. This is an absurd and downright dangerous idea – but in a strange way it is the natural consummation of our modern dread of fattening foods.

that the dieting industry works because diets don't. Nearly every dieter who loses weight puts it all back on again within two years – and so is straight away back in the market for a new method of weight loss.

And we're all getting fatter …

The average weight of an American adult went up by almost 2lb in every decade from the 1940 to 1980 and then suddenly rocketed by 8lb between 1985 and 1995. At the same time, the perceived ideal of the perfect body grew ever skinnier. Miss America 1921 was 5'1" tall, weighed 108lb and had a 25-inch waist; Miss America 1981 was five inches taller and had a 22-inch waist – but she weighed almost the same as her predecessor, to whom she would have looked like a freakish, emaciated beanpole.

So the gap between the body shape that people admire and the body that most of us have is now so wide as to be unbridgeable. The diet industry operates inside this yawning chasm. But the fact is, for all the millions of words written about dieting and the billions of dollars spent on it, everything anyone needs to know about slimming can be expressed in one sentence: if, over a sustained period, you expend more energy in your daily activities than you consume in your daily food, then you are certain to lose weight.

'I really hated what I looked like as a teenager … They called me an elongated matchstick.'

Twiggy

GIBSON GLORY Created by the American illustrator Charles Dana Gibson in the 1890s, the Gibson Girls epitomised the tall, narrow-waisted, feminine ideal.

SUPER MODEL Twiggy's waifish silhouette and gamine looks earned her the title of the world's first supermodel. A Sixties' icon, she became the face of Swinging London.

The fast food revolution A huge proportion of the food we now eat comes cooked in an instant form. Why is this, and who invented fast food in the first place?

It is often said that fast food was born on 12 December 1948 in the city of San Bernardino, California. On that day Dick and Mac McDonald opened their refurbished hamburger stall with a shiny new kitchen and an equally brilliant new concept: the Speedee Service System. Their intention was to increase profits by offering a limited range of food produced in an efficient, reliable way. In the reconfigured McDonald's kitchen there were no chefs turning out finished meals. Instead, there were dedicated burger-flippers, French-frymen and milkshake shakers. There was also a person who did nothing but wrap the burgers in paper, and someone on the till to take the money.

What Dick had done was apply the logic of the modern motorcar production line to the American lunch. His kitchen was now turning out 'henryfordburgers'; like the Model T Ford car the burgers were identical every time and in every detail. The key elements that define fast food were there: low costs and correspondingly low prices; a quick turnaround of customers; disposable packaging; a product that is easy to eat with the fingers, and that must be consumed more or less straight away. Most of the dishes we think of as fast food have these things in common.

Fast food before McDonalds
But the birth of McDonald's – like most historic turning points – was not quite as revolutionary as it now appears. For decades, America's entrepreneurs had been searching for ways to feed the country's legions of hungry, impatient construction workers and clerks during their short lunch breaks. One early experiment was Horn and Hardart's Automat, which opened in Philadelphia in 1902. This was a self-service cafeteria with a bank of hundreds of small pigeon holes along the wall. Each compartment contained a dish, visible behind a glass window that could be opened by putting the right money in a coin slot. These swift, impersonal restaurants thrived for a generation: there were 85 outlets in 1950. They went into decline as hamburger restaurants sprouted like cacti in the American landscape – most were converted to Burger Kings.

A more immediate ancestor of the McDonald's approach was a chain called White Castle, established in Wichita in 1921. White Castle restaurants produced a narrow range of dishes – mostly hamburgers – in spotlessly clean, partially automated kitchens. All outlets were made to look identical: every branch was dressed in the same white cladding with false battlements in order to make the brand as recognisable as possible – McDonald's golden arches have the same function. White Castle also organised its own supply chain in order to guarantee the cheap, standardised fare that people wanted.

Burgers around the world
The White Castle method was much copied in the 1920s, as was the White Castle image. Among the copycat chains were White Tower, White Hut, White Dome and Royal Castle.

> All outlets were made to look identical: every branch was dressed in the same white cladding

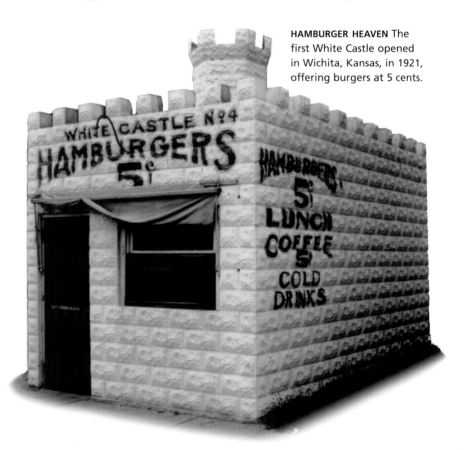

HAMBURGER HEAVEN The first White Castle opened in Wichita, Kansas, in 1921, offering burgers at 5 cents.

GOLDEN ARCHES The global expansion of McDonald's began in 1967 in Canada; today, it has outlets in more than 100 countries, including Saudi Arabia.

skilled labour had to be removed from the equation, so that no human intervention could affect the end product; the pizza or burger served by a franchisee in Detroit had to taste exactly the same as the pizza or burger served in an outlet in Tokyo – because that was the only way to protect the brand. Only a giant organisation can exert this kind of control over the supply chain and the production process, and most of the corporations that made a success of it arose in the conducive commercial climate of the USA. The result is that in many people's minds, fast food is synonymous with globally branded American food.

The Pig Stand in Dallas, Texas, set itself apart in 1921 with a concept that combined the new American love of the motorcar with the Tennessee barbecue pork sandwich. The first restaurant – a simple stand on a Dallas turnpike was staffed by 'carhops' who ran to greet the cars and take orders. As the owner predicted, customers were delighted to be served in their cars, and by 1934 there were over 120 Pig Stands across America.

Global control

The Pig Stands brand survived an impressive 85 years in the USA and White Castle still flourishes, but it has been eclipsed by the global success of McDonald's. In 1955, Ray Kroc, who had been supplying the McDonald brothers with milkshake machines, made a deal with them to sell the McDonald's brand. He duplicated their methods, and by 1960 had opened 200 franchises bearing the McDonald's name. A year later he bought out the McDonald brothers. In 1963, the billionth McDonald's hamburger was consumed live on television – 'fast food' had well and truly arrived.

Other businesses rushed to adopt the streamlined McDonald's model – among them hamburger restaurants such as Wendy's and Burger King, and suppliers of fast foods, such as pizza, fried chicken, doughnuts, sandwiches and tacos. Ingredients had to be highly processed to ensure uniform quality;

Moveable feasts worldwide

Fast food may be a modern industrial phenomenon, but every country has its portable foods – dishes that can be eaten on the hoof. Britain has the Cornish pasty, said to have evolved as a food for tin miners: the thick encasing pastry functioned as an edible lunch box with a crust they could hold with toxic fingers, then discard.

Food on the run

The frankfurter in a roll known as a 'hot dog' came to America from Germany, as the name of the sausage suggests. Hot dogs are said to have got their name in 1906 when a cartoonist drew a dachshund in a bun, and captioned it 'hot dog' because he couldn't spell the animal's name in German. This is a myth: the cartoon has never been identified and the snack was in any case called a hot dog long before 1906.

Street food, unlike fast food, has an ancient history and is usually produced by small traders using fresh ingredients that are bought daily and as a result is usually far more nutritious. This is true of the many exotic dishes of Asia – the hot shrimp soup of Thailand and the fried rice of Indonesia. And to a lesser extent it applies to Britain's traditional fish and chips, a staple of the urban masses since the 1860s at least.

GREATEST SHOW ON EARTH

3

How did sport become so important to so many? For millions of people around the world sport is a daily obsession. Why did we first start playing sport and how did it become so central to our lives?

The object of golf is to hit a little plastic-coated ball, using an expensive and specialised set of golf clubs, into small holes distributed around a giant obstacle course laid out over swathes of land that could be productively used for agriculture or forestry. Some may feel that there must be more constructive ways to spend one's time and the American writer Mark Twain dismissed the game of golf as 'a good walk spoiled'.

But he lived in an era before golf professionals, devoting their entire working lives to the game, could win £1 million in a single tournament.

For kicking air-filled balls over turf, professional football players in top European clubs can expect to earn at least £1,000,000 in a year, nearly five times as much as the President of the United States. Through salaries, prize-money, performance-related bonuses and, above all, sponsorship deals, the highest paid sports personalities earn tens of millions of dollars a year.

These colossal figures alone demonstrate the high status accorded to sport in the modern world. And in our passion for sport, as participants or as spectators, we take for granted the absurdities of the sporting

disciplines to focus on the objectives: the demonstration of skills and creativity, and the pursuit of fitness, personal achievement and even glory.

Old habits

Sport has not always been divorced from practical purpose. In ancient Greece and Rome most sporting disciplines – athletics, wrestling, javelin- and discus-throwing, chariot-racing – coincided with the demands of military training. Vigorous team sports, such as the Roman 'small ball game' *harpastum*, a violent, forerunner of football, also helped to keep fighting men fit for combat. When the rival, warring city-states of ancient Greece sent their top athletes to the Olympic Games, they were doing battle by proxy.

These habits laid the foundations of organised sporting events. At the same time, there was also a general understanding of the link between physical fitness, good health and a sense of well-being. Across the Roman Empire, activities such as wrestling, ball games, weightlifting, gymnastics and swimming, were practised in the area of the public baths called the *gymnasium* as part of a Roman citizen's daily routine. Sport in the ancient world had a spiritual side, too: the Greeks placed great emphasis on athletics, and the four Panhellenic Games – Olympic, Pythian, Nemean and

NATIONAL PRIDE The football World Cup inspires patriotism like no other sport, with supporters donning national colours and whole countries spurring on the team.

Isthmian – were also important sacred and religious traditions.

The collapse of the western Roman Empire in the 5th century AD led to the virtual extinction of organised sport in Europe. In the Middle Ages, sports became localised, with their own traditions and rules. They were often centred on religious feast days and could become riotous occasions. Shrove Tuesday football games in England involved hundreds of players, who rampaged and brawled through city streets and across the countryside in pursuit of an inflated pig's bladder that was both kicked and carried.

Team sports

This kind of event was not unique to Europe. Lacrosse began as a Native American game. It involved two teams of hundreds of players battling over an area of at least 2.5km² (1sq mile)

and lasting several days. Polo was played in Central Asia by huge teams of horsemen, sometimes using the carcass of a dead sheep, goat or calf in place of a ball.

In Europe, countless edicts were issued, to little effect, to try to ban the 'mob football', which caused injury to players and damage to people's property. In the late medieval period, more orderly games started to evolve, emphasising skill but also delivering the pleasures of entertainment combined with physical exercise. They included real tennis, an indoor sport played by the nobility from the 15th century, notably in France. Golf developed in Scotland at about the same time (page 95). Cricket was one of the first of the modern team sports; records begin in the 17th century. During the 18th century, the landed gentry put together teams and enjoyed gambling on match results. In order to

ensure an even footing for such events, the rules of cricket were codified in 1744 by the men from the London Cricket Club and first printed in 1775.

Fair play and sporting rules

In the early 19th century, most ordinary working people did not have spare time to indulge in sports. But Britain became the source of a number of modern team sports as a result of social division. Its private schools for the wealthy recognised the advantages of games as a means of providing physical exercise, a form of healthy competition and an outlet for aggression. Sport was considered to be character building: it promoted

CROWD CONTROL The first FA Cup Final at the new Wembley Stadium in 1923 far exceeded capacity. Mobs flooded the pitch, only eased back by off-duty policeman PC George Scorey and his horse Billy. The match was delayed by 45 minutes.

fortitude and discipline under pressure, and an opportunity to demonstrate the virtues of team spirit and fair play. The words of the Roman writer Juvenal: *Mens sana in corpore sano* summed up the attitude to sport at the time. Though it translates literally as 'a sound mind in a sound body', the phrase is better known as 'healthy in body, healthy in mind'.

For fair play to flourish, there had to be an agreed set of rules – for matches within the school and against other schools. In 1845 Rugby School produced a code of rules for the ball-handling kind of football that now bears its name. A cascade of rulebooks followed, many produced by schools and universities. Rules for a football game using only the feet (except by the goalkeeper) were formulated at Cambridge University in 1863. The British Football Association adopted

the new rules when it was founded that same year. (The 'Assoc.' later gave rise to the term 'soccer'.) In boxing, brutal bare-knuckle fights gave way to a combat played under the Marquess of Queensberry Rules, published in 1867. They included many of the stipulations of the modern sport, such as the use of padded gloves and rounds limited to three minutes.

American advances

Similar developments were taking place in North America. The rules of baseball – which probably evolved from old English bat-and-ball games – were first codified in the USA in the 1840s; the rules of American football in the 1870s. Students of McGill University in Montreal devised the first set of seven rules for ice hockey in 1877 after an indoor game of lacrosse on ice skates.

On the crest of this enthusiasm for organised sport, new games were invented or shaped out of old ones by a new set of rules. Lawn tennis, a spin-off of real tennis, was launched in the 1870s. Basketball was created at Springfield College, Massachusetts, in 1891 by the Canadian James Naismith who sought an energetic indoor team sport for the winter. Netball began in Britain in 1895 as a women's version of the game. Also in Massachusetts and inspired by Naismith, William Morgan created 'Mintonette' in 1895, as

HORSING AROUND A polo match, 17th-century style: the Mughals brought the game from Egypt to India, where it was discovered by the British in the 1850s.

a less athletic alternative to basketball that would suit all physical shapes; it was later renamed volleyball.

The health of the nation

Organised sport was considered useful as part of military training by the colonial powers of the 19th and 20th centuries. It chimed with the values of empire. New sports travelled to far-flung corners of the Earth, and were played by officers and other ranks of the army, by the administrators and tradesmen who accompanied them, and by those whose countries they ruled.

Recruitment for the Second Boer War (1899-1902) revealed the shocking health of volunteers. National and local government were goaded into promoting sports at schools and providing sports facilities in public parks. Factory owners set about creating sports clubs for their workforces. In 1895, the owners of the Thames Ironworks and Shipbuilding Company founded West Ham United Football Club in east London. Germany concentrated on the development of gymnastics for similar reasons. The Soviet Union promoted sports actively as centrally directed government policy from the 1920s, in order to encourage fitness in the workplace and among the military.

The fear that poor physical health can lead to spiritual and moral decline inspired a number of Christian groups to promote sport. Members of the Villa Cross Wesleyan Chapel in Aston, Birmingham, founded the Aston Villa Football Club in Birmingham, England, in 1874. James Naismith and William Morgan were physical education instructors for the Young Men's Christian Association. And Christian missionaries helped to spread sport around the globe.

By the second half of the 19th century, factory workers were beginning to have Saturday afternoon off, leisure time that could be devoted to sport, either as participants or as spectators. The network of trains and trams that arrived with the Industrial Revolution permitted teams to travel further to meet rivals, supported by their fans. The rise of spectator sport was rapid. The first FA Cup Final (the final of the Football Association knock-out cup competition) in 1872 was attended by 2,000 spectators; over 73,000 watched in 1899; and about 200,000 at the new Empire Stadium at Wembley in 1923. Baseball, the working-class sport of the USA, experienced a parallel rise as a spectator sport; the word 'fan' was first used of baseball enthusiasts, in around 1889.

If the public was willing to pay for tickets, then professional sport began to make sense. Sports clubs could attract the best players by paying them an attendance fee, or a share of prize money, or compensation for time taken off work, or a salary. The first professional baseball team was the Cincinnati Red Stockings, founded in 1869. The first professional football players emerged in the 1880s. This caused serious rifts in some sporting circles: there was still a strong belief that the true spirit of sporting endeavour belonged to the gentleman amateur, pursuing sport for its own sake, and that the very concept of professional sport tainted the ideal. The game of rugby split over this issue in 1895, producing rugby union and rugby league. The modern Olympic Games, launched in 1896, in theory remained closed to professional sportsmen until the 1970s.

National glory

Governments since ancient times have understood the crowd-pulling power of sports, and have sought to manipulate it. Roman leaders staged spectacular games to curry favour with their citizens. These were usually gladiatorial 'games', such as the 123-day extravaganza at the Colosseum in Rome in 106 AD, marking the Emperor Trajan's victory over the Dacians. Chariot-racing was also a crowd-

pleaser: an estimated 250,000 spectators would turn up to watch the races at the Circus Maximus in Rome. Juvenal attributed the public's lazy acceptance of this kind of political bribery to its desire for free *panem et circenses* – 'bread and circuses'.

Adolf Hitler attempted to turn the 1936 Olympic Games in Berlin into a tool of Nazi propaganda and a demonstration of Aryan racial superiority. The triumphs of the black American athlete Jesse Owens, who won four gold medals in athletics events, effectively made a mockery of Hitler's presumption.

During the Cold War, the Soviet Union invested heavily in sports academies in order to nurture excellence, which could stand as a shining example of the Communist way at international sporting events like the Olympic Games. Victorious Soviet sportsmen and women were granted a lifestyle commensurate with their heroic status, which inspired millions to emulate them. The pressure to succeed also led to abuses, such as the use of performance-enhancing drugs by East German athletes in the 1970s and 1980s.

Sporting celebrity

Since ancient times, spectator sports have fostered a cult of celebrity, and money has always been involved. Winning athletes at the Olympic Games in ancient Greece would be handsomely rewarded by their home city. Star gladiators fighting in the Colosseum could escape from slavery into a life of wealth and luxury, and celebrity status. This pattern re-emerged with the growth of organised sports in the 19th century.

W.G. Grace was the first cricketing superstar, reaching his peak in the 1870s. In the early decades of the 20th century, newsreel footage played at cinemas helped to ensure that every sport had its heroes. In cricket there was the Australian Donald Bradman; in baseball Babe Ruth; in tennis the

A GLOBAL COMMODITY? Switzerland's Roger Federer signs autographs after a tennis match. Today's sports stars have become worldwide brands, giving their names to all manner of merchandise.

Frenchman Jean Borotra, the Englishman Fred Perry, and one of the earliest female sports stars, the French player Suzanne Lenglen.

The passion for spectator sports has been fuelled by the relentless growth of the global media in all their forms. When Gene Tunney beat Jack Dempsey in a championship boxing bout in Philadelphia in 1926, he was watched by 140,000 spectators. The next year Tunney triumphed again at the return match in Chicago. It was known as 'The Battle of the Long Count' and was watched by 104,000 people, and heard by 50 million radio listeners.

Eighty years later a television audience of 715 million watched Italy win the 2006 World Cup football final in Berlin – and officially the 64-match tournament had a cumulative total of 26.29 billion viewers in 214 countries. No other activity, not even a religion, has this breadth of appeal.

Shaping the beautiful game Why are there
11 players in a football team?

The size of a football team is rooted in its links with cricket, which is also played with teams of 11 players. In the mid-19th century a number of cricket clubs in England adopted football as a winter sport, to give the cricketing gentlemen a way of keeping fit through the cold months. Football games were often played on the same pitch as cricket was in the summer. Several of the best-known football clubs were founded in this way. Sheffield Wednesday was an offshoot of The Wednesday Cricket Club. When it was established in September 1867, the club was at first renamed the Sheffield Wednesday Cricket and Football Club.

Just the right number

So why is cricket played with teams of 11 players? In the evolution of team sports, from their rough-and-tumble origins to an ordered structure governed by rules, the optimum number of players emerged naturally. Only well-balanced teams could provide a satisfactory contest. If there

> **Only well-balanced teams could provide a satisfactory contest**

were too many players, the game became bogged down in a tangle of bodies, or too physical for participants to show their skill. Too few, and the players became exhausted: imagine a five-a-side football match played on a full-sized pitch. So the size of the pitch became an essential element in the rules of team sports. The origins of cricket go back to the 13th century. By the time that the first reliably recorded cricket match took place in 1697, the 11-player team was established.

When the rules of rugby were beginning to take shape, in the mid-19th century, team sizes varied. Sometimes there were 11 players in the team, sometimes 25 – or many more. Clubs would negotiate the number of players before the start of each match, until the Rugby Football Union (RFU), established in 1871, set the standard at 20 players per team. This was reduced to 15 in 1877. Northern clubs split off from the RFU in 1895 because they wanted to use professional players. Over the next few years they

Why do some sports use oval-shaped balls?

When football was a crowd game in which both kicking and carrying the ball were permitted, it did not matter what shape the ball was. But the evolution of the kicking-only game of football in the mid-19th century called for a ball with a smooth, spherical shape.

In contrast, an oval shape suited ball-handling games such as rugby: it was aerodynamic for passing, and did not roll far when dropped. It also bounced oddly, so did not encourage football-style dribbling; and, after a long-distance kick, the ball would stop fairly close to where it landed. All in all, oval-shaped balls ensured that ball-handling remained the best option for retaining possession of the ball.

The oval ball was adopted by all the games that developed out of rugby: rugby union, rugby league, American football, Canadian football and Australian Rules.

JUBILEE GAME The 50th anniversary of Marylebone Cricket Club (M.C.C.) was commemorated in a historic match on July 10, 1837. The match was recorded for posterity on a painted plaque.

developed a slightly different game with 13 players per team; this became known as 'rugby league' (as opposed to 'rugby union').

American football evolved in parallel to rugby. At Harvard University it was played with teams of 11 men, the maximum number their playing area would accommodate. In Canada, McGill University in Montreal played with 12 men per team on a larger pitch. American football teams still have 11 players on the pitch at any one time; the slightly different game of Canadian football has 12 players per team.

The numbers of players correspond roughly to the sizes of the pitches used. Rugby union is played on a pitch 100m long by 70m wide. Rugby league uses a pitch of similar proportions. The field for Canadian football is 101m long by 59m wide, while for American football it is rather smaller, at 91m long by 49m wide. Australian Rules football, based on rules codified in 1858, is played with teams of 18: here the playing field is oval (because the game was designed to be played on a cricket oval during winter), and can measure up to 185m long by 155m – considerably larger than a rugby union pitch.

Covering the field

Such ratios have shaped all team sports. Field hockey has 11 players per side for similar reasons to football: it was developed by cricket clubs in the late 19th century for winter exercise (using a cricket ball). Ice hockey, played over a much smaller area, has just six players a side. When basketball was invented in 1891, there were as many as nine players on each team, but by the end of the century five players were thought sufficient to cover the court.

In most sports, the women's game has the same number of players as the men's. There is one exception: men's lacrosse has 10 players per team, while women's lacrosse – a slightly different, less physical game – has 12.

Where do the strange names of sports teams come from?

The names of teams are badges that give a compressed summary of their origins and territory. The London-based football club Arsenal was founded in 1886 by workers at the Royal Arsenal in Woolwich. It had built cannons since 1717, giving the team its nickname, 'The Gunners'. Tottenham Hotspur ('Spurs') was founded in 1882 by grammar-school boys who played cricket on a ground associated with Sir Harry Percy – the character Sir Harry Hotspur in Shakespeare's *Henry IV*.

Founded in 1874, the Edinburgh football team Heart of Midlothian ('Hearts') met at a dance hall which was named after Sir Walter Scott's novel *The Heart of Midlothian* (which itself took its name from a prison; a cobbled heart marks its location today). The Wanderers began as a successful team in northeast London called the Forest Football Club, before they 'wandered' south of the Thames to Wandsworth in 1864. The Dutch football team, PSV Eindhoven was founded in 1913 by the electronics company, Philips. Its initials stand for Philips Sport Vereniging ('Union'). The American team Green Bay Packers, from Green Bay in Wisconsin, was founded in 1919 by the workers at the Indian Packing Company. The name of the Pittsburgh Steelers refers to the city of Pittsburgh's reputation as a major centre of steel manufacture.

Before they moved in 1960, the basketball team Los Angeles Lakers were the Minneapolis Lakers, so named because of the many lakes of Minnesota, while the New York

THE GUNNERS' BADGE Arsenal football club, from the Royal Artillery in Woolwich, London, reveals its origins in its distinctive club badge.

Knickerbockers, the legendary Knicks, chose their name from the Dutch short-length breeches traditionally associated with the city. Until 1974, the American basketball team the Denver Nuggets was called the Denver Rockets. It had to change its name because the American National Basketball Association (NBA) already had the Houston Rockets. The Philadelphia 76ers ('Sixers') adopted this name in 1963 to celebrate the signing of the Declaration of Independence in Philadelphia in 1776.

Eastern European football teams founded in the Communist era adopted names evoking industrial zest such as FC Lokomotiv Moscow, founded by a group of rail workers. The energetic metaphor of the dynamo inspired the name of the influential Dynamo Sports Club of the Soviet Union, founded in 1923. It also proved a popular choice for football teams, such as Dinamo Minsk (1927), Dinamo Zagreb (1945) and Dinamo Bucharest (1948). Juventus – the football team founded in Turin, Italy, in 1897 – used the Latin word for 'youth' in its title.

Many American football teams have chosen images of energy, power and aggression, to inspire members and supporters. Among them are the New York Giants, Oakland Raiders, Detroit Lions, Denver Broncos and Chicago Bears. The New York Jets used to be called the New York Titans until their move to the stadium of the baseball team, the New York Mets – a stadium familiar with the roar of jets using nearby LaGuardia Airport.

Why have the Brazilians won the football World Cup more often than everybody else?

Brazil has won the World Cup five times, in 1958, 1962, 1970, 1994 and 2002. It is also the only nation to have qualified for every World Cup finals tournament – 18 times since the competition was inaugurated in 1930. Unusually, this prowess does not provoke rancour among rival nations so much as delight and admiration: at its best, Brazilian football has a grace and style that all fans admire. Pelé, one of its greatest players, remarked: 'I don't believe there is such a thing as a "born" soccer player. Perhaps you are born with certain skills and talents, but quite frankly it seems impossible to me that one is actually born to be an ace soccer player.' But is there something in the way that football is played in Brazil that explains its continued success?

The best Brazilian players not only show exceptional skills with their feet, and pinpoint accuracy in passing the ball, but also a seemingly innate ability to create spaces for the ball. Many of the great Brazilian footballers, such as Pelé and Ronaldo, learnt their skills from barefoot games as young children, in the backstreets or on the beach, which taught them deft ball-control techniques and the merits of invention.

Brazil's infectious fervour for football dates to the late 1880s when the game was introduced by English expatriates. It now calls itself 'o país do futebol', 'the land of football'. Competition is intense, but there is a carnival atmosphere among the crowds that rewards imaginative play.

In recent years, attention has turned to another ingredient in the game. Many great Brazilian footballers, such as Rivelino, honed their technical and creative skills through futsal (futebol de salão), an indoor five-a-side game invented in Uruguay in 1930. Its fast pace and non-stop action make it a hit with spectators. A similar game was developed on basketball courts in Sao Paulo. Played with a smaller, less bouncy ball than a football, it teaches young players a unique sense of spatial awareness, coordination and rhythm.

LATIN MAGIC Brazil's Ronaldo storms past Thomas Linke of Germany in the 2002 World Cup final.

Man versus beast Is bullfighting a fossilised vestige of the Roman arena?

The bull is an ancient symbol of virility and fertility, feared and idolised for its ferocity and power. The most famous bull-cult of the ancient world coincided with the myth of the Minotaur, a monster – part man, part bull – kept in a labyrinth by King Minos of Crete and killed by Theseus. When the royal palace of Knossos in Crete, dating to about 1500 BC, was excavated in the early 1900s, frescoes were found showing young men and women grabbing the horns of sacred bulls and vaulting over them – a pursuit of daring athleticism known as 'bull-leaping'.

Harnessing aggression

The Spanish fascination with exploiting the aggression of the bull dates to before the Roman era. In ancient Spain, goaded beasts were sent stampeding through enemy lines in warfare. Bull-running – as at Pamplona – may have begun as training to face this tactic. In the Roman Empire, bulls were among many ferocious animals sent into the ring for entertainment: there are examples of Roman bullrings in Spain at Mérida and Tarragona. Amphitheatres for such spectacles were built throughout the empire. Between the 1st and 4th centuries AD, the cult of Mithras became popular among Roman soldiers and a form of bull-fighting (tauromachy) played a central

EARLY GYMNASTS During Minoan bull-leaping events acrobats would vault the bull's back, dive between its horns and somersault before the distracted animal.

role in its practices. At the same time, bull sacrifice called 'taurobolium' was a feature of the worship of Cybele, the Great Mother of the Gods.

Other theories suggest that the Visigoths, rulers of Spain from AD 415 to 711, founded the tradition of bullfighting. By the 11th century, when the Moors were battling for superiority against the Christians in Spain, bull-lancing tournaments, on horseback, were held in city amphitheatres and plazas. As with jousting, this was a pursuit deemed worthy of knights and the ruling classes. In Portugal, the tradition of mounted bullfighting has persisted to this day as a showcase for equestrianism; here the bull is not killed in the arena.

In the modern form of the Spanish bullfight, commoners took centre stage, fighting bulls on foot, armed with a cape and sword. The pioneer of this tradition was Francisco Romero. The story goes that in 1726, Romero, an employee at the Royal Riding School at Ronda, in Andalusia, rushed

BRAVURA SPORT This 1892 painting by Paredes captures a matador in classic pose, challenging the bull.

to help a nobleman knocked from his horse during a bullfight. Distracting the bull with his hat, he performed a number of passes that wowed the audience – a practice that he, and a dynasty of Romero offspring, later made popular all over Spain, but using a cape (*muleta*) instead of a hat.

Modern ways

King Fernando VII of Spain (ruled 1808-1833) promoted the Romeros' style of bullfighting as an elevating public spectacle of heroism and founded the Royal School of Bullfighting in Seville. Purpose-built, circular bullrings were erected across Spain for the ritual of the *corrida de toros* ('running of bulls'). Costumes – notably the matador's *traje de luces* ('suit of light') – paid homage to its 18th-century origins. Aficionados of bullfighting think of it in terms of art and culture, not sport, and look back nostalgically to the 'Golden Age' of the *corrida* in the early 20th century, when Juan Belmonte devised the technique of standing very close to the bull, and performing moves of balletic elegance.

Recently, partly because of criticism about the cruelty of bullfighting, bull-leaping has re-emerged, both in Spain and southern France, which has similar bullfighting traditions. In scenes recalling Knossos, teams of *recortadores* (in Spain) or *sauteurs* (in France) perform acts of great daring – vaulting or pole-vaulting bulls or heifers, which are neither wounded nor killed.

Faster, higher, stronger The Olympics comprise an odd collation of sports. How is it decided which ones to include? Why is there tennis but not squash; synchronised swimming but not ballroom dancing; equestrian sports but not horse racing?

In 2005 the International Olympic Committee (IOC) voted to remove baseball and softball from the list of Olympic sports. The IOC is the supreme authority of the Olympics, its 115 members selected by other members and drawn mainly from the world of sport and its organisations.

These were relative newcomers: baseball first appeared as an official sport at Barcelona in 1992, and softball at Atlanta in 1996. Baseball fell foul of the IOC because Major League Baseball in the USA refused to release the best players, diminishing the status of the Olympic competition. Softball apparently lost favour because the USA won all the gold medals. But, as the members of the IOC vote in secret, the millions of disappointed fans and players can only speculate as to how their fate was decided. It was the first time any sport had been removed since polo was dropped after 1936.

The original series of Olympic Games began in around 776 BC, and was held at the sanctuary of Zeus at Olympia in Greece. The origins of the games were shrouded in myth and legend even then – including the tale that Hercules won a race at Olympia and insisted that games should be held there in perpetuity. The rival city-states of Greece set aside their differences and sent their best athletes to the festival every four years; the intervening period was known as an Olympiad. The event was much more than a sporting contest. Tests of strength and stamina were interspersed with religious ceremonies.

Olympic ideals

Winning athletes gained personal prestige and honour for their own towns. At first, the programme consisted entirely of running races, but later other sports were added, such as wrestling, boxing, javelin, discus and chariot-racing. The Olympic disciplines reflected the needs of the military, with events aimed at

STRENGTH AND GRACE Sports such as discus-throwing had a military as well as a sporting purpose.

developing qualities that would be required in battle. The competitors, all male, performed naked and women were not even allowed to watch. But, from the 6th century BC, women had their own, separate competition at Olympia, the Heraea Games. By this time the four-year cycle of the Olympic Games was underlined by three other sets of games held in the intervening years. Known collectively as the 'Panhellenic Games', all four combined sporting prowess with devotion to the gods. It was because of their pagan associations that the Christian Roman emperor Theodosius I abolished them in around AD 393.

During the 19th century, a number of groups in Europe attempted to revive the games in some form. Dr William Penny Brookes pioneered an 'Olympian Games' movement in the small town of Much Wenlock in Shropshire, England, from 1850. Greece held its own 'Olympic Games' in Athens in 1859. But it was the drive and imagination of the French educationalist, fencer, boxer and rower, Pierre de Frédy, Baron de Coubertin, that forged the modern concept of the

SYNCHRONISED SWIMMERS Russia won both gold medals at Athens in 2004 in this all-female sport.

Olympic Games. De Coubertin saw the pursuit of sporting excellence as a way of achieving a mental and physical ideal, and viewed international competition as a route to universal peace. He chose as the Olympic motto the phrase *Citius, Altius, Fortius* ('Faster, Higher, Stronger'). He formed the International Olympic Committee in 1894, and the first games were held two years later, in Athens.

Selected sports

The first games involved nine sports (aquatics [swimming], athletics, cycling, fencing, gymnastics, shooting, tennis, weightlifting and wrestling), contested in 43 events by 280 athletes from 12 countries. The selected sports had been whittled down from many more that had been proposed, including football and cricket.

At the Paris Olympics of 1900, the list had grown to 18 sports contested in 95 events by 997 participants (including six female archers). While the core group (including athletics, swimming, gymnastics, equestrian sports and fencing) has remained constant, the total number of sports has kept growing. Among others, basketball was added in 1936, judo in 1964, table tennis in 1988 and beach volleyball in 1996. Further disciplines or subcategories of the main sports have also been introduced: trampoline (gymnastics) in 2000; BMX (cycling) in 2008. The Summer Olympics now cover 28 sports contested in 302 events by 10,625 participants from some 200 nations.

The Winter Olympics was launched as a separate event in 1924. They originally took place in the same year as the summer games, but after 1992 have been held two years later. Smaller in scope than the Summer Olympics, their programme has remained more constant, but there have been newcomers: short-track speed skating joined in 1992; freestyle skiing in 1994; and snowboarding in 1998, the year that curling was re-admitted after

Olympic experiment and extinction

Since the start of the modern Olympic Games in 1896, a large number of sports have been tried and tested – and found wanting. Sports now gone from the official programme include cricket, croquet, golf, *jeu de paume* (real tennis), Basque *pelota*, roque (an American form of croquet) and tug of war (below).

Display and experiment

Some have never even got beyond the demonstration phase, such as American football, the French martial arts *la canne* (stick-fighting) and *savate* (kickboxing). For the Winter Olympics, *skijoring* (a skier pulled by dogs) was demonstrated in 1928, and sled-dog racing in 1932. But neither made it onto the official programme.

The 1900 Paris Olympics was probably the most experimental. The official programme included underwater swimming (up to a distance of 60m, timed), and the swimming obstacle race (200m, scrambling over a pole and a row of boats, then swimming under another row of boats). Also showcased were boules, ballooning and motorsport. So too was live pigeon shooting, but the carnage horrified onlookers, and quickly put paid to any hopes of future Olympic glory for the shootists.

THE SWEDISH TUG OF WAR TEAM AT THE 1912 OLYMPICS IN STOCKHOLM

a 74-year break. In the past, sports that were not on the official Olympic programme could be showcased as 'demonstration sports' in a bid for their inclusion. Baseball appeared six times in 76 years before it was accepted as an official sport for the 1992 Olympics. The martial art Tae Kwon Do was a demonstration sport in 1988 and 1992, and made its first official appearance in 2000.

These days, the route into the official Olympic programme is via the category known as 'recognised sports'. If a sport has an international federation with the necessary qualifications, it may be allowed to join the current list of 35 recognised summer and winter sports. All of these, in principle, stand a chance of

becoming an official Olympic sport – provided they can win a two-thirds majority vote from IOC members. The list of recognised sports includes ten-pin bowling, dancesport (ballroom dancing), sport climbing, sumo, billiard sports (pool, snooker) and even the card game bridge. Many sports – lawn bowls, darts and horse racing among them – are not recognised and remain outside the Olympic orbit.

In 2002, the IOC decided to limit the total number of Summer Olympic sports to 28. So, when it dropped baseball and softball in 2005, two places in the list of 28 became vacant. Any of the recognised sports stand a chance of being voted back in again for the 2016 games – including perhaps baseball and softball.

The improbable sport Sumo wrestlers make unlikely athletes. What is the origin of their strange fighting contest?

Commodore Matthew Perry's 1854 expedition to Japan first brought sumo wrestlers to the attention of the wider world. As part of the exchange of gifts, the Japanese gave the Americans 100 sacks of rice, each weighing 57kg (125lb). The official report recorded how 'the attention of all was suddenly riveted upon a body of monstrous fellows, who tramped down the beach like so many huge elephants.' The 25 *sumotori* each casually shouldered two of the sacks and deposited them ready to be shipped. The Americans were astonished by the bulk, strength and fitness of the wrestlers, by their status and privileged lifestyle – and by the exhibition match of their ritualistic sport to which they were then treated.

Weighing in for the gods

Modern sumo wrestlers weigh around 180kg (400lb), and the heaviest weigh 270kg (600lb). The accumulation of bulk is part of an ancient tradition of feeding, coaching and sleeping in the highly disciplined environment of the sumo training 'stable' (*heya*), to which

every wrestler (*rikishi*) is attached. Sumo is several thousand years old and is one of a number of traditional sports associated with the Japanese religion of Shinto; others include kyudo (archery) and kemari (an ancient kind of football). Wrestling bouts were performed in shrines as a kind of ceremonial temple dance to entertain the *kami* (Shinto deities), in the hope of winning their protection and good harvests. It was a ritual confrontation expressing the necessary clash of forces that underpins balance and harmony.

The format of this ritualised contest – requiring physical dominance delivered in short bursts of high energy – made heaviness an advantage. Wrestlers developed techniques of eating and resting to put on weight. The practice was adopted as court ritual; emperors, shoguns and *daimyo* (warlords) became enthusiasts, rewarding champions with wealth and samurai status.

During the Kamakura Shogunate (1192-1333), sumo was formalised as a martial art and developed as a professional sport, often contested by

CLASH OF TITANS Sumo bouts take place in a clay circle or *dohyo* that has been purified by salt. Fights are brief, often lasting no more than a few seconds.

cash-strapped *ronin* (masterless samurai). The strict hierarchy of professional rankings was introduced in the 18th century; the samurai topknot (*chonmage*) hairstyle still worn by the rikishi also recalls that era.

Sumo, like Shinto, is closely bound to Japanese national identity. But foreign rikishi in recent years have earned access to sumo training stables and – controversially – have achieved the highest ranks of the sport.

Who first jumped off a precipice attached to a rubber band?

DEATH-DEFYING DIVING An initiation rite in Vanuatu performed for the visit of Queen Elizabeth II.

For centuries, young men on Pentecost Island, Vanuatu, in the South Pacific, have performed a high-risk ritual to ensure good crops and gain entry to adulthood. They hurl themselves from a specially built tower to the ground with a strand of vine attached to each ankle. The aim is to brush their heads on the soil below, trusting careful preparations to keep them safe.

A BBC film of the ritual inspired the Dangerous Sports Club in Britain to

emulate the feat, using elastic ropes: in 1979, four members jumped from Clifton Suspension Bridge, Bristol. When New Zealander A.J. Hackett saw televised footage of the feat from the Royal Gorge Suspension Bridge in Colorado, he decided to create a safe version of the sport. To emphasise its safety, Hackett made an illegal leap from the Eiffel Tower in Paris in 1987. He also performed the first building jump from the Auckland Stock Exchange in 1988. With Henry van Asch, he opened the first commercial bungee-jumping operation in 1988 at Kawarau Bridge, New Zealand.

Why does golf have its own language?

Golf has a curious vocabulary. Technical terms include birdie, eagle and bogey. Old club names, like mashie-niblick, are equally strange.

Although similar games were known in China and the Netherlands, Scotland is the acknowledged home of golf. It is first mentioned in Scottish records in 1457, but may have been played 200 years before this. Musselburgh Links, east of Edinburgh, claims to be the world's oldest golf course still in use.

Mashie-niblick

Many of the old names for clubs were Scots, sometimes known as lowland Scots. Mashie (roughly equivalent to a five-iron) came from 'mash', a kind of hammer. Cleek (two-iron) came from a verb meaning to hook or grab. Baffy (four-wood) relates to 'baff', to hit or slap with the back of the hand. A niblick was originally a short-nosed wood, designed to get a ball out of an awkward spot like a cart rut; 'nib' meant beak or nose. The word survived in mashie-niblick (seven-iron).

All these clubs were somewhat different to the modern equivalents and there was little standardisation: golfers assembled their own set from

PUTTING GAMES Coloured engraving of St Andrews golf course in 1800. Players used hand-crafted clubs and balls of leather stuffed with feathers.

different makers. It was only in the 1920s, when golf clubs were first mass-produced in complete sets, that the old names were replaced by one-iron, two-iron, three-iron and so on.

The Scots language also gave us putt, from a word meaning to propel forward. Caddie came from the Scots form of cadet, a young man. The warning call 'Fore!' may come from the old habit of employing 'forecaddies' to walk ahead down the course to watch where the ball landed.

Eagles and albatrosses

Golfing terminology is not exclusively Scots. Fairway was adapted from the English marine term for the navigable part of a river or harbour. Bogey (a score for a hole of one over par) was coined at Great Yarmouth Golf Club in 1890. Originally, it meant the target score for each hole and is said to be derived from the mischievous monster, the bogeyman, whom the successful golfer had to vanquish. With improved golf balls, good golfers regularly could beat the bogey, so a new term 'par' (meaning standard, from the Latin for equal) was introduced for a lower target score. Eventually, bogey came to mean a score of one shot over par.

The term 'birdie' (one below par) comes from the USA, where golf has been played since the 17th century. The story goes that, in around 1900, some players at the Atlantic City Country Club in New Jersey declared a shot that led to such a score to be 'a bird' (good), and the name stuck. Two under par then became an 'eagle', and three under par an 'albatross'.

Colonel Bogey

The 'Colonel Bogey March', one of the world's most famous marching tunes, has a direct golfing connection. It was written in 1914 by Kenneth J. Alford, the pseudonym adopted by Lieutenant Frederick J. Ricketts (1881-1945), bandmaster of the Argyll and Sutherland Highlanders from 1907 to 1927. When stationed at Fort George, near Inverness, he played golf at a local course. Another golfer – some say a forthright colonel nicknamed 'Bogey' – whistled a two-tone signal in place of shouting 'Fore!' This gave Ricketts the first two notes of his march, which he named after his golfing inspiration.

The sound of success   Why do audiences clap to show their appreciation? It's a curious habit, bristling with unspoken rules. Is clapping a natural instinct? And if not, who started it?

When Beethoven conducted the premiere of his Ninth Symphony at the Imperial and Royal Court Theatre of Vienna in 1824, the audience was in an ecstatic mood. They clapped and cheered after each movement, and even applauded the entrance of the timpani in the Second Movement. But though he was gesticulating to keep the tempo, Beethoven was by this time profoundly deaf and had his back to the audience. The orchestra and singers were actually following the man beside him, the theatre's musical director, Michael Umlauf. When the symphony finally came to its triumphant close, the audience went wild, but Beethoven – head still down in the score – continued conducting. Eventually, the contralto Caroline Unger stepped forward and turned him around to the audience, which erupted into a noisy standing ovation, waving handkerchiefs in the air. It must have been a strange, disorienting experience for Beethoven, but he would probably find the reactions of a modern audience even stranger. Today, the movements are separated by heavy silences, filled only by coughing and creaking seats. Clapping – enthusiastic but measured – must wait until the last note has been played.

RITUAL APPRECIATION
A theatre audience in 1951 applauds spontaneously. Showing appreciation is a ritualised custom dependent on time and place.

Throughout most of history, the behaviour of audiences has been raucous rather than respectful. It is only in the last 150 years or so that appreciation at the theatre or at concerts has been ritualised into applause limited almost exclusively to hand clapping. Isolated in this way from other forms of audience expression, the habit of clapping seems decidedly peculiar. So is it a natural impulse?

Animal researchers studying primates have looked for signs of clapping. Like human beings, gorillas, chimpanzees and orang-utans can all make some kind of clapping sound by smacking the palm of one hand against the other, or against the body. Though chimpanzees learn to clap when in captivity, in the wild it seems that primates clap their hands only very occasionally, and then simply to

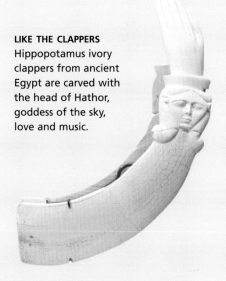

LIKE THE CLAPPERS
Hippopotamus ivory clappers from ancient Egypt are carved with the head of Hathor, goddess of the sky, love and music.

express alarm or to draw attention – not as an expression of appreciation.

Rhythmic clapping was probably an integral part of the first human music. Ancient Egyptian paintings show people clapping alongside musicians. Artificial clappers, which intensified this sound, were developed. Made from wood and ivory, they often had hands carved on the upper surface.

Audience participation

But to become a tradition, the ritual of applause needed something else: a large audience. For applause is essentially the expression of the crowd. The acoustically perfect open-air theatres of ancient Greece, which seated as many as 15,000, were ideal. The Romans followed Greek practices, coining the word *applaudere* – to clap in approval. But neither Greek nor Roman audiences simply clapped: they also booed, hissed, shouted and threw food. Roman audiences also snapped their fingers and, if transported with delight, would wave handkerchiefs and the flaps of their togas.

Public theatres were equally rowdy in Shakespeare's day, and even Mozart fully expected his audiences to applaud, chat and eat throughout his concerts in the 18th century. As enthusiastic applause became the benchmark for success, composers and playwrights often included showy sequences in their work in order to

'trap' applause. When their intentions were too transparent, such gimmicks were dismissed by critics as 'claptrap' – the origin of that expression.

The claque

A time-honoured way to generate applause is to plant friendly – and noisy – supporters among an audience. The Roman emperor Nero loved to sing and recite his poetry in public, and inflicted marathon performances on audiences, who were forbidden to leave. Though famously untalented, he guaranteed himself rapturous approbation by employing a huge corps of professional applauders.

This practice was resurrected in 19th-century Paris. After 1820, theatres and opera houses hired 'claques' – teams of professional *claqueurs* (clappers) – to manipulate the mood of the audience. They did not just clap: *rieurs* specialised in leading the laughter for comedies, and *pleureuses* would sob loudly during melodramas. Agents for the claques negotiated deals with the theatres, priced according to the number of interventions required, and the levels of enthusiasm to be exhibited. The claque could subtly raise an audience's appreciation, especially for a new or difficult work. But the practice was widely deplored as artificial.

Furthermore, some claques used extortion, threatening to turn up and boo unless hired – and paid sufficiently well – to do the opposite; and rival claques sometimes clashed in the theatre, causing mayhem. The phenomenon has not entirely died out: claques of supporters still endeavour to influence audience reaction in opera houses, notably in Italy.

Clapping offers the comfort of the herd, and the herd likes to be led: audiences are uncomfortable if they think they ought to clap, but are not sure. It is not traditional to clap in a church, but does that apply to concerts performed in a church? In modern theatre where no curtain signals the end of a performance, only a blackout, the audience can be similarly discomfited; it may require a member of the production crew to trigger clapping. Television takes no such risks with live audiences: flashing 'Applause' signs signal when to clap – the modern version of the claque.

Refined applause

The fashion for restrained, clapping-only applause filtered down from the royal courts: in the salons of the great palaces of Europe, such as Versailles, courtiers attending a concert would obediently follow the lead of the king or queen in showing their appreciation of a performance. To suggest an artistic sensibility, the tone was always delicate, dignified and restrained. Instead of clapping, ladies in the audience would flutter their fans.

In public venues, restrictive conventions of applause evolved more slowly, but during the 19th century there was growing pressure on audiences to show more respect for the artistic integrity of performances.

Composers of the late-Romantic era, such as Mahler, were concerned to evoke mood, often ending the successive movements of a suite, concerto or symphony on a delicate note, which would be shattered by applause. Audiences gradually began to toe the line, sitting in silence and clapping only when the entire piece was finished, not after each movement – but this convention did not become fully established until the early 20th century.

The language of clapping

Numerous other conventions have developed over time. The volume and insistence of an audience's applause signals to a production how many curtain calls are needed to satisfy its desire to show appreciation. By collective instinct, it knows if a standing ovation is appropriate. In opera, it is permissible to clap after a well-performed aria, and even to shout out 'bravo!' or 'brava!' In jazz concerts, the audience is expected to reward each contribution by a soloist with a round of applause.

Although clapping occurs in most cultures, the language of applause is not universal. In Britain, slow hand clapping may be interpreted as a statement of mass disapproval or impatience, while in Germany, tennis fans will slow-hand-clap to give their stars encouragement. In Indian classical music, any clapping – even at the end of a performance – is considered boorish: it breaks the spell.

Today, clapping may seem an insufficient expression of appreciation. Younger audiences will also whoop and cheer – a growing habit since the 1990s, probably influenced by American television chat shows and sitcoms. But they are also echoing traditions of the ancient Greeks.

PAID TO CLAP The claque in a Paris theatre in the 1830s. The applause of the paid hands aimed to raise audience appreciation.

Who did the first Mexican Wave?

'I and 47,000 Oakland A's fans invented the first wave in history on October 15th, 1981– two weeks before the University of Washington documents their first wave.' Thus professional cheerleader 'Krazy George' Henderson states his claim in a bitter controversy. So did the 'audience wave' come into being at a game of Major League Baseball, at the Oakland Coliseum or was it instead at an American football game at the Husky Stadium in Seattle, as his rivals claim?

At least the date and location are consistent: October 1981 in the western USA. The 'wave' took off from there. Vertical ripples circulated around sporting venues across North America, as audiences – initially encouraged by cheerleaders – stood and threw up their arms and sat down again in sequence, and delighted in the novelty of behaving like a single organism. The 'wave' featured at the Los Angeles Olympics in 1984, but it was at the FIFA World Cup soccer tournament, held in Mexico City in 1986, that it came to international attention. For the English-speaking world outside North America, it was then dubbed the 'Mexican Wave'. But in Spanish-speaking countries it was known as 'La Ola', which means 'the wave'; ola! is also what you can shout as you stand up, creating an audible as well as visual ripple. Many other countries, including Germany and France, likewise call it 'La Ola'. The Mexicans themselves claim they were doing 'La Ola' at the 1968 Olympics in Mexico City. And in Latin America, many football fans say that it has been a feature of their stadia since the 1970s. Like the wave, the controversy ripples on.

KING, QUEEN AND KNAVE
Cards by the 17th-century
Parisian card-maker, Hector
de Trois. The designs were
partially driven by the
printing technology: flat
block colours and simple
shapes made for easy,
inexpensive manufacture.

A pack of kings and queens
Why do playing cards have royalty on them?

In the late 14th and early 15th centuries playing cards spread suddenly across Europe. The new craze led to many calls for card games to be banned, mainly because of fears of the 'evil' of gambling. But suppression was impossible. With the ready availability of paper in Europe from 1400 and the printing revolution of Johannes Gutenberg in Germany in the 1450s, playing cards were soon being mass-produced. Lavish decks were hand-painted for the rich; cheap versions were run off on a single sheet to be cut up by the purchaser.

The origins of the court cards
Playing cards were reported in China in the 12th century and they may have reached the Middle East via the Silk Road. The Mamelukes, rulers of Egypt from 1250 to 1517, had a game known as *Nayb*, *Naibbe* or *Naips*. It used a 52-card deck, with four suits: swords, batons (curved clubs), coins and cups. Each suit had 'spot' cards numbered 1–10 and three 'court cards', called the king, the viceroy (deputy, or *na'ib* for whom the game is named) and the second viceroy. The use of high-ranking figures for the highest value cards seems to have been a kind of visual shorthand. Surviving examples have geometric, non-figurative designs, but

the court cards have inscriptions to indicate their value. The game became popular in Italy and Spain by the early 1400s. At about this time, perhaps inspired by these 'Saracen' cards, European playing cards developed along similar lines, except that the court cards bore illustrations of kings, knights or queens, and knaves (servants).

Knights, queens and four suits
In the early days of European card manufacture, a variety of local traditions emerged. In Italy the three court cards usually comprised the king, the *cavallo* (horse, with rider) or *donna* (lady), and the *fante* (infantry soldier). In Germany, the suits were sometimes depicted as hunting animals (ducks, falcons, stags, hounds), but later resolved as hearts, bells, leaves and acorns.

In France, by about 1480, the four suits had become hearts, diamonds, spades and clubs. The court cards began as the king, chevalier (knight) and valet (knave), but the queen replaced the knight to form the now-familiar trio of king, queen and knave. During the early 16th century, card-players in Rouen in northern France devised representations of these characters that became the basis of the standard Anglo-American deck: the

King of Hearts holds a sword over his head; the Queen of Spades a sceptre; the 'one-eyed' Jack of Spades, Jack of Hearts and King of Diamonds are pictured in profile. The ace is another French device, named after the Latin word for a basic unit (*as*). From earliest times, the lowest card was sometimes played as the highest card.

The game of tarot was widely played in mainland Europe with a full set of cards and a set of 22 picture cards known as the *trionfi* (triumphs, hence modern trumps). The Joker is the only survivor of this tradition in the Anglo-American deck, recalling the Fool of the tarot.

Blue-chip origins

Well-established, reliable, large-scale companies with vast capital value are often referred to as 'blue-chip' companies. Their shares are likewise referred to as 'blue-chip stocks'. They are usually considered low-risk and solid, yielding dependable dividends in good times and bad. But the origin of the term 'blue-chip' has little to do with dependability: blue was the colour of the highest-value chip used in casino games, notably poker, in the days when only white, red and blue chips were used. The term was probably coined simply to denote the high value of the stock and its promise of the best long-term return on investment, but it serves also as a sobering reminder that all investment is ultimately a form of gambling.

INFERNAL ROW Hector Berlioz, the subject of many caricatures, conducts noisy brass instruments – and a cannon – while the horrified audience shy away and cover their ears.

Sweet harmony Is it inevitable that the classical orchestra looks the way it does, or might it have been composed of entirely different instruments?

As a young man in 1822, the French composer Hector Berlioz was reluctantly training to be a doctor in Paris. One day he went to the opera to see *Les Danaïdes* by Antonio Salieri. It was a life-changing experience. As he later recalled in his *Mémoires*, 'The blended harmonies of orchestra and chorus ... put me in a troubled state of exultation, which I cannot begin to describe. I was like a young man with the natural instincts of a navigator who, having only ever seen rowing boats on the mountain lakes of his homeland, suddenly finds himself on board a three-decked sailing ship on the open ocean.'

Berlioz went on to become one of the central figures in the shaping

of the modern orchestra, composing and directing spectacular works that enriched and extended the range of orchestral sound. To mark the closing of the *Exposition Universelle* in Paris in 1855, he conducted a spectacular

concert involving 1,200 musicians. In his influential book *Treatise on Instrumentation*, published in 1844, Berlioz discussed the tonal qualities, range and limitations of instruments, and the role each of them could play in achieving the ultimate goal in the development of the symphony orchestra: a sumptuous, smooth and balanced sound.

Traditional combinations

All traditions of music have a tendency to expand to the fullest sound possible, finding their natural boundaries according to the nature of the music and their audience. The gamelan orchestras of Bali in Indonesia accompany temple ceremonies and sacred dance. They have no more than 20 musicians playing a range of xylophone-like instruments, kettles, gongs, drums and sometimes a stringed instrument and flute. The rippling music is based on a five-note scale spread over the octave, with an intricate interplay of rhythms. More instruments would add nothing.

The complexity of Arabic music, with its 24 quarter-tones to an octave, and the delicacy of traditional

BALI SOUNDS Gamelan musicians in Bali play a range of local instruments. The *suling* is a simple bamboo flute whose tone can be manipulated by the speed of the airflow.

instruments such as the oud (lute), qanum (zither) and ney (flute), tends to limit orchestral groups to between 20 and 40 musicians, and even then the sound may have to be filled out by western strings.

The traditions of western music, with scales restricted to 12 semitones within the octave, have encouraged a more complex multi-layering of instrumentation. Over time, patrons and the paying public have been willing to fund the exploration of an ever-larger sound.

Building the sound

The development of the modern western orchestra began in the 17th and early 18th centuries. Composers such as Jean Baptiste Lully in France, Johann Sebastian Bach in Germany and the German-born George Frideric Handel in England were creating ever more elaborate music. Such music was performed in churches, to accompany ballet and opera, and to entertain the courts of the nobility.

Typically, the collection of instruments played consisted of strings (violins, violas, cellos and a violone or contrabass), wind instruments (flutes, oboes, recorders, horns, bassoons), and a harpsichord to play the underlying structural chords of the 'basso continuo'. Orchestras had about 20 musicians, but the precise composition of the group depended on whoever was available on the occasion, and the music was adapted to fit.

During the later 18th and early 19th centuries, opera theatres and aristocratic courts began to employ full-time orchestras. The more stable arrangement produced a closer bond between musicians, more opportunities for rehearsal and, as a result, a more refined sound. Clarinets, trumpets and timpani were added to the complement of instruments, and composers such as Wolfgang Amadeus Mozart and Joseph Haydn could create more ambitious pieces, knowing precisely

how they would sound when performed. The word 'orchestra' entered common currency at about this time, from the Greek word meaning 'dance space'.

Composers of the later 19th century created an even bigger, richer sound, pioneered by Ludwig van Beethoven and embellished by Hector Berlioz, Felix Mendelssohn, Richard Wagner,

Johannes Brahms and Gustav Mahler. During this period, orchestras grew to about 100 musicians and included more wind and brass instruments, such as piccolos, double bassoons, trombones, tubas and harps.

Now regularly performing purely musical concerts in public halls and theatres, orchestras began to take on more or less the shape they have

Why can't modern violin-makers match the quality of a Stradivarius?

Antonio Stradivari (1644-1737) was the greatest of a series of violin-makers working in the northern Italian city of Cremona in the 17th and 18th centuries. Any of the 600 or so 'Stradivarius' violins ('Strads') that survive fetch extraordinary prices at auction: in 2006, his violin called 'The Hammer' sold for a record-breaking US$3.5 million.

The elusive secret
For centuries, makers, musicians and scientists have attempted to discover what makes a Strad so special. Could it be the shape – the curves and subtle changes of thickness, meticulously carved from solid blocks of wood – or the f-holes on the front plate; or the internal structure? Perhaps it is the quality of the wood: Stradivari would have selected pine, maple, willow, or poplar and tested it throughout construction for its resonance. A recent theory suggests that the period when Stradivari was working coincided with a mini Ice Age, which made the wood

unusually dense. Or did he perhaps treat the wood with a special primer?

For a long while, it was believed that the secret lay in Stradivari's varnish, its formula now lost. But most Strads have been re-varnished since the 18th century. And most examples have been adapted to some degree to suit the changing demands of orchestral scores: in the 19th century they were given longer necks and higher bridges to allow them to play more complex music.

The advantage of time
Modern scientific analysis has failed to prove conclusively why Strads are exceptional. The answer seems to lie in the combination of elements in their construction, and in their great age. Violins need time to mature, and their tone is enhanced by use: this is a factor that modern violin-makers cannot reproduce.

But some leading violinists suggest that Strads are beginning to reach the limit of their golden years and it is their collectability, mystique and value that sustain their reputation.

today. Strings came at the front, wind instruments behind and percussion at the rear. Many city symphony orchestras were founded during the 19th century. A number of them adopted the name 'philharmonic', from the Greek meaning 'music-loving'; they included the London Philharmonic, Vienna Philharmonic and New York Philharmonic.

The right balance

Instruments evolved to match the new orchestral demands. They had to have a distinctive voice that contributed to the overall sound, sufficient but not strident volume and the ability to play with pitch-perfect precision. So the Baroque viols, a family of bowed and fretted, gently humming stringed instruments, were soon replaced by the more robust sounding violin family. The harpsichord disappeared because its sound was too soft; the piano now appeared as a solo instrument in concertos. Thousands of now redundant harpsichords were burnt as firewood during the French Revolution in the late 18th century.

Some of the most radical changes occurred among wind instruments. The reeded shawm of Renaissance times became the hautbois, and later the oboe; the rackett was replaced by the bassoon; the sackbut evolved into

Why is the leader of the orchestra a violinist?

From the 16th to the 18th centuries, orchestras were led and directed by one of the musicians, usually the first violinist. The violin was the most important solo instrument of the Baroque period (c.1600-1750) when a wide repertoire developed, much of it written by composers who were also violinists. The instrument's pre-eminence and appeal to composers continued into the 19th and 20th centuries; and there are more violins in the orchestra than any other instrument, all factors which may have made a violinist a natural choice to lead the orchestra.

The leader of the orchestra was known as the Konzertmeister in Germany and Austria; 'concertmaster' is still the term used for the first violinist in the USA and Australia. As

orchestras became larger at the start of the 19th century, a non-playing 'baton-conductor' was appointed to beat the time, but the first violinist was still in charge of the musical arrangements and interpretations.

During the late 19th century, the conductor's role grew. But the first violinist has kept the pivotal position of leader of the orchestra, sitting at the front in the 'first chair', just to the conductor's left. It is not simply an honorary title. The leader is usually one of the most experienced musicians, and can provide a vital bridge between the orchestra and the conductor when differences occur.

On other occasions, the conductor's place may be taken by a singer rather than the first violinist.

the trombone. During the 18th century, levered keys helped to extend the range of notes for wind instruments and assisted precision. Keys were added to flutes; the chalumeau, which had five finger holes and two keys, was upstaged by the clarinet, with five or more keys. Keys released trumpet players from the need to rely solely on their lips,

facial muscles and tongue to form the right notes. The serpent, a snaking wooden instrument, clad in leather with a deep bass sound, was supplanted by a new keyed, brass bugle called an ophicleide, later replaced by the euphonium and tuba.

Valves and pistons added greater precision to brass instruments such as cornets, trumpets and horns, giving a

MUSICAL MAP Musicians in an orchestra sit in a standard arrangement – the bass instruments to the right and the treble to the left.

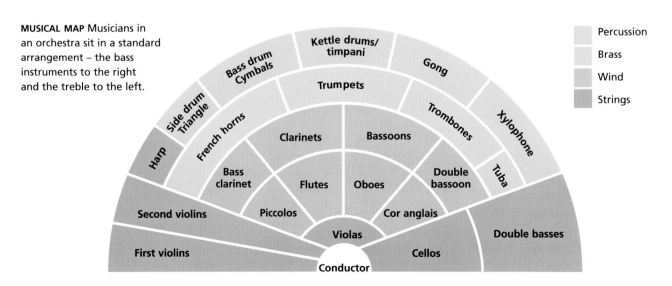

Percussion
Brass
Wind
Strings

smoother, fuller sound to an orchestra and allowing the brass section to take on the melody.

Also-rans

New instruments also appeared. According to legend, the Belgian Aldophe Sax was mending an ophicleide in his workshop in about 1840 when he decided to attach a reed to the mouthpiece. The result was the inspiration for the saxophone – a novel combination of woodwind and brass, fully keyed. But despite its success in bands, it never became a mainstream orchestral instrument. Numerous similar inventions did less well, such as the sudrophone, a large, buzzing trumpet whose tone could be changed at will. This was invented in 1892 by the French instrument-maker François Sudre.

Xylophones were accepted into the percussion section of the orchestra in the 1870s and tubular bells in the

1880s; temple blocks and gongs followed in the 20th century. But orchestras and composers showed scant interest in the new electronic instruments, such as the theremin

(invented 1919), the ondes Martenot (1928), or the Moog synthesiser (1964). Since the early 20th century the classic symphony orchestra has been able to make all the sounds it needs.

OLD AND NEW The sackbut (left) was a mellower, more versatile version of the trombone, while the serpent (right) has survived the centuries – even being included in modern pieces.

Why do major and minor keys have a similar effect in virtually all musical forms?

When you're near there's such an air
of Spring about it,
I can hear a lark somewhere begin
to sing about it,
There's no love song finer,
But how strange the change
from major to minor,
Ev'ry time we say goodbye.

Cole Porter's famous song 'Ev'ry Time We Say Goodbye' (1944) exploits one of the great mysteries of Western music. In the line 'But how strange the change from major to minor', the music shifts from a major chord to a minor chord – and from happiness to melancholy.

In Western music, bright, happy, positive, bold and heroic compositions are usually played in a major key. Handel's 'Hallelujah Chorus' and Schubert's sweeping and joyous

Symphony No. 10 are in major keys, as are the melodies of 'Here Comes the Bride' and 'Happy Birthday to You'. Minor keys tend to be associated with sadness, gloom, longing, doubt, or mystery. A classic example is Chopin's 'Funeral March', which he adapted from his *Piano Sonata No.2 in B-flat Minor*. They also express passion, however, as in Rachmaninov's famous *Piano Concerto No. 2 in C minor*, by turns driven, energetic and lyrical.

Flattening the mood

Musicologists and psychologists have struggled to explain why the minor keys evoke darker emotions. It appears to have something to do with the structure of scales. The intervals between the notes in major scales go: *tone-tone-semitone-tone-tone-tone-*

semitone. But in minor scales they go: *tone-semitone-tone-tone-semitone-tone-tone*. Semitone intervals flatten the ensuing note, depressing the brightness of the sound – and semitones are more prominently located in the minor scale.

Our response to a minor key may echo the way we express emotion when we speak. Say, 'It's been smashed!' with joy, as if a long-held Olympic athletic record has just been broken. It has quite a different resonance from saying the same thing when you have just found out that you have been burgled: your tone of voice will most likely drop.

However, not all minor-key compositions are sad. The jolly Christmas carol 'God Rest Ye Merry, Gentlemen' is usually sung in E-minor.

Pop's magic number Why are most pop songs three-and-a-half minutes long?

JUKEBOX JIVE Taking its name from the southern American 'jook' or 'dance' joint, the jukebox helped spread pop music to a new, appreciative audience.

The best pop songs contain a mysterious ingredient that makes them comfortingly familiar and endlessly fascinating. They engage the emotions and reflect humans' natural sense of rhythm. Most modern songs are based on variations of a verse followed by a chorus, a pattern which repeats three or four times within the song.

The structure allows for variations in light, shade and volume and gives the composer and singer the opportunity for switches in melody and emotion within a short time frame. Not all songs follow this pattern – The Beatles' 'Yesterday', which divides into two distinct musical sections, is a famous example. But most are almost exactly the same length. Why is this?

The birth of pop music coincided with the switch to vinyl for record production in 1948. Before this, records were made in brittle shellac, in a 10-inch or 12-inch format, played on gramophones at 78 revolutions per minute (rpm). A 10-inch '78' lasted three minutes; a 12-inch '78' could last for five. Vinyl was more durable, had better sound quality, lower surface noise and was cheaper to produce. The 7-inch (18cm) vinyl disc, run at 45rpm, was introduced in 1949 to replace the 78 which could only play one song on each side – a 'single' – and it quickly became the chosen format for pop songs.

Single success

Crucially, 7-inch vinyl discs were well suited to jukeboxes. Installed in clubs, cafés and dance halls, jukeboxes played a key role in binding pop to the emerging youth culture, for which the discussion, selection and sharing of new music was a defining feature. By the late 1950s all successful pop songs were being published as 7-inch singles.

But the format of records does not alone explain why most pop songs last three to three-and-a-half minutes.

A 7-inch record can accommodate songs twice that length. Long hits include The Beatles' 'Hey Jude' at 7:05 minutes and Queen's 'Bohemian Rhapsody' at 5:55 minutes long, but they are exceptions. The formats of records were designed to fit the songs, not the other way round.

Three-and-a-half minutes may be simply a measure of the natural attention span of listeners. The most famous operatic arias tend to be short: the 'Habanera', from Bizet's Carmen (1875), usually lasts about three-and-a-half minutes. 'La Donna e Mobile', from Verdi's Rigoletto (1851), lasts less than three minutes. Operetta songs such as 'When I was a Lad', from Gilbert and Sullivan's HMS Pinafore (1878), are about the same length, as are popular songs such as 'O Sole Mio' (1898), as well as church hymns and Christmas carols.

Hooking the business

Modern commercial pressures have reinforced the preference for the three-and-a-half-minute song. In the face of intense competition, songwriters and performers must grab the listener and radio producer's ear immediately. They may do this with an alluring musical hook, a toe-tapping dance rhythm or by capturing their imagination with the lyrics. Such demands also explain why pop songs usually have a simple structure and content, consisting of verses and a repeated chorus, kept within a narrow musical range. John Lennon's 1971 hit 'Imagine' (3:01 minutes) is a classic example.

Commercial radio in particular demands that pop songs be succinct. If listeners become restless, they switch stations and miss the advertising that finances the enterprise. Three-and-a-half minute songs ensure plenty of advertising breaks.

With CDs and downloads musicians can produce songs of virtually any length using a uniform format – but the ones that reach the charts still end up about three-and-a-half minutes long.

Who really invented pop music – Elvis Presley or someone else?

There has always been popular music. In the days of the travelling minstrel, the medieval nobility could request the most popular songs of the time, such as French troubador-composer Bernart de Ventadorn's 'Can vei la lauzeta mover' ('When I see the lark beat his wings', c.1170). The musicians learned the songs from fellow troubadours and committed them to memory.

Printed sheet music appeared 20 years after the development of modern printing in the 15th century; this helped fix and circulate standard forms of compositions. The words of popular songs such as 'Greensleeves' were printed as 'broadsheet ballads' or 'broadsides'. By the 18th century, sheet music and songs were sold by street hawkers and in the 19th century, music-hall hits quickly reached the local public house or the domestic parlour through printed sheet music. In New York, from around 1885, the music publishing business created a hothouse of popular musical composition in a district of Manhattan nicknamed 'Tin Pan Alley' – allegedly because of the racket produced by a host of cheap, tinny pianos.

Recorded music

In the 19th century, music for popular songs was transposed onto metal discs and cylinders for musical boxes, street organs and fairground organs. After 1900, songs were recorded on paper rolls to be played at home on 'Pianolas' – pianos fitted with pedal-driven mechanisms. As the roll turned, words appeared, printed next to the holes that played the appropriate notes, so the Pianola-player could sing along.

In 1877 gramophones – known in the USA as phonographs – became available for the first time. They could record and play live music and by the 1890s were bringing the sounds of star performers into private homes. The novelty caught on rapidly. The first record to sell a million copies was Enrico Caruso's 1902 rendition of the aria 'Vesti la Giubba' ('Put on the Costume'), from the opera *Pagliacci* (Clowns) by Ruggiero Leoncavallo.

The combination of readily available records and the spread of radio led to a growing passion for popular music. In 1942 Bing Crosby produced 'White Christmas', one of the biggest selling singles of all time. Hit charts were established as the bellwether of musical fashion in the early 1950s. In the mid-1950s, the charts included songs such as '(How Much is that) Doggie in the Window?' by Patti Page, 1953; 'Wanted' by Perry Como, 1954; the first rock-and-roll hit, 'Rock Around the Clock' by Bill Haley and His Comets, 1955; and 'Sixteen Tons (and what do you get?)' by Tennessee Ernie Ford, 1955/6.

Pop music

Elvis Presley's first big hit, 'Heartbreak Hotel', raced to Number One in the US charts in 1956 and was followed by five more hits over the next 18 months. His success symbolised the shift into the age of 'pop music'. The new term embraced style and fashion, the cult of the teenager and the new celebrity of the 'pop stars', as well as the popularity of the form. Rock 'n' roll, launched in 1951, played a key part in this development. Based on the 12-bar blues, with gospel and country thrown in, it repackaged black dance music for a young white audience. When authority figures labelled the new sound unseemly, suggestive and 'the Devil's music', it became a vehicle for the young to express themselves and emphasise the growing generation gap.

There were plenty of stars involved, such as Chuck Berry, Little Richard, Jerry Lee Lewis and Buddy Holly. But Elvis Presley was unquestionably the iconic figure – 'The King'. By the time The Beatles launched their string of hits with 'She Loves You' (1963) and 'I Want to Hold Your Hand' (1963 – one million copies sold in just 10 days in the UK), the foundations of pop music had been laid.

MUSIC THAT SHOOK THE WORLD
Elvis Presley's 'rock 'n' roll' redefined music for a generation.

Under the Big Top

A unique collection of acts comes together in a circus – but who decided that clowning was great entertainment – and that it should go together with acrobats and animals doing tricks?

The story of the modern circus begins with trick horse-riding. In 1768 Philip Astley, a former cavalry sergeant-major, began giving displays of horsemanship in London. The next year he helped George III subdue a frisky horse and as a reward he was granted a formal licence to perform. Astley now erected a canvas-covered arena. In the morning he taught riding, and in the afternoon he entertained the paying public.

Though the enterprise was a huge success, Astley had to bring in more variety to entice audiences back. From 1769 he introduced acrobats, jugglers, fire-eaters, tightrope walkers, clowns and performing dogs. Such traditional, popular entertainers have existed since ancient times. Across Europe they had enthralled and amused the public at medieval fairs and markets, earning their living by passing round the hat. Now they were brought together in a new kind of spectacular show.

In 1772 Astley took his equestrian show to France, to perform at the court of Louis XV. During the rest of the decade, he developed a purpose-built

RAISING THE ROOF Horsemen wowed audiences at Astley's Amphitheatre with equestrian stunts: the riding master, whip in hand, became the ringmaster.

arena in London called Astley's Amphitheatre. The performance area was a ring 13m (43ft) in diameter. This shape and size gave horses the space to achieve a constant gallop and the centrifugal forces created assisted the riders as they performed stunts. Stalls and tiers of galleries for the audience surrounded the ring, inspiring its grand name. This size and layout served as the model for all circuses to come.

Grand visions

Astley opened the Amphithéâtre Anglais in Paris in 1782. After the French Revolution, it was bought and run as the Cirque Olympique by

HORSES FOR COURSES Chariot-racing in the Circus Maximus was fast and furious, and riders were often killed trying to thwart their opponents.

Antonio Franconi, an equestrian performer, juggler and one-time bullfight impresario credited as the founder of French circus. Also in 1782 a rival show appeared in London, when Astley's former colleague Charles Hughes – in partnership with the actor and author Charles Dibdin – opened The Royal Circus and Equestrian Philharmonic Academy.

With grandiose names like Circus and Amphitheatre, both Astley and Hughes were evoking the wonders of ancient Rome. An amphitheatre was a circular arena, designed to mount spectacular shows, such as gladiator fights, combats with wild animals and even sea-battles. A circus was a round or oval-shaped hippodrome (a track for horse-racing), also used for chariot-races and athletics – the name simply meant a circle in Latin.

The largest amphitheatre in Rome was the Colosseum, seating 50,000 people; and the largest circus was the Circus Maximus, said to be able to accommodate 250,000 spectators. Astley and Hughes' shows were more modest, but were sensational in their day. In addition to familiar circus acts, they offered staged sword fights,

Just clowning around in pantomime

There are two main types of clown. The typical circus clown has a red face and red nose, with lips and eyes surrounded by large patches of white greasepaint, plus a fright-wig of orange hair, a baggy suit and giant shoes. This character is called an 'auguste' and causes mayhem by pursuing a course of madcap antics, often well-intentioned but with disastrous results. The other type is a 'whiteface' clown, with finer features and sometimes bald with a completely white head, topped by a conical white hat. Whiteface clowns may display the wily intelligence of a bossy schemer. Many clowns are a combination of the two types.

These clowning traditions emerged in the 19th century, but their origins go back much further, and their story is linked to both pantomime and mime.

Commedia dell'arte

In 16th- and 17th-century Europe groups of touring actors, originally from Italy, performed improvised farces known as 'Commedia dell'arte'. Their characters included the clown, sometimes played as the naive, love-struck, white-faced servant called Pedrolino or Pierrot.

In English theatres, a Commedia dell'arte performance was sometimes preceded by a silent 'dumbshow' to introduce the characters. Called a 'harlequinade' after the mischievous servant character, Harlequin, it involved acrobatics and plenty of knockabout fun, typically using a split baton that made an exaggerated slapping sound – the origin of the term 'slapstick'. Such dumbshows were also called pantomines, after the Greek and Roman tradition of the pantomimos ('mimicking all'), a silent, solo dancer performing a humorous commentary on life to music.

Stories and mime

Harlequinades often related fairy tales; over time these evolved into shows of their own, called pantomimes, usually devised as family entertainment. Joseph Grimaldi, 'the father of modern clowning', made his name in pantomimes in the early 19th century, playing a white-faced character based on the antics of Harlequin.

Modern mime came out of a tradition that adhered more closely to the pantomimos concept. The French performer Jean-Gaspard 'Baptiste' Deburau (1796-1846) created a white-faced mime character based on Pierrot, founding a tradition that was maintained in the 20th century by Marcel Marceau.

THREE CLOWNS IN TRADITIONAL DRESS

melodramas with mounted knights or highwaymen, shadow plays, ballet pieces, fireworks – all punctuated by bursts of music from an orchestra. After the storming of the Bastille at the start of the French Revolution, Astley caused a public sensation by displaying Madame Tussaud's waxworks of severed royalist heads.

Bricks and mortar

The tradition of staging circuses in permanent, purpose-built venues carried on into the 19th century. Following successive bouts of rebuilding after fire damage in 1794 and 1803, Astley's Amphitheatre became as grand as an opera house. Charles Dickens wrote admiringly of it in *Sketches by Boz* (1833):

'We defy anyone who has been to Astley's two or three times ... not to be amused with one part of the performances at least ... we know that when the hoop, composed of jets of gas, is let down, the curtain drawn up for the convenience of the half-price on their ejectment from the ring, the orange-peel cleared away, and the sawdust shaken, with mathematical precision, into a complete circle, we feel as much enlivened as the youngest child present; and actually join in the laugh which follows the clown's shrill shout of "Here we are!" just for old acquaintance' sake.'

The Cirque Napoléon was built in Paris in 1852, a 20-sided polygon designed to seat 4,000; it became the Cirque d'Hiver (Winter Circus) in 1870, the name by which it still goes today. The London Hippodrome was built as late as 1900 to host mixed music hall and circus entertainment.

Although circuses are thought of as popular entertainment, these permanent establishments set out to appeal to all echelons of society. Paintings of the French circus in the

1880s by Henri de Toulouse-Lautrec and Georges Seurat show audiences with men in top hats and bow ties and their elegantly dressed womenfolk.

The Big Top

This setup suited big cities, where there was a large potential audience to draw from. But from the beginning of the 19th century, smaller circus troupes realised that they could make a living by travelling from town to town, particularly in North America.

In the USA the circus dates back to 1793. John Bill Ricketts, an equestrian performer at Hughes Royal Circus, founded an enterprise in Philadelphia that was similar to Astley's. The President, George Washington, attended one of the first performances. Ricketts then toured with his troupe, erecting temporary wooden arenas, usually open to the sky, in cities along the East Coast.

Travelling circuses in the USA continued like this until 1825, when Joshua Purdy Brown began to tour with a large tent. This was the forerunner of the Big Top, a canvas version of the Amphitheatre-style circus building. Now the circus became not only more mobile, but could guarantee shelter from bad weather and perform six days a week. Travelling circuses could follow the expansion of US settlement west; and by the same means, circuses now spread around the world.

Wilder and weirder

By the 1860s European and American troupes were travelling to China and Japan. China had an ancient tradition of gravity-defying acrobatics, balancing acts and plate-spinning. In 1866 the French performer Louis Soullier introduced the first Chinese troupe of acrobats into a European circus.

Showmen had to keep the public constantly thrilled. The inventor of the modern trapeze act was the Frenchman Jules Léotard, an acrobat

> **Philip Astley's Amphitheatre became as grand as an opera house**

TINY PRESENCE At just 2ft 1in tall, General Tom Thumb achieved international fame singing and dancing for Barnum's circus.

at the 19th-century Cirque Napoléon. He was the first to use the flying trapeze (leaping from one trapeze to another) and to turn a somersault in the air. His trademark costume, designed to give his limbs freedom of movement, was later adopted for ballet. Léotard performed in whatever venue would have him, often flying over the heads of the public (the safety net was not introduced until 1871). In the same way, his fellow countryman Charles Blondin took his skills as a circus tightrope walker to the extreme in 1859-60 by stretching a rope across Niagara Falls and crossing while performing a variety of feats including cooking, pushing a wheelbarrow and carrying his manager.

By the 1830s, the tradition of exhibiting exotic animals in touring menageries had become part of the circus. Animal acts, such as lion-taming, were introduced. Many circuses were also freak shows, exhibiting dwarves, giants, Siamese twins and people with alarming deformities. The original touring show of Phineas T. Barnum, one of the renowned names in American circus history, included, among many others: Joice Heth, a former slave, who claimed to be more than 160 years old and to have nursed the infant George Washington; the hairy-faced 'Jo-Jo the Dog-Faced Man'; and the midget 'General Tom Thumb', who performed before Queen Victoria on a tour of European tour in 1844.

The travelling show

In 1871 Barnum joined forces with two circus entrepreneurs to create P.T. Barnum's Museum, Menagerie and Circus, a travelling show with exhibits of exotic animals and human oddities as a 'sideshow'. Winston Churchill recalled that when he was taken to Barnum's as a child, 'the exhibit ... which I most desired to see was the one described as "The Boneless Wonder"'.

The circus reached its zenith in the USA. By the mid-19th century it had become the most popular form of public entertainment; and by the end of the century there were 100 travelling circuses, many of them touring by rail.

In 1881 Barnum merged with James Bailey to form the Barnum & Bailey Circus. Operating in three rings simultaneously, it advertised under Barnum's slogan 'The Greatest Show on Earth'. After Bailey's death, the Barnum & Bailey Circus was bought by another major circus that had been founded in 1884 by the seven Ringling brothers; in 1919 they merged the two circuses to form the Ringling Bros and Barnum & Bailey Circus. With a colossal touring operation that included 300 tents, it dominated the American circus scene in the 20th century. Since 1957, it has toured as two groups performing in indoor arenas, each with their own private circus trains, specially equipped to carry animals.

Audiences for traditional circuses have dwindled since the Second World War, and have struggled to provide

the kind of spectacle that can compete with cinema and television. In the Soviet Union, circuses were promoted by the state as upstanding examples of popular culture, but since the collapse of Communism in the 1990s they have been deprived of funding. In Europe and elsewhere, a public distaste for animal acts, on the grounds of welfare and cruelty, has made it harder for circuses to provide a full bill of entertainment.

There are exceptions, the most prominent being the Cirque du Soleil. Founded in 1984 by Canadian street-performers Guy Laliberté and Daniel Gauthier, it has grown to be the world's greatest force in modern circus, employing 3,500 people in 15 touring shows and its six resident troupes at Las Vegas, Nevada, and Orlando, Florida. It creates highly theatrical theme-based spectacles through its distinctive blend of costumes, lighting, live music and exhilarating versions of traditional circus acts (juggling, trapeze, plate-spinning, trampoline, clowns). But unlike Astley's original circus, no animals are used in its performances, only humans.

A GLOBAL GATHERING With its roots in Canadian street entertainment, Cirque du Soleil now brings together circus talent from across the globe.

The camera never lies Or does it? We now see the broader world through the camera's lens. How did our understanding of the world change as a result of the invention of photography?

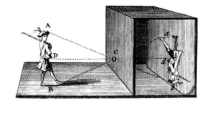

'Photography is a marvellous discovery, a science that preoccupies the highest intellects, an art that fascinates the shrewdest minds – and whose practice lies within the grasp of the simplest imbecile ...' declared the dynamic French photographer Nadar in 1857, adding that, 'Photographic theory can be learnt in an hour, the basic technique in a day.' He encapsulates the wonder, fascination, surprise and fear that accompanied the development of photography. Here was a new, science-based technology that could record reality with unique precision. And at first photography seemed to pose a threat to the livelihood of those who previously had a monopoly on capturing images of the world. The French painter Paul Delaroche declared, on seeing some of the earliest photographs, 'From today, painting is dead!'

Capturing light

The first photographs appeared in the 1820s, but many people were already familiar with the 'camera obscura' (named after the Latin for 'dark room'), which exploited a natural phenomenon in which light passing through a small aperture into a darkened space can project a full-colour view from the outside onto a flat surface or screen. Artists used a small camera obscura to project an image onto paper and trace a drawing from it. Painters such as the Dutchman Jan Vermeer and the Italian Caravaggio may have used them to master the complex perspective of their work. A camera obscura could also be a room-sized darkened chamber into which outside views were projected via a mirror. The phenomenon was often exploited as a fairground attraction. Customers could see clear colour images of the real world outside, transposed onto a screen. It was a two-dimensional

PIONEER PHOTOJOURNALIST In the 1870s John Thomson made 'the camera a constant companion' and recorded the ordinary citizens of London's streets.

picture that they could believe in, produced without the interpretative intervention of an artist.

The technique of projecting three-dimensional scenes of the world onto a two-dimensional surface was therefore well known. What was needed was a means of capturing and printing the projected image. The French inventor Joseph Nicéphore Niépce made a leap forward in 1826, producing a photograph using a copper plate coated with bitumen and lavender oil. But it needed an exposure lasting eight hours. He went into partnership with a painter called Louis Daguerre, who by 1838 was printing photographic images onto copper plates coated with silver and treated with iodine vapour. He called these 'daguerreotypes'. The technique reduced exposure time to 30 minutes and produced remarkably crisp images. Protected by glass, and framed like portrait miniatures, they became an instant success. Light from the real world had been captured and preserved: daguerreotypes showed how people really looked, albeit in black and white.

In England at the same time, William Henry Fox Talbot was devising another method. In his 'calotypes' (from the Greek for 'beautiful impression'), first produced in 1840, the image was first captured as a negative, then light was passed through the negative onto sensitised paper to create the positive,

the final image. Although at first less sharp than daguerreotypes, any number of prints could be taken from the negative. Daguerreotypes by contrast were one-offs – and within 20 years had fallen from favour. Photography quickly became an international profession and attracted support from those in high places; Queen Victoria and Prince Albert, for example, were noted enthusiasts. The first daguerreotype studio in the USA opened in 1840, while photographs displayed at the 1851 Great Exhibition in London fuelled public excitement and wonderment about the new technology.

Cartomania

A succession of technical advances included the wet-collodion process, invented in 1851. Glass plates were coated with cellulose nitrate and plunged into a silver nitrate bath just before the photograph was taken.

Say cheese!

Try holding a smile for five seconds: within moments the bright flicker of spontaneity begins to cloy. This was a problem in the 1860s, when the wet-collodion plate required exposure times of several seconds. Photographers asked their sitters to look straight-faced and dignified; some studios were even equipped with head-clamps to keep the sitters still. It is hardly surprising that our forebears often appear dour and humourless, peering sternly out of their sombre world of black (or brown) and white.

Monkeys and kimchi

During the 1870s, mechanical shutters and improved light-sensitive materials brought faster exposure times, but the real change came after 1888 with the launch, in the USA, of the handheld

Kodak box cameras, invented by George Eastman. His slogan was, 'You press the button, we do the rest'. The Kodak Brownie (below) came onto the market in 1900. Soon, the term 'snapshot' was common currency, and smiles appeared more regularly. But it was hard to break a habit: to persuade their subjects to smile, photographers asked them to say words that had the same visual effect. In the English-speaking world, this instruction became the formulaic: 'Say cheese!'

The English expression followed snapshots around the globe. But some places have chosen their own quirky formulae to produce a smile. In Korea, subjects say 'kimchi' (pickled cabbage). In China, 'quiezi' (aubergine); and in France, 'ouistiti', a marmoset (a small monkey).

Although cumbersome and messy, it produced high-quality negatives with an exposure time of just a few seconds rather than minutes. The negative images could be transferred to the new, high-quality albumen paper (so called because the chemicals were bound by egg white).

But an invention by the French photographer Eugène Disdéri made photography into a worldwide craze. His 1854 wet-collodion system created a series of portrait poses on the same plate from which sitters could choose their favourites. Individual portraits were printed and mounted on boards the size of a visiting card, 90 x 57mm.

These cartes de visite were relatively cheap and became even cheaper. Soon almost every town in the western world had several professional studios, churning out an estimated 300 million carte de visite portraits every year throughout the 1860s. By the end of the decade, portrait photographers were so numerous that even people of modest means could afford to join the craze. A term was coined for the phenomenon: 'cartomania'.

Photographs were collected in family albums, and posted to relatives abroad. They marked every stage in life, from birth to death. Photographs of the famous – royalty, politicians, war heroes, inventors, poets, composers, actors and actresses – were widely traded and circulated. Abroad, and in the colonial empires, photographers made studio pictures of local people in their costumes. There were humorous joke cards, artistic compositions and historical reconstructions, and female nudes for the 'gentleman connoisseur'.

Facing reality

What captivated the public imagination was the cheapness and accuracy of photographic portraits. Previously, the only portraits available were paintings or drawings, or silhouettes cut from black paper. Professionally painted portraits were

EYES AVERTED In an early instance (1855) of photography as propaganda, Roger Fenton's carefully posed groups taken in a break in the fighting portrayed the Crimean War quite differently from the accounts given by the newspapers.

beyond the means of most people. Photographs seemed more real than the work of artists, who could flatter a sitter, or simply fail to capture a true likeness. And it was now possible to see what royalty and other well-known people looked like, without actually witnessing them in the flesh.

The notion that photography portrayed reality more truthfully and reliably than painting was quickly and widely accepted. During the Crimean War (1853-56), the British government was heavily criticised because of fevered press reports of military incompetence and the shameful neglect of the nation's troops. In response, the government despatched a photographer to the war zone to counter these reports – to carry out a task normally performed by war artists.

Early photojournalism

Roger Fenton, his two assistants, a mobile darkroom and 36 cases of equipment arrived in the Crimea in 1855, a year after the Battle of Balaklava and the Charge of the Light Brigade. The long exposures of wet-collodion photography and the cumbersome photographic equipment made capturing battle scenes impossible, but he made 360 plates of camps, harbours and fortifications that showed the reality of the setting from which the negative reports had emerged. In contrast to the heated newspaper reports, the photographs showed the calm, ordered, if battle-bruised reality of the campaign. After their exhibition in London, *The Literary Gazette* affirmed the reassurance that this provided: 'It is obvious that photographs command a belief in the exactness of their details which no production of the pencil can do.'

More shocking images emerged from the American Civil War (1861-65), taken by Mathew Brady and the team of photographers he assembled for the

ILLUSION OF DEPTH Photographic stereograms added depth to a 2-D plane, allowing viewers to see world-famous sights from the comfort of their own home.

purpose. 'Harvest of Death' (1863) by Timothy H. O'Sullivan shows the bodies of Union soldiers strewn over the battlefield of Gettysburg – in marked contrast to the glorifying traditions of battle paintings.

These early war photographs were designed to sway public opinion: the public's acceptance of photographs as reality was already being exploited for propaganda purposes. But sitters were aware that the camera does not tell the whole truth. Studio portraits used backgrounds and props to imply that sitters lived in a grand home, were reading in a park, at the seaside, or standing on the deck of a ship. Trick photography was sometimes used for deliberate deception – to create images purporting to show ghostly apparitions, spirit entities at seances and fairies. Even as respected a figure as Sir Arthur Conan Doyle could be fooled. He endorsed as genuine the 'Cottingley Fairies' photographed in 1917 by two schoolgirls posing with paper cutouts of fairies, images that were the subject of dispute for decades.

Because it could reproduce convincing, detailed images of reality, photography was widely used for documentary record. Subjects included news events and their aftermath, newly explored places abroad, ancient

> **Sitters were aware that the camera does not tell the whole truth**

Egyptian monuments, exotic peoples, paintings, diseases, criminals, strange animals, plants, the microscopic world – and, after 1895, X-rays. It could also show the realities of social deprivation, but was rarely used for this purpose in the 19th century. The French photographer Charles Nègre was an exception, making pictures in the 1840s and 1850s of beggars, street urchins, organ grinders and chimney sweeps, while Jacob A. Riis, a Danish-American journalist, photographed the slums of New York in 1888 using the newly invented flash powder.

In 1872, the English photographer Eadweard Muybridge, working in California, was asked to resolve a dispute about how horses gallop. A railway tycoon, Leland Stanford, was convinced that there were moments when galloping horses had all four hooves off the ground. Others said this was impossible. In 1877, after inventing a camera using an unprecedented shutter speed of 1/500th of a second, Muybridge was able to prove Stanford right. He had shown what the human eye simply could not see. Muybridge continued work at Stanford's ranch, using a specially built outdoor studio with a

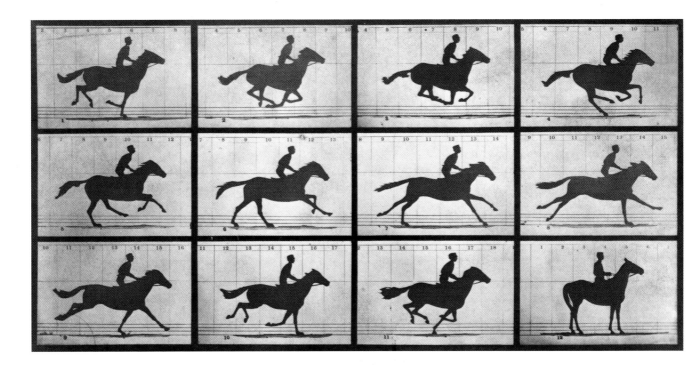

HORSE POWER Known as 'the man who split the second', Muybridge shot this sequence of a galloping horse for the US tycoon Leland Stanford.

line of cameras (with shutter speeds of 1/2000th of a second) triggered by tripwires, to record the full motion of horses. He proved for the first time that they did not move with the 'flying gallop', with front legs and back legs splayed outwards, as previously portrayed in paintings. Similar series on the movement of various animals and humans were published in the 1880s to great acclaim.

Art photography

From its earliest days, photography had a complex and fraught relationship with the art world. Some artists considered it a cold, scientific medium, unable to express the interpretation, judgement and sensitivity of painting, while the long exposure times of early photographic portraits often made sitters look lifeless or tense. Others, such as the French Romantic painter Eugène Delacroix, embraced photography, and sketched from photographs of models. The

1840s coincided with the development of Realism in French painting, notably in the work of Gustave Courbet, which chimed with the objectivity of the camera lens. Edgar Degas saw how the casual composition and framing of photographs echoed similar virtues that he so admired in Japanese prints. In their immediacy, photographs could portray the world as we glimpse it, unposed and unprepared.

Photography pushed the pace of change in art. The Impressionists recognised the rival claims of photography to create realistic likenesses of landscapes. They abandoned meticulous accuracy and instead used dabs of colour to capture the 'fleeting moment' of changing light on landscape. The Symbolists of the late 19th century carried painting beyond reality, into the world of the imagination, dreams and subconscious association, where photography could not easily go. A number of early photographers did

WONDERFUL LIFE From 1936, *Life* magazine brought photojournalism to the masses. Its minimal text alongside 50 pages of glossy photographs proved to be an instant hit.

demonstrate the capacity of photography for artistic expression. In the 1860s, the British photographer Julia Margaret Cameron produced portraits of depth, grace and delicacy. Landscape photographers such as Peter Henry Emerson, who worked in East Anglia in the east of England in the 1880s, showed a similar sensibility.

Until the 1880s, if publications were to include photographs, they had to use real photographs 'tipped in', that

is, literally glued onto the pages. Fox Talbot had foreseen the possibilities of breaking photographs into dots to make plates for printing, but it was not until the 1880s that the 'halftone' process was properly developed – from afar, the eye reads the varying-sized dots as a continuous tone.

During the 1890s, crudely printed photographs began to appear alongside engravings in magazines and newspapers. In the 20th century, picture-oriented magazines, such as the British *Illustrated London News*

and *Picture Post* and the American *Vanity Fair* and *Life*, put photography before the public as never before.

At the same time, photography established itself as an independent art form with its own terms of reference. Individual photographers developed distinctive styles that opened the public gaze to new ways of seeing. American photographers such as Edward Weston, Paul Strand and Ansel Adams revealed a poetic majesty in landscapes and in intricate, close-up details from nature. Dorothea Lange

showed the universality of suffering in her penetrating portraits of migrant sharecroppers during the Great Depression of the 1930s – her most famous, 'Migrant Mother', became an iconic image of the era. The French photographer Henri Cartier-Bresson found multiple points of focus that have the viewer's eye dancing around the image. He called his small Leica camera the 'extension of my eye': the camera does not lie, but there is a human mind behind it that manipulates how and what it sees.

How did early moving pictures develop, and what were they used for?

An 1896 handbill for a showing of the new Cinematograph in Dublin rang with excitement at the possibilities of the new medium. 'To-night! To-night! Something special! ... First presentation in this City of the most wonderful exhibition on earth. THE CINEMATOGRAPH ... produces with the most absolute correctness in every minute detail animated representations of scenes and incidents ... in everyday life ... Taking one of the scenes depicted – that of a very busy railway terminus ... the effect ... is so realistic that for the moment one is almost apt to forget that the representation is artificial.'

A year earlier, the French brothers Auguste and Louis Lumière had mounted the first projected film show before an audience in Paris. Just the sight of 'moving photographs' amazed the public, regardless of their content.

The wonder of moving pictures

Moving images were not new. Throughout the 19th century, magic-lantern shows included painted 'slipping slides' that appeared to show movement. Artwork presenting sequential images could be seen to move in flicker books, or when set inside the revolving cylinder of a zoetrope, invented in 1834. Prints of Eadweard Muybridge's photographs

of galloping horses were mounted onto zoetropes, and, after 1879, on glass discs for his own 'zoopraxiscope'.

The invention of durable, emulsion-coated celluloid film in the late 1880s suggested how photography and this early technology might be combined. Inventors in a number of countries worked on cameras that could open and close a shutter repeatedly.

The road to cinema

In 1891, William K. Dickson produced the 'Kinetoscope', a combined camera and viewing method. Viewers had to watch his short films by peering into a box. The projection system pioneered by the Lumières made the real breakthrough. It was called the Cinématographe, from the Greek *kinema* (motion) and *graphein* (to write).

Moving pictures spread rapidly worldwide and were presented in theatres, public halls, fairgrounds and mobile cinematograph vans. Many film-makers won audiences by filming the public during the

day, then inviting them to see themselves on film that same evening. Subjects included workers flowing out of the factory gate, supporters at football matches, or promenaders at the seaside. A firm of British film-makers, Mitchell & Kenyon, produced hundreds of such films between 1897 and 1913. Recently discovered and restored, their films present a unique and haunting insight into a bygone age, especially when they are played at the original, life-like speed of a hand-cranked projector.

WHAT FUTURE? Though effectively inventing cinema along with his brother, Louis Lumière deemed it 'an invention without a future'.

Why is the US film industry in Hollywood?

The global film business was born in an obscure settlement on America's West Coast, not in one of its great cities. Why did it start out here in the desert?

TEXAN THRILLS A production still from *The Texans*, 1938; Paramount's big budget feature about an ex-Confederate soldier.

In 1910 one of the greatest directors of the silent era, D.W. Griffith, working for the Biograph Company, came to Los Angeles with a film crew and troupe of actors including Mary Pickford and Mack Sennett, future founder of the Keystone Company and director of Charlie Chaplin. They produced a series of movies in a matter of weeks. Then one day Griffith travelled into the countryside, through the citrus groves, to a small settlement called Hollywood. Just seven miles outside Los Angeles, it had a hotel and a reputation for being an agreeable place to stay. He brought his troupe out from Los Angeles and they filmed *In Old California*, a 17-minute historical tale set in the era of Mexican rule in the early 19th century. Despite its short length it was Hollywood's first real movie.

The birth of cinema is a tale of astonishing whirlwind success. In 1895, the French Lumière brothers, Louis and Auguste, staged an exhibition of moving images projected from celluloid film, in Paris – an event widely cited as the first public screening of movies. Within a few

DIRECTOR'S CUT D.W. Griffith on the set of *Intolerance*, 1916. One of the greatest – and most expensive – films made in the silent era, its four parallel stories of political, social and religious intolerance span over 2,000 years. While it proved a commercial failure, it was a triumph of cinematographic innovation and artistry, influencing generations of film-makers.

years, scores of films were being produced for public entertainment, and shown in makeshift cinemas in public halls and shops. In the USA, customers were charged just five cents (a nickel) to enter. In just three years between 1905 and 1908, 10,000 'nickelodeons' were created in the USA, catering for an audience of some 26 million customers.

Grasping the opportunity
Cinema was a goldmine. Dozens of paying customers could be entertained by just one man and an assistant with a projector, and a pianist. The films were 'silent', so they could appeal to audiences of any language group. It opened up a global export market for the film-makers, but in the USA, silent movies also appealed to a huge immigrant population many of whom had a fragile grasp of English. All they needed was an endless supply of films.

Until 1910, films were short 'one-reelers', lasting around 10 minutes, shown in varied programmes covering all the genres: drama, romance, documentary, suspense thrillers, Westerns, horror and the hugely popular slapstick comedy. The films were churned out by studios at an extraordinary rate, using small teams of actors, directors and technicians.

In 1909 alone, Mary Pickford acted in 51 films. All films were made using natural light, out of doors, or on rooftops, or in purpose-built studios with retractable roofs. On the east coast of America, film-makers were often hampered by bad weather – or forced to adapt the story to fit the prevailing conditions on the day.

Thomas Alva Edison, the American inventor, held patents for much of the equipment used in film-making. To protect his patents, in 1908 he brought together nine of the leading film studios with one of the main film distributors and Eastman Kodak, manufacturers of raw film; they formed the Motion Picture Patents Company (MPPC), also called the 'Edison Trust', or simply 'The Trust'. The MPPC laid down a code of operation for the film industry, and aggressively pursued its patent rights through the courts, making life difficult for independent film studios.

Go west!
It was partly to escape The Trust that several film-makers headed to California. The Selig Polyscope Company, founded in Chicago in 1896, began working in Los Angeles in 1907, and set up a permanent

A UNITED FRONT Mary Pickford and Douglas Fairbanks at the gate of their own 18-acre lot in Hollywood. The husband-and-wife team gained valuable early experience as film producers in 1919, when they entered into partnership with Charlie Chaplin and D.W. Griffith to form United Artists, the first film company run by independent artists.

Who had the bright idea of turning humble actors into global marketing machines by making them stars?

Until 1910, film actors were not credited by name in their films, or in the publicity for those films. Many were happy with the arrangement as films were then considered a low-class form of entertainment. The nine film companies of the dominant 'Edison Trust' (see left) maintained the tradition, knowing that actors, if they became known by name, would demand more money.

But audiences became thirsty for more information about the actors. Florence Lawrence, a successful Canadian actress onstage since the age of three, was known simply as 'The Biograph Girl', because she appeared in films made by the Biograph Company. When Carl Laemmle, the head of Universal Studios persuaded her to join his Independent Motion Picture Company (IMP) in 1910, he spread the rumour that she had been killed in a streetcar accident, before announcing that Florence Lawrence was in fact alive and well and making a new movie called *The Broken Oath* with IMP.

From then on, the major studios selected actors to be turned into stars. They were often given new names and fictitious backgrounds. When they demanded enormous salaries, the studios acquiesced happily. Soon the stars began to lead ultra-glamorous lives, living in mansions and being chauffeured around in limousines. Cinema magazines gloried in stories of their lavish lifestyles and private lives. As early as 1915, Quigley Publications had an annual list of the stars that drew the biggest cinema audiences.

Soon, filmgoers could be drawn to a movie by the star names that appeared 'on the marquee'.

A number of silent-era actors attained dizzying fame under the 'star system', notably Douglas Fairbanks (Douglas Ulman), Mary Pickford (Gladys Smith), Rudolph Valentino (Rodolfo Guglielmi), Gloria Swanson (Gloria Swenson) and Greta Garbo (Greta Gustafsson). In 1917, Charlie Chaplin, the 'Little Tramp', was the first to sign a $1 million contract The 'star system' became a feature of the highly controlled 'studio system' that reached its zenith after the arrival of 'talkies' in 1927. Stars were contracted for rolling terms of five to seven years; contracts even stipulated codes of moral behaviour. The system was broken up by Supreme Court anti-trust (anti-monopoly) action in 1948 and by the late 1960s the 'star system' was dead.

BLONDE BOMBSHELL Her onscreen poise belied Lana Turner's hectic private life: she married seven times.

ALL THAT JAZZ Though billed as the first 'talkie', the first speech in *The Jazz Singer* did not start until 17 minutes into the film.

170 minutes, cost $110,000 to make, and was a massive hit that brought the theatre-going middle classes into the cinema.

In 1912 and 1915 Supreme Court interventions caused the Edison Trust to lose control of its patents. From then on, studios were free to innovate, and rapidly introduced new techniques and technology. Camera dollies and cranes, and back projection brought a whole new look to films. Shooting under artificial lighting became more common after 1914; this called for make-up, which, for black-and-white movies, required the use of sometimes bizarre and counterintuitive colours – an art pioneered by Max Factor, a Polish immigrant who moved to Hollywood in 1909.

At around this time, many of the major film studios merged, and a handful of big film companies began to dominate. Universal Pictures and Paramount Pictures Corporation were both founded in 1912, the Fox Film Corporation in 1915, Warner Brothers in 1923, and Columbia Pictures and Metro-Goldwyn-Mayer in 1924. They built large studios, signed up a stable of stars to contracts worth millions of dollars, and took complete control of them, as well as the entire production process from script to cinema screen. The studio bosses were businessmen, and were often autocratic and temperamental. It was to free themselves of such constraints that Charlie Chaplin, Douglas Fairbanks,

studio there in 1909. The climate, with long hours of daylight and up to 320 sunny or clear days a year, was another major draw. A number of companies relocated to California each winter to escape the frozen east coast weather. They soon realised that conditions were excellent for year-round filming. A range of settings lay within easy reach: urban Los Angeles, the coast at Santa Monica, agricultural land and sagebrush scrub country for Westerns.

After the release of *In Old California*, the story of Griffith's discovery of Hollywood attracted other studios. In 1911 the Nestor Film Company came to Hollywood and director Al Christie turned a derelict tavern at the end of a dusty road called Sunset Boulevard into the first Hollywood studio. By the end of the year, there were 15 other studios in Hollywood, and within two years Hollywood had become the leading film production centre in the USA.

Between 1905 and 1914, the world's most productive studio was not in the USA, but Gaumont, in Paris. But the First World War caused severe disruption to all the European film studios, and the film-makers of Hollywood stepped into the gap. The shift westward coincided with the growth of the 'feature film', the name given to any film running more than 40 minutes.

In the early days of motion pictures, film-makers believed that audiences would not be prepared to concentrate on a story for longer than two reels (about 20 minutes). But in 1914 Cecil B. de Mille's silent western *The Squaw Man* was released. Running for 74 minutes, it is regarded as Hollywood's first feature film.

In 1915 D.W. Griffith released *The Birth of a Nation*, a stirring – and now highly controversial – story of the American Civil War, packed with ground-breaking techniques. It ran for

> **Christie turned a derelict tavern at the end of a dusty road called Sunset Boulevard into the first studio**

Why are the Oscars so named?

'Academy Awards of Merit' are the awards handed out by the Academy of Motion Picture Arts and Sciences (AMPAS). The annual awards ceremony each spring is Hollywood's most glamorous public occasion, when the stars and key players in the film industry assemble to see who has won the top award in each of the 25 categories.

Ever since the first Academy award ceremony in 1927, winners have received a copy of the gold-plated, Art-Deco-style statuette of a naked man with a crusader sword standing on a film reel. The statue was designed by MGM's influential art director Cedric Gibbons and sculpted by George Stanley, using the Mexican actor Emilio 'El Indio' Fernández as a model. But why is it called an Oscar?

Uncle Oscar

There are four main theories. Margaret Herrick was Executive Director of the Academy from 1943 to 1971, but she started her career as the librarian. In 1931 she commented that the statuette reminded her of her uncle, Oscar Pierce. Her colleagues picked up on this, and casually referred to the award as an Oscar, a nickname that gradually took hold over the years.

Hollywood columnist Sidney Skolsky challenged Herrick's story. He put the name Oscar in print in 1934, when referring to Katharine Hepburn's best Actress Award that year. He claimed that this was a reference to a vaudeville joke: a comedian would say 'Will you have a cigar, Oscar?' to the orchestra leader, but it was an empty gesture – like, he implied, the Academy Awards. Skolsky continued using the name Oscar in the coming years, and it stuck.

Bette Davis, who won her first Best Actress award in 1936, also laid claim to the nickname. She said that she called her award Oscar because it reminded her of her husband, bandleader Harmon Oscar Nelson. This was probably just a playful boast, and one that she later retracted.

Wilde speculation

Another tale is that the award is named for Oscar Wilde. When asked about winning the Newdigate Prize for Poetry, Wilde replied, 'Yes, but while many people have won the Newdigate, it is seldom that the Newdigate gets an Oscar.' When Helen Hayes won her Best Actress award in 1932 for *The Sin of Madelon Claudet*, her husband apparently called it 'her Oscar' in reference to this.

Even the Academy, which began to use the term Oscar officially only in 1939, does not know the name's origin, but it tends to favour the Herrick story. In any case, it seems to suit Hollywood, the 'dream factory', to have an award that the whole world knows by an affectionate nickname whose origins are surrounded by myth.

EMILIO FERNANDEZ, ACTOR AND OSCAR MODEL

Mary Pickford and D.W. Griffith broke free by forming their own film studio, United Artists, in 1919.

You ain't heard nothin' yet!

Perhaps the greatest technical breakthrough occurred in 1927, when Warner Brothers produced *The Jazz Singer*, the first feature-length movie with synchronised sound. 'Wait a minute, wait a minute,' exclaimed the star, Al Jolson, in the first of the brief snatches of speech, 'you ain't heard nothin' yet!' The 'talkies' transformed the film industry, opening up the possibilities of a much more complex form of entertainment. They were also the ruin of many silent movie stars, whose voices were too heavily accented, failed to match their glamorous personae or who simply had no talent for acting with speech. Cinema audiences also had to adapt: they learnt to sit quietly and listen.

Synchronised sound dealt a further blow to continental European film-makers. Whereas silent-era films could be sold anywhere in the world, now their markets shrank to the areas where their language was spoken. Hollywood, on the other hand, could feed the burgeoning English-language market with big-budget movies that exploited sound to the full, such as the lavish musicals of Busby Berkeley. When colour film came of age in 1935, with the release of *Becky Sharp* – the first feature filmed in full three-colour Technicolor – again it was Hollywood that was able to make the most of the innovation.

The years from 1927 to 1950 are considered the 'golden age' of Hollywood, before cinema began to be challenged by television. But with its ceaseless invention, access to funding, energy and scale, Hollywood has managed to retain its dominant position in world cinema. Though production facilities have shifted to other parts of Los Angeles, Hollywood is the unquestioned spiritual home of American film.

It's just a load of senseless daubs Has modern art always alienated the public? Ever since the Impressionists, new trends in art have often been greeted with shock and outrage. Why do people find it hard to embrace a new way of looking at the world?

When the American artist Jackson Pollock first came to public notice in the late 1940s, many art critics were ecstatic. Here, they claimed, was an entirely new way of producing painting: Pollock laid his huge canvases on the ground and danced around them in a trance-like state, spattering the surface with drips, dribbles and splashes of industrial paint. Not only was this Abstract Expressionism, it was 'action painting': an art form where its merit lay as much in the method of production as in the finished result. An admiring article in *Life* magazine

in August 1949 asked provocatively, 'Is he the greatest living painter in the United States?'. The readership strongly disagreed, arguing that Pollock's work was not art: house decorators across America had dustsheets that looked like his canvases. Chimpanzees could do it. The press's jokey nickname chimed better with the public mood of dismay: 'Jack the Dripper'.

Jackson Pollock has a secure place in the history of western art and his drip paintings now fetch more than US$10 million. His work was a vital step in the establishment of complete

freedom from figurative art, as well as from the rational design of earlier abstract painters such as Piet Mondrian.

The entire history of postwar art is the story of action and reaction. For a while, the art world was abuzz with Abstract Expressionism. Then came the reaction, Pop Art, which first surfaced about 1956. Among its disciples, Andy Warhol made multiple copies of familiar commercial products, such as Campbell's soup tins and cartons of Brillo pads, deliberately minimising all signs of personal artistic flair. Roy Lichtenstein

INFINITE ART One critic commented that Pollock's paintings, such as *Number 6, 1948*, had no beginning or end. 'He didn't mean it as a compliment,' said Pollock, 'but it was.'

produced hugely enlarged copies of comic-strip images. Was this art? Though collectors dived in, large swathes of the public – if they gave any thought to that matter at all – dismissed Pop Art as another blatant attempt at attention seeking by the world of contemporary art.

A more extreme reaction to Abstract Expressionism was Minimalism – where art was reduced almost to the bare process of selection. In 1966, the American artist Carl Andre produced a series of sculptural pieces called *Equivalents*, consisting of nothing more than rectangular arrangements of industrial firebricks. In 1972 London's Tate Gallery caused a public furore by purchasing *Equivalent VIII* for an undisclosed sum. 'Whichever way you look at Britain's latest work of art,' screamed the *Daily Mirror*, 'WHAT A LOAD OF RUBBISH.'

And the story continued: 1991 saw the unveiling of *The Physical Impossibility of Death in the Mind of Someone Living* by the British artist Damien Hirst, a dead shark pickled in a tank of formaldehyde. *My Bed* (1999) by Tracey Emin was an installation consisting of her soiled, unmade bed. Was the public being hoodwinked? Were these pieces the art world's version of the Emperor's new clothes?

Public property

The views of the public have never had much influence on the course of art. While artists shape its evolution, it is steered by the big collectors who support and promote them. It is only since the 19th century that the public's views about art have been heard at all.

From the Renaissance of the 15th century to the 19th century, a closed circle of artists and their patrons – the church, aristocracy and wealthy

merchants – dictated taste. Though there had been controversial swings in style along the way, the public were not in a position to complain. The Italian master, Michelangelo, painted Biblical scenes on the Sistine Chapel ceiling using especially robust, muscular and sculptural figures – but they were sanctioned by the Pope and so readily accepted. Slightly later and even more individualistic were the emotionally charged and brightly coloured 'Mannerist' paintings of El Greco, but the church in Spain was his patron.

France, and Paris and Versailles in particular, became the starting point for trends in European art from the 18th century onwards. After the French Revolution, art was democratised. It

came into the public domain via the Salons in Paris – yearly shows of new works selected by the Académie des Beaux-Arts. New art movements were conceived in the Salons, which always opened to feverish excitement.

At an 1819 Salon, Théodore Géricault caused controversy with his dramatic *The Raft of the Medusa*, which depicted the desperate survivors of the wreck of the ship *Medusa*, a recent news story with strong political undertones. Viewers were stunned to see so controversial a subject in a work of such scale: they were used to uplifting scenes of the past. At the 1851 Salon, Gustave Courbet exhibited his *Burial at Ornans*, a large, anti-Romantic painting of his grandfather's

When did fine art become a valuable commodity? Is it anything to do with putting pictures in frames?

The 15th-century Flemish painter Jan van Eyck is sometimes called the 'father of oil painting'. He did not invent the technique, but he was one of the early masters. From his studio in Bruges, he produced exquisitely detailed religious works and portraits, such as *The Arnolfini Portrait* (1434). They were painted on wood panels, so they could be picked up, carried out of the studio, framed and hung on walls.

Panel paintings were not a new concept: they had been produced since Byzantine times, but using encaustic (pigment mixed with beeswax) or egg tempera (pigment mixed with egg) – both laborious and complex processes. Oil paints were richer, had a wider range of colours and were easier to apply and work with. Flemish oil paintings became highly treasured, portable commodities. They were bought by rich merchants like Giovanni Arnolfini and transported along the trade routes that spanned Europe. The *Portinari Triptych* (1475),

for example, which is now in the Uffizi Gallery in Florence, was commissioned from the Flemish painter Hugo van der Goes by Tommaso Portinari, a Florentine banker.

Mark of status

Flemish oil paintings transported to Italy in the 15th century were much admired. Previously most of their work had been in fresco or tempera, produced mainly for the church. Artists such as Giovanni Bellini in Venice, and Leonardo da Vinci in Florence, quickly mastered the skill of oils, bringing to it a new subtlety and delicacy. Instead of their work remaining *in situ*, they could now paint beautiful, portable works for the rapidly growing merchant classes who had money to spend and saw patronage of the arts as a mark of status. In this way, the framed painting – then on wood panels and later on stretched canvas – became the main currency of the art trade.

funeral. It was a statement of Courbet's desire to 'paint the world as it is', the essence of the Realism movement. The public was horrified: such an everyday scene was not a subject for art.

Fuelled by public interest, the French art world was showing signs of frenzy. In 1863, the Académie rejected so many works for the Salon that the artists caused a public outcry. Napoleon III felt obliged to step in and sanctioned an exhibition of the rejected art called the Salon des Refusés. The public came to see it, many expecting to be entertained by art that they could ridicule. They were not disappointed.

A scandalous painting

One work in particular drew attention: *Le Déjeuner sur l'herbe* ('Luncheon on the Grass') by Édouard Manet was a contemporary picnic scene, with two Parisian men lounging next to a nude woman who gazed flirtatiously at the viewer. The public scoffed, the critics railed. The painting was considered a scandal, a deliberate provocation – despite Manet's clear debt to a classic work, *Fête Champêtre* by the Venetian

painter Titian, which hung in the Louvre. In London, the Pre-Raphaelite Brotherhood caused a similar reaction This tight-knit group set out to paint historical, religious and moral pictures in the finest detail, in a manner, they claimed, that reflected the purity of European art before it was corrupted by the High Renaissance elaboration of Raphael and Michelangelo.

In 1850, John Everett Millais created a highly realistic picture called *Christ in the House of His Parents*, depicting Jesus as the child of an ordinary carpenter. Today, we might find it idealised and sentimental: many at the time found it sacrilegious – a shocking demotion of the Holy Family to the status of crude artisans. Charles Dickens described it as 'the lowest depths of what is mean, odious, repulsive and revolting'.

The history of western painting until the mid-19th century reflected the struggle to create the illusion of a three-dimensional space on a two-dimensional panel. During the 19th century, many artists were already beginning to reject the pursuit of purely representational art, exploring instead the poetic and expressive possibilities of a freer style of brushwork. In Britain, J.M.W. Turner took a radical approach to the depiction of light and weather in his painting, *Rain, Steam and Speed – The Great Western Railway* (1844). A similar freedom appealed to the group of French artists who became known as the Impressionists. Claude Monet, Pierre-Auguste Renoir, Alfred Sisley and

A QUESTION OF ART
Marcel Duchamp set out to challenge convention by creating art from a mundane industrial object: the urinal. Though its subject matter was considered 'immoral', it was intended to be controversial and to provoke reactions from critics and public alike.

Camille Pissarro wanted to paint the real, modern – and usually agreeable – world that surrounded them. Unusually for the time, they painted out of doors (*en plein air*) and, to capture the 'fleeting moment', they worked quickly, applying dabs of colour with broken, rapid brushstrokes.

When Monet exhibited *Impression, Sunrise* in 1874, a critic mocked the group as 'impressionists' and the name stuck. Most public opinion was equally dismissive and suspicious, regarding Impressionism as an offensive kind of anti-art, with its disregard for the hard-won technical brilliance of academic painting.

In Britain, there was a notorious public spat over an impressionistic painting called *Nocturne in Black and Gold: The Falling Rocket* (1874, left)

COURTING CONTROVERSY
At his libel trial, Whistler said *The Falling Rocket* was only ever meant to be 'an artistic impression'.

FRAGILE EXISTENCE Damien Hirst explores the themes of life, death, love, loyalty and betrayal in his 'Natural History' works.

by the American-born artist James Abbott McNeill Whistler. The influential art critic John Ruskin saw it for sale and publicly declared that he 'never expected to hear a coxcomb ask two hundred guineas for flinging a pot of paint in the public's face'. Whistler ill-advisedly sued Ruskin for libel. Though he won the case, he was awarded a derisory farthing in damages. The press lampooned his work, and dismissed it as devoid of the moral value required in art. His career was, for the time being, ruined.

Slowly, however, the Impressionists in France began to change the public's opinion, and by the 1880s they had become successful and established. When Monet died in 1926, he was the grand old man of art, a French national treasure. But by this time, the art world had experienced a dozen further bouts of turmoil. The trajectory of the Impressionists from public mockery to triumph provided a template for later art movements. Shock the public, win the attention of the critics and collectors who matter, and see your fortunes rise. Bourgeois taste was derided in artistic circles, so *épater la bourgeoisie* ('shock the middle classes') became a rallying cry.

Against this background, in 1905 the French artist Henri Matisse and others painted landscapes in vivid, non-naturalistic colours. They were dismissed as *fauves* ('wild beasts') by a critic, and so adopted the name Fauvism for their movement. Pablo Picasso, a Spanish artist working in Paris, and Georges Braque began their counterblast two years later with splintered images giving simultaneous, multi-angled views. By 1908 the method had been labelled Cubism. Both movements showed a new way of recording the visual world; both perplexed the public.

Abstract art, which made little or no reference to the real world, came to the fore from about 1910. Then in 1917 the French artist Marcel Duchamp, working in New York, presented *Fountain*, an industrially manufactured urinal, signed R. Mutt 1917. In the work he boldly stated what has become the governing principle for conceptual artists ever since: 'This is art if I say it is.'

Duchamp was also associated with Surrealism, a cultural as well as an artistic movement that appeared after the First World War. Its practitioners, including Man Ray, René Magritte, Max Ernst, Salvador Dalí and Joán Miró, explored elements of surprise and unexpected juxtapositions of objects through a wide range of media.

Reflection and acceptance

After the initial shock of each successive art movement, the public tends to accept the narrative of the history of art, either retrospectively reaching an understanding of the merits of the avant-garde, or at least warming to it for its familiar, iconic celebrity. The process of acceptance can take several decades.

At the 1900 Paris Universal Exposition, the French President, Émile Loubet, was being conducted around the art exhibition at the Grand Palais by Jean-Léon Gérôme, an artist of the old school, famous for his sensuous historical and oriental pictures. It was 26 years since the launch of Impressionism. But as they reached the room displaying Impressionist work, Gérôme tried to block the way and expressed a still widely held view by declaring: 'Do not stop, Monsieur le Président, for herein lies the dishonour of French art!'

RELIGION AND IDEAS 4

Invisible truths Adam's apple, the Three Wise Men and the Holy Trinity. None of these things are mentioned in the Bible, so where did the ideas come from?

The Bible is not a single book; it is more like a small and patchy library. It consists of 66 works, mostly by different authors, and in various genres, such as law, history, poetry, prophecy, letters and biography. The books of the Old Testament were written over a period of about 1,000 years and mostly in Hebrew. The books of the New Testament were all written in the space of one lifetime, and were composed in Greek.

The Psalms are about as different from the Acts of the Apostles as the poems of Russian writer, Alexander Pushkin are from the speeches of former US president, Ronald Reagan. Christians believe that these disparate works, taken together, are a coherent revelation of God in the world.

Millions of words have been written down the centuries to support the idea that there is a divinely inspired unity in the Bible's message. Along the way stories been told and doctrines proposed, which (whether or not one believes them to be true) are not present in the Bible. Theologians have extrapolated ideas from the revered texts; writers have elaborated upon them; and the centuries have overlaid them with the rich patina of tradition.

The fruit of knowledge

At the simplest level, this process has involved nothing more than filling in some obvious gaps in the narrative. Some of the best-known Bible tales are frustratingly short on detail. The

Genesis story says that Adam and Eve ate the fruit of the tree of the knowledge of good and evil, but does not say what kind of fruit it was. The Jewish scholars of the Talmud took various

guesses – that the fruit was a fig, a grape or even wheat – while another ancient Jewish text mused that it might have been a tamarind. Some Muslim thinkers have suggested it was

MODESTY FOUND German artist Lucas Cranach the Elder's 16th-century painting contains many popular elements of the Adam and Eve story: the tempting serpent, the apple tree and the fig leaves they used to protect their modesty.

most likely an olive. For Jews and Muslims, the exact nature of the fruit was a purely scholarly matter.

But for Christians the problem was real and pressing because artists needed to know how to depict the scene: paintings of religious episodes were forbidden in Islam and Judaism, but they were a central part of Christian worship.

The early church was divided: the Latin-speaking west was inclined to believe Adam's fateful fruit was a grape, while the Greek-speaking east favoured the fig. A third option, that Eve's gift might have been an apple, gained currency early on – partly as a result of a pun: the Latin for 'apple', *malum*, is also the word for evil. In addition, the apple – originally a native of Asia – was the most commonly found fruit in the unconverted lands of northern Europe. The apple had a long history as a mystical symbol of knowledge, and the first Christian missionaries, with their knack for co-opting pagan ideas and imagery, made clever use of this ancient association when preaching. By the

12th century, the apple was firmly established in the Christian imagination as the fruit that led to the fall.

Who were the Three Wise Men?

If an undefined fruit was the source of such curious speculation, how much more so was the identity of the many anonymous but significant human characters in the Bible? There are numerous unnamed bit-players in the gospels: the flock-watching shepherds, the thieves on the cross, the righteous centurion. But none of these have generated so many stories as the wise men who followed the Star of Bethlehem. The 'Magi' feature in only one of the four gospels (Matthew) and their part in the story is just 12 sentences long. Even then, the Bible story does not state how many of them there were; it does not describe them as kings, and it does not give their names.

As Christianity spread, people naturally wanted to know more about the mysterious, alluring foreigners who were the first to worship Jesus. The 3rd-century Egyptian theologian Origen

BEARING GIFTS A painted wooden relief clearly shows the wise men as kings, each of different ethnic origin and with a precious gift.

said that there must have been three wise men, because three gifts are mentioned – but there is no reason to suppose that the wise men brought one gift each. There are early traditions that give their number as two, four or eight. In Middle Eastern churches it was held that there were 12 wise men and each of them was known by name.

Nevertheless, the notion that the wise men were three in number was accepted in the west by the 6th century. The idea that they were also kings was first suggested by the Roman writer, Tertullian, who was roughly contemporary with Origen. He said tentatively that they were 'well-nigh kings'. His hesitancy derives from the fact that the Bible says nothing of the sort – but Tertullian was looking for a fulfilment of a prophetic line in the Psalms that says: 'The kings of Tarshish and of the isles shall bring presents; the kings of Sheba and Seba shall offer gifts.' The names of the Three Wise Men are first given in a fragment of text written around AD 550. It says: 'During the

Why do we traditionally pray with our hands together

We know from tomb art that the first Christians prayed with their arms raised and the palms of the hands held upwards – a position known as the 'orant'. 'I want men everywhere to lift up holy hands in prayer', wrote the author of the Book of Timothy. It is not clear when Christians began to put their hands together to pray, but the practice may derive from the medieval ceremony of 'commendation', in which a vassal pledges allegiance to a king. From a devotional point of view, clasping hands and closing eyes are a way of cutting oneself off from the world, in order to create an oasis of stillness for the soul.

HANDS OF AN APOSTLE BY ALBRECHT DÜRER

his gift of myrrh testified to the Son of Man who was to die.'

The idea that each of the wise men belonged to a different race is poetic licence. It is an elaboration of the symbolic role they play in the story of the nativity, where they represent the Messiah's lordship over the Gentiles as well as the Jews. Their names are invented. Balthazar is a version of the name given to the prophet Daniel in Babylon; Melchior is like the Hebrew for 'king of light'; and Gaspar is a corruption of Gundaphorus, a name given to the king of India in the apocryphal Gospel of Thomas. Other Christian traditions ascribe different names to them. If the wise men existed at all, they were most likely to have been priestly astrologers from Persia – for whom but an astrologer would look at the stars and deduce that a king had been born in a distant land?

Three in one and one in three

The Three Wise Men are not the only Biblical trio to have been extrapolated from the text of the New Testament. The crucial concept of the Trinity – God as Father, Son and Holy Spirit – is also not elucidated in scripture. Neither Jesus nor the apostles used the word 'Trinity' and it appears nowhere in the pages of the Bible. So how did this central tenet of Christianity arise?

The apostles were devout Jews and were steeped in the belief that there is only one God. Christianity inherited that monotheism unquestioningly. At the same time, the first Christians believed that Jesus was the Messiah and 'the son of God' and that he died to save them from sin – which implied that he was in some sense divine. There was a difficulty here for the first

reign of Augustus, the magi brought him [Jesus] gifts and venerated him. The magi are called Bithisarea, Melchior and Gaspar.' A document written in Britain 200 years later adds some flesh to these bare biographical bones. 'The magi were the ones who gave gifts to the Lord. The first is said to have been Melchior, an old man with white hair and a long beard, who offered gold to the Lord as to a king. The second, Gaspar by name, young and beardless and ruddy complexioned, honoured Him as God by his gift of incense. The third, black-skinned and heavily bearded, named Balthazar, by theologians of the new-minted Christian religion: if Christ was created by God the Father, as the phrase 'son of God' might imply, then surely he was in some sense inferior to God; if so, how could he forgive sin? But if he was God in his own right, alongside God the Father, how did that tally with the idea that there is one God? Their belief in God's omnipresence on Earth as the incorporeal Holy Spirit – the force behind the words of the prophets and the virgin birth, represented 'descending like a dove' at Christ's baptism and as a mighty wind and tongues of fire on the first Pentecost – only made things more complex.

The precise nature of Christ and the Holy Spirit was the subject of much lively debate in the first two centuries of the Christian era. But the need for a theological resolution to the question became acute in the 4th century, when under Constantine, the first Christian emperor, Christianity became an accepted religion of the Roman Empire. By now the discussion had come down to two opposing views, both supported by reference to the Bible. Most bishops said that Christ and the Holy Spirit had always existed along with God the Father, and that

FAVOURITE TALES Some Bible stories, such as that of Jonah and the whale, may have had little basis in fact but were popular because of their power as fables.

they were three persons in one Godhead. But there was a strong minority belief, articulated by an Alexandrian theologian named Arius and held by many ordinary Christians within the Empire, that only the Father was God, that Christ was subservient to him and the Holy Spirit subservient to Christ. The bishops defined Christ in Greek as *homoousian* – 'of the same essence' as God, and so 'uncreated'. Arius and his followers said that Christ was *homoousion*, a word which differs by just one letter, and means 'similar in essence' to God – that is, created by God.

This history of the Christian faith turns on that single Greek iota. In AD 325 a council of 300 bishops was called at Nicaea to settle the issue. Arius attended, but he was overruled and his faction outvoted. The bishops drew up a list of words that defined the essentials of Christian belief. That document is the Nicene Creed, which is still recited in churches today: 'We

believe in one God, the Father, the Almighty ... We believe in one Lord, Jesus Christ, the only Son of God ... begotten, not made, of one Being with the Father ... We believe in the Holy Spirit ... who with the Father and the Son is worshipped and glorified ...' At Nicaea the doctrine of the Trinity was made the touchstone of Christian orthodoxy. The Arians lost the argument, and were declared heretics and persecuted out of existence.

Who decided which books should go in the Bible?

The first Christians were Jews, and they used the existing Jewish scriptures in their worship. That is to say, Christianity inherited the Old Testament from Judaism and treated it as a holy scripture from the start. But there were a number of spoken and written accounts of the life of Jesus circulating in the earliest Christian communities, a fact alluded to in the first lines of Luke's gospel: '... many have undertaken to set down an orderly account of the events that have been fulfilled among us.' The best of these biographies were later gathered together and used for devotional purposes.

Within a century or so of Christ, the four gospels we know today were being used as aids to devotion. They were joined by the letters of Paul, which were collected together and read out at church services. Most Christians took the view that the new works – the gospels and the epistles – were at least as sacred as the Hebrew Bible, that they constituted a 'new testament' from God to complement the 'old testament' given to the Jews. Some doubt remained over one or two of the minor letters, as well as the Book of Hebrews and the allegorical 'Revelation' of John. At the same time, some dubious accounts of Jesus'

early life and theologically unsound collections of 'sayings' were rejected. By AD 250 most of the contents of the New Testament were gathered together as a single entity. About a century later, in AD 367, Athanasius, Bishop of Alexandria, wrote out a list of New Testament works, which corresponds exactly to those we know today. In 393, Athanasius' list of books and the Septuagint (the Greek translation of the Jewish scriptures) were 'canonised' at the council of Church leaders, known as the Synod of Hippo. The Church identified these works as the Word of God, and bequeathed them to posterity.

The geography of faith Why is northern Europe predominantly Protestant and southern Europe mostly Catholic?

PAPAL PRAYERS Pilgrims throng St Peter's Square to receive Pope Benedict XVI's Christmas Day blessing.

It is an odd fact about Europe that nations where Germanic languages are spoken lean towards the Protestant faith, while those with Latin-derived languages tend to be Roman Catholic. So Germany, Britain, the Netherlands and Scandinavia are all, broadly speaking, Protestant. France, Spain and Italy turn their face to Rome. There are exceptions – in Germany there are predominantly Protestant and predominantly Catholic areas, but any map of the religious affiliations of western European nations, not least in Germany, would show a clear north-south divide.

Germany and the Reformation

The geographical divide in European Christianity is the long-lasting legacy of the religious reformation of Europe in the 16th century. It goes back to the start of Protestantism and its instigator, Martin Luther. A well-known story tells how Luther, an obscure German monk, went to the castle church in Wittenberg on 31 October 1517 and nailed his '95 Theses' to the door. This document (so the story goes) was a damning critique of corruption within the Roman Catholic church, and effectively a manifesto for a new form

a bulletin board for academics at Wittenberg University, and the 'Theses' was a discussion document for their eyes only. Moreover, it was not intentionally divisive: Luther's aim was to encourage reform of the Catholic church, not to create a new one.

But Luther's 'Theses' did contain the seeds of a religious revolution. His main criticism was directed against papal corruption in Rome, in particular the sale of indulgences. The church taught that people could shorten the time their souls would spend in Purgatory, before they could ascend to Heaven, by paying priests to intercede for them, or for souls already departed. But Luther said that these so-called indulgences were nothing

but extortion of the poor. He added that they were theologically brash: God's forgiveness could not be bought with paupers' pennies, because the Bible taught that salvation was given to all the faithful. And no priest – up to and including the Pope – had the right to place himself between a Christian and his Father in Heaven.

Luther's 'Theses' were soon translated into German. The new technology of printing enabled copies to be swiftly circulated. The presses also churned out explanations and defences of the Lutheran position written by him and others in the ensuing months and years. Crucially, the printing press made it possible to disseminate Luther's own translation of the New Testament, made in 1522. (His translation of the whole Bible was published in 1534.) German speakers could read it for themselves, without the mediation of priests versed in Latin. Perhaps nothing did

of Christianity. That episode at Wittenberg probably never happened. Luther never wrote about it and there are no reliable accounts. If it did occur, then it was not the populist act of defiance it is often portrayed as being. The church door functioned as

more to undermine the Catholic priesthood than Luther's German Bible. Most of the people who read his words – or heard them read – did not grasp the theological subtleties. But they did understand the general point that the Church hierarchy (and, they assumed, also the temporal hierarchy) was unjust and exploitative. Luther's stance on the Church – his resistance to priestly authority – coincided with eruptions of anti-authoritarianism everywhere. In 1524, peasants across Germany rose in a rebellion that swept through Franconia and Swabia. Their demands covered such social concerns as the right to elect their own pastors and reform of the system of rents and leases.

The new Lutheran thinking did not only appeal to proletarians and peasants. It also attracted the semi-independent rulers of the Holy Roman Empire. These grandees were glad of a reason to throw off papal law and tax, and some of them saw the chance to grab church property. The princes of Hohenzollern, Hesse, Brandenburg and Schleswig were among those to adopt Protestantism for themselves and on behalf of their subjects. Cities such as Magdeburg, Nuremburg, Bremen, Strasbourg and Frankfurt did the same. The Emperor Charles V remained staunchly Catholic. But he was distracted by external wars against France and the Ottoman Empire, and his power over lesser German princes was limited. His empire was not an autocracy; it was more a kind of aristocratic federation. If the princes favoured Lutheranism and published Luther's work, no edict could stop it.

The spread of Protestantism

There was nothing to prevent the northward advance of the new ideas, and within a generation Protestantism had become entrenched in Germany. In 1555 Protestant and Catholic states reached a truce that recognised the *status quo*: the Peace of Augsburg legalised Lutheranism inside the Holy Roman Empire in the cities and principalities where it had already been adopted. Parts of Switzerland, Bohemia and the Netherlands had adopted the cerebral, uncompromising form of Protestantism advocated by the French reformer John Calvin. Bavaria and Austria, the German-speaking places closest to the Papal States in Italy, chose to remain Catholic.

The Holy Roman Empire could not contain the new Protestant movement. In England, Protestantism came about because Henry VIII, formerly hailed as 'Defender of the Faith' by the Catholic church, saw it as a means of dodging papal objections to his plan to divorce and remarry. Most Catholic churches became Anglican with their own Prayer Book. Scotland, under the influence of Calvin's cohort John Knox, adopted a form of Calvinism that came to be known as Presbyterianism. The Calvinists also made inroads in

Why does most of Christian eastern Europe subscribe to the Orthodox faith?

Eastern Orthodoxy is the child of Byzantium. In the third and fourth centuries, the Roman Empire comprised two entities: a Latin-speaking western empire with its capital at Rome; and a Greek-speaking eastern empire with its capital at Byzantium (later renamed Constantinople, now Istanbul). The division of the empire was at first political, but over time the Latins and Greeks developed divergent religious practices. The Latins called themselves catholic, or 'universal', while the Greek speakers called themselves orthodox, or 'right-thinking'.

When the rulers of the eastern Slavs – the ancestors of the Russians and the Ukrainians – decided to adopt Christianity, they turned to Byzantium because they already had long-standing trading links with the Byzantine Empire. Missionaries were sent to convert the Slavs and translate the Bible into their native tongue. According to tradition, the work was done primarily by two brothers, Saints Cyril and Methodius. The former gave his name to the Cyrillic alphabet, in which Russian, Ukrainian, Belarusian and Serbian are written. Today, the Russian Orthodox Church, with 145 million members around the world, is by far the largest Orthodox congregation in Eastern Europe.

ONION DOMES OF A RUSSIAN ORTHODOX CHURCH

Calvin's homeland of France. Here they were known as Huguenots, a term of uncertain origin that may have made fun of their secret night-time services by comparing them to 'Le roi Huguet', or evil ghosts who roamed the Earth at night. Their influence involved them in a series of persecutions, then civil war. A brutal massacre of Huguenots occurred in France in 1572. The French religious wars continued, ending only when the Huguenots emigrated, giving up their fight for a Protestant France.

In Italy, the spiritual heartland of the Catholic faith, the Lutheran revolution made little impact. Luther's German Bible, which was his secret weapon inside the Holy Roman Empire, was useless in territories where other, Latin-based languages were spoken. And the Italian church proved good at keeping Luther's work out of their lands.

No European state remained more staunchly Catholic than Spain. King Ferdinand of Aragon and Castile had only recently driven the Muslim Moors out of the Iberian peninsula when Protestantism surfaced. Spanish rulers kept tight control of their Church, and believed themselves to be commanders in the front line of the battle for the 'True Faith'. The Church and the Crown had developed ways of deterring those who undermined the faith. The Church published its own list of banned books – at least as strict as the Vatican's; students were forbidden to study abroad, and unlikely to be infected by Lutheran ideas; Jews were expelled or forced to convert: no alternative to Catholicism could prosper or take root on Spanish soil.

Spain's strongest weapon in the fight for Catholicism was its ideological police – the Spanish Inquisition. All the techniques that the Inquisition had used to uncover Spanish Jews masquerading as Christians were now applied to the task of winkling out Protestant heretics. So the Protestant faith never gained even a foothold in Spain and Portugal. Lutheranism, Calvinism and Presbyterianism turned out to be best suited to the cool, temperate climes of northern Europe; Catholicism, like the fruit of the vine, flourished better in the hot, parched earth of the south.

PUBLIC SHAME The Spanish Inquisition parades heretics in Plaza Mayor, Madrid, in 1680 in an *auto da fé*, at which the sentence, usually burning at the stake, would be announced.

Why is the Pope based at the Vatican in Rome?

In Catholic tradition, Rome's pre-eminence derives from the fact that its Christian community was founded by the apostle whom Jesus named Peter, declaring that 'on this rock I will build my church'. According to the New Testament, therefore, Christ himself nominated Peter as the first Pope, and his authority has been passed down to every pope since.

But there is no archaeological or Biblical evidence that Peter ever went to Rome. And if he was leader of the Roman Christians, then it is odd that he is never mentioned as such in the letters of Paul the Apostle. The claim that Peter preached and died in Rome arose only in the 2nd century AD, and the tradition that he was Bishop of Rome does not appear until after Emperor Constantine legalised the Christian faith in the 4th century. The bishopric of Rome was by that time the wealthiest in the church.

Rome became the centre of the faith because it was the centre of the empire. Its importance grew after the 7th century, when the places described in the New Testament fell into Muslim hands. Pilgrims could no longer walk in Christ's footsteps in the Holy Land, but they could come to Rome and worship on the Vatican Hill where Peter was said to have been martyred.

In the Middle Ages, the Pope became in effect a powerful worldly prince as well as head of the Church hierarchy. He controlled a vast swathe of central Italy – the Papal States – and from 1506 employed a Swiss Guard for protection, a role that continues to this day.

After the unification of Italy, the extent of the Papal States shrank to the tiny Vatican City state of today, within the city of Rome. Yet it remains sovereign and independent and the Pope has full legal, executive and judicial powers. It has its own banking system and communications, with the Pope's voice heard by millions of Catholics worldwide on Vatican Radio.

CIVITAS·IHERVSALEM

HOLY CENTRE In 1483 a German nobleman called Bernhard von Breydenbach made a pilgrimage to the Holy Land. On his return he published a description of his journey illustrated by this map of Palestine with Jerusalem at its centre. The city is drawn as it would be seen looking westwards from the Mount of Olives.

The thrice-holy city Is it a coincidence that Christians, Jews and Muslims alike regard Jerusalem as a holy city?

Jerusalem is in the world's news almost every day and probably has been for most of its history. From the earliest times it has been portrayed visually as the centre of events: one of the oldest and most detailed maps in existence is the Madaba mosaic dating from the 6th century AD. Its representation of 'The Holy City of Jerusalem' is one of the most accurate early city maps. A 1471 map of Israel had Jerusalem at its symbolic centre, while a 1581 'clover-leaf map' went still further, showing the city as the absolute hub of the three continents of Europe, Africa and Asia.

Perhaps the most miraculous thing about Jerusalem is that it still exists at all. The ancient part is tiny, so that you could walk round the present-day walls in about half an hour. And in its long history, the city has been besieged or attacked dozens of times and completely destroyed at least twice. It could easily have disappeared

altogether, like the fabled city of Troy or Tenochtitlán, the capital of the Aztec Empire. But it has survived, to become the most contested and revered location on the face of the Earth today.

The holy city of the Jews
Jerusalem's ascent to holiness began 3,000 years ago when it was held by a tribe called the Jebusites. When David, King of Judah, captured the city from them he made it the capital of his kingdom. Later, his son Solomon built a great temple to house the Ark of the Covenant, which contained the tablets on which were written the Ten Commandments. For Jews, the Ark was so holy that it was almost as if God himself resided within it. It could almost be said that in the Jewish imagination the Ark emitted a form of sacred radiation that completely imbued the temple and was felt to permeate the entire city. Solomon

declared: 'The places to which the ark of the Lord has come are holy.' In c.586 BC, Jerusalem was overrun by the Babylonians. The temple and the city were destroyed, the Ark was carried off and a large proportion of the Jewish population was deported. The disaster served only to heighten the Jewish sense of devotion to Jerusalem. It also inspired one of the finest poems ever addressed to a city.

'By the rivers of Babylon – there we sat down,' wrote one of the Jewish exiles, 'and there we wept when we remembered Zion … If I forget you, O Jerusalem, let my right hand wither! … if I do not set Jerusalem above my highest joy.' These sad verses, which now form Psalm 137, have sustained generations of Jews in times of tribulation. It is as if all the hardships suffered by Jews since ancient times were echoes of the destruction of the city. The act of 'remembering Jerusalem' became a means of keeping the faith.

The city of Christ
Christians took the Jewish belief that Jerusalem is somehow the dwelling-place of God, and transmuted it into a metaphor for heaven, or for a better world to come on Earth. The author of Revelation, the last book of the Bible, wrote of 'the new Jerusalem that comes down from my God out of heaven'. The idea of a new Jerusalem

ON THE ROCK The Mosque of Omar stands on the rock, which previously bore the Roman Temple of Jupiter and before that, the two temples of the Jews.

WALL OF PRAYERS Orthodox Jews pray at the Western (or Wailing) Wall, a remnant of the wall that once enclosed the Second Temple.

The four quarters

Jerusalem's old walled city is traditionally divided into four districts, or quarters, each with a distinctive religious and cultural identity.

1 Dome of the Rock
2 Al Aqsa Mosque
3 Antonia Fortress
4 Church of St Anne
5 Via Dolorosa

6 Church of the Holy Sepulchre
7 Citadel
8 Church of St James
9 Western (or Wailing) Wall

Christian quarter
Armenian quarter
Jewish quarter
Arab quarter

MEETING POINT The Church of the Holy Sepulchre, or Church of the Resurrection, has been a site of Christian pilgrimage since the 4th century AD.

has inspired Christians down the ages, most notably the English poet William Blake, who hoped to 'build Jerusalem in England's green and pleasant land'.

But the Christian reverence for Jerusalem is only partly to do with its Old Testament symbolism. Christians' interest in Jerusalem derives mostly from what might be called its holy history. Here Jesus spent the last week of his earthly life. The momentous events that included the last supper, his trial and crucifixion, and his resurrection all took place in Jerusalem. The actual locations within the city where these events took place were long ago fixed by tradition and have been sites of pilgrimage for almost 2,000 years. Two of the most significant sites: Golgotha, the place where Christ's cross was placed, and the tomb where he was laid are both conveniently located within the same building: the venerated Church of the Holy Sepulchre.

Sacred to Islam

For Muslims, the holiness of Jerusalem is bound up with a tale told in the Koran. This story recounts how Mohammad was visited at night by the archangel Gabriel. The prophet was given a winged horse that carried him 'to the farthest mosque', where he met with all the previous prophets and was then carried into the presence of Allah.

Though the location of the farthest mosque is not stated, Muslim tradition, based on the interpretation of learned commentaries, holds that the term denotes the site of Solomon's Temple in Jerusalem. Muslims also believe that Temple Mount (also known as Noble Sanctuary) is the site where Abraham was commanded by God to sacrifice his son. These are all later traditions; Jerusalem is not mentioned by name in the Koran. But the city was always a sacred place for Islam: in the first days of the faith it was to Jerusalem, not Mecca, that Muslims turned to pray.

Why is Abraham a major figure in all three faiths?

RELIEF ON THE DOORS OF THE BAPTISTRY IN FLORENCE, SHOWING THE SACRIFICE OF ISAAC

Judaism, Christianity and Islam all trace their lineage back to the holy figure of Abraham. He is the shared locus from which their differing traditions emanate. For Jews, Abraham is the father of the nation and a founder of the faith. The promises that God made to Abraham are bestowed on all Jews because he is the ancestor of all Jews. Abraham's son Isaac was the father of Jacob, who became the father of Joseph and his 11 brothers. The 12 grandsons of Abraham were the progenitors of the 12 tribes of Israel.

But Abraham (or Ibrahim as he is known in Arabic) is also the ancestor of every Arab. The Bible recounts how Abraham believed that his wife Sarah was barren. At her own suggestion, he lay with a slave-girl, Hagar, who bore him a son. This boy was named Ishmael and he became the father of the Arab people. According to the Biblical account, Sarah persuaded Abraham to send Hagar and Ishmael away after she herself became pregnant. Muslim tradition says that mother and son settled near Mecca, and that Abraham was reunited with them there. Together, Abraham and Ishmael built the Kaaba in Mecca, Islam's holiest shrine.

Muslims also believe that it was Ishmael, not Isaac as described in the Jewish scriptures, who came close to being sacrificed by his father. God stayed his hand at the last moment and told him to sacrifice a goat instead. The Christian view of this troubling test of Abraham's faith is that it symbolises and prefigures God's plan to sacrifice his own son to redeem the sins of the world. So the Christian link to Abraham is not literal and genealogical as it is with Jews and Muslims, but metaphorical and spiritual.

Why are cows sacred to the Hindu religion?

Cows are not worshipped in Hinduism, but they are profoundly revered, because they are seen as a living metaphor for the bounty of nature and the benevolence of the gods. The overwhelming feeling that Hindus have for the cow is one of gratitude for the five gifts it is held to bestow. These gifts are milk; yoghurt; *ghee*, the clarified butter used in lamps and in cooking; *gobar*, or cow dung, which is used as fuel, a building material and an insect repellent; and *gau mutra*, cow urine, which is an important element in traditional Indian Ayurvedic medicine.

The provision of all these good things depends on the cow being alive, which is probably the root of the Hindu prohibition on killing or harming cows. In ancient times cows were just too valuable as an asset to slaughter. 'Let not the cows run away from us', says one of the Vedic hymns of the Rig-Veda, the ancient collection of hymns to the gods. 'Let no thief carry them away … Let them not fall into the hands of a butcher or his shop.' In this verse, we can see how the early economic importance of the cow is closely linked with the taboo against making use of it as meat.

The mythical cow

Reverence for the cow is expressed in countless tales of Hindu mythology. Krishna, an incarnation of the supreme being Vishnu, is said to have been a cowherd in his youth and once raised a mountain to shelter a herd. His epithets include *bala-gopala*, 'child who protects cows', and *govinda*, 'the one who brings satisfaction to cows'. Other stories tell how Lakshmi, the goddess of wealth, arose Venus-like from a churning sea of milk. And the hour when the sun is setting and the cows come home is known as *godhuli* – 'cow dust'; it is held to be the best time of day for a wedding.

But in Hindu thought the cow is more than a piece of walking folklore. There is a moral dimension in the Hindu attitude to this gentle animal. 'The cow is a poem of pity,' said Mahatma Gandhi. 'She is the mother to millions of Indian mankind. Cow protection means protection of all that lives and is helpless and weak in the world. I would not kill a life, be it ever so precious.'

HARVEST THANKS Garlanded with flowers, a cow takes part in the festival of Pongal, held on 14 January to celebrate the traditional end of the harvest.

Other sacred animals in Hinduism

Animals were considered sacred by many ancient societies and religions. Ancient Egyptians worshipped cats, considered to be demi gods, while the Plains Indians came to regard the horse, introduced by Europeans, as sacred. As well as the cow, Hinduism reveres a wide range of creatures that includes:

Monkey A manifestation of the god Hanuman, they were traditionally encouraged around temples and are fed and protected.

Turtle In his second earthly incarnation, Lord Vishnu took the form of a gigantic turtle and sat at the bottom of the ocean where he helped the Hindu spirits attain the nectar of immortality from the celestial ocean by holding Mount Mandara on his back.

Ring-necked parakeet Sacred to the goddess Meenakshi, who holds a parakeet in her right hand. At the Meenakshi temple in Tamil Nadu, parakeets are trained to repeat the goddess's name.

Black bear In the Hindu epic poem, the *Ramayana*, Jambavantha the bear helps Lord Rama to find his abducted wife Sita.

Elephant The great beasts are sacred to Hindus. Many temples have special elephants that carry the deities during festival processions.

Cobra In Hindu tradition, Lord Shiva often wears a cobra coiled around his neck, a symbol of his power over the deadliest creatures. Lord Vishnu also rests on a coiled cobra, the Adi-sesha, asked by Lord Brahma to bear the weight of the entire world on its head.

A faith divided The two main branches of Islam are the Shias and the Sunnis. How did they come about, how are they different and why are they frequently in such conflict?

Like a tree that is forked at the root, Islam split almost as soon as it came into being. The division of the Islamic world into two denominations, Sunnis and Shias, came about almost immediately after the death of the Prophet Mohammad. Both groups grew out of a murderous wrangle over the leadership of the Muslim community, and the consequences of that ancient conflict are still keenly felt to this day. The differences between Sunni Muslims and their Shia brethren are rooted in the tale of the early days of the faith.

Mohammad is the undisputed leader of the movement he

created. In AD 610, when he was 40 years old, he had abandoned his life as a merchant in Mecca to preach a simple new revelation: that there is one God, Allah, and that the true path lies in 'submission' (*islam* in Arabic) to Him. Mohammad and his first followers, who called themselves the 'submitters' (*muslims*), were persecuted for their ideas and driven out of Mecca. They went to Medina, where Mohammad was welcomed as a man of wisdom. Here the faith found many new converts, and in 630 Mohammad was able to

march back to Mecca at the head of an army and take the city where he was born. Within a couple of years his ideas and his soldiers had conquered most of the Arabian peninsula and Mohammad himself had been recognised as a prophet. More than that, he was the 'seal of the prophets', the last and greatest of a line that stretched back through Jesus and King David to Abraham, Moses and Adam.

In 632, Mohammad fell ill and died. His uniquely pre-eminent position made it hard to know who could succeed him, and Mohammad himself

HOLY CITY Imam Ali Mosque in Najaf, Iraq, is the third most holy Shia site after Mecca and Medina. Imam Ali is interned in the mosque and the devout bring their dead to his tomb before burial.

had left no clear instructions on that score. It was generally agreed that the next leader would have to come from the Prophet's inner circle. But as the matter was discussed, differences began to emerge as to what the succession meant.

Faction allegiance

Most of Mohammad's longest-serving lieutenants and disciples, the men who had been with him since the difficult first days of the faith, thought that the new leader should be the person who most closely followed Mohammad's example (*sunna* means 'precedent' or 'way' in Arabic). The person would not be a spiritual leader to rival the Prophet, but the political head of the Islamic community and the commander of the Muslim armies. Their candidate was Abu Bakr, who was Mohammad's close friend and the father of the prophet's wife, Aisha.

A much smaller faction, consisting primarily of members of Mohammad's family, thought that the succession should remain with Mohammad's bloodline. Their champion was

Mohammad's cousin Ali, who was also one of the prophet's first converts.

For the 'followers of Ali' (*shi'at Ali*, hence *shia*), there was a factor even more important than the bond of kinship: Ali was married to Mohammad's daughter Fatima, and so his sons were the grandsons of Mohammad. The Shia saw a dynasty of descendants of Mohammad stretching into the future – an eternal, living link with the Prophet Mohammad. Soon after Mohammad's death a meeting was called at Medina to discuss the succession. It took the form of a kind of parliament of elders in the city, and many long-standing associates of Mohammad attended.

Both Abu Bakr and Ali were absent, but Abu Bakr learned of the meeting, and rushed to the place where it was being held. He spoke to the gathering and made a general recommendation that the new leader should be a man who could unite the whole Muslim world, not just someone who was

acceptable to the people of Medina. Whether he intended it or not, the result of this speech was that he was elected on the spot, and everyone present pledged allegiance to him. He became the first caliph – a word that is derived from *khalifa*, the Arabic for 'successor'.

Both sides agree that Ali was deeply distressed at being passed over – and not even consulted on the succession. But from this point on, the accounts grow more partisan. Sunnis say that Ali became reconciled to Abu Bakr, gave his allegiance, and served as an adviser to him and the next two caliphs. Shia accounts say that if Ali gave his allegiance at all – which is by no means certain – then it was under threat and duress, and only in order to maintain unity within the

> ## The next leader would have to come from the Prophet's inner circle

umma, the Muslim community as a whole. There is a Shia tradition that Ali's pregnant wife Fatima was injured when Abu Bakr's men forced their way into her house, that she miscarried as a result of this and died of her injuries soon after.

The occluded Imam

What is certain is that from the start of Abu Bakr's rule, the supporters of Ali felt themselves to be an oppressed minority within a wider Sunni world. This sense of struggle was reinforced by subsequent events. Ali was passed over as successor two more times. He became the fourth caliph, but was assassinated in 661. The caliphate passed back to the Sunnis and open war broke out between the two factions. Ali's son Husayn continued the struggle against Yazid, the ruling Sunni caliph, but Husayn and his supporters were massacred at the Battle of Karbala in 680, in a heroic last stand beside the River Euphrates in what is now central Iraq.

Husayn's death has become the central event of Shia legend; he is seen as a blameless martyr in a righteous cause. Both Husayn and Ali came to be revered as Imams, which in this context means a figure akin to a Christian saint. Most Shias believe that there was a succession of 12 godly Imams, that the last of them was 'occluded' (hidden from sight by Allah) in the year 874, and that he will return one day to raise up his followers and usher in a new age. This belief is, one might say, a natural corollary of a faith based on a history of disinheritance (and it is akin, though few Muslims would approve of the comparison, to the Jewish people's longing for the messiah). Until the return of the Hidden Imam, the spiritual life of Shia Muslims is regulated by a hierarchy of clerics. At the pinnacle of this hierarchy are the *ayatollahs* (the Arabic title means 'Sign of God') – high-ranking, learned figures analogous to Christian archbishops or cardinals.

A golden age

One should not stretch the analogy, but Sunnis view these Shia beliefs in a manner that is not unlike the Protestant view of Catholicism. For a Sunni, the reverence accorded by Shias to the 12 Imams is almost idolatrous, and the clergy system is an unnecessary complication of the straightforward Muslim faith. To the Sunni way of thinking, an imam is a leader of prayer and an interpreter of the law: functions that can be fulfilled by any qualified Muslim.

Their meritocratic view chimes with the Sunni stance on Abu Bakr's succession, but it is also rooted in the Sunni view of Islam's later history. The years in which the somewhat melancholy Shia world view was formed look totally different from a Sunni perspective. To Sunnis, the first centuries after the death of Mohammad are a kind of golden age. A Sunni dynasty, the Umayyads, ruled an empire from their base in Damascus in modern-day Syria that stretched from Spain through to Africa and Persia. Even when this empire fell, Sunni rule persisted through the Abbasid and ultimately the Ottoman empires.

As a result of this political success, the Sunni version of the Islamic faith became the doctrine of most Muslims around the world. Today, 85-90 per cent

AWE-INSPIRING A 17th-century portrayal of the Umayyad Mosque in Damascus, one of the oldest Sunni mosques in the world.

of Muslims are Sunni. The Shias constitute a minority within Islam now, as they always have done.

Few countries have a Shia majority; they include Iran, Iraq, Bahrain and Azerbaijan. In Iran, the Ayatollah Khomeini took the Shiite yearning for spiritual justice and turned it into a revolutionary theology that demanded political justice. When Khomeini came to power in 1979, he superimposed the Shia clerical hierarchy on the government infrastructure. Iran became a nation ruled by Islamic law (*Sharia*) – though under Khomeini and his successors the country is not so much a religious republic as a totalitarian theocracy.

Polarisation and moderation

In Iraq the Shia majority was brutally treated by Saddam Hussein. A Sunni himself, he ruled through a military elite made up mostly of fellow Sunnis. In 2003, Saddam and his government were toppled by a US-UK invasion force, which, in the aftermath, was unable to prevent the oppressed Shia from taking vengeance on their oppressors. A self-perpetuating cycle of civil strife has been the result.

Events in these countries have had the unfortunate effect of resurrecting a historic suspicion of Islam in the western world. This has been exacerbated by the rise of a vocal anti-western strain of political opinion within Muslim society – a militant trend that most Muslims consider ill-conceived and deeply un-Islamic.

To judge Islam by these extremist manifestations would be as unfair as assessing Christianity on the evidence of the violent sectarianism that took place in Northern Ireland during 'the Troubles'. After all, many Sunnis and Shias are disinclined even to use those denominational labels, preferring instead to be known simply as Muslims – those who surrender to the will of God.

What are the other forms of Islam?

Sunnis and Shias together constitute the vast majority of Muslims worldwide. But there are other beliefs and practices within Islam, other ways of submitting to Allah. Sufism is a thoughtful, mystical tradition. Like the monastic orders within Christianity, it came about as a reaction to the growing wealth and power of Muslim society in the early days of its expansion. Like Buddhist ascetics, Sufis use techniques of methodical repetition to induce the state of spiritual ecstasy known as *sukr* or 'intoxication'. They might, for example, recite the name of Allah over and over again. The Turkish sect known in the west as the 'whirling dervishes' are Sufis, and their dance is a meditative and symbolic practice towards attaining selfless love. Sufist traditions are also prevalent in north Africa.

At the opposite end of the religious spectrum is Wahhabism. A strict, austere interpretation of Islam, it is named after an 18th-century Muslim scholar named Muhammad Ibn Abd al-Wahhab. He deplored what he saw as the moral laxity of fellow Muslims and spoke out against the veneration of shrines and the blind devotion to non-Koranic medieval texts. He saw these as distractions from the central truth of Islam: that there is no God but Allah. In many ways, Wahhabism is a kind of Puritanical Islam. Like Puritanism in 17th-century England, it was a militant political movement as well as an uncompromising religious creed. Followers of al-Wahhab razed Sunni and Shia shrines in the same manner and for much the same reasons as Cromwell's Roundheads smashed statues of saints in English churches. An early ally of al-Wahhab was Muhammad Ibn Saud, an Arab tribal chief whose descendants became the rulers of Saudi Arabia. Wahhabism remains the most influential strain of Islam within Saudi Arabia today.

There are other minor breakaway groups in Islam. Examples are the Ismailis in India; the Mahdists of the Sudan; the Alawites in Syria; the Zaidis in Yemen; the Kharijites and Ibadites in Oman and parts of Algeria and Tunisia; and the Druze in Lebanon and Syria.

SPINNING AROUND A whirling dervish performs the *Sema*, a ritualistic dance in which the blessing of heaven is transferred to Earth.

Where did terrorism come from? How did the idea arise that killing innocent people, not enemy combatants, is a legitimate way to achieve a political end?

One man's terrorist, it is said, is another man's freedom fighter – and there is some truth in that old political cliché. Nelson Mandela was called a terrorist by his opponents and thrown in jail for it. The French Resistance used classic terrorist methods to fight the Nazi occupation during the Second World War, and its members were considered heroes.

But there is a crucial difference between a terrorist and a freedom fighter. The distinction lies in the willingness or otherwise to use *indiscriminate* violence, to carry out acts that run the risk of hurting or killing people unconnected to the

FOILED PLOT In November 1605, Guy Fawkes and fellow conspirators sought to blow up the Houses of Parliament in London and assassinate James I.

REPRESSED REBELS Social unrest in Russia reached boiling point and in 1881 rebels assassinated Alexander II. A first bomb halted his carriage; as the Tsar alighted to comfort the injured, he was killed by a second blast.

cause. In this regard, the freedom fighter/terrorist is faced with two separate questions that require an answer. The first is practical: is it acceptable that some innocent people

will get caught in the crossfire of the armed struggle? The second is ideological: is it a good and useful strategy to target innocent people if it will further the cause?

The practical question arose once the power of bombs and grenades became available to political assassins. Using bombs for terrorist attacks meant that bystanders were liable to be killed along with (or instead of) the real target.

The Russian revolutionaries of the 19th century were among the first to grapple with the problem. In 1879, a group called the 'People's Will' planned to assassinate the tsar, Alexander II. At first they favoured using a knife, or at most a gun, in order to limit the danger to others of any assassination attempt. When they found it was not possible to get close enough to kill the tsar by these means, they resorted to bombs – though were at first concerned about carrying out an attack if anyone was nearby. But there were always people around the tsar, so they overcame this scruple.

One bomb, planted below the dining room of the Winter Palace, killed nearly 70 people in the tsar's absence. In the end he died when his carriage was targeted by several bombers at once. The one who struck Alexander was also fatally injured.

Modern strategy
Many present-day terrorist organisations have used bombing as part of their strategy, and have not baulked at terrorist acts that are liable to result in the deaths of civilians. That said, organisations such as the IRA generally issued warnings so that civilians could be evacuated before the bomb went off. Massive disruption, not mass murder of non-combatants, was their main aim. But some ideologies do not recognise that there is any such thing as a non-combatant. The actions of Palestinian suicide bombers on Israeli buses have been justified on the grounds that Israel has universal conscription, therefore every Israeli citizen is – previously, presently or potentially – an enemy soldier and so a fair target.

More generally, the aim of some terrorists is not so much to effect

The Assassins: killers for a cause

In modern parlance, an assassin is a practitioner of political murder. His sole function is to damage the machinery of state oppression by removing certain fundamental cogs: the president, the chief of police, the king or queen.

This was precisely the function of the *hashshashin*, the 11th-century sect whose name gave rise to the word 'assassin'. The original Assassins were a kind of guerrilla group formed from disaffected elements within the Ismaili branch of Shia Islam, and their principal enemy was the Sunni Empire of the Seljuk Turks. Their intention was to kill their man as publicly as possible – often in a mosque or a marketplace. They sometimes worked singly, sometimes in groups, and they often made clever use of disguise to get close to their targets. When the moment came they would ambush their victim and stab him in the heart. Once the deed was done, they did not try to escape nor try to defend themselves: they stood by and waited to be cut down – belatedly – by their victims' bodyguards or family members. They were, in a sense, the original suicide terrorists.

The sect's enemies gave it the name *hashshashin*. The word probably denoted a renegade or an outlaw, but its literal meaning is 'hashish takers'. There is no evidence that the Assassins used drugs, but the literal sense of the word gave rise to all sorts of stories (retold in lurid detail by Marco Polo) about how they used the drug to induce visions of the martyrs' Paradise that awaited them after their act of self-sacrifice. For their contemporaries, such tales went some way to explaining their baffling and chilling indifference to death.

ASSASSINS ENJOY THE DELIGHTS OF PARADISE, FROM AN ILLUMINATION, C.1412

change but to inflict punishment. This was certainly the case in the 9/11 attacks of 2001 (page 149). In this instance, the deaths of the passengers on the planes and the people in the buildings that the planes struck were not considered 'collateral damage' by the terrorists, but an essential element of the plan – namely, to inspire terror in entire populations, to imbue people everywhere with the sense that no one is ever entirely safe. In this goal, at least, the latest generation of terrorists has been entirely successful.

BECOMING A LEADER Osama bin Laden (standing far right) with members of the mujahidin in Afghanistan in the 1980s.

Though the man himself has not been seen in public for many years, the grave, ascetic face of Osama Bin Laden, the Saudi Arabian leader of al Qaeda has become one of the most familiar on the planet. And what an arresting face it is: the steady gaze that seems to mark him out as a man of contemplation; the long, greying beard, making him look older than his years; the gaunt cheekbones. If you didn't know better, you might take him for a monk or a guru, because Osama Bin Laden does not have the air of a mass murderer.

But more noteworthy than Bin Laden's appearance is his rise to global notoriety. Ask anyone what they know about Bin Laden, and they will tell you he is the head of a worldwide network of Islamic terrorists called al Qaeda, and the

Osama's war Hardly anyone had heard of al Qaeda until the events of 9/11. So where did the world's most feared terrorist organisation spring from?

AFGHAN AMBUSH The aftermath of an ambush by mujahidin fighters in 1985, which destroyed a convoy of more than 80 Soviet and Afghan tanks.

author of the deadly attacks that took place on 11 September 2001. Ask the same people what they knew of al Qaeda before 9/11 and the chances are they will say 'nothing at all'. So what is al Qaeda? Where did the organisation originally come from and why has it declared an all-out war on America and its allies?

What is al Qaeda?

The word *al-qaeda* is difficult to translate from Arabic. It is usually rendered as 'the base' in the sense of a camp or headquarters, but it can also mean the foundation of a house, or the foot of a column. More figuratively, the word *qaeda* can denote a method or a model, a principle or a pattern. But if the word is a hard thing to define, then the radical movement that bears the name is even harder to grasp. The way the word *al-qaeda* is used by politicians and the media might lead one to think that al Qaeda is an organised paramilitary group akin to the IRA or the Basque separatist movement, ETA. But it is at least as true to say that al Qaeda is not a clearly defined group, but rather a revolutionary set of ideas. The lack of clarity about the exact nature of the organisation is one of a number of factors that has continued to hamper the effective waging of a 'war on terror'.

Al Qaeda had its roots in the war that the Soviet Union fought in Afghanistan from 1979 to 1989, in which Russian troops battled the *mujahidin*. This word, meaning 'freedom fighters resisting invaders', was used to describe Afghan guerrilla groups resisting the invasion. During the war, the mujahidin received support from many quarters. They were supplied with arms and money by the American government because it saw them as anti-Communist freedom fighters. The government of Saudi Arabia, like the government

of Pakistan, backed the Afghan fighters as fellow Muslims at war with an atheistic, infidel army; and among the Saudis who joined the mujahidin was Osama Bin Laden, an extremely wealthy young man whose father had made a fortune in the construction industry.

A recent graduate of King Abdul Aziz University, he had been influenced by a radical Egyptian teacher at his school in Jedda. He set himself up in the Pakistani city of Peshawar, close to the Afghan border. At first, like most of the Arabs who went to aid the mujahidin, he had little direct involvement in the fighting. He functioned as a kind of charity worker. He handed out cash and food parcels to wounded fighters, and he helped out at the offices of an Islamic newspaper called *Al-Jihad* ('The Struggle'), which was published by a charismatic Palestinian preacher called Abdullah Azzam, a man whose words had a powerful impact on the young Bin Laden.

Bin Laden's front-line experience helped to radicalise him

The radicalisation of Bin Laden

His association with Azzam turned Bin Laden into a radical militant, deeply involved with the military side of the mujahidin cause. With Azzam he set up Maktab al-Khidamat (MAK), or 'The Office of Services', which set out to recruit committed fighters from all over the Muslim world, and get them into Afghanistan.

Bin Laden became a soldier himself, pledged to an Afghan *jihad* to fight for the holiest of causes. He used his wealth and contacts to set up training camps inside Afghanistan to which he recruited volunteers from almost every Muslim country, whatever its form of government. He believed that the struggle had forged links between Muslims in the world at large and the consciousness of unity had to be maintained and developed.

TERROR MASTERMIND Abu Azzam was al Qaeda's commander in Iraq and deputy to al-Zarqawi, Iraq's most wanted terrorist. He was killed by coalition forces in 2005.

By 1986, Bin Laden's mentor Azzam himself began to consider what would happen after Soviet troops were driven out of Afghanistan. He envisaged a kind of permanent jihad, an ongoing struggle for the reunification of the Muslim world in which his Arab Afghans would play a leading part. 'Fighting is compulsory for every Muslim,' he wrote. 'This duty will not end with victory in Afghanistan. *Jihad* will remain an obligation until all the lands that were Muslim are returned to us so that Islam will reign again: before us lie Palestine, Bokhara, Lebanon, Chad, Eritrea, Somalia, the Philippines, Burma, southern Yemen, Tashkent and Andalusia.'

Two years later as Soviet troops retreated, he published an article in *Al-Jihad* that was entitled *Al-Qaeda al-Sulbah* – 'The Solid Base'. 'Every principle needs a vanguard to carry it forward,' he wrote, 'to undertake difficult tasks and make tremendous sacrifices. It is the Solid Base that constitutes this vanguard.' He did not explain how it would work.

A proposition rejected

In 1989, the year that the Soviet Empire collapsed in Europe, Azzam was assassinated by a car bomb. Bin Laden took over the leadership of the Arab-Afghan network that Azzam had termed *Al-Qaeda al-Sulbah*, facing a

after civil war in 1996. A year later it changed the name of the country to the Islamic Emirate of Afghanistan: Saudi Arabia and Pakistan were two of the three countries in the world to recognise it, but the Saudis remained as opposed to Bin Laden as ever, not least after he took to issuing *fatwas* (edicts or rulings on Islamic law) against the United States – something he did not have the authority to do. He was particularly fired up by what he saw as outright American support for Israel's occupation of Palestinian land and called for the re-establishment of a Muslim caliphate. It was, he sought to ordain, incumbent on all Muslims, to 'kill Americans and their allies,

new situation in his own part of the world in 1990 when the Iraqi leader Saddam Hussein invaded Kuwait. He approached the Saudi government and offered his Arab Afghans as a defensive army should Saddam then move against Saudi Arabia. Instead, the Saudi government turned down his proposal and allowed American forces to deploy on Saudi territory.

Bin Laden, deeply affronted, considered the presence of American forces in the country of his birth a defilement of Islam's most holy shrines and thereafter he attacked the Saudi royal regime as well as the Americans. His angry statements on the subject attracted the attention of the Saudi secret police, and he was forced to go into exile.

Towards a notion of jihad

The first Arab country to which Bin Laden went was the Sudan, where an Islamic fundamentalist general had seized power in a coup of 1989. Bin Laden was able to set up a training camp there, but he did not discover the personal security he had hoped

for and there were a number of attempts on his life.

Bin Laden decided, therefore, to return to Afghanistan, where there had been significant political changes since he had left the country. The Taliban, an extreme Islamist student movement formed by exiles in Pakistan, had taken over the country

INTERNATIONAL APPEAL A supporter in Kenya. Despite attempts to kill Bin Laden, his influence is growing.

military and civilian'. Such statements attracted a number of supporters from Europe and elsewhere around the world, many of whom were Muslim converts. A prominent supporter of Bin Laden was Ayman al-Zawahiri, a member of the Muslim Brotherhood in Egypt, who had also found refuge in Afghanistan. The Muslim Brotherhood had been founded as early as 1928 and it operated as al Qaeda did, under a series of different names in a number of countries. Egypt's president, Hosni Mubarak, was as hostile to the Brotherhood as Saudi Arabia was to Bin Laden.

However, the notion of a jihad that Bin Laden called upon his supporters to join was not the kind of jihad that all Muslims believed in. An important detractor was the influential Sayyid al-Sharif, al-Zawahiri's mentor, who complained that Bin Laden was seducing Muslim youth.

Terrorism in New York

The plan to mount a spectacular, devastating attack against the USA may not have been devised by Bin Laden himself. We do not know who exactly had the idea of simultaneously targeting symbolic sites on American soil, but he and the circle surrounding him evidently saw its immense propaganda potential and took a special interest in it.

Holed up in a mountain hide-out on 11 September 2001, Bin Laden must have listened intently as the planes his supporters had hi-jacked turned their noses that morning to target Washington and the Pentagon, and New York and the twin towers of the World Trade Center.

A number of supporters of Bin Laden's jihad were involved when a series of bombs went off on London's transport system on 7 July 2005, killing and injuring civilians. But the 'battle against terrorism' was now taking new forms, as – with the worldwide communication permitted by the internet – was terrorism itself.

What lay behind the 9/11 attacks?

The four aerial terrorist attacks of 11 September 2001 were so shocking and so unexpected that they looked like a totally new form of terrorism. But for all its enormity, the assault on mainland America was not an entirely new departure for al Qaeda. It might better be described as the culmination of a number of trends in the strategy of terror.

Symbolic targets

The use of aeroplanes as 'flying bombs' was mooted by Islamist militants as early as 1994. It was a tactic made possible by the willingness of terrorists to die along with their victims. On 11 September, al Qaeda took the familiar practice whereby a suicide bomber crashes a car full of explosives into a military checkpoint or similar target, and elevated it to a new level of technical expertise and a new height of atrocity.

The targets were chosen for their symbolic value. To al Qaeda, the World Trade Center was a symbol of American arrogance and this was not the first time it had been targeted. In 1993, Islamist terrorists had detonated a car bomb in the basement garage of the WTC, hoping to topple one tower into the other. The Pentagon, as the HQ of the US Defense Department and perhaps the real seat of American power, should have been the most secure building in the country; if al Qaeda could land a blow there, then they could hit anything. The fourth target seems to have been the White House, the headquarters and home of the American President.

COMMUTERS FLEE AS THE SECOND TOWER OF THE WORLD TRADE CENTER COLLAPSES

We are all green now Thinking ecologically has become a kind of civic or even moral obligation. Who decided that we should all start to be green?

A generation ago, no one recycled, the car was an unquestioned boon of modern life, and nobody had heard of global warming, yet awareness of mankind's harmful effect on the environment is centuries old. In 1661, the English horticulturalist and diarist John Evelyn wrote a treatise about the pollution caused by the use of sea-coal as fuel. That work – *Fumifugium, or the inconveniencie of the Aer and Smoak of London dissipated* – was one of the first pieces of writing with an ecological theme, and it set a pattern: from the start, environmentalism was a response to technological progress.

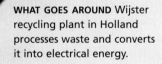
CND LOGO

Into the atomic age

Complaints became more frequent and more urgent as industrialisation gathered pace. In 1798, the English demographer Thomas Malthus warned that unchecked population growth was likely to lead to famine and disaster sooner or later. In 1852, the Scottish chemist Robert Angus Smith discovered a link between air pollution and what he called 'acid rain'. Later, societies for the protection of animals sprang up throughout the western world in response to practices such as the large-scale slaughter of the American bison.

In the middle of the 20th century, one spectacular technological advance sparked the modern environmental movement – nuclear fission. Between 1945 and 1962 Britain, France, the USA and the USSR carried out a total of 423 nuclear tests – mostly for military purposes. Small groups set up protests against this arms race: the first and most significant was the Campaign for Nuclear Disarmament (CND), formed in Britain in 1958. At first it was the obliteration of the planet in a nuclear exchange that worried protesters, but soon they objected to the irradiation of the Earth that was already occurring. Some of the grassroots environmentalists – the activists who went on to join Greenpeace or Friends of the Earth – were people who had cut their teeth in the anti-war movement.

The nuclear nations signed a partial test-ban treaty in 1963, but by that time other troubling environmental problems had come to the fore. Among them was the widespread use of the pesticide Dichloro-Diphenyl-Trichloroethane, or DDT, which had successfully been used to control mosquitoes spreading airborne diseases in the early years of the Second World War. Its catastrophic effects on wildlife and local people had been highlighted in 1962 in the book *Silent Spring*. Its American author, Rachel Carson, pointed out that DDT poisoned the very crops it was supposed to protect, and that it killed insect life indiscriminately, depriving birds of their main source of food. Future springtimes would be silent, because there would be no birds alive to sing. Carson's book became a bestseller because her message had the simple force of a Biblical parable: by exploiting the Earth for our own benefit, we were destroying it. The American government took note. In 1963 one of President Kennedy's administration wrote that: 'America today stands poised on a

WHAT GOES AROUND Wijster recycling plant in Holland processes waste and converts it into electrical energy.

ICE MELT Arctic sea ice melts unseasonally early as a result of global warming, a process which has also caused glaciers to recede.

pinnacle of wealth and power, yet we live in a land of vanishing beauty, of increasing ugliness, of shrinking open space, and of an overall environment that is diminished daily by pollution and noise and blight.'

Over the next 25 years, successive scandals and disasters highlighted the dangerous liberties that humanity was taking with Earth. In 1967, the tanker *Torrey Canyon* hit a reef off the Scilly Isles, southwest of the British mainland, and spilled an estimated 119,000 tons of crude oil, polluting hundreds of miles of Cornish coastline. In the 1960s, Japanese chemical factories were found to have been discharging mercury and other metals into Japan's rivers and seas for years, poisoning wildlife and people. In 1972, the UN Conference on the Human Environment argued for a set of 'common principles to inspire and guide the peoples of the world in the preservation and enhancement of the human environment'. The worst fears were realised when a reactor exploded at the Chernobyl nuclear power station in the Ukraine in 1986, sending a toxic, radioactive plume across the western Soviet Union and into northern Europe and Scandinavia.

Scientific proof

Catastrophes like these increased awareness, but at the same time they were terrible yet isolated incidents that could have been avoided. In the 1970s and 1980s, scientists began to argue that the gravest threat to the planet's future came from a different source: a cumulative effect of the everyday activities of billions of people. In 1985, the British Antarctic Survey at the South Pole found a 'hole' in the ozone layer that shields the Earth from the Sun's radiation. This was caused by global use of chlorofluorocarbons, non-toxic chemicals used as refrigerants and aerosol propellants.

Scientists also found that worldwide temperatures were rising, almost certainly due to the volumes of 'greenhouse gases' released into the atmosphere by burning fossil fuels. Even a small degree of global warming might lead to irreversible climate change, with violent weather and floods causing crop failure and the loss of vital ecosystems. The environmental 'vandals' were the people who drove cars, heated their houses, used machinery or flew in aeroplanes. This dawning acceptance of collective responsibility had turned environmentalism into a political issue by the 21st century. Global agreement was necessary but there were different opinions, with the west on one side and developing countries like China and India making claims for their own requirements.

In 1979, the ecologist James Lovelock proposed the 'Gaia hypothesis', which treats the planet as a single living entity, and says that Gaia instinctively knows how to adjust conditions so Earth remains a hospitable place. His good news is that life will surely go on whatever damage we do to it. The bad news is that Gaia may have to arrange things so that it goes on without us.

Who invented political correctness? Where did 'political correctness' come from, and how did politically correct terms, such as 'African-American', establish themselves?

In its simplest and least contentious form, 'political correctness' is no more than a social courtesy, an insistence on the language of tolerance. If society holds that every citizen has equal rights, then it is wrong – 'politically incorrect' – to use words that imply some groups are of less worth than others. So terms that were once common currency – 'darkie', 'wop', 'spastic' – come to be disapproved of, or even outlawed.

Why words become offensive

The troublesome characteristic of politically correct language is that it is not static. Words and phrases that have been touted for their social neutrality can themselves slip down the verbal scale and become offensive. This process, known as 'pejoration', can be seen in the string of terms used to describe physical disability: crippled, lame, handicapped, differently abled, disabled, physically challenged. A new term will surely be required soon, since the cry of 'challenged!' has been noted as a taunt in school playgrounds.

In each generation, new politically correct terms are coined to replace words worn out by pejoration. 'Colored' was a more or less respectful term for Americans of African descent

in the first years after the emancipation of the American slaves and survives in fossil form in the name of the National Association for the Advancement of Colored People (NAACP), founded in 1909. But the leaders of the civil rights movement that emerged in the 1950s disliked the word 'colored', because it defined their race as distinct from the white-skinned norm. The civil rights leader Martin Luther King favoured the word 'Negro' and used it routinely ('The new Negro says he doesn't like the way he is being treated …'). During the civil rights struggle, 'Negro' had an honest ring about it. It did not sound politically loaded as it came from the ostensibly non-political science of ethnography.

In the 1960s, another term came to the fore. That term was 'black'. The surprising thing about the adoption of the word 'black' is that it had long been used by white people as an insult. Yet this was precisely what made it attractive to more radical young activists, such as Malcolm X. 'Reclaiming' the word was felt to be an act of defiance, and it was flown as a kind of banner in phrases such as 'Black Power' and in the slogan 'black is beautiful'. In 1968, the soul singer

James Brown had a hit with a song that spelled out the new attitude to the word: 'Say it loud – I'm black and I'm proud.' The older term 'Negro' fell out of use and was seen as degrading in casual conversation.

Shared heritage

Within a decade or so, however, the word 'black' was questioned just as the word 'colored' had been: it defined Americans of African descent in terms of their difference from the Europeans who had once been their oppressors. And the term did not recognise that people of African descent can have a range of complexions. What we share, said some thoughtful black Americans, is not so much skin colour as an African heritage.

Ramona Hoage Edelin, a lecturer at Northeastern University in Boston, USA, had been using the term 'African-American studies' (rather than 'black studies') to describe her courses. In 1988, Edelin attended a meeting of black leaders chaired by Jesse Jackson, the veteran civil-rights leader and associate of Martin Luther King. At that meeting she suggested that 'African-American' could replace the increasingly unsatisfactory 'black'.

BLACK AND PROUD In his 'I Have a Dream' address of 1963, Martin Luther King declared that 'the life of a Negro is still sadly crippled by the chains of discrimination.'

Jackson agreed, and at a press conference announced that 'African-American' was to be the preferred term for describing his community. 'To be called African-American has cultural integrity,' he said. 'It puts us in our proper historical context. Every ethnic group in this country has a reference to some land base, some historical cultural base. There are Armenian-Americans and Jewish-Americans and Arab-Americans and Italian-Americans; and with a degree of accepted and reasonable pride, they connect their heritage to their mother country and where they are now.' Jackson's eloquence gave the word wings. It was adopted by the American press and spread into the English-speaking world.

Adopting 'political correctness'

It was in feminist circles that the term 'political correctness' first took hold. In 1970, the writer Toni Cade Bambara wrote in an essay that 'a man cannot be politically correct and a chauvinist too.' This is one of the first uses of the term in a sense close to its modern usage. But Bambara had not made it up; she had taken it from the pages of Marxist philosophy, in which the phrase was used to describe a comrade who always followed the party line. She was saying wryly that committed feminists could sometimes be as ideologically bigoted as a functionary of the Chinese communist party.

The term 'politically correct' was too useful to be just a passing quip. It soon began to be used in the negative – 'politically incorrect' – to describe words that perpetuated discrimination against women. Feminists pointed to gender-specific nouns, such as 'policeman' and 'headmaster', that implied that only men could do the job (political correctness demanded the gender-neutral 'police officer' and 'head teacher'). They also highlighted masculine bias in western society, for example, honorific titles for a woman – Miss and Mrs – showed her

availability as a spouse. The inelegant title Ms was invented as a female equivalent of the male term Mr.

Many countries soon introduced legislation banning discrimination against women, racial minorities and people with disabilities. Businesses and government departments found themselves in danger of being sued if their practices appeared to be biased against any such groups. Personnel departments – rebranded Human Resources – took to making rules and publishing guidelines intended to pre-empt the possibility of legal action.

As they took the form of diktats from above, such guidelines looked very like the kind of prescriptive authoritarianism that Bambara had joked about. Some even described 'political correctness' as 'cultural Marxism'. Certainly, many examples of PC rule-making emerged from left-wing organisations and stories about 'political correctness gone mad' were a staple of right-wing commentators. Some of the criticism was fair, focusing on the sheer idiocy of many PC phrases: 'temporarily abled' for physically fit and 'deferred success' for exam failure. Other stories were distortions or untruths, such as the claim that the nursery rhyme 'Baa baa black sheep' had been banned because it was considered racist.

'Political correctness' has led to a refashioning of everyday expression. Where once there was a single undisputed word there are now a range of options. What is the proper way of addressing the woman in charge of a business meeting: Chair? Chairwoman? Chairperson? Madam Chairman? None of the variants can be said to be entirely correct or incorrect, but all of them are political.

Indians and Eskimos

The re-naming of ethnic groups has long been a preoccupation of political correctness, but in some cases it has proved impossible to satisfy everybody. The word Indian, when used to refer to the pre-European inhabitants of the USA, was challenged on the grounds that it is geographically incorrect and a blanket term that takes no account of the ethnic and cultural diversity of the people it is applied to. The PC 'Native American' was adopted in the 1970s – in the teeth of protests that anyone with a generation or two of American ancestry, indeed anyone born there, is entitled to call themselves a Native American. 'Amerind', from 'American Indigenous', lured no one. Many think the best term is 'American Indian': its meaning is clear and there is nothing obviously offensive about it.

Canada, faced with the same issue, has opted for the phrase 'First Nations' though individual members tend to describe themselves by their tribal name and the expression does not apply to all Canadian natives. The people of the frozen north are seen as separate. They are Inuit, rather than Eskimo, because their activists viewed the word 'Eskimo' as insulting, saying it came from an Algonquin word for 'eaters of raw meat'. That is probably untrue, but the word 'Eskimo' went out of fashion all the same. Awkwardly, there are Eskimos in Alaska and Siberia who are not Inuit, and don't want to be termed so. In situations like this, only an expert ethnographer can be sure of not putting a foot wrong.

INUIT HUNTER BUILDING AN IGLOO, CANADA

By the people, for the people
Who decided that democracy was the only acceptable political system? Where did the belief in the superiority of democracy come from?

Democracy literally means 'rule by the people'. In practice this simple definition covers a wide variety of political traditions and structures, but it is a fact that today nearly every state in the world claims to be democratic. The few nations that do not consider themselves democracies include most of the countries of the Arabian peninsula, the military dictatorship of Burma and the papal theocracy of Vatican City.

Some states, as if to advertise their commitment to democracy, include the word 'democratic' or 'people's' in the official name. Curiously, these tend to be the least democratic countries of all.

So democracy claims almost universal political legitimacy among most people around the world (even if in some cases they are only paying lip service to the idea). This is odd, because for most of history democracy has not had a good reputation.

Athenian democracy
The original Greek word *demokratia* had none of the positive associations it carries today. It was at first a purely descriptive term, first used in the 5th century BC to describe the machinery of government that evolved in Athens and spread to many city-states in Greece. In the writings of Plato and

Aristotle, the greatest political thinkers of the ancient world, the word democracy is sometimes used in a decidedly pejorative way, and might better be translated as 'mob rule'.

Democracy in ancient Athens was very different from the modern understanding of the word. If the Athenian city-state existed today it would be condemned as deeply oppressive. It required a large population of slaves in order to function; without them free citizens would have had neither time nor leisure to invest in public affairs. Women were by definition not citizens: only adult men were eligible

ANCIENT BALLOT Part of a *kleroterion*, or 'allotment machine', used to select jurors in ancient Athens. Identity tickets of wood or bronze were slotted in. Small bronze balls poured into a funnel then selected rows of tickets at random.

to take part in the democratic process. 'Rule by the people' was rule by a fraction of the population – perhaps 10 or 15 per cent. But the lucky few were intensely involved in the political process. They were all entitled to attend the *ecclesia*, the town meeting where laws were made. And they were all eligible to serve as city officials and judges. Candidates for office were not usually chosen by holding elections, but through the casting of lots, rather like the selection process for jury service today.

The road to Rome

The Athenian method was unwieldy, but it worked so long as the number of eligible voters was small. Aristotle said the city should never grow so large that the voice of the town crier could not be heard by the whole assembly. It never occurred to the Greeks that they might elect officials who would serve as representatives of the people, and carry out the business of state on their behalf. They would have thought parliamentary democracy a dangerous practice. At best, it would tend towards oligarchy, or rule by an elite few. At worst, it might lead to tyranny – rule by a despot.

That worst-case scenario of Greek political thought came to pass with the rise of Rome. The early Romans thought of their state as a *res publica*, a loose term literally meaning 'a thing of the people'. To the Romans, the essence of res publica was a balance of power between the elite who debated policy in the Senate and the *populus*,

the ordinary, uneducated masses. The two part system was acknowledged in the slogan on Roman military standards: SPQR, abbreviated from *Senatus Populusque Romanus* – 'the Senate and People of Rome'. Their relationship was summed up by Cicero as *potestas in populo, auctoritas in senatu* – 'power lies with the people, authority with the senate'. In practice, senators knew that they had to keep the common people on side: Roman rulers lived in constant fear of the rabble.

But power might accrue to any strong man who could carry the people with him. Julius Caesar was just such a man. Caesar's ambition and hunger for power turned Rome from an oligarchic republic into the full-blown imperial tyranny it became under his successors. With the rise of the Roman Empire, democracy disappeared from the political vocabulary, and from the European mindset. The word was barely uttered in the course of the next 1,500 years.

Medieval progress

It was not true, however, that no progress was made towards democracy during that time. In the medieval states of Europe, there were constant power struggles between kings on the one hand and their aristocratic backers on the other. Kings tended to want absolute power, while barons and bishops were determined to share that power in return for raising the king's taxes and providing his armies. In many parts of Europe, the kings

won out and absolute monarchies, such as those of Louis XIV of France and Peter the Great of Russia, were the result. In England, the aristocracy gained the upper hand. The Magna Carta, sealed by King John in 1215, was a contract that limited the right of the king to lord it over his barons, knights and merchants, and even, to an extent, his peasants, or villeins. That document, frequently reinterpreted, set the tone for a struggle that culminated 400 years later in the English Civil War.

Parliament, which by that time had broadened its power base to include members of the minor country gentry, such as Oliver Cromwell, declared war on Charles I primarily because he insisted on behaving as an absolute monarch. Parliament won and the English monarchy was abolished. Though it was restored just 11 years later, it never regained anything approaching its previous political power. Parliament was king in England now.

It is only in retrospect that these events can be termed democratic. That

LORD PROTECTOR Oliver Cromwell ruled England between 1649 and 1658. But his austere regime was no more popular than the deposed Charles I and the monarchy was restored when he died.

word was never part of the political discourse of the time. But there was a key democratic idea at the heart of the English Civil War: namely, that a man – and it was still only men – had a right to a say in how he was governed, and that he could decide for himself how he should go about worshipping God, and how he should conduct his life. It was more than 100 years before the attitudes implicit in the English Revolution were ready to be spoken out loud – and when the time came, it happened in America.

The first act of the American Revolution was the 1776 Declaration of Independence, a resounding statement of democratic principle that has never been bettered: 'We hold these Truths to be self-evident: That all Men are created equal, that they are endowed by their Creator with

America's struggle for self-determination inspired people in the Old World

certain unalienable Rights, that among these are Life, Liberty and the Pursuit of Happiness. That to secure these Rights, Governments are instituted among Men, deriving their just Powers from the Consent of the Governed …' An intriguing point about the declaration is the word 'self-evident'. The American revolutionaries were not putting forward new concepts, but restating ideas that already had wide currency in Europe and the American colonies. Those ideas were mostly derived from the 18th-century French philosopher Jean-Jacques Rousseau, who had proposed that civil society rests on an unwritten 'social contract'. Since laws are necessary to protect

each individual's freedom, each individual citizen has a duty to take part in appointing lawmakers. These lawmakers (in this case, governments) are obliged to ensure that the law is an expression of the general will of the people. If government fails to fulfil its part of the bargain, then the people are entitled to remove it – by force if necessary. The American Revolution was the first instance in history of a nation going into action on a breach of the social contract.

Revolutionary times

The drama of America's struggle for self-determination inspired people in the Old World. In 1789 the French people, armed with the democratic slogan 'Liberty, Equality, Fraternity', overthrew its absolute monarchy. They beheaded the king (as England had done a century earlier) and instituted a

VIVE LA RÉVOLUTION In 1792, the newly elected National Convention declared France a republic. The former king, Louis XVI, was tried and found guilty of 'crimes against the people' and guillotined on January 21, 1793.

republic (as America had done). In some parts of the world, monarchy came to be seen as incompatible with freedom. To many, a republic, in which the head of state was chosen by the people rather than by accident of birth, seemed inherently more democratic.

Many of the new republics that emerged in the 18th and 19th centuries modelled their political institutions on a rose-tinted vision of the Roman republic – especially if they had, like Rome, arrived at republican status by overthrowing an established monarchy. In calling their upper house 'The Senate' and its members, 'senators', Americans were paying deliberate homage to the system used in ancient Rome.

Votes for all

In the 19th century, many countries evolved a deeper, more inclusive understanding of the democratic ideal. In Britain, the flexible institution of parliament adapted itself organically to the huge social changes wrought by the Industrial Revolution. Through a series of reform acts the right to vote was extended to working-class men. British women over 30 gained the vote in 1918 and finally achieved electoral equality with men in 1928.

In America, slavery was a blight on democracy and made a mockery of the Constitution's lofty claim 'That all Men are created equal'. The Civil War (1861-65) abolished that wrong, but more than a century of struggle passed before the descendants of America's slaves won the right to be treated as equal to white Americans. In many parts of the world where there was no liberal tradition and no voluntary institutional infrastructure, democracy never won through. Absolute monarchy clung on in Russia into the 20th century when it was replaced by 'a dictatorship of the proletariat', a Marxist concept adapted by Lenin.

In the decade leading up to the Second World War, the democratic ideal came under attack from Adolf

One man, one vote

The ballot box is part of the paraphernalia of a modern democracy. Before it came into use, it was customary for voters to attend a mass meeting and shout their preference to an election official (having first sworn on the Bible that they had not voted once already). Alternatively, or sometimes in addition to their verbal vote, voters might be asked to submit a paper provided by one or other candidate or party. Clearly, this system was open to massive fraud. Dishonest electoral officers could easily manufacture votes without being detected; and voters were liable to be bribed or intimidated by agents of one party or another.

The uniform, anonymous ballot slip, along with the sealed box into which it was deposited, did away with that kind of electoral abuse. The first such secret ballot was held in December 1856 in the Australian colony of Victoria, and the poll in question was an election to the Victoria State Legislature. The man behind this new voting system was an English-born judge named Henry Samuel Chapman. He was a friend of the English reformer John Stuart Mill, and was steeped in radical politics. Chapman's innovation met with resistance at first – some people felt that it was more honest to declare one's political allegiance openly – but

the system was swiftly adopted by the administrations of other Australian colonies, then by New Zealand, England and Canada. Many of the American states had embraced Chapman's idea before the end of the century. Even now in the USA, a secret vote using a sealed box and a 'neutral' list of candidates is sometimes termed 'an Australian ballot'.

As for the box itself, it takes many forms throughout the world. There are polished wooden ballot boxes like pirate chests, and disposable cardboard ballot boxes that resemble fruit cartons. Some ballot boxes are not boxes at all, but tamper-proof bags. But in countries all around the world, the very term 'ballot box' serves as shorthand for the fundamental democratic ideal of free and fair elections.

COIN SHOWING A ROMAN CITIZEN VOTING

Hitler, who held democracy in open contempt. The war against Nazism was seen at the time as a confrontation between democracy (the definition of which was diplomatically stretched to include the USSR) and its enemies. The victory of the Allies was likewise incontrovertible evidence of democracy's inherent superiority. Later, as the Cold War came to a dramatic end in the late 1980s, many of the Eastern

European states that had formerly been opponents of the democratic western alliance queued up to join it, and to reinvent their own political systems in the western image. They knew well that democracy, which allowed citizens to change their governments, was (in Winston Churchill's words) 'the worst form of government except for all the others that have been tried.'

The end of an empire The USSR was a global superpower to rival America. No one expected it to crumble easily. So why did Soviet and Eastern European Communism collapse when it did?

On 25 December, 1991, the red hammer-and-sickle flag was lowered over the Moscow Kremlin for the last time and in that moment the Soviet Union ceased to exist. The 15 republics that made up the USSR became 15 new-minted independent nations and the world order changed forever. The striking of the red flag was seen to mark not only the demise of the world's first Communist state, but the defeat of the Communist idea itself. This collapse came about with remarkable and, to the outside world at least, unexpected speed.

Ten years before, in 1981, the USSR looked like the 'indissoluble Union' it claimed to be in its national anthem. Its superpower status and military might were undeniable. The country had a huge arsenal of nuclear weapons to challenge those of western nuclear powers, while the nations of Eastern Europe were ruled by Communist governments that had been forged in Moscow's image.

The Soviet Union was feared or respected by every government in the world. But it had troubles, the greatest of which was its 'command economy'.

All production and distribution were planned from the centre. Factories and businesses worked not to make profit, but to meet targets that were handed down from Moscow. These were often impossible to achieve because machinery was worn out, or the management was incompetent and

A SPEEDY COUP On 19 August, 1991, Boris Yeltsin stood on top of a tank, urging the Russian people to resist a hardline takeover of the government. Later he became the first freely elected president in Russian history.

idle, or part of the workforce was habitually absent.

Every manager had to lie to the centre about having met his targets, when in every sector except the military the wheels of the Soviet economy had almost stopped turning. Russians joked mirthlessly that 'They pretend to pay us, and we pretend to work.' Shops across the USSR were almost empty much of the time, and building projects were left unfinished for years. Standards of living inside Russia spiralled downwards in the early 1980s. Poverty led to cynicism, which engendered indolence and more poverty. So while the Soviet state was strong, Soviet society was suffused with tensions.

Gorbachev and perestroika

Little of this was apparent to the outside world, which saw only Communism's imposing facade. But by the late 1970s, Russians had a living picture of the state of the nation in the person of their leader: the moribund and confused figure of Leonid Brezhnev who had suffered a series of strokes. He died in 1982, but his successors were barely less ageing and ailing: both Yuri Andropov and Konstantin Chernenko died within a year or so of becoming General Secretary of the Communist Party.

The annual round of state funerals was becoming farcical – and the top ranks of the party knew that the next leader they chose must be a man of

some life and vigour. Their choice fell on a 54-year-old career Communist named Mikhail Gorbachev.

The new man's first instinct was to enforce a little 'Leninist discipline' in the workplace, the main thrust of which was a concerted campaign to tackle the long-standing problem of excessive drinking. Gorbachev restricted the sale of vodka and brought in new

punishments for alcohol-related absenteeism. The media pumped out anti-drink propaganda, and the vines of the wine-producing republics of the Caucasus were torn up. The 'dry laws' had a number of negative effects, each of which weakened the Soviet edifice. They created a universal black market for alcohol, boosting the income of the nascent Russian mafia. They cost the Soviet economy billions of roubles in lost revenue. Most of all, they earned Gorbachev the distrust of the working class and the peasantry, for many of whom vodka was a comfort in a life of hardship. Gorbachev was

Why is the colour red associated with revolutionary or left-wing causes?

The red flag has been linked to popular revolt since the French Revolution. A red flag was the signal used by the National Assembly to advertise a declaration of martial law. Hung from the windows of government buildings, it warned demonstrators to depart peaceably. In 1791, there was an incident in Paris during which the red flag was raised, and while it flew the National Guard charged the crowd, killing many people. In the aftermath, crowds of republicans took to waving red flags to goad the government. One banner from that time was inscribed with the words: 'The martial law of the people'. The red flag became the symbol of the political outrage of the common man.

The flag reappeared in Paris during the political upheavals of 1830 and 1848, but was not yet a specifically left-wing banner. Its association with socialist causes began during the Paris Commune of 1871, when the city was taken over by a workers' government. The uprising was crushed, but became one of the heroic episodes in the history of the Left. In their writings, Karl Marx and Friedrich Engels extolled

LA FRANC-MAÇONNERIE & LA COMMUNE.

the 'communards', and in his tomb Lenin was draped in a red flag taken from the barricades of the Commune. The red flag was no less meaningful for western socialists. It was the symbol of the British Labour Party until the 1980s (when it was replaced by a red rose) and the anthem 'The Red Flag' was sung at the annual party conference until 1999: 'Though cowards flinch and traitors sneer/ We'll keep the red flag flying here.'

barely more popular with other sections of Soviet society. The *nomenklatura*, the cadres of middle managers and party functionaries, suspected – rightly – that Gorbachev's vague criticisms of corruption and bureaucracy were directed at them, so that they would be the losers in the new policy called restructuring (*perestroika*). Since Gorbachev had emerged from their ranks, his attack on the administrative class looked like treachery.

Then there was the intelligentsia – the doctors and agronomists, teachers and journalists, the people who would queue in the snow for theatre tickets or the chance to buy a translation of Oscar Wilde. Though these people were in a sense Gorbachev's natural allies, they were dubious about his sloganeering and repelled by his rural southern accent.

A more open regime?

Yet all that western leaders and their people saw was a man of immense personal charm who talked in sensible and conciliatory tones about nuclear disarmament and the Berlin Wall. Country after country succumbed to 'Gorbymania'.

The hard truth behind Gorbachev's foreign policy was that his country could no longer afford to pursue the arms race or maintain garrisons in its satellite states in eastern Europe. In 1988, Gorbachev announced an end to the so-called 'Brezhnev doctrine', that is, the right of intervention in the internal affairs of any state in the Soviet bloc to safeguard the common interests of the rest. Instead, he adopted a line that the Soviet foreign ministry dubbed the 'Sinatra doctrine': Communist states to which they had been closely linked, such as East Germany, Czechoslovakia and Poland, would be allowed to 'do it their way'.

At home, Gorbachev pursued a correspondingly liberal policy that was given the title *glasnost* – 'openness' or 'frankness'. He realised that government had to be honest about the problems that his economic reforms were intended to address, because this was the only way to rally the people behind perestroika. So he licensed the press to discuss failures and abuses of power.

Revisiting the past

Glasnost was a means to address the most glaring falsehoods of Soviet propaganda and win back the support of the intelligentsia. Newspapers and journals discussed the horrors of Stalin's rule and published long unavailable or illegal works by émigré Russian writers.

Brezhnev's years in office became officially designated 'the era of stagnation', and the press, television and populace at large could speak openly about matters previously discussed behind closed doors. Russians read books on the metro that a few months previously would have had them arrested for possession of anti-Soviet propaganda.

But as the first flush of novelty wore off, the discussions unleashed by glasnost took a wider and more critical scope. The critique of Stalin's regime led to unanswerable questions about Communist regimes in general. The key issue was: if Stalin was a brutal dictator, by what right did Stalin's successors continue to rule? The peoples of Eastern Europe, pursuing glasnost locally, quickly concluded that the governments foisted upon them by Stalin at the end

of the Second World War had no legitimacy at all.

In 1989, with the leader of the Soviet Union no longer giving any support to the hardline Communist government of East Germany, its citizens tore down the Berlin Wall, opting joyfully for reunification with their fellow Germans in the west. Poland and Hungary, never comfortable within the Soviet empire, took little time to shake free of its influence. The Solidarity movement in Poland had already begun to erode Communist power during the 1980s, while Hungary had made moves towards

HOLE IN THE WALL When the Berlin Wall came down in 1989, many people saw their close neighbours for the first time in a generation.

The break-up of the USSR

After the countries of Eastern Europe chose democratic governments, in 1991 the Soviet republics claimed their independence. With Russia they formed the Commonwealth of Independent States for mutual economic and political support.

■ Present-day Russian Federation

■ Former republics of the USSR
(now members of Commonwealth of
Independent States)

■ Former republics of the USSR
(now EU members)

■ Former European Warsaw Pact members
(now EU members)

democratic government from 1987. The Czechoslovak government relinquished power in the so-called 'Velvet Revolution', while Bulgarians rejected their government and held free elections for the first time since 1931.

In Romania, where the Communists clung to power, a short but bloody revolution ended with the summary execution of party leader Nicolae Ceausescu. To the astonishment of the rest of the world, within a few weeks eastern Europe had broken free from Soviet control to make its own destiny.

The final loss of confidence

In May 1989, Gorbachev visited Beijing to celebrate the restoration of relations between China and the USSR. Because of his reputation for openness, his visit focused media interest on China's pro-democracy movement and gave it legitimacy. Soon after, the Chinese moved with swift brutality to crack down on protesters in Tiananmen Square, but for Gorbachev it was impossible to turn back the changes he had initiated.

Within the Soviet Union, the Baltic republics were making exactly the same demands as the Eastern Europeans. But Gorbachev would not countenance the secession of Soviet

republics, and in 1991 he sent tanks into Lithuania to put a stop to nationalist rallies – which yet did not smother the republics' demands.

Meanwhile, Gorbachev tried to sidestep growing criticism of the Communist Party, of which he was the head, by taking on the non-party role of president of the USSR. It was as if he was trying to place himself above and beyond the rising tide of protest and discontent. In the summer, the Russian people elected Boris Yeltsin to the newly created post of President of the Russian Federation. A former ally of Gorbachev's, Yeltsin had fallen out with his boss over the pace of reform: he believed change was not happening nearly fast enough.

In August 1991, Communist hardliners in Gorbachev's government staged a coup against him in an attempt to prevent the break-up of the USSR. Gorbachev was confined to his holiday dacha, while in Moscow Yeltsin led the people who came out onto the street to resist. The army refused to subdue the protesters, and the coup petered out. Yeltsin, the hero of the hour, used his new

authority as Russian president to ban the Communist Party and forced a tired and humiliated Gorbachev to countersign the decree.

In December 1991, Yeltsin and the presidents of the other Soviet republics took a joint decision to dissolve the USSR. On 25 December, Gorbachev resigned from his post as president of a Union that had now ceased to exist. Yeltsin moved into Gorbachev's office that same day – and ran down the red flag in the evening. Few outside had foreseen that so monolithic a power as the USSR could collapse so quickly and comprehensively.

Whether or not it was Mikhail Gorbachev's great achievement to dismantle the Soviet Union – as has been claimed – the process he helped to set in motion proved unstoppable.

Reasoning things through
When did people start trusting in scientific fact more than in religious belief?

The word superstition comes from the Latin *superstitio* meaning 'fear of the supernatural'. In ancient Rome, Cicero wrote that the superstitious were so called because they spent the day praying and offering sacrifices that their children might survive them. Medieval churchmen contrasted heathen superstition with true faith. St Augustine wrote: 'Thou strikest the first chord in the worship of one God, and the beast of superstition hath fallen.'

The challenge to the church
During the Reformation, the church's own practices came under fire. Protestants began to condemn Catholic veneration of relics, censing, rosaries and holy water as superstitious. Repudiating the rites and authority of the church in Rome, they took the Bible as sole authority. But were the scriptures that they themselves relied on free of the superstition they decried?

During the 16th and 17th centuries, scientists were exploring the natural world with ever greater curiosity. In Italy, despite a church ban, Leonardo da Vinci made hundreds of detailed anatomical sketches of humans and animals. Galileo Galilei was persecuted for insisting that the Earth revolved around the Sun, a theory that contradicted not only the teaching of the church in Rome but the scriptures too, for verses in the Bible imply that the Sun revolves around the Earth.

In effect, science was separating itself from religion. This was a major development in human thought. The new quest for knowledge was based on empirical observation: experience formed through analysis and experiment in the natural world. Science began to represent a challenge not only to organised religion, but to a more general belief in the supernatural. Superstition and science both hold that there is a connection between events that occur. But whereas superstition relies on intuitions and revelations that cannot be proved, empirical science only accepts truth that can be tested and verified.

The Enlightenment
In 1665, as a young scientist studying at Cambridge in England, Isaac Newton performed an experiment in a darkened room. A hole in his window shutter allowed a beam of sunlight to enter the room. Newton put a glass prism in its path and

INDISTINGUISHABLE FORCES Richard of Wallingford, a 14th-century English monk, used mathematics, astronomy and astrology to design a huge clock that accurately predicted lunar eclipses.

discovered that the sunbeam created a rainbow-like band of light. He then placed another prism upside-down in front of the first. The colours combined again into white sunlight. Newton now had empirical evidence that white light is made up of all the colours that we can see.

Experiments like these opened up a world of understanding – and led to new inventions of practical use to humankind, such as Newton's own reflecting telescope. A surge of optimism accompanied further scientific advances in the 18th century. When applied to manufacturing, it led to the development of coke-fuelled blast furnaces to make cheap iron at Coalbrookdale (1709) and the steam engine pioneered by Thomas Newcomen (1712). As the Industrial Revolution dawned, the problem-solving potential of man's own intellect seemed limitless.

In France, a body of intellectuals known as the *philosophes* ('philosophers') emerged, thirsting for the freedom to pursue their enquiries untrammelled by censorship or unproven dogmas of any kind. Through their movement, known as the 'Enlightenment', empirical science and rational thought became tools to

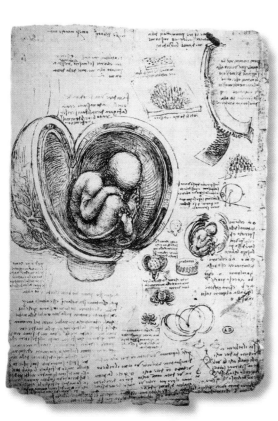

DARING DRAWING Da Vinci's drawing of a foetus flew in the face of a Church ban on the study of human anatomy.

attack the cruel, obsolete and unjust in Europe's old, hierarchical regimes.

From the Enlightenment came the spread of knowledge through the great compendium known as the *Encyclopédie* (page 220). The *philosophes* had faith in the dignity and perfectibility of man. 'If the laws are good,' said the *Encyclopédie*'s founder, French philosopher Denis Diderot, 'morality is good'. The American Declaration of Independence (1776) was framed in this spirit. Rule by divine right was replaced by the idea of constitutional government and the document named 'life, liberty, and the pursuit of happiness' among the 'unalienable rights' of man.

The ideals of the Enlightenment contributed to the French Revolution of 1789 and were exported across Europe by Napoleon. By celebrating the common man over the entrenched interests of priests and tyrants, the movement radicalised politics and law.

In economics, enlightened thinking contributed to the abolition of archaic tariff boundaries between and within nations. Just as ideas should circulate freely, it was felt, so too should manufactured goods. Rationalising trade led to the metric system of weights and measures (page 224).

As for religion, many of the *philosophes* were Deists. Men like Voltaire, Jean Jacques Rousseau and Diderot believed in one God but doubted all reported phenomena that could not be empirically tested. So they challenged the existence of miracles, supernatural events and even the authority of the scriptures. They hoped that the triumph of reason would bring the end of persecutions by rival faiths and restore a sense of God that they deemed natural to mankind. Taking their cue from the *philosophes*, French revolutionaries even attempted to create a rational religion. Maximilien Robespierre organised a Festival of the Supreme Being in Paris on 8 June 1794. The spectacular pageant, intended to inaugurate a new state religion for France, featured artillery salvos, tricolour flags, men bearing branches of oak and women bouquets of roses. It failed to catch on; soon afterwards Robespierre himself fell to the guillotine.

> The *philosophes* had faith in the dignity and perfectibility of man

Separating church and state

Instead of a rational religion, the concept of a secular state emerged – separating government entirely from church institutions. The United States government has been legally separated from religion since the First Amendment to the Constitution in 1791: 'Congress shall make no law respecting an establishment of religion, or prohibiting the free exercise thereof'. In 1905, France declared itself a secular country and many others followed suit. Turkey in 1924 was the first and most important, although in the 21st century the government is moving away from the strict secularism of the previous 80 years. Nepal, which was the world's only Hindu kingdom, declared itself a secular state in 2006, but does not operate as one in practice.

Many religious leaders support the secular state as a guarantee of freedom of worship to all groups. A compromise has evolved, allocating scientific and religious beliefs to their separate spheres in life. But traditional faiths that repudiate scientific findings have proved more enduring than 18th-century rationalists might have imagined. Recently, the world has witnessed a resurgence of fundamentalism, whereby adherents refer to a strict set of beliefs, derived from the religion's first principles – and often openly rejecting of 'reason'. And in the United States, the model of church-state separation, religious groups are staking a greater claim to a role in the public sphere.

SEEING THE LIGHT Isaac Newton's experiments in the 1660s on the refraction of light met with initial hostility. He therefore did not publish his great work, *Opticks*, until after his critics had died.

All in the mind
We freely use terms such as 'inferiority complex', 'introvert' and 'unconscious' to explain human behaviour, but barely a hundred years ago no one would have known what we were talking about. Where did these ideas originate?

Today, we are all psychologists to a greater or lesser degree. We want to know what other people think of us, why we are sad, whether love is going to last, what made us the person that we are. Words have always been available to express and explore these questions. But the jargon of modern psychology has provided a rich new vein of verbal possibilities. Everyday speech has borrowed widely and deeply from the pioneering psychoanalytical

works of Sigmund Freud, Carl Jung, Alfred Adler, William James and others – and no other scientific vocabulary has pervaded common parlance more thoroughly. The result is that we have ways of expressing feelings and categorising behaviour that were unknown to our grandparents. Until the 1960s, no one would have known what it means to go on an 'ego trip'. And many people are still taken aback to hear mildly fussy individuals routinely described

as 'anal'. The oldest psychological terms come from medieval theories on temperament, and are so deeply embedded that they are no longer recognised as medical or pseudo-medical turns of phrase.

The medieval 'humours'
The best known of those words is 'melancholy', from the Greek for 'black bile', one of the four bodily fluids or 'humours' that, until the 17th century, were believed to rule personality. An excess of black bile in the spleen made a person prone to unhappiness – hence the modern sense of the word. The other three humours – blood, yellow bile or choler, and phlegm – were just as central to the belief, and have also left their mark on the language in describing different temperaments: 'sanguine' (optimistic, due to excess blood); 'choleric' (angry,

MELANCHOLIC SAINT
A pensive St Augustine, father of the early church, in one of four sculptures around the 1480 pulpit of St Stephen's Cathedral, Vienna. Each sculpture depicts a 'humour' – this is melancholy.

16TH-CENTURY WOODCUT SHOWING THE FOUR HUMOURS

INVENTOR OF THE COMPLEX Carl Jung, seen here at Lake Zurich, developed the practice of analytical psychology and explored how the mind worked through a number of abstract areas, including dreams, art, mythology and philosophy.

bumptious self-importance. The other two parts of Freud's 'psychic apparatus', the 'id' and the 'superego', have faded into the background.

Freud's concept of 'libido' was similarly misrepresented. To him it meant the energy of the mind, the drive that makes us want to create memories, write poems, climb mountains. It is also the engine of our sexual urges – and it is this sense that has completely eclipsed the others. Freud said that in children the libido focuses on different parts of the body as the body grows. Babies are orally fixated while they are being breastfed. When the time comes for them to be potty-trained, their libidal attention becomes transferred to the intriguing business of controlling the rectum and they become for a time anally fixated.

Finally, as a person grows to maturity, the libido homes in on the genitalia, which is where it ultimately belongs. But if something goes wrong for a child in the toilet-training phase, when the task is to learn when to let things go, that child may grow into an adult who is unable to 'let go' in any life situation. That person may become a hoarder, or be unwilling to delegate tasks to others, or grow obsessive about little details. In short, they may never grow out of the toddler's entirely normal anal fixation.

Describing behaviour

Among the other Freudian concepts that have become part of pop psychology is the idea of being 'in denial'. In Freud, the term denotes the desperate struggle of the ego to suppress the unpleasant memories and feelings that rise up from the unconscious during psychoanalysis; but in the language of teenagers today

due to too much yellow bile); and 'phlegmatic' (calm, due to an excess of phlegm).

It is instructive to follow the uneven traces left on our understanding by the medieval theory of humours, because the newer scientific psychology has come down to us in exactly the same partially absorbed, semi-digested way. Beginning at the turn of the 20th century, odds and ends of the new science of the mind percolated into the consciousness of the general public.

The first idea to do so was the biggest of all: that of the unconscious. Freud did not invent the word, but he popularised the notion that some of our mental processes are hidden from us. Today, no one is surprised if a friend starts to overeat in the wake of an unhappy romance, because we know that on a deep level food equates with love. The reason for this (said Freud) is that we all have a distant memory of the security and

love we felt at our mother's breast. Buried deep in the human unconscious is a strong association between feeding and affection, so when affection is withdrawn food can become a substitute for it.

The misrepresentation of Freud

Such ideas are commonplace now, but they were often shocking to Freud's Edwardian contemporaries because they implied that sexuality was rooted in childhood. As is often the case with new intellectual concepts, most people heard about Freud not from his own writing but from attacks on him published in more easily accessible media, such as newspapers. The apparently outrageous parts of his work were drawn to people's attention first, usually in a distorted form. This process of debasement goes some way to explaining how Freud's subtle and inventive concept of 'ego' (page 167) came to mean nothing more than it is often no more than a refusal to go along with the opinion of the rest of the gang. The term 'complex', taken to mean a tangled unconscious knot of psychological issues, belongs to Freud's friend and pupil Carl Jung. (The well-known 'inferiority complex' was named and investigated by his contemporary, the Austrian psychologist Alfred Adler.) It was also Jung who coined the terms 'introvert' and 'extrovert' for personalities whose personality looks inwards or outwards, respectively. The word 'egocentric', now a mere synonym for 'conceited', was first used in the pioneering work of child psychologist Jean Piaget, to describe a toddler's inability to understand that his or her own view of the world is not shared by everyone. For example, a child who announces to a stranger on the street that 'Ruby likes pink', without thinking to explain that Ruby is her sister, is being egocentric.

All of these ideas have found their way into the language because they fulfil a need – even if it is only to criticise someone else's behaviour in a novel and authoritative way. But certain scraps of psychological thinking have found a place in the language for a different reason: because they are such redolent turns of phrase that people cannot help playing with them and teasing new meanings from them.

One such is 'stream of consciousness', an expression invented by the American psychologist William James. What he meant by it was that the mind is never turned off, and so it makes more sense to think of it as a flowing, ever-changing river of thought than as a box of separate compartments where thoughts and memories are stored. This idea appealed to avant-garde artists – notably to the Irish writer James Joyce. His novel *Ulysses* purports to record all the currents of his character's mind, a literary technique that was much imitated and which is known as 'stream of consciousness' in homage to William James.

Another psychological term that sings with possibilities is 'the pleasure principle'. Coined by Freud, in his work it is paired with 'the death instinct',

> **Freud's 'pleasure principle' and 'death wish' have been adopted as the titles of books and films.**

often mistranslated or misquoted as 'the death wish', a far more evocative phrase. They are concerned with the psyche's longing to repeat happy experiences, along with its apparently contradictory urge to revisit unpleasant ones. These arresting phrases have been adopted as the titles of books and films – none of which has anything to do with Freud's psychology.

The Freudian slip

The best known and most fruitful psychological idea to find its way into common parlance is the one Freud termed *Fehlleistung* – 'faulty action'. The world knows it better as the 'Freudian slip', the tendency to make unconscious errors in speech or action that betray one's inner state: the reluctant jogger who comes home and absent-mindedly throws his shorts in the toilet instead of the laundry basket; the would-be Lothario who says he is hoping for a win on the 'premium blondes'.

Like most of Freud's thought, the Freudian slip is viewed with scepticism by present-day psychologists, who question whether such a phenomenon exists. Freud, with Jung and most pioneers of modern psychology, are in the position of early explorers who, through trial and error, discovered hidden shores that are now accessible to the most casual visitor. But if their thinking has been revised or superseded, that does not lessen their achievement. Their groundwork established the core truth of psychology: that the mind, like the heart, has reasons that reason does not know.

THE POWER OF DREAMS Part of a dream sequence designed by Salvador Dalí for Alfred Hitchcock's 1945 film, *Spellbound*, set in a mental asylum. The film's producer, David O. Selznick, had gone into analysis two years earlier and brought his own experience to bear on the film. He even invited his psychotherapist, May Romm, along to the set to act as an adviser.

Freud was not the first to study the human mind, so why is he now considered the father of psychoanalysis?

Sigmund Freud's great achievement – the accomplishment that earned him his place in history – was to bequeath to humanity its first useable map of the unconscious mind.

He proposed that the mind consisted of three parts: 'id', 'ego' and 'superego'. The id is the animal drive inborn in us all, the babyish desire to have our appetites satisfied above all. The ego is the part of the mind that grows to understand the world and interact with it, and which knowingly seeks out ways of getting the id what it wants. The superego equates to the conscience: it is the sophisticated knowledge that satisfying the id can sometimes bring consequences that are worse than leaving it unsatisfied – in other words, it is the adult

realisation that you can't always have what you want.

Freud spent many years investigating different routes to the unconscious, ways of delving below the surface of conscious thought and uncovering the hidden mechanisms of the mind. Among his experimental methods were hypnosis and 'free association' – prompting patients to respond to single words with the first word that came into their head. But his greatest methodological success was the interpretation of dreams. He saw that a person's dreams are replete with symbolic significance, that their narratives, props and characters are the means by which the unconscious mind sends coded messages and warnings to the waking, conscious

self. In his landmark work, *The Interpretation of Dreams* (1900), Freud wrote that this was 'the royal road to the unconscious'. Psychologists and psychoanalysts have been traversing that road, and its many twisted byways, ever since.

ON THE COUCH The image of the couch has become indelibly associated with psycholanalysis in popular culture, as in the 1985 *Punch* cartoon (top right).

ON THE COUCH Sigmund Freud poses next to his couch c.1932. Although inviting patients to lie on a couch was considered very daring at the time, Freud believed that lying down helped to free them from conventional patterns of thought.

Once upon a time ...
Tens of thousands of novels are published worldwide every year. But why do we like reading about events that never happened?

Anyone who reads a Harry Potter book knows that the events described within the book never happened and could not possibly have happened. Yet in the process of reading, silently and systematically scanning the black marks on white pages, Harry and his friends become so alive that the reader grows fearful for their safety and desperately wants to know what becomes of them. The fact that the narrative is an elaborate falsehood does not in any way diminish the emotional power of the reading experience.

Tales of the gods
Storytelling is almost as old as language itself. Some of the oldest stories – the mythologies of various times and places – have survived to this day and still have the capacity to captivate and move us. Every civilisation has had its myths. These shared tales, known to the whole community, served the same purpose everywhere: to bind the members of the group together in a common vision of the world. All mythologies tend to deal with the same themes – the origin of the universe, mankind and the natural world, and the special place of one's own culture within the grand scheme of things. The Greeks' tales of Zeus and his dysfunctional coterie of gods perform this function, as do Aboriginal

IMAGINARY HEROES Dressed like characters from the books, fans of the Harry Potter series wait for the release of the final novel.

fables of 'Dreamtime', and the Hebrew stories – Adam and Eve and the Garden of Eden – that we find in the first chapters of the Old Testament.

Today, we recognise that the world's mythologies are collections of made-up stories. The reality of religious experience for many is no longer based on acceptance of the literal truth of humankind's earliest attempts

CAPTIVE AUDIENCE Rudyard Kipling reads his *Just So Stories* to a group of children in 1902. A reviewer wrote: 'It strikes a child as the kind of yarn his father or uncle might have spun if he had just happened to think of it; and it has, like all good fairy-business, a sound core of philosophy.'

to make sense of their world. But in the minds of the ancient peoples who created and recounted myths, the distinction between spiritual truth and fact was much more blurred. The people who first heard and told the biblical tale of David and Goliath would have seen it as true because it contained a universally held belief of their people – that with God's help, the weak can overcome the strong. No Israelite is likely to have said of the Bible account, as a modern person might: 'Well, I like the story, but I'm not sure it really happened that way and I don't believe that Goliath could possibly have been three metres tall.'

The founding stories of western literature, works such as Homer's *Iliad*, work in the same way. Modern archaeology has proved that Homer's account of the war between the Greeks and the Trojans contains entirely accurate details of armour and weaponry, though the text was not written down until hundreds of years after the events that inspired it. To a modern mind this is deeply impressive – it means that we can say Homer's account is true in a historical sense. It would be all too easy to dismiss the parts of the account that deal with rivalries between the gods of Olympus as a picturesque legend. But these are the very parts of the story that represent universal themes, such as destiny, love, loss and power. The insights that Homer has on these eternal subjects would be true even if there were not one historical fact in the tale.

The essential difference between the *Iliad* and the stories of the Old Testament, what makes Homer's tale a milestone on the road to modern

HIGH SEAS ADVENTURE A 17th-century French painting of a scene from the *Iliad*: Odysseus returning the maiden Chryseis, who had been stolen by Agamemnon, to her father.

fiction, is that the *Iliad* is intended as a popular entertainment. It is more about men and women like us than it is about God or the gods. The same can be said of the hero-stories of other lands and later ages. Among the national epics that echo the Homeric sagas are the *Mahabharata* in India, *Beowulf* in England, the *Nibelungenlied* in Germany, the *Chanson de Roland* in France and the *Poema de Mío Cid* in Spain. All of these epics grew out of an oral tradition, which is why they were all originally composed in an easily remembered rhyming form. Most of the European epics were committed to the page in the 11th and 12th centuries, but well into the Middle Ages, storytelling continued to involve a performance and an audience. It was necessarily a communal activity that took place round a fire, on a village green or sometimes more formally in a theatre,

> The first stories to be published as books were not fiction as we understand it today

for the benefit of people who could not read books.

The first stories to appear in book form were manuscripts, each one painstakingly transcribed by hand. The invention of printing and the subsequent rise of literacy transformed the business of storytelling and brought books to the masses. The reader – not the narrator – was now in control: you can't easily stop a bard or a troupe of actors in full flow, but it is easy to put down a book.

The popular romance
The first popular stories to be published as books were not fiction in the form we understand it today. Many of them were verse tales of love and chivalry – 'romances' as they were called at the time. In English, these include the many versions of the King Arthur story (Malory's *Le Morte d'Arthur*, published in 1485, is the outstanding example). But over time, the poetic rhyming form was dropped in favour of prose. Now that there was no need

to help a bard remember thousands of lines of narrative, there was no need to force the story into the straitjacket of a rhyme scheme. The rise of prose was a definitive break with the oral tradition, and an important move towards a form of story that is best contained in the covers of a book.

The first novel

The first fiction of any psychological depth is the *Satyricon*, a comic, picaresque novel that follows the escapades of a trio of disreputable heroes, which was written in the 1st century AD in lively, colloquial Latin and attributed to the Roman author Petronius Arbiter. This book, along with *The Golden Ass* written by Lucius Apuleius in the 2nd century AD, paved the way for what we know as the modern novel.

In 1605, the Spanish author Miguel de Cervantes published the first volume of a two-part book called *Don Quixote* – a work that has since been identified as the first novel in western literature. Its opening sentence – the very first words in the canon of

modern fiction – reads as follows: 'In a place at La Mancha, the name of which I have no desire to recollect, not very long ago, lived a noble – one of those nobles who keep a lance in the lance-rack, an ancient shield, a skinny old horse, and a fast greyhound.' The Don Quixote of the title is, in other words, a clapped-out version of the very heroes traditionally found in the romances. Cervantes is satirising those now tired old tales. and at the same time demonstrating a new way of telling a story – one that deals in real people who inhabit the

ANCIENT KNIGHT Statues of Don Quixote and his servant, Sancho Panza, in Madrid. The story of their adventures is the most frequently translated text after the Bible.

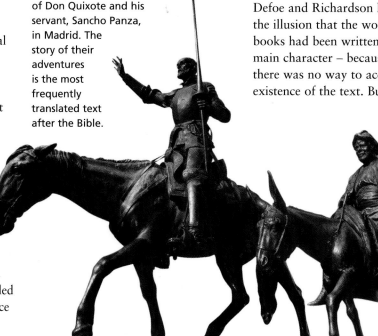

present age and who live lives not unlike those of the intended reader. From now on (Cervantes is saying), stories can be about the here and now, and they can be realistic.

Fact and fancy

Cervantes' book was translated and plagiarised throughout Europe. But almost a century passed before his pioneering realism was carried forward, and this happened in England. Many of the earliest English novels were disguised as factual accounts, because the reading public was not yet ready for the idea that a narrative might be nothing more than the writer's fancy.

Robinson Crusoe is often said to be the first true novel in English. But when it was published in 1719, it pretended to be a factual memoir written by Crusoe himself. The author, Daniel Defoe, let the public believe that he had merely edited a manuscript that had fallen into his hands by chance. Samuel Richardson's *Pamela*, published in 1740 and a rival candidate for the title of 'first English novel', takes the form of a series of letters and diary entries written by the young servant girl of the title. Both Defoe and Richardson had to create the illusion that the words in the books had been written down by the main character – because otherwise there was no way to account for the existence of the text. But writers and

AN AUTHOR AND HIS CHARACTERS
An etching of Charles Dickens
(1812-70) surrounded by some of
his colourful creations including
Oliver Twist (centre left) and the
Cheeryble brothers from *Nicholas
Nickleby* (bottom centre).

readers soon grasped the limitations
of this clumsily realistic approach.
A novel based on memoirs or letters
can only ever give one point of view,
and can only recount incidents that
the main protagonist witnessed. To
tell more ambitious tales, authors
needed to be able to step outside the
narrative, to read the thoughts of all
the characters, to have a panoramic
overview of events both big and
small, to zip backwards and forwards
through time at will. The author
needed to be omniscient.

Meanwhile, the god-like liberties
taken by authors required a
corresponding shift in attitude on
behalf of the reader, who now had to
be willing to 'suspend his disbelief'
(a phrase invented much later by the
poet Samuel Taylor Coleridge).

Understanding the language

Readers learned the new conventions
very quickly. In Henry Fielding's *Tom
Jones*, published in 1749, the author is
already omniscient: Fielding knows
everything about the circumstances of
his bawdy hero's life. But he still needs
to apologise for it and intrudes in the
narrative to explain what is happening
next, and what period of time is going
to be covered. It is as if the writer
feels he has to hold the reader's hand
because readers are not yet used to
this kind of narrative. It took a while
longer for the omniscience of the
author to be taken entirely for
granted. At the beginning of the 19th
century, Jane Austen still occasionally
pokes her head round the curtain and
addresses her 'dear reader' directly.

By the middle of the 19th century,
outstanding writers, such as Charles
Dickens in Britain, Honoré de Balzac
and Gustave Flaubert in France and
Leo Tolstoy in Russia, had made the
novel into the magnificent, infinitely
versatile storytelling instrument that
we all now recognise and understand.
In their novels – as in most subsequent
works of fiction – the narrator does
not feel the need to announce his
presence and the reader is usually
happy to take for granted that the
story is made up. Readers, then as
now, knew that they were being
artfully lied to, and were prepared to
accept this falsehood for two reasons
that are as old as storytelling itself.

The first reason is that good stories
(like good music, food or art) are an
enjoyable temporary escape from the
mundane and the familiar – and for
most readers that is, in itself, a
sufficient return on the investment of
effort. The second is that truly great
fiction – whether it be a novel or a
film or any other narrative genre –
says something profound and
worthwhile about the world and the
people in it – something more than
is implied by the actions of the
imaginary puppets on the page. Ernest
Hemingway, a master storyteller,
summed up the purpose and the point
of fiction when he said: 'All good
books are alike in that they are truer
than if they had really happened.'

DISCOVERY AND CHANGE

5

Under the skin Human beings are genetically almost identical yet superficially diverse. How did this variety come about?

The streets of any great world city now throng with an extraordinary diversity of ethnic types. Yet research suggests that every one of them – indeed, everybody on the planet – has inherited a small piece of genetic material (mitochondrial DNA), from one woman who lived over 190,000 years ago in Africa. So how did our phenomenal physical variety come about?

DNA is the main molecule in the nucleus of every living cell, and determines all our inherited physical characteristics. Mitochondrial DNA (mtDNA) is a tiny circular string of genetic material, similar to nuclear DNA, but found only in mitochondria, outside the nucleus of cells. We inherit exact copies of mtDNA only from our mothers and it is not contaminated by or mixed up with male genes in any generation. That is why it can be used to trace right back to our earliest female ancestor.

About once in every 200 generations a small mutation occurs in mtDNA. Each mutation is inherited by subsequent offspring and forms a new branch on the mtDNA tree. This maternal tree of descent has been accurately reconstructed back to its root about 200,000 years ago, by comparing variation in mutations in mtDNA backwards from many living people around the world.

The mtDNA tree can be laid out on a map of the world, rather like spreading ivy on a wall, with different branches extending into particular continental regions. This makes it possible to plot ancient migrations using the spread of branches from the root of the gene-tree in Africa. Because the rate at which the mutations occur can be measured, it can be estimated when each of them took place. The timings and locations of the mutations show when and where the earliest migrations happened and how the world was populated.

The genetic tree of our maternal ancestors stretches back nearly 200,000 years to a type of mtDNA found only in Africa, the 'mitochondrial Eve'. This term has given rise to the concept of an African Eve, or 'first mother' of modern humanity. The term is misleading in that it suggests that all of our DNA derives from one

> **The mtDNA tree can be laid out on a map of the world, like spreading ivy on a wall**

single African woman and her partner. This is not true. The woman carrying our root mtDNA type would have lived in a human group numbering thousands, arising from earlier humans. But while mtDNA from contemporary females has not survived, other parts of the human genome almost certainly do come from members of that early population. Also, the mtDNA evidence does not necessarily suggest that she represented a new species, rather a particularly successful local 'race' of humans, which went on to replace all the others in the world.

Where in Africa did she live? The mtDNA evidence suggests that it was in East Africa. This ties in with the fossil evidence: the earliest skulls with characteristic features of *Homo sapiens sapiens*, or 'Anatomically Modern Humans', are found in the southern end of the Great Rift Valley in East Africa.

Migration 'Out of Africa'

East Africa does, then, seem to have been the cradle of humanity. But when did we leave sub-Saharan Africa; from where, and how many exits were there? Were Europeans a separate branch? The most current widely accepted theory was suggested by Oxford-based researcher Stephen Oppenheimer in his book, *Out of Eden*, in 2003. Its reconstruction suggests that, following an abortive migration to the Eastern Mediterranean and Middle East 125,000 years ago, only one group of humans emigrated successfully from Africa. They then gave rise to all modern non-Africans. He believes that this group left Africa in a single, southern exit, across the mouth of the Red Sea to the Yemen around 85,000 years ago. From there they travelled

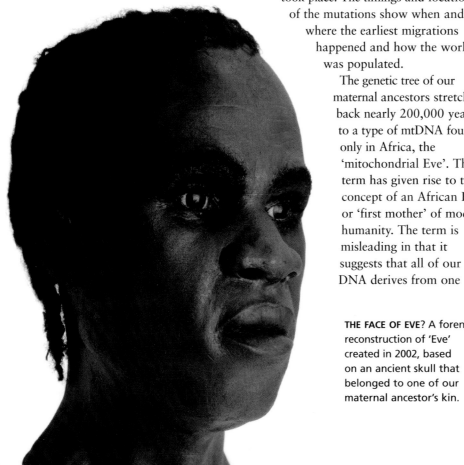

THE FACE OF EVE? A forensic reconstruction of 'Eve' created in 2002, based on an ancient skull that belonged to one of our maternal ancestor's kin.

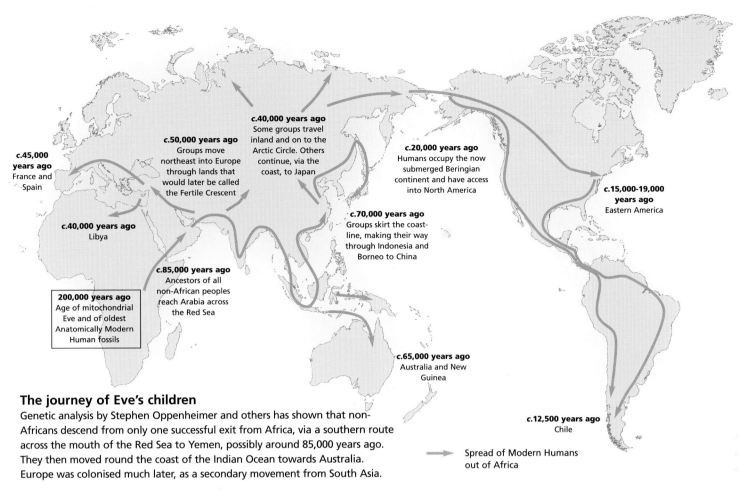

c.45,000 years ago
France and Spain

c.50,000 years ago
Groups move northeast into Europe through lands that would later be called the Fertile Crescent

c.40,000 years ago
Some groups travel inland and on to the Arctic Circle. Others continue, via the coast, to Japan

c.20,000 years ago
Humans occupy the now submerged Beringian continent and have access into North America

c.15,000-19,000 years ago
Eastern America

c.40,000 years ago
Libya

c.85,000 years ago
Ancestors of all non-African peoples reach Arabia across the Red Sea

200,000 years ago
Age of mitochondrial Eve and of oldest Anatomically Modern Human fossils

c.70,000 years ago
Groups skirt the coast-line, making their way through Indonesia and Borneo to China

c.65,000 years ago
Australia and New Guinea

c.12,500 years ago
Chile

→ Spread of Modern Humans out of Africa

The journey of Eve's children

Genetic analysis by Stephen Oppenheimer and others has shown that non-Africans descend from only one successful exit from Africa, via a southern route across the mouth of the Red Sea to Yemen, possibly around 85,000 years ago. They then moved round the coast of the Indian Ocean towards Australia. Europe was colonised much later, as a secondary movement from South Asia.

to South Asia, and round the Indian Ocean coastline by land bridges to Bali and ultimately overseas to Australia by 65,000 years ago. Humans may have spread to East Asia around 75,000 years ago, later entering the Americas across the Bering Strait, which formed a huge continent around 20,000 years ago. Europe was not colonised directly through North Africa but around 50,000 years ago, as an offshoot of the Asian trail from the Gulf through Iran and Iraq.

Genetic evidence

The genetic evidence for the recent 'Out of Africa' movement suggests that wherever the emigrants travelled, they replaced pre-existing human species, such as Neanderthals and *Homo erectus*. It is clear from the genetic trails across Eurasia that when the explorers colonised a new region or sub-continent, they tended to stay put, and their descendants still live in those places.

The question remains as to whether there was interbreeding between modern humans and the Neanderthals

and *Homo erectus* they encountered. The mtDNA and male Y chromosome evidence shows no interbreeding, but these are small parts of the human genome and cannot, on their own, provide the final answer.

Modern humanity's diversity blossomed as regional populations were separated from each other geographically, but the degree of differentiation is overstated by references to 'racial groups'. A typical scheme classifies modern humans into five major races – Caucasoid, Mongoloid, Negroid, Khoisanoid (referring to African bushmen) and Australoid. Biologically, race means an inbreeding group with a set

ONE ADAPTING SPECIES Humans' physical appearance is shaped by the environment and coded in just a few genes. This means changes can occur rapidly – today's racial differences may date back just 20,000 years.

of physical and genetic features that differentiate it from other groups. It is now clear that there is insufficient anatomic or genetic variation between regional groups of humans to warrant the label 'races' in the same way in which the word applies to other species of mammals.

Humans' recent dispersal throughout the world means there is actually

more variation within groups than between them. So, how is it that we can often identify peoples' regional origins so easily? The most important reason is our powerful ability to recognise faces and subtle variations between them, while the second reason is that there are significant regional variations between populations, which result, not from isolation of groups, but from regional adaptation to sun and climate.

The colour of our skin

The most immediately obvious of these adaptations is loss of skin colour, which is not unique to any population, but varies with latitude. The darkest skins are found in areas closest to the Equator (such as Ugandans in Equatorial Africa and Tamils in South India) and the palest nearer the poles (such as Scandinavians in the north and San Bushmen in South Africa). These characteristics evolved in relation to the strength of sunlight. Melanin – the pigment in skin – is a natural sunscreen and its presence in dark skin serves as protection from UV light, which causes burns and skin cancer.

If protection against UV light were the only factor selecting for darker skin colour we would all have black

ADAPTED FOR THE TROPICS A Dinka man of southern Sudan surveys his cattle close to the River Nile. Dinka physique is ideally suited to hot, dry environments.

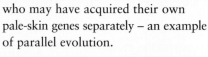

NORTHERN EXPOSURE The Mongoloid 'epicanthic' eye fold may be a protection against freezing wind. People of the extreme north have more sweat glands on their faces than their bodies – an evolutionary response to being permanently clothed.

skin, but we do not. There are evolutionary disadvantages to having dark skin in low sunlight. Sunlight activates the synthesis of vitamin D in the skin, preventing vitamin D deficiency and rickets. The latter is a bone disease, which may be lethal in infancy and is commoner in migrants to Europe with dark skin colour than in pale-skinned locals.

Genetic adaptation to low sunlight would explain why people in high latitudes are naturally paler and find it harder to tan in the sun. At least a dozen simple mutations have been found that are associated with paler skin. These interfere with normal melanin production in Europeans and are most common in Scandinavia. Research has shown that these bleaching mutations have been recently selected for in Europe, but are rare in other

pale-skinned groups like the Chinese, who may have acquired their own pale-skin genes separately – an example of parallel evolution.

Human traits

Other human traits are also related to climate. It has been suggested that Mongoloid eyes are of benefit in cold countries; those of the hunters of the Arctic are specially adapted to the freezing wind conditions, having an extra ('epicanthic') protective fold of skin over the upper lid. The compact shape of their bodies also conserves heat.

In contrast, the tall, slim build of Sudan's Dinka tribesmen and the Masai of Kenya and Tanzania is believed to be an adaptation that prevents overheating: the high ratio of surface area to volume allows them to radiate a lot of warmth. The diminutive stature of the Pygmies is argued to be an adaptation to forest dwelling.

A population's gene pool is influenced by natural selection, which can take many forms. Sexual attraction is one, and involves an element of choice, whereby members of a given population prefer to mate with individuals who possess desirable characteristics, which then become more prevalent. So, if a rarity such as blue eyes becomes a standard of beauty in a given population, more blue-eyed babies may be born.

A larger proportion of genetic variability stems from chance events, such as flood, famine and disease, may, for example, devastate a population. If a large percentage is killed off, the survivors will have a different gene pool from the original population. Similarly, if a group divides and one group moves away, the two populations will differ as genetic differences accumulate over successive generations.

Has human evolution come to a stop, or are we still evolving?

Modern humans first appeared about 200,000 years ago. They had brains that had undergone their greatest evolution in size between one and two million years earlier. But are we still evolving? Or do we have much the same intellects, personalities and motivations as our human ancestors in Africa?

Natural selection is an ongoing process, and this is most evident in the fight against disease. There is good evidence that regional evolution has affected resistance to malaria among all populations where malaria is transmitted, particularly in tropical and sub-tropical regions. In the last 10,000 years the move towards sedentary living and more crowded settlements, together with rising temperatures and humidity, favoured malaria-carrying mosquitoes. Much of the human population died of infection; others were saved by genetic mutations that gave resistance to malaria. Those with the mutations survived and passed on their genes to their offspring. So while humans may have spread globally, there has also been local evolution.

Climate is an important factor in human evolution. For example, European immigrants to Australia with pale skins are particularly at risk from skin cancer. It is now the commonest cancer among Australians, and will be a powerful evolutionary force in the future in selecting for genes which allow more effective melanin production. Over many generations this will result in Australians of European extraction becoming progressively darker skinned.

Change in human behaviour leads to physical and mental adaptation – not the reverse. (Far from increasing in size, our brains have actually shrunk over the past 150,000 years.) Reaction to the stresses of survival in an ever-changing climate has been the great drive in our mental development, leading to innovative ways of thinking and living: boat-building in times of flood, or new ways of hunting and finding water in times of drought. These cultural innovations are cumulative; they have been accelerating sharply in the past few thousand years, and are still accelerating. They culminated in the development of music and writing c.5,000 years ago – but in terms of evolution these milestones are purely cultural. Single new mutations could not be responsible for such recent cultural achievements as musical notation, writing and computer programming, unless they were confined to the region in which they were invented.

Why have different languages evolved?
So much human communication is universal – the wave of the hand, the raised eyebrow greeting – so why don't all humans speak the same mutual tongue?

It is a question that has bemused people throughout history and numerous myths evolved in explanation. One of the most famous is the story of the Tower of Babel, told in the first book of the Bible. The descendants of Noah had just one language – a result of the Great Flood, which wiped out the rest of humanity. They decided to build a huge tower, tall enough to reach heaven. God recognised the dangers in this human talent for cooperation mixed with overweening ambition and promptly put a stop to it, confounding the builders by endowing them with a multiplicity of languages and scattering them all over the Earth.

The essence of this myth is remarkably similar to modern ideas about the original spread of languages. The widely accepted theory is that humans evolved in Africa, and spread from there to the rest of the world (page 174). There were probably two phases of migration. The first took place 1.7 million years ago and involved *Homo erectus*, tool-making ancestors of modern humans. Around 200,000 years ago, *Homo sapiens sapiens* evolved – again in Africa – and, 100,000 years later, moved into the wider world. By the end of the last Ice Age, about 12,000 years ago, they had spread southwards through the Americas. It is quite possible that these early migrants from Africa – like the descendants of Noah from the Old Testament story – spoke one language as they set out, but evolved their own languages as they settled around the world.

Such conclusions are based on the theory that languages have an ancestry that resembles a family tree. The 6,000 or so languages of today have been divided into about a dozen major families that each share similarities in structure, grammar and vocabulary. It is easy enough to trace how such families have evolved in recent history. The best examples are Romance languages, derived from the Latin of

SIGN LANGUAGE Buffalo Bill Cody and an American Indian chief communicate with signs and gestures at Buffalo Bill's Wild West Circus encampment in the early 1900s.

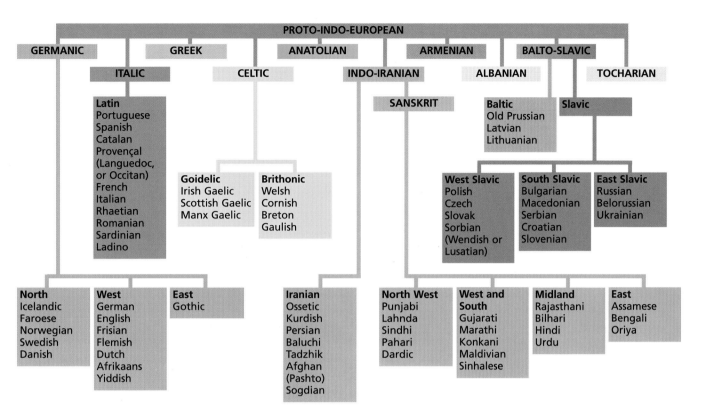

PROTO-INDO-EUROPEAN						

GERMANIC — **GREEK** — **ANATOLIAN** — **ARMENIAN** — **BALTO-SLAVIC**

ITALIC — **CELTIC** — **INDO-IRANIAN** — **ALBANIAN** — **TOCHARIAN**

SANSKRIT — **Baltic** / **Slavic**

Latin
Portuguese
Spanish
Catalan
Provençal
(Languedoc,
or Occitan)
French
Italian
Rhaetian
Romanian
Sardinian
Ladino

Goidelic
Irish Gaelic
Scottish Gaelic
Manx Gaelic

Brithonic
Welsh
Cornish
Breton
Gaulish

Baltic
Old Prussian
Latvian
Lithuanian

West Slavic
Polish
Czech
Slovak
Sorbian
(Wendish or
Lusatian)

South Slavic
Bulgarian
Macedonian
Serbian
Croatian
Slovenian

East Slavic
Russian
Belorussian
Ukrainian

North
Icelandic
Faroese
Norwegian
Swedish
Danish

West
German
English
Frisian
Flemish
Dutch
Afrikaans
Yiddish

East
Gothic

Iranian
Ossetic
Kurdish
Persian
Baluchi
Tadzhik
Afghan
(Pashto)
Sogdian

North West
Punjabi
Lahnda
Sindhi
Pahari
Dardic

**West and
South**
Gujarati
Marathi
Konkani
Maldivian
Sinhalese

Midland
Rajasthani
Bilhari
Hindi
Urdu

East
Assamese
Bengali
Oriya

MOTHER TONGUE Most modern European tongues, and many of those of southwest Asia and India, can be traced back at least 6,000 years to a language known as Proto-Indo-European. Many linguists now believe it was the tongue of farming people who settled in northeastern Europe.

the Roman Empire: they include Italian, French, Spanish, Portuguese, Catalan and Romanian.

The Romance languages belong to the biggest family of languages, known as Indo-European. This incorporates the Germanic languages, including German, English, Dutch and Danish; it also takes in Indo-Aryan languages, such as Sanskrit, Hindi, Bengali and Punjabi. Linguists can show common features in the structures of these languages that point to a common origin.

Like a family tree, tracing languages back in time leads to an ever-diminishing number of ancestors. Taken to its logical conclusion there would be just one original language – the 'proto-language' – at the earliest point that humans started talking. But hard evidence of the early history of language begins only with the development of writing around 3500 BC.

Linguists, by analysing the structures of early written language, can be fairly confident of their history to about 10,000 or 15,000 years ago but, beyond that, the picture is murky.

It is not even clear exactly when humans started speaking, though it occurred sometime after early humans split off from an ape-like ancestor, shared with chimpanzees, seven million years ago. One of the branches of the human family, *Homo erectus*, was fairly sophisticated socially and technologically – they were the first hunter-gatherers and tool-makers – so it is highly likely they would have

CREATION MYTH The Tower of Babel by Pieter Brueghel, 1563, illustrating the story from Genesis. According to the Bible, the great city of Babel, or 'God's gate', was never built. Other cultures, such as the Greeks, the Bantu in Africa and the Aztecs, had their own language creation myths.

communicated in some way, probably with a combination of sounds and gestures, in order to coordinate their activity as a group. But it is unlikely they spoke to each other as we would understand the term today.

The capacity for speech requires certain anatomical features – most significantly, an L-shaped vocal tract, a larynx positioned relatively low in

Why are there 26 letters in the English alphabet?

The alphabet we use today is a 'phonographic' system in which the symbols stand for the speech sounds that make up a word. But the earliest forms of writing were 'logographic', with each symbol standing for an entire word. They were made up of 'pictograms' (symbols, which physically resemble what they signify – such as a picture of the Moon for 'Moon') and 'ideograms' (graphic symbols, which represent ideas – today's '£' for 'pound'). The earliest recorded language system is the simple cuneiform used by traders in Mesopotamia in the 9th century BC. This developed into the more sophisticated Sumerian cuneiform from the middle of the 4th century BC. At around the same time the hieroglyphic system, which contained over 700 different symbols, appeared in ancient Egypt. Today, Chinese is the nearest we have to a logographic language system – it has approximately 50,000 characters, of which 4,000 are in regular use.

In contrast, the human voice uses only a limited number of distinct sounds in speech. The International Phonetic Alphabet identifies more than 100 of these, but most languages manage with fewer than 35. In around 1900 BC, scribes in the Middle East began to use writing that imitated speech, with a symbol for each sound. The Semitic people of Upper Egypt produced an alphabet of 22 consonants – all that was needed to represent their entire language. The symbols were formed of pictures of words with that sound:

SUMERIAN CUNEIFORM CLAY TABLET, C.2250 BC, RECORDING THE GIFT OF A SLAVE AND A HOUSE

'Aleph, meaning ox, became A, and was represented by a picture of an ox's head; Beth (B), a house, and so on.

The language was adopted by the Phoenicians, and was in turn taken up by the ancient Greeks. The Greeks recognised the alphabet's efficiency, adopting 19 Phoenician letters and adding five vowel sounds. They called their first letter alpha and their second letter beta – the origin of the term 'alphabet'. Through trade and settlement, they spread their alphabet around the Mediterranean. Later the Romans adopted the Greek alphabet and in turn spread it across Europe.

The Roman alphabet had 23 letters; it did not distinguish between I and J, used V for U, and lacked a W. They wrote in capitals until the introduction of lower case letters from around the

3rd century AD. Even after the fall of the Roman Empire in the 5th century, Latin was the lingua franca of Europe for a thousand years, largely because it was the language of the Church, which dominated education and writing.

In northern Europe, Medieval scribes enlarged the alphabet to take account of the different sounds of their own languages. They made I and U into vowels, and J and V into consonants. In English, the W sound was originally represented by the Anglo-Saxon wynn, with its P-shaped symbol, but during the Renaissance this was replaced by W.

In this way we ended up with the 26 letters of the alphabet we use today, which, with the help of accents in some cases, covered the sounds that most European languages speakers needed.

THE EVOLUTION OF 'A'
The letter 'A' owes its form to the proto-Sinaitic alphabet, used around 1900 BC in Upper Egypt. Inspired by Egyptian hieroglyphs, the proto-Sinaitic letter name was 'Aleph, meaning ox.

PROTO-SINAITIC   PHOENICIAN   EARLY GREEK   ETRUSCAN   ROMAN

THE LANGUAGE OF GOD Frederick II (1194-1250), German King and Holy Roman Emperor, performed an experiment on a group of babies, instructing them to be raised in silence to see what 'natural' language they might grow up to speak. Without a means of self-expression, the children failed to thrive and, according to the Medieval chronicler Salimbene di Adam, they all died in infancy.

the neck, and plenty of nerve links between the tongue and the brain. Drawing on fossil records of archaic human remains, some linguists believe that our ancestors only evolved these features as *Homo sapiens sapiens*, and that the earliest speech was therefore around 200,000 years ago. Before then, they argue, early humans were simply anatomically incapable of producing recognisable speech, only a range of vocal sounds.

Gift of the gab

There is a mystery, too, about how and why humans learned to speak at all. What took them from ape-like grunting to the plays of Sophocles and the speeches of Martin Luther King? Humans are the only animals that possess anything like this kind of sophistication in language. With its potential for communication and the conveying of accumulated knowledge, language was a key feature in the package of evolutionary advantages that gave the human race its dominance and its ability to develop the urban-based, technological civilisation that we know today.

Humans have a unique ability to think in abstract terms. This was useful for early humans: they could knap a piece of flint to make a spearhead, fix it into the split end of a wooden shaft and bind it on with strips of hide while picturing the food they were going to obtain with it. Language equally depends on abstract thought or the expression of imagination, seen in a statement like 'We will eat bison

tomorrow.' Studies of the human brain suggest that connections between the various lobes relating to sight, touch and sound – and their links to the part of the brain that operates the complex muscles needed to voice speech – may have directly influenced the original formation of words. So the human brain, on seeing or thinking about something, may be predisposed to express it vocally in a way that seems to correspond. The neuroscientist Vilayanur S. Ramachandran has pointed out that words for 'small' frequently lend themselves to being pronounced in a pinched, high-pitched way: little, tiny, minuscule, *petit* (French), *piccolo* (Italian), *winzig* (German). Whereas words for 'big' require a more booming and expansive vocal performance: huge, enormous, *grand* (French), *grosso* (Italian), *ungeheuer* (German).

How language is learned

There is no direct correlation between what we see and how we speak about it; if there were, we would all speak the same language. To judge from the way children learn language and the structure of simplified languages like pidgin that have evolved so people from

different language-groups can trade, early language began with a basic structure of subject-verb-object ('We kill bison') and developed from there.

Recently a gene, FOXP2, has been discovered that, according to some scientists, is intimately connected to language and speech. Human infants seem to be born with an innate ability to learn language very fast. They pick up vocabulary and string the words together into grammatical sentences with an instinctive sense of how the system works.

This natural ability to create an infinite number of sentences from a finite number of words is common to all languages, an observation that led the American linguist Noam Chomsky to conclude, in the 1960s, that languages work on two levels. The sentences uttered, in whatever

STANDING ORATION The Orator, c.90 BC, an honorific statue of Aulus Metellus, master of the Etruscan language and Roman official. Language – most especially public speaking – was an art in ancient Rome and political careers were made or broken according to the orators' skill and power over a public audience.

language, are the 'surface structure', but beneath this lies a 'deep structure' hardwired into the brain – a kind of universal grammar that is common to all languages. But despite this 'hardwiring', languages still have to be learned.

If humans started with one, universal proto-language, it did not last. From that original source, languages split and evolved into thousands of different strands. No language remains static and there are no universal words common to all languages. Two almost qualify: mama and papa (or similar sounding words) are widely found – but this may simply be because these are two of the most common sounds a baby begins to play with; then the mother sees a reference to herself and encourages the baby to make the connection. In some languages 'mama' is taken to mean 'food', although, in some roundabout way, this might also be linked to the mother's role as a provider of milk.

From one, many

Language families may have some words in common, but generally the tendency is for individual languages to follow their own unique path. Papua New Guinea has some 830 different languages – the largest number of any country of the world, relative to its size and population (6 million). The

reason for this diversity is the social isolation, over a long time, of numerous groups in the remote, forested mountain valleys. It also gives us a clue as to how so many languages came to be created throughout the world. Over many thousands of years, starting with the migrations out of Africa, small groups and clans of hunter-gatherers stuck together, inhabiting a distinct geographical region and evolving their own languages.

It is likely that the total number of languages in the world peaked during the first millennium AD. But we will never know the total number, because languages that are not written down leave no trace. A reverse process set in with the growth of empires. Over

UNIVERSAL LANGUAGE The virtues of Esperanto depicted on a Hungarian postcard of 1918. Its creator, Ludwik Zamenhof, hoped to unite the world with an international tongue.

several generations, minority languages tended to die out or became assimilated as empires spread – not so much through conquest, but because adopting the dominant language was a route to social advancement. This was the case with Latin in the Roman Empire, and Arabic with the spread of Islam. When European countries fanned out to colonise much of the world after the 15th century they took their languages with them, often smothering native languages.

And one for all

The complications caused by the multiplicity of languages inspired Ludwik Zamenhof, a multi-lingual Polish doctor, to invent Esperanto ('one who hopes'), a simplified amalgam of various European languages, designed to serve as a

The language of our ancestors

A handful of words have come down to us directly from Proto-Indo-European and so can be termed among the oldest living words in the world. They include some of the most primal utterances – 'mother', 'father', 'night', 'Sun' and 'Moon'. 'Mother', for example, is *mutter* in German, *mater* in Latin, *meter* in Greek, *mat'* in Russian and *matar* in Sanskrit. Night is *nacht, noctis, nuktos, noch'* and *náktam* in the same sequence of languages.

Many words for nature, and some plant and animal names, can be traced back to their root language – snow, for example, comes from *sneigwh-*, a word that has also given us *neige* in French, *nieve* in Spanish, *snö* in Swedish, *sne* in Danish and Norwegian, *snjór* in Icelandic and *schnee* in German.

More unexpectedly, earthier words such as 'ale', *alut-*, and 'fart', *perd*, also share the ancient Proto-Indo-European source.

common international language. But it never caught on, partly because no one spoke Esperanto as a mother tongue. Besides, people become attached to their own language: it is part of their identity and culture. Indeed, language can be said to frame the way we think: we form and organise our thoughts according to the words and grammatical structures we have available. The ambitions of Esperanto to create a universal language may, in any case, be achieved naturally. Of the 6,000 or so languages that exist today, only 200 have more than one million speakers. Many languages have very few speakers and are on the verge of extinction. In 2008 it was reported that only eight people now speak the Central American language of Ixcatec, and the United Nations has calculated that the world loses 26 languages every year. Mass-communications, radio, television and the internet all have the effect of bolstering dominant languages at the expense of minority ones; this homogenising effect is only likely to increase in the future as technology accelerates and advances.

Who invented sign language for the deaf?

The deaf did. In fact, sign language is barely related to the spoken language at all: it is a language all of its own, using hands, gestures and facial movement to convey meaning and a quite different grammar.

Sign language has been used by deaf communities since ancient times. Each group developed its own set of signs, although some of these have become standardised to a degree at national level in recent times. But the result is that there are numerous different and mutually unintelligible systems around the world. American Sign Language is very different from British Sign Language, and the Irish, Danish, Malay and Brazilian languages are all quite different again. An international sign language, originally called Gestuno, was invented for delegates at the first World Games for the Deaf, held in Paris in 1924, and is still used at international occasions.

Specialised schools

For centuries deaf children were dismissed as unteachable but in the early 17th century the Spanish priest Juan Pablo Bonet was given the task of teaching the deaf-and-dumb children of his wealthy employer. He developed a system of signing the alphabet, which he published (with illustrations of the gestures) in 1620.

More than a century later, Abbé Charles-Michel de l'Épée set up a school in Paris where a structured method of signing played a key role. It became the influential National Institution for Deaf-Mutes, which soon had numerous affiliated schools across Europe. After visiting the school, Reverend Thomas Hopkins Gallaudet returned to the USA with one of its former pupils, Laurent Clerc, to found, in 1816, the American School for the Deaf at Hartford, Connecticut. His son, Edward Miner Gallaudet, later founded what would become Gallaudet University for the deaf in Washington, D.C. on land given by local businessman Amos Kendall. These institutions helped to establish American Sign Language, in part based on the French system.

In Britain, sign language was well established by 1720, and was widely used in the growing number of deaf schools and clubs in the 19th century.

Signing setback

Many hearing teachers of the deaf took the view that sign language held deaf children back. They favoured the 'oral system': teaching deaf children to speak. From the 1880s signing was virtually banned for nearly a century in deaf schools and even in families in many parts of the world.

In the 1970s, damning reports revealed the ineffectiveness of the oral system, and the pioneering work of Doctor William C. Stokoe at Gallaudet University demonstrated that sign language possessed enough features to be considered a language in its own right. Since then, signing has regained its respectability around the world. It has been reintroduced into schools, and now appears on television and at theatre performances, but still with all its diverse national – even regional – variations.

FOUNDING FATHER Abbé Charles-Michel de l'Épée, whose work and teachings led to the formulation of an official French sign language. He wrote two books on his schooling methods, together with a signing dictionary.

The web of knowledge

Fifteen years ago, relatively few people had heard of the internet. How did it so rapidly become the phenomenally powerful medium that it is today? And whose idea was it?

CROP PRICES ONLINE Multinational company ITC has set up free internet kiosks in remote villages in Madhya Pradesh, India, for locals to access detailed crop information. Similar schemes are in operation in rural areas across the country.

Like the 'space race', the internet was a by-product of the Cold War. In the early 1960s, when the world was haunted by the vision of nuclear war, the United States was shielded by a radar-based early-warning system that depended on the best computers of the day – large mainframe machines that filled a room. As part of its drive to leapfrog Soviet technology, the US Department of Defense set up the Information Processing Technology Office (IPTO) at its Advanced Research Project Agency (ARPA). It was given the task of finding a way to link all these computers into a secure network – one that would continue to operate even if part of the network were destroyed by a nuclear attack. The scattered computers of the tracking system known as the Semi-Automatic Ground Environment (SAGE) were linked by modems, but the dedicated telephone lines that connected them were still vulnerable to attack.

Packet switching

In 1962, J.C.R. Licklider was appointed head of the IPTO. He proposed an 'Intergalactic Computer Network', with implications beyond defence needs. It was a premonition of the internet. But how could it be achieved? Attention turned to a technique devised simultaneously by researchers in the United States and Britain. By using 'packet switching' for transmission along telephone lines, each block of computer data could be treated like the electronic equivalent of a 'packet' in the mail. The destination address was attached to the packet at the sending computer; it then travelled to its destination along the quickest route, via a series of computer 'nodes'. If a node could not forward the packet directly, it would select another route. One way or another, the package would reach its destination. Individual transmissions could also be broken up into a number of packets before despatch and, according to availability, take different routes before reassembly at the destination.

Packet switching made optimum use of transmission capacity; and it was secure, flexible and robust enough to survive partial obliteration of the network. In 1969, the theory was tested for the first time in a network of four nodes: computers at the University of California, Los Angeles (UCLA); the University of California, Santa Barbara; the Stanford Research Institute; and the University of Utah. The so-called ARPANET was designed primarily for the military. But such computer links also offered university researchers the chance to share their findings. Other major American academic and research institutions soon joined ARPANET, and by 1972 it had 37 nodes. Meanwhile, parallel networks were created, linking other communities of computers.

Electronic mail

Users of these networks found them particularly useful because they could carry 'electronic mail'. In 1971, Ray Tomlinson, an American programmer at a company in Massachusetts, sent the first such message within a network – between two computers in the same room, linked to the ARPANET. He was also the first to adopt the @ symbol in the address.

Email, as it became known, could be flicked between the new personal computers (PCs) and workstations that appeared from about 1975. Designed for use by one person, they were equipped with 'visual display units' (VDUs) – screens displaying text.

The early networks were a province of a highly specialised, technical world, operated by computing experts. One of their most pressing tasks was to refine the methods, or protocols, that prepared information for transmission and allowed other computers to receive it. The earliest protocols were designed to link computers within a network. The next challenge was to devise protocols that could link one network to other networks: an 'internet'.

In 1974, Vinton Cerf, a computer scientist at Stanford University, proposed a radically new way of restructuring the protocols to link networks: the Transmission Control Protocol (TCP), which breaks up data packets for transmission and reassembles them; and the Internet Protocol (IP), which sees that the packets find their way to the right destination. After nearly a decade of refinement, on 1 January 1983 ARPANET switched to TCP/IP, and TCP/IP soon became the standard set of protocols for networks, and remains so today. The internet had arrived. Computing still seemed remote to the general public, but it was beginning to enter the office. By the end of the 1970s, electronic typewriters were being edged out by 'word-processors'. These had a

Why are the letters on the QWERTY keyboard arranged that way?

When Ray Tomlinson sent the world's first email within a network in 1971, the content was, he recalls, 'entirely forgettable … QWERTYUIOP or something similar'. This might seem like computer gobbledegook – but it is simply the top line of letters on most of the world's keyboards. So where did the curious arrangement come from?

An American printer, Christopher Sholes, invented the first practical typewriter in 1867, arranging the keys in alphabetical order. Pressed down by the fingers of the typist, each key sent a metal rod hammering into the ink-ribbon to print its letter on the paper. Fast typists soon found that adjacent rods, if activated in quick succession, collided and jammed. To solve the problem, Sholes redesigned the keyboard so that the rods of the most frequently used letters or letter combinations were separated by less frequently used ones. He therefore ended up with an arrangement that made QWERTY the first six letters at the top left of the keyboard. Most countries accepted this arrangement as they took delivery of their American-produced typewriters in the 19th century. For some languages the arrangement was altered slightly: so the Germans have QWERTZ, and French have AZERTY.

The problem of jamming hammer rods vanished with the arrival of electronic keyboards in the 20th century. There is no reason at all to preserve the QWERTY layout for computer keyboards, except that this is the pattern that millions of people around the world have learnt to use. Quirky it may be, but it would be far too complicated to change now.

THE LETTER ARRANGEMENT ON A VINTAGE FRENCH TYPEWRITER

memory capacity that enabled pre-printing correction and, after 1979, spell-checking, and electronic storage of documents and addresses. In the 1980s, word-processors had VDUs that allowed the user to see the document they were preparing without looking down. It was only a short step from here to PCs, which performed all the word-processing functions and carried more ambitious programs to produce documents using 'desktop publishing' (DTP), a process previously requiring a typesetter and printing press.

Home computing

The idea of installing an office computer at home was still of limited appeal, since it offered little more than advanced typewriting, help with accounts and primitive games. But manufacturers were keen to promote the concept of home computers, which began to take off with cheaper, consumer-targeted products, such as the Sinclair ZX80 in 1980 and the Amstrad CPC range in 1984.

In 1988, the internet was opened to commercial traffic, and the first Internet Service Providers (ISPs) sprang up to give access to the internet to subscribers. But it still could not deliver the futuristic vision of an 'information society' that everyone could access. The breakthrough came from an unexpected source. The Geneva-based European Organization for Nuclear Research (known as CERN after its French name: *Conseil Européen pour la Recherche Nucléaire*) is the world's largest particle physics laboratory and was the biggest internet node in Europe.

During the 1980s, Tim Berners-Lee, a British computer scientist, was working at CERN trying to develop a more efficient way for particle physicists around the world to share research. He recognised the main difference between computers and the human brain: computers work in a linear way, churning through the information supplied to them; humans gather and build information by association, and select paths of information according to their need.

How could he get computers to present information in a way that reflected how the human brain works? The answer, he felt, lay in 'hypertext', an on-screen system that allows users, equipped with a mouse, to point-and-click on highlighted words to access another document. The technology for hypertext and the mouse had been developed in the mid-1960s by Douglas Engelbart at the Stanford Research Institute. Berners-Lee proposed using hypertext to create a 'web of links' – a system that he named the World Wide Web. He devised the HyperText Transfer Protocol (HTTP); the HyperText Markup Language (HTML); and the familiar labelling system, using what is now called a Uniform Resource Locator (URL), which gives each website a unique address (such as http//:www.readersdigest.co.uk).

Berners-Lee persuaded CERN to back the development of the World Wide Web, which was finally launched on the internet in 1991. Three years later, it was placed in the public domain royalty-free, for the use of all.

To link into the internet and access the World Wide Web, and to locate, download and display web documents (or 'pages') and navigate between them, personal computers needed software called a 'browser'. In 1993, Marc Andreessen and Eric Bina, graduates of the University of Illinois, created the most effective and easy-to-use browser yet, called Mosaic. In 1994, re-launched as Netscape Navigator, it became the browser for 90 per cent of PC users and facilitated the new fad of 'netsurfing'.

The information superhighway

Suddenly, the true potential of the internet became apparent. The US government began to promote the vision of an 'information superhighway' of benefit to all. As personal computers

Timeline

The internet has enabled people in the remotest corners of the world to communicate anywhere, in minutes.

1965
Hypertext a clickable text system is invented by Douglas Engelbart

1969
ARPANET goes live with four linked computers

1972
First email management program written by L.G. Roberts

1975
MSG email program developed by John Vittal

SINCLAIR ZX80
HOME COMPUTER

1980
Sinclair ZX80 goes on the market

1983
ARPANET switches to TCP/IP. Domain name system introduced

1960s

1961
Packet switching, a revolutionary system of data transmission, first described in a paper by Leonard Kleinrock, UCLA Professor of Computer Science

1964
Packet switching independently described by computer scientist Paul Baran

1970s

1967
Plan for ARPANET, world's first packet switching network, published by computer scientist L.G. Roberts

1971
First email sent by US programmer Ray Tomlinson. @ sign chosen for 'at'

1974
TCP/IP, a new system of transmission, proposed by computer scientist Vinton Cerf

VINTON CERF

1980s

1982
The term 'cyberspace' coined by writer William Gibson

became faster and more efficient, prices fell and modem connection speeds improved; computing programs started to look more user-friendly to consumers. In 1995, Microsoft introduced the browser Internet Explorer as an add-on package to Windows 95, and it became an integral part of Windows 98, as Microsoft rose to take up its dominant position in PC operating systems.

Many businesses saw the value of having a web presence. As new web pages of all kinds poured in, finding a path to the information sought became trickier. But 'search engines' came to the rescue, some using automated 'web crawler' systems to browse web pages for keywords and create indexes. Yahoo! was launched in 1994; AltaVista in 1995; Google in 1998.

In the early days of the internet, users mainly looked up information from web pages, just as they might consult a printed encyclopedia or catalogue. But two-way interaction between users and websites, and improved security encryption, opened up the possibility of 'e-commerce': on-line shopping, banking and reservations. By 2000, interest in the internet reached fever pitch as a large number of start-up companies raced to establish new business models, heavily funded by speculative capital.

When many failed to match their expectations, the result was the 'dot-com' crash that quickly ensued.

Access all comers

Since then the most successful internet businesses have tended to focus on the communication potential of the Web, benefiting from the willingness of users to provide content, a development known as Web 2.0. Wikipedia, the online encyclopedia, was founded in 2001. Written, edited and updated by users assisted by automated systems, in April 2008 its articles numbered 10 million in 253 languages.

The internet is now a network linked not just by copper telephone lines, but by electrical coaxial cables, wireless Local Area Networks (LANs), satellite links and superfast optical fibre circuits. Increased bandwidth has permitted the transfer of huge files containing soundtracks, photographs and video clips, even whole films. The potential has been exploited by social networking sites, such as MySpace (2003) and Facebook (2004). The video-sharing site, YouTube, was created in a garage in February 2005; in November 2006, Google bought it for US$1.65 billion. By 2008, it carried more than 70 million videos.

An essential factor in the internet's success is its openness: anyone can use

it, or add to it, or try out ideas on it, without asking permission. The only overarching organisation is the Internet Corporation for Assigned Names and Numbers (ICANN). There is otherwise no governing body; the Internet Service Providers are the main gatekeepers. This can lead to abuse, but the broad consensus is that the advantages outweigh the disadvantages.

World wide phenomenon

In 1995, seven million computers were connected to the internet and there were more than 20 million web pages; by 2000, 95 million computers could access a billion web pages. By 2008, the internet had 1.3 billion users world wide – some 20 per cent of the world's population and more than 30 billion web pages. The same year, CERN launched the Grid, a service for sharing computer power and data storage capacity over the internet. The Grid is intended to go far beyond communication between computers, aiming to turn the mighty global network of computers into one vast computational resource.

The ideal of its early pioneers – the dream of democratised knowledge to which anyone can have access and can contribute – no longer looks like science fiction. It no longer looks like a luxury either, but a necessity.

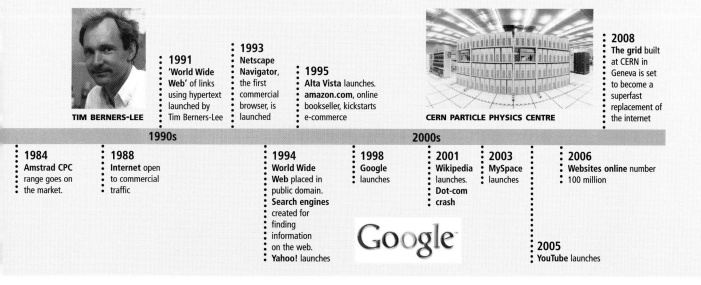

TIM BERNERS-LEE

1991
'World Wide Web' of links using hypertext launched by Tim Berners-Lee

1993
Netscape Navigator, the first commercial browser, is launched

1995
Alta Vista launches. amazon.com, online bookseller, kickstarts e-commerce

CERN PARTICLE PHYSICS CENTRE

2008
The grid built at CERN in Geneva is set to become a superfast replacement of the internet

1990s

2000s

1984
Amstrad CPC range goes on the market.

1988
Internet open to commercial traffic

1994
World Wide Web placed in public domain. Search engines created for finding information on the web. Yahoo! launches

1998
Google launches

2001
Wikipedia launches. Dot-com crash

2003
MySpace launches

2006
Websites online number 100 million

2005
YouTube launches

Google

I'm on the train! Mobile phones have killed off the telephone box and the telegram, and made it almost impossible to be out of touch. How did the mobile revolution so rapidly conquer the world of communications?

The Motorola DynaTAC 8000x was a highly desirable, technological marvel. In 1983, after decades in development, it became the first mobile phone to win the approval of the US Federal Communications Commission, opening the door to a new era of wireless telephony. Not for nothing was it nicknamed the 'brick phone': it was 25cm (10in) long, excluding the antenna, and weighed nearly 800g (1lb 12oz). If charged for 10 hours, it could support calls lasting 30 minutes to an hour, but after eight hours it needed recharging.

Despite its price tag of US$3,995, Motorola struggled to satisfy the public's demand.

Cells and mobility

DynaTAC stood for 'Dynamic Adaptive Total Area Coverage', a clue to the development that brought about the telephone revolution. A mobile phone transmits and receives radio waves, communicating with an antenna at the nearest base station, which makes the link to the phone of the other party. The area within range of the base station is called a 'cell'. At first, these cells were large with limited capacity. But in the 1980s telephone companies created networks of smaller cells, which could carry more traffic. The new 'cellular' phone technology allowed users to move freely from one cell to another, a

IT'S NO SECRET The first mobile phones were bulky creations and lack of encryption meant conversations could be overheard.

process called 'handover' or 'handoff'. The Global System for Mobile Communications (GSM), established in 1982, set the standards that permitted 'roaming' between different mobile phone service providers.

The early, 'first generation' (1G) mobile phones were based on analogue radio signals. In the second generation (2G), launched in 1991, signals were converted from analogue to digital communications, the language of computers. The third generation (3G), launched in 2001, extended the digital capabilities with high-speed data access to embrace email and internet links. Meanwhile, mobile phones became cheaper, smaller and more efficient, soon acquiring a cluster of advanced

ECONOMIC IMPACT Mobile phone technology is now so sophisticated that communication is possible almost anywhere. Local economies benefit all over the world, even nomadic desert ones.

features previously found on separate gadgets, such as a clock, calculator, camera and camcorder, video games console and MP3 music player. In 1984, there were 300,000 mobile phone subscribers in the world; by 2000 there were 550 million; now there are 3.5 billion and cell phone networks are accessible to 80 per cent of the world's population.

Telehistory

Mobile phones are the most recent chapter in a long history that tracks the human desire to communicate over long distances. Developments in telecommunication systems were often driven forward by the needs of war. Early systems from the 1790s linked European capitals to their naval ports via a chain of visual signalling stations on hilltops. In the 1840s, the invention of electrical telegraph systems and Morse code gave rise to the telegram, printed onto paper by the receiving office and taken to the addressee by hand. In the 1870s, the telephone was the first telecommunication device to convey the sound of a real voice over a long distance.

Landline telephone systems held sway for 100 years. But in the 1940s, inspired by the development of handheld radio telephony ('walkie-talkies') in the Second World War, inventors began looking for ways to liberate telephones from wires. By the 1950s, 'mobile' (radio) car phones were commercially available. And during the 1970s, 'cordless phones' – radio handsets linked to a landline base in the home – let users wander around the house and even into the garden while making a call. But it was the 1G cell phones of the 1980s that gave genuine mobility to phone technology.

The freedom to be accessible

The explosive expansion of mobile phone networks around the world owes much to their freedom from landline cables, which are expensive to install and maintain. With the advent of cellular telephony, countries without extensive landline systems – for historical, geographical or economic reasons – have been able to join the modern telecommunications revolution. The fastest growing mobile phone markets today are in Africa and Asia. Mobile phones satisfy the human instinct to have a permanent link to others, enabling users to make calls from anywhere and also be contacted wherever they are. Privacy is both threatened and reinforced: formerly, while telephone conversations were conducted from fixed points of access (in the hall, in the office, at a telephone box), privacy was often compromised; it is now possible to be much more secretive, especially when texting.

These changes have called for new codes of social conduct and etiquette – for example, to prevent ringtones causing a distraction in public places. Mobile phones are banned from some railway carriages, so passengers do not have to listen to overloud conversations – conversations that often begin with that cliché of the modern age of telephony: 'I'm on the train!'

Who invented the text message and why did it take off?

On 3 December 1992, an engineer at the Airwide Solutions communications company in Britain used a computer to send a message to the mobile of a contact at Vodaphone. This was – it is claimed – the first ever text message, sent using the Short Message Service (SMS) on a GSM network. It said: 'Merry Christmas'.

The theory of sending text messages between handsets had been explored in the 1980s, and the SMS standards, limiting messages to 160 characters, were agreed in 1985. The first technology appeared only in the form of one-way pagers or 'beepers', which sent alerts to recipients telling them to call the number given on the display. Engineers behind the earliest SMS text messages could never have envisaged the global escalation of text messaging: in 2000, 17 billion messages were sent; by 2008, 2 billion users sent some 2.3 trillion messages.

Text messages dispense with the time-consuming social exchanges of telephone conversations. They can be sent at any time and can be stored if the recipient's phone is turned off or out of reach of a signal. Most of all, they cost a fraction of a voice call.

The first Short Message Service Centres (SMSCs), specialising in text message traffic, were set up in 1993, but as hundreds of messages can be sent in the time it takes to transmit a single call, changes in technology were needed to make SMS messaging profitable. At first, messages could only be sent to others on the same network. But when inter-network texting became possible in 1998, the market took off, driven by young users. Their enthusiasm was restricted only by their budgets – explaining the popularity of the short-form language called 'txtspk'. The sheer volume of text messages reaped considerable revenue for the mobile phone operators, creating a business now worth some US$60 billion a year.

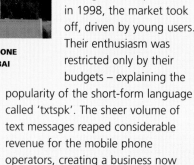

A MOBILE PHONE MAST IN DUBAI

Just like my office Why did the computer desktop come to be arranged like an office filing system?

Using a computer is a bit like driving a car. We know how to make it work, to carry out the tasks we need it for, but most of us have no idea *how* it works. This was the challenge for computer developers in around 1980, at the cusp of the personal computer (PC) revolution. How could they explain the benefits of computing without scaring potential customers with the complexities of computer programming? The breakthrough came with what is known as the 'paper paradigm' – the idea of making the screen appear just like print on a piece of paper.

The desktop metaphor

Early word processing programs such as WordStar, launched in 1978 by MicroPro International, presented the text on screen in one typeface and needed codes (commands entered from the keyboard via the alphabetic keys and the 'control' key) to create italic, paragraph indents, and so on. It took the technology of WYSIWYG ('What You See is What You Get'), introduced in the 1980s, to show on

screen exactly how the text would look when printed out on paper.

But already in the early 1980s, personal computers could do far more than just word processing. To provide a link to the various applications and files, their opening screens showed symbols and pictograms ('icons'), which the user clicked onto. The technology for this kind of interactive screen – called a 'graphical user interface' (GUI) – had been forged during the 1960s at the Stanford Research Institute by a team led by Douglas Engelbart, originator also of the mouse. It was refined further in the 1970s by the Xerox PARC research and development company, based in Palo Alto, California. The now-familiar WIMP interface emerged from this: 'window, icon, menu, pointer' – a combination that first appeared in 1981 in the Xerox Star Workstation.

As a way of structuring these GUI symbols and icons in an orderly and approachable way, companies such as

Xerox adopted the image of a desk in an office. This was partly because personal computers were still primarily bought for the office or for office work in the home so the 'desktop metaphor' seemed appropriate. It was another way of making computers more 'user-friendly' – a term that was rapidly gaining currency at the time. A primitive two-tone image of an office was used as the GUI for 'Magic Desk', word-processing software produced in 1983 for the Commodore 64 – one of the most successful early PCs. The picture showed an office desk with a filing cabinet standing next to it. By manipulating a joystick to move a pointing hand over the image, users could press a trigger to click on the symbols – for instance, the typewriter on the desk to access the word-processing program. They could store files by dropping them into the drawers of the filing cabinet – or delete them by dropping them in the wastebasket that was pictured on the floor beneath. 'Imagine using your computer to type, file and edit personal letters and papers,' ran the

> **GUI technology and the desktop metaphor only began to grab the public in 1984**

KEYSETS AND MICE Douglas Engelbart's first mouse of 1964 (right) had just one button and was encased in wood. It was designed for use with workstations (left). The contemporary keyboard allowed the user to enter codes quickly, making text manipulation more efficient.

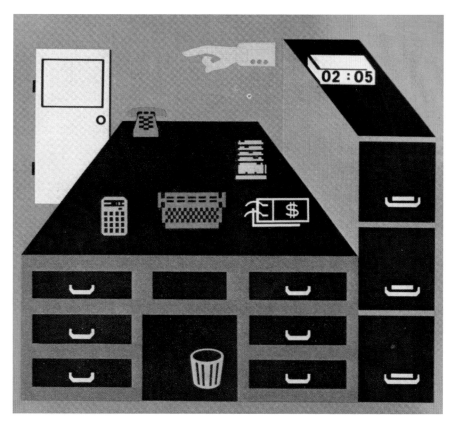

TOP DESK Magic Desk was marketed as 'the next generation of user-friendly software'. Created for the Commodore 64 home computer, the utility cartridge enabled the user to 'point' to the required feature with an animated onscreen hand, moved by means of the joystick and trigger.

Alternatives were tried and tested. In the early 1980s, Amiga used the workshop metaphor, in which programs were 'tools', files were 'projects', and directories appeared as the drawers of a workbench. In an attempt to embrace the multitasking capabilities of PCs, Xerox introduced the idea of 'Rooms' in 1986. Packard Bell developed a virtual 'Living Room' image: the GUI of their Navigator 3.5, launched in 1995, pictured the sophisticated interior of a home, with active, clickable symbols (printer, phone, fax) on a desk, on bookshelves (software library, electronic reference books, games), on a music centre mounted on the wall, and in side rooms (the 'Info Room' and the 'Software Room'), which offered internet access and tutorials.

Office bound

But by this time the office image – made so pervasive by Microsoft – had become familiar to the majority of PC users; it framed their mental approach to how computers operate. Where once files and folders, cutting and pasting and even the desktop itself, were understood as helpful metaphors, now the electronic application of these terms took over as the first meaning. Email extended the office analogy to the post room (address books, forwarding, the paperclip symbol for an attachment).

The internet brought with it a dilution of the office analogy as numerous other terms quite unrelated to general office life came into play, such as viruses, surfing, phishing and mashing. But in computing, as in real life, there is still always an office somewhere in the background.

publicity, '*without learning any special commands!*' But this early commercial application of the WIMP interface had technical limitations and was not a great success. The combination of the new GUI technology and the desktop metaphor only really began to grab the public imagination in 1984 with the enhanced graphics might – on a 9-inch monitor – of the Macintosh 128K personal computer.

Folders and files

In the 1960s, computer programmers had laid the foundations of this office analogy by speaking in terms of computer 'files'. When the first personal computers were equipped with screens in the 1970s, GUIs showed pictures of tabbed suspension files (like those used in filing cabinets) to represent files, folders, or programs. In the 1980s, the office image became more elaborate, as WYSIWYG technology led to the more ambitious layouts of 'desktop publishing'. The 1990s meant word-processing programs not only

had directories structured like filing cabinets, with folders, documents and files, but also the tools of a print studio that allowed users to choose fonts, rules, borders and colours.

The desktop metaphor went hand in hand with Microsoft's MS-DOS (Disk Operating System) and its Windows software operating system, which dominated the PC market in the 1990s. Microsoft Word 97 even included an 'Office Assistant' – an animated paperclip that popped up with help screens at any potential point where advice or assistance might be useful to the user.

Since the 1980s, much of the expansion of PC ownership can be attributed to the success of the desktop metaphor in rendering computing accessible to newcomers. But there was no good reason why the office should be the only mind map for PC structures, especially given that PCs were increasingly being used in the home – for entertainment purposes as well as work.

The spread of AIDS More than 33 million people globally may be infected with HIV, the virus that causes AIDS. Yet 30 years ago no one had heard of it. Where did it come from?

In 1981, a number of young, mainly homosexual men in California and New York, were treated for aggressive versions of formerly rare infections and tumours. These included Kaposi's sarcoma, a relatively slow-growing skin cancer that usually affects older people, and pneumocystis carinii pneumonia (PCP), a lung infection. The new forms stubbornly resisted all forms of standard medical treatment. Around the same time there were reports from France and Belgium of a people of central African origin with similar infections. Doctors working in parts of Zambia and Zaire also noticed the emergence of a form of Kaposi's sarcoma, which, unlike previous variants, was often fatal.

It became clear that the victims were all suffering from a similar syndrome that caused their immune systems to become compromised, leaving them vulnerable to tumours and infections of all kinds. But what exactly was the new syndrome, where had it come from and how was it caused?

It became known as AIDS, an acronym for Acquired Immune Deficiency Syndrome. Just 181 cases of AIDS were reported in that first year, but within a couple of years the disease had become widespread in central Africa and it swiftly became a global pandemic, affecting people of all ages from every stratum of society.

It is now believed that the disease originated in the 1950s, or even earlier, and began to spread in the mid- to late-1970s, although it was not known within the medical community before 1981. Later that year, cases were reported among intravenous drug users as well as

IN REMEMBRANCE The Circle of Remembrance at the National AIDS Memorial in San Francisco will, on completion, be engraved with the names of more than 2,000 victims of the disease.

homosexuals. The next year a case occurred in a child following multiple blood transfusions, suggesting that the cause was an infectious agent, though the means of transmission was still unknown. In 1983, reports of infected women with no other risk factors raised the spectre of transmission among heterosexuals, and public anxiety increased.

By 1997, the United States Agency for International Development was describing the spread of AIDS as 'a crisis of staggering proportion, that is going to affect not only the future of

BUILDING ACCEPTANCE Diana, Princess of Wales, in 1992 with William Drake, a patient at the London Lighthouse, a dedicated facility for people with AIDS. In the early years of the disease, AIDS patients were regarded with fear and often hostility. The princess's 'hands-on' approach was an important factor in helping to remove the stigma of AIDS and allowing sufferers to reintegrate into the community.

these countries [but] … the entire global network of trade, diplomacy and development. What we are talking about here is something that has never been seen before, which is countries with one-sixth to one-quarter of all children without one or both parents.' To date, 25 million men, women and children have died of the condition worldwide.

What is AIDS?

AIDS is caused by HIV – the Human Immunodeficiency Virus. By 1984, separate research teams at the National Cancer Institute in the USA, the Pasteur Institute in Paris and the University of California had each identified a specific virus, later to be named HIV, as the cause of AIDS. The discovery of the virus was a vital breakthrough since it meant scientists around the world now had a target to aim at. In 1985, a blood test for HIV became available.

HIV is transmitted through contact with bodily fluids (such as blood or semen) and may be passed on through sexual intercourse, especially anal intercourse. Other possible means are through blood-to-blood contact, so

intravenous drug users who share needles are at risk, as were those requiring blood transfusions – such as haemophiliacs – in the early years of the disease before blood was screened for HIV. A pregnant woman with HIV can pass it on to her child while it is in the womb, during birth or later in her milk when she is breastfeeding.

HIV is now known to be a retrovirus, a kind of virus that stores its genetic information in an unusual way and can break down the DNA of human cells and use it to replicate itself. It attacks a type of white blood cell in the immune system that would normally help the body to fight infections. These cells become severely depleted, impairing the body's immune response and eventually allowing specific cancers and infections characteristic of AIDS to take

THE SHAPE OF THE VIRUS An electron micrograph of a T-lymphocyte blood cell, which has been infected with the HIV virus (coloured red). The virus eventually leads to the death of the cell, reducing the body's ability to fight infection.

hold. Such infections are called 'opportunistic' as they take advantage of the weakened immune system, which would normally be able to control them. Along with certain types of cancer, they are known as AIDS-defining conditions – someone who is HIV-positive with a low white cell count is diagnosed as having AIDS if one of these conditions develops.

How long the transition from HIV to AIDS takes varies from person to person. The infection goes through a long latent period – on average 8-10 years before symptoms appear – so most people in the world infected with HIV are unaware that they have the virus, though they may pass it on to others during this time. The American basketball star Magic Johnson tested positive for HIV in 1991 and announced his retirement from competitive sport, but at the time of writing had not developed AIDS.

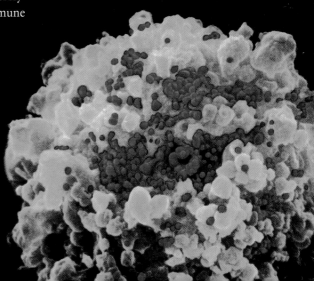

There are two types of HIV virus – HIV-1 and HIV-2 – and many subtypes of each. HIV-1 is the more virulent and causes most HIV infections. The earliest blood sample that has tested positive for HIV-1 dates from 1959. HIV-2 is still largely confined to west Africa, though it, too, is spreading.

Origin of the viruses

For many years scientists speculated that HIV originated in primates, from a virus that somehow jumped species. A retrovirus called Simian Immuno-deficiency Virus (SIV) was found in 1985 in captive monkeys suffering from an immunodeficiency disease very similar to AIDS. Although SIV does not infect humans, it had remarkable similarities to HIV.

In 1999, scientists announced that they had identified the original source of HIV-1 as an almost identical SIV strain from a subspecies of chimpanzee from west equatorial Africa, where the animals were hunted for food. They proposed that the virus was transmitted to humans as a result either of carrier animals being killed and eaten, or from their blood getting into open cuts and wounds on the bodies of their hunters.

A particular strain of SIV found in these chimpanzees is closely related to HIV-1, while HIV-2 is now known to be related to a strain of SIV that infects sooty mangabeys, a type of African monkey. Most scientists now believe that HIV is a descendant of SIV.

Other theories of HIV's origins seem less likely. One is that an oral polio vaccine called CHAT, tested in the Congo, Rwanda and Burundi in the late 1950s, had been grown in cultured monkey cells contaminated with SIV. Another argues that the spread of HIV, perhaps from hunters who had acquired SIV from chimpanzees, was caused by the widespread re-use of disposable plastic syringes and contaminated needles across the African continent, which allowed the quick transfer of any viral particles directly into the bloodstream, giving the viruses the chance to mutate and replicate almost immediately.

Precisely where the transfer from apes to humans took place has not been firmly established. Some claim the original source of the contagion as southern Cameroon, but it is not clear how HIV spread from there to the Congo and from Africa to the Americas. The most recent theory is that a migrant worker returning from the Congo probably carried it to the Caribbean island of Haiti in the mid-1960s and that from there the disease was brought to the USA around 1969.

A global pandemic

While the medical profession battled to understand the cause of the new disease and how to treat it, AIDS continued to spread. As reports of outbreaks poured in – from Africa, Haiti, Europe, Asia and the Americas – it became evident that the world was facing a global pandemic.

In Britain, the first two AIDS victims were admitted to hospital in December 1981 and January 1982 and many more soon followed. Dr Anthony S. Fauci, Director of the

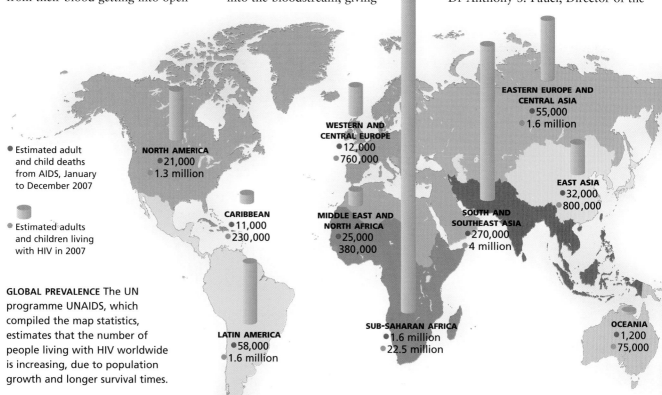

● Estimated adult and child deaths from AIDS, January to December 2007

● Estimated adults and children living with HIV in 2007

GLOBAL PREVALENCE The UN programme UNAIDS, which compiled the map statistics, estimates that the number of people living with HIV worldwide is increasing, due to population growth and longer survival times.

NORTH AMERICA
● 21,000
● 1.3 million

CARIBBEAN
● 11,000
● 230,000

LATIN AMERICA
● 58,000
● 1.6 million

WESTERN AND CENTRAL EUROPE
● 12,000
● 760,000

MIDDLE EAST AND NORTH AFRICA
● 25,000
● 380,000

SUB-SAHARAN AFRICA
● 1.6 million
● 22.5 million

EASTERN EUROPE AND CENTRAL ASIA
● 55,000
● 1.6 million

EAST ASIA
● 32,000
● 800,000

SOUTH AND SOUTHEAST ASIA
● 270,000
● 4 million

OCEANIA
● 1,200
● 75,000

PROVIDING CARE Young children and their families at a monthly HIV/AIDS day in Uganda where they are screened and tested as part of a charitable programme to improve care, education and training.

National Institute of Allergy and Infectious Diseases in the USA, wrote that 'it was like living in an intensive care unit all day long'. Despite the best efforts of doctors and nurses, most of the victims died. It was clear that a massive research programme was needed. Dr Fauci recalled: 'I made the decision that we would have to switch over to research on AIDS because, as every month went by, I became more and more convinced that we were dealing with something that was going to be a disaster for society.'

Advances in treatment

Billions of dollars have been spent on attempts to find effective ways of treating HIV and AIDS, but no definitive cure for either condition has been discovered. Understanding of how the HIV virus attaches itself to an immune cell and replicates itself enabled the development of anti-retroviral drugs that could suppress HIV replication. The first, zidovudine, was approved in 1986, and others followed.

But although individuals varied in their response, single drug treatment was not very effective – it could delay disease progression but not prevent it, and the high doses needed provoked severe side-effects.

Research showed that HIV, like many viruses, may undergo tiny genetic changes that make it resistant to antiviral agents. After 1995, treatment efforts moved to using combinations of drugs, in lower doses, to stop the development of resistant strains. This gave both a dramatic improvement in efficacy and a reduction in side-effects.

Combination therapy using different types of drug, known as 'highly active antiretroviral therapy' or HAART, became the standard treatment after 1997. Triple or quadruple HAART therapy along with better treatment of opportunistic infections has greatly reduced both the speed of progression of HIV to AIDS and the death rate from AIDS. But total elimination of HIV has not happened and may be almost impossible, as the virus is now known to 'hide' in reservoirs inside the body, shielded from attack by the immune system or by drugs.

The development of a truly effective HIV vaccine may still be a decade away, and several trials were halted in 2008 when initial results of field studies of the most promising candidate suggested that not only did it not protect people but may have slightly increased the risk of infection.

Other more radical approaches that may prove useful in the future include the development of gene therapies whereby new genes are incorporated into the human genome to create new proteins that can combat HIV.

A major problem is that all the drugs developed so far are very costly. It can be prohibitively expensive to use the latest therapies in the countries where they are needed the most and many in need are denied treatment. In 1998, 39 drug companies filed a law suit against the South African government to contest legislation aimed at reducing the price of medicines. In 2005, the World Health Organisation revealed that in sub-Saharan Africa only about 50,000 out of the 4.1 million people who needed treatment with the drugs – just over one per cent – were receiving it.

An end in sight?

AIDS is still incurable. In 2008, Nobel Prize winner David Baltimore, a leading authority on the disease, warned that such was its complexity that scientists were no closer to a vaccine now than when they first linked it with HIV more than 25 years ago.

But there is hope on the horizon. In 2005, world leaders at the G8 summit pledged to provide universal access to anti-retroviral drugs by 2010. At the UN World Summit the same year, it was agreed to scale up HIV prevention, treatment, care and support with a goal of universal access by 2010.

WHO statistics indicate that the number of HIV and AIDS cases has declined slightly over the last couple of years. This is probably due to improved detection of HIV in its early stages and greater awareness of the risks that lead to contraction of both diseases. Today, HIV detection, whether by a saliva or blood test, is relatively quick and simple and extremely accurate. At least this means that someone who is HIV positive can take the necessary steps to avoid transmitting the disease.

The death of a disease In past centuries, it would have been an everyday occurrence to encounter people who had been disfigured by the effects of smallpox. Now, this killer disease is virtually unknown. Why does no one get smallpox any more?

Known as the 'speckled monster' in the 1700s, smallpox has a long, dark history. The 19th-century English historian, T.B. Macaulay vividly described its effects: 'The smallpox was always present, filling the churchyards with corpses ... leaving on those whose lives it spared the hideous traces of its power, turning the babe into a changeling at which the mother shuddered, and making the eyes and cheeks of the bighearted maiden objects of horror to the lover.'

Ancient threat

In the course of the 20th century, 300 million people worldwide perished from the disease. Its origins are uncertain, but smallpox may have appeared as early as 10,000 BC in the Nile Valley and Mesopotamia. In 1157 BC, Pharaoh Ramses V of Egypt was its first recorded victim; the traces of the pustules are still visible on his mummified remains. The disease quickly spread from the Middle East, reaching India during the first

millennium BC. From there, it entered China and eventually Japan. Crusaders brought smallpox to Europe from the Holy Land and in the late 11th and 12th centuries it became endemic throughout Europe.

By 1700, around 400,000 Europeans were killed by smallpox every year. Rank and power were no protection: the Holy Roman Emperor Joseph I, Tsar Peter II of Russia and Louis XV of France all died from the disease. Smallpox is a viral condition. It is caused by the variola virus, which enters the body through the lungs and is carried in the bloodstream to the body's other internal organs, which it then infects. It spreads to the skin, where it causes the characteristic rash.

Incubation is usually 12-14 days, after which victims start to suffer from fever, headache, backache and vomiting. The rash appears three days later, starting off as small pink spots that quickly grow bigger and slightly raised. By the third day, they turn into blisters, that leave a sunken scar, the pockmark. Death is usually as a result of blood poisoning, internal bleeding or secondary infections after the first affected cells die and the virus moves into the spleen, bone marrow and lymph nodes. There is still no effective treatment once symptoms appear.

Prognosis and prevention

Smallpox kills around a third of the adults it infects and up to half the children. Even if it doesn't kill, victims may be left blind and with joint problems that can lead to limb deformities in children. It spreads most quickly among peoples who have not encountered it before and have no inbuilt resistance.

When the Spanish conquistadors arrived in South America in the 16th century, they brought smallpox with them. Neither the Aztecs nor the Incas had any immunity and many thousands perished. By 1520, just a year after the Spanish arrival, a third of the Aztec population had died. The same thing happened in North America where European settlers infected native peoples. Australian Aboriginals suffered several catastrophic epidemics in the 18th and 19th centuries, from contact with Indonesians or Europeans.

The search for a way of controlling the disease began early. A procedure called variation was first practised in the 10th

CENTURIES OF A DISEASE
The Egyptian Pharaoh Ramses V of the 12th century BC (above) and the Somalian Ali Maow Maalin are the first and last known sufferers from smallpox.

GODDESS OF THE POX A bronze statue of Mariyamma, the Indian goddess of smallpox and pestilence.

century AD in India and China. Pus taken from the pockmarks of a sufferer was injected into a healthy person. The result was usually a mild case of smallpox, but the benefit was a lifelong immunity. Lady Mary Wortley Montagu, the wife of the British ambassador to the Ottoman Empire, who herself survived smallpox, is credited with introducing variolation to Britain in 1721. She learned of the practice from the Turks and described the process in a letter.

'They make parties for this purpose, and when they are met … the old woman comes with a nutshell full of the matter of the best sort of smallpox and … with a large needle … puts into the vein as much venom as can lye upon the head of her needle. The children … play together all the rest of the day and are in perfect health till the eighth. Then the fever begins to seize them and they keep their beds two days, very seldom three … in eight days time they are as well as before the illness …

'There is no example of any one that has died in it, and you may believe I am very well satisfied of the safety of the experiment since I intend to try it on my dear little son …' Having had her children variolated, Lady Mary persuaded her friend, the Princess of Wales, to do the same. The royal example encouraged the upper classes to follow suit. But the procedure was unaffordable to most people, and thousands continued to die of smallpox. Nor was variolation totally reliable. Medical science at that stage could not always identify a suitable strain of the disease and deaths from the procedure were not uncommon.

Jenner and vaccination

The breakthrough in the fight against smallpox occurred in 1796, when Edward Jenner, an English doctor,

CONTROVERSIAL COWPOX Jenner's new procedure was viewed with suspicion. A cartoon from 1802 shows miniature cows erupting from the pustules of those who have been inoculated.

QUEUEING FOR PROTECTION In April 1947, New Yorkers responded to an appeal to come and be vaccinated against smallpox.

discovered a new way of protecting people against infection. His discovery owed much to folklore. Many country people believed that a milkmaid who had had cowpox, a far milder infection, could never fall victim to the disease. Jenner decided to investigate.

In May 1796, a dairymaid called Sarah Nelmes consulted Jenner about a rash on her hands that he diagnosed as cowpox. She confirmed that one of her cows had recently contracted the condition and Jenner seized the chance to test his theory. James Phipps, the eight-year-old son of Jenner's gardener, was the guinea pig. Jenner made some

scratches on one of the boy's arms and rubbed pus extracted from pockmarks on Sarah Nelmes' hands into them. A few days later, James became mildly ill with cowpox, but quickly recovered. The next step was to test whether James was now protected from smallpox. On 1 July, Jenner variolated the boy. As he had anticipated, James did not develop smallpox.

Jenner was quick to realise the significance of his discovery. In 1801, he wrote: 'It now becomes too manifest to admit of controversy that the annihilation of the Small Pox, the most dreadful scourge of the human species, must be the final result of this practice.'

> **Bavaria was the first country to make smallpox vaccination compulsory**

Yet his vaccination technique – the term comes from *vacca*, the Latin for 'cow' – was relatively slow to catch on. There were several reasons. Cowpox did not occur widely. Samples were often contaminated because those handling it worked in smallpox wards or practised variolation. Many doctors were opposed to the new idea because it threatened the livelihoods they made from treating the disease. Others were against it on religious grounds. But there was no stopping its spread. Bavaria was the first country to make smallpox vaccination compulsory, in 1807. Denmark followed in 1810, Prussia in 1835 and Britain in 1853.

It was over a century before Jenner's confident prediction was fulfilled globally. Although the adoption of vaccination in Europe and North America largely wiped out the established strains of smallpox, these regions still suffered outbreaks imported from other parts of the world where smallpox was endemic.

In 1947 a Mexican businessman, unaware that he was incubating smallpox, travelled to New York where he collapsed. Once evidence of smallpox was confirmed, the US authorities reacted immediately. They ordered the mass vaccination of six million New Yorkers. As a result, only 12 people contracted the disease, of whom two, including the carrier, died. Six more died from an adverse reaction to the vaccine. Decisive action had avoided an epidemic.

Global action

In 1972, a Muslim pilgrim returning to his village in Kosovo, Yugoslavia, from the Middle East unwittingly spread the disease to family and friends. Misdiagnosis meant the infection spread into Serbia. When a doctor raised the alarm, Kosovo was completely isolated. No one was allowed in or out of the region without being vaccinated or producing proof of previous vaccination. All public events, meetings and even weddings were banned. In all over 170 cases resulted, and by the time the outbreak was under control, almost the entire population of Yugoslavia had been vaccinated against the disease.

The Yugoslavian incident gave teeth to a global campaign against smallpox first proposed by the World Health Organisation (WHO) in 1965. Now the time had come for decisive action. Every time an outbreak of the disease was reported, a WHO team was despatched to the scene to vaccinate and isolate all those who were ill, and trace and vaccinate all their contacts.

The idea was to ring-fence the disease and stop it spreading. An outbreak in Somalia in 1977 was tackled exactly like this. It began in October, when a hospital cook contracted the disease. As the result of an extensive campaign, 54,777 people were traced and vaccinated over the next 14 days and the outbreak halted in its tracks. Two years of close monitoring followed, until, in 1980, the WHO announced that the disease had been eradicated worldwide.

A new threat

Four years later, it was agreed that only two laboratories – one in the United States and one in the then Soviet Union – should be allowed to keep stocks of the deadly smallpox virus for research purposes. Though officially eradicated, smallpox is still a latent menace. Most people have lost what natural immunity they possessed and have never been more vulnerable should it ever recur.

Because of this, smallpox as a potential biological weapon is more potent than ever. In 1992, Kanatjan Alibekov, a top Russian scientist, moved to the USA. He told US intelligence that he had overseen an illegal programme to utilise the smallpox virus in just such a way. The Kremlin believed, said Alibekov, that smallpox could be 'the most powerful and effective weapon ever created to eliminate human life'.

Dealing with disease

In 1880 the French scientist Charles Chamberland hit upon the notion of using inoculation as a way of preventing all kinds of disease. Like many important discoveries, it came about by chance. When Chamberland accidentally left a batch of chicken cholera bacteria exposed to the air, and then injected it into some chickens, they survived and were found to be immune to further infection. The weakened strain of chicken cholera had given them immunity to the condition.

Another Frenchman, Louis Pasteur, was also a great pioneer of disease control. He produced effective vaccines against anthrax in 1881 and rabies in 1885. Later, Albert Calmette, a French physician, and Camille Guérin, a vet, developed the BCG vaccination against tuberculosis, while a German doctor, Emil von Behring, conquered diptheria.

More recently, American scientists developed two different kinds of polio vaccine. One, pioneered by Jonas Salk, uses an unactivated – killed – virus. The other, devised by Albert Sabin, relies on a live, but attenuated (weakened) virus. The former is injected, the method used in many European countries and the USA; the latter is administered orally in drop form.

Today, there are more than 300 vaccines for about 30 different diseases, including measles, mumps, rubella and hepatitis B. Some are highly effective and long-lasting; others must be administered regularly to maintain immunity.

SUGARING THE PILL
Albert Sabin's oral polio vaccine is often given on a sugar cube.

Just a speck of blood DNA profiling makes it possible to identify a person by analysing just a spot of blood or a drop of saliva. But who came up with the idea that this process would be invaluable in tracking down criminals and solving crimes?

On 6 June 1983, 32-year-old Rachel Kosub was found raped and strangled in the interior design shop where she worked in San Antonio, Texas, USA. Her murder remained unsolved for 20 years. But in 2003, detectives sent evidence that had been taken at the scene for DNA testing. The DNA evidence matched that of a man called Mike Dossett. Interviewed soon after the murder, Dossett had told detectives about a 'dream' he'd had that related to Rachel's death, but, though he remained a suspect for many years, there had never been any hard evidence that linked him to the crime scene. Dossett was tried for murder in January 2005, found guilty and sentenced to 40 years in jail. Without DNA profiling, the case against him would probably still be unproved. Thousands more criminal cases have been closed with the aid of this silent biological witness. But how did it all start?

Forensic breakthrough

Sir Alec Jeffreys, a geneticist at Leicester University, invented 'genetic fingerprinting' in 1984. The process he developed is based on the fact that small sections of human DNA repeat themselves and that different people have different numbers of repeats. These repeats, known as genetic stutters, can be counted to produce a highly specific sequence of 20 numbers. The odds against the numbers in a DNA sample taken from anyone other than an identical twin matching the numbers of a sample taken from anyone else are reckoned to be about a billion to one. So each of us possesses a genetic profile – or 'fingerprint' – that is totally unique.

'It was a "eureka" moment,' Jeffreys said of his discovery. 'We could immediately see the potential for forensic investigations.' To create genetic profiles, forensic investigators collect tissue samples, such as hair and body fluids, from a crime scene and any suspects. The DNA is extracted and analysed to create the profiles required and they are then compared. At first, fairly large amounts of

A FORENSIC REVOLUTION Alec Jeffreys holds aloft a comparison of DNA profiles in his office at Leicester University, England, in 1987. He published the first paper on DNA fingerprinting in 1985.

biological material were needed but the technology is now so sophisticated that only a tiny number of cells are needed to create a profile.

Tracking a murderer

Jeffreys' hypothesis was put to the test less than two years later when he used his profiling techniques for the first time in forensic history. The result was the first murder conviction to be obtained through DNA evidence. Colin Pitchfork, a Leicestershire baker, was found guilty of the separate killings of two 15-year-old girls, Lynda Mann and Dawn Ashworth, who lived just a few miles apart.

At first, the Leicestershire police were convinced that Richard Buckland, another local man, had committed both crimes, but, though Buckland confessed to the second murder, he refused to admit to the first. Jeffreys was called in to bolster the police case. But, after comparing samples taken the crime scenes with a blood sample from Buckland, he came up with a stunning conclusion. He proved that, though the same person had murdered both teenagers, it was impossible for Buckland to have been the perpetrator in either case. There was no DNA match.

The world's first mass DNA screening followed. Men in three villages were asked to volunteer blood or saliva samples to be tested. Some 4,582 complied. One who did not was Colin Pitchfork, who bribed a friend to supply a sample for him. When that friend was overheard bragging about what he had done, police followed the trail from him to Pitchfork. This time, Jeffreys established a complete match. Pitchfork's conviction followed.

Soon, forensic scientists around the world were mastering the techniques of DNA profiling. In 1987, Florida rapist Tommie Lee Andrews became the first American to be convicted as a result of the DNA evidence produced by the prosecution at his trial. The following year, Timothy Spencer was

Forensic science and fingerprints

As early as 1247, Song Ci, a notable Chinese judge, produced a book called *Yi Yuan Ji Yu* ('The Washing Away of Wrongs') that described how death by drowning and death by strangulation could be distinguished.

Fingerprints may have been used to establish identity as early as the 7th century AD, when an Arab merchant of the time described how it was customary for a debtor's fingerprints to be appended to a bill, which was then given to the lender. The bill was legally recognised as proof of the validity of the debt.

Modern fingerprinting dates from the 1880s, when the British scientist Sir Francis Galton devised a method of classifying fingerprints by grouping their patterns into arches, loops and whirls. He built on the work of Henry Faulds, a British surgeon who worked in Japan, and Sir William Herschel, chief magistrate in the Hooghly area of Bengal, India. Galton was able to prove scientifically what Herschel and Faulds had suspected: that fingerprints never

change during the course of a lifetime and that no two fingerprints are exactly the same. Galton calculated the chances of two individuals sharing a fingerprint as 64 billion to one.

Later, Sir Edward R. Henry, Chief Commissioner of the Metropolitan Police in London, improved on Galton's work. The result of these improvements was the Galton-Henry system of fingerprint classification. Officially adopted by Scotland Yard in 1901, the system is still universally accepted as the best way of classifying fingerprints.

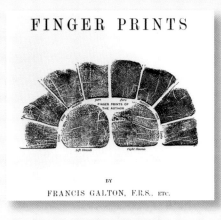

SIR FRANCIS GALTON'S FINGERPRINTS

the first person to be sentenced to death for murder in the USA as a result of DNA profiling.

Solving old crimes

It seemed to its advocates that the powers of the new technique were almost limitless. It also became clear that crimes did not have to be fresh for DNA profiling to be used to conclusive effect.

In Britain, James Lloyd terrorised women in the Rotherham area of South Yorkshire between 1983 and 1986. After sexually assaulting his victims, he stole their shoes and was nicknamed the 'shoe rapist'. For more than 15 years, he escaped justice until developments in forensic technology

meant that scientists could link his DNA to the crimes. In 2006, he was convicted and jailed.

The previous year, in Australia, DNA obtained from deep inside the homemade ropes he had used to tie up one of his two victims was crucial in the conviction of Bradley Murdoch for murder. In July 2001, Murdoch flagged down British backpackers Peter Falconio and Joanne Lees in their camper van in Alice Springs. He shot Falconio dead and tied up Lees, who eventually managed to escape. Despite Murdoch's protestations of innocence, the jury at the trial believed the scientists, who said that the DNA they had found in the ropes was 100 million times more likely to

GATHERING EVIDENCE Crime scene investigators or forensics officers wear protective clothing to avoid contaminating the evidence they collect. They comb the crime scene for samples of skin, hair and body fluids that can be used as sources of DNA for testing.

have come from him than anybody else. In 2008 in Britain, DNA evidence was similarly the key to securing the conviction of Steve Wright for the killing of five Ipswich prostitutes. All the other evidence produced in the case against him was purely circumstantial. There have been occasions, on the other hand, when the technique has been questioned. The most celebrated instance was in 1994, when US prosecutors relied on DNA evidence to link American football star O.J. Simpson to the killing of his ex-wife and an acquaintance.

When the case came to court, Simpson's lawyers convinced the jury that the DNA evidence was questionable. They attacked the way in which the evidence had been collected, claiming that there were problems with the manner in which blood samples had been processed and that the blood itself had become severely degraded during storage. Despite the testimony of experts from three crime laboratories, all of whom

agreed that the DNA in the drops of blood found at the scene of the crime matched that of Simpson, he was acquitted. Since then, a number of other lawyers have questioned the accuracy of results produced by the latest versions of the technique, particularly because samples put through analysis can now be extremely small. Even more controversial is the way in which a number of governments around the world have made it official policy to build up national DNA databases. In 2007, the USA's Combined DNA Index System held around 4.5 million records; the British DNA database holds about the same number.

> **A number of lawyers have questioned the accuracy of results produced by the technique**

Civil liberties

Many critics claim that the retention of such records in perpetuity amounts to an infringement of civil liberties and an attack on the rights of the individual. For their part, the agencies concerned point out that, while matching DNA profiles is invaluable

in linking people to a crime or crime scene, they can equally be used to clear innocent suspects. Official statistics show that around 30 per cent of the DNA profiles currently carried out by the Federal Bureau of Investigation result in the exclusion of suspects, and therefore DNA profiling is just as powerful and important a weapon in confirming innocence as it is in proving guilt.

Proving innocence

The Innocence Project in the USA was set up to investigate the cases of those who may have been wrongfully convicted or imprisoned in the past, and thanks to its efforts more than 200 people have had their convictions overturned. One of their main weapons has been the use of DNA evidence and all potential clients are carefully screened to see if DNA testing could prove their innocence.

One such was Eddie Joe Lloyd, who was convicted in 1985 of the murder of a 16-year-old girl in Detroit. Suffering from mental illness, he was arrested after he wrote to police with suggestions for solving several recent crimes. He was fed details of the crime by police and convinced to confess with the suggestion that he was in fact helping to unearth the actual killer. Seventeen years later his false conviction was overturned when DNA evidence showed that he could not have been the killer.

DNA solves mysteries of history

DNA profiling has helped to answer some enduring historical riddles. In 1994 the procedure finally satisfied most of the scientific community that the supposed remains of Tsar Nicholas II and the rest of the Russian royal family, executed by a Bolshevik firing squad in 1918, were genuine. In July 1991, bones were exhumed from a shallow grave outside Ekaterinburg, Russia, and the DNA compared with blood samples from living Romanov descendants, including Prince Philip, the Duke of Edinburgh. A series of tests confirmed that the bodies were those of the tsar, his wife and children. They also proved that Anna Anderson, a woman who had claimed to be the Grand Duchess Anastasia, was a fraud.

In December 1999, French royalists were disappointed when a myth of the French Revolution turned out to be just that. It had been claimed that the Dauphin, son of the executed French king, Louis XVI and his queen, Marie Antoinette, had escaped the revolutionaries. DNA from a heart

said to be that of the Dauphin was compared with samples from living and deceased members of the French royal family, including a lock of Marie Antoinette's hair. The samples matched closely, leading to the

NOT THE DAUPHIN Charles-Louis-Edmond de Bourbon with a picture of his ancestor, Carl Wilhelm Naundorff, whom he claimed was the lost Dauphin.

conclusion that the Dauphin had most likely died in a Paris prison in 1795.

In 1992, the technique was used to prove that a man calling himself Wolfgang Gerhard, who had drowned in a boating accident in Brazil, was none other than Dr Joseph Mengele. The notorious doctor, wanted for Nazi war crimes, had been in flight from justice since the collapse of the Third Reich in 1945.

LOST TSAR A gaunt Nicholas II in the woods following his abdication. The location of his body, and those of the rest of his family, remained a mystery for nearly 80 years.

FALSE CLAIMS In 1920, a woman known as Anna Anderson, a patient in a German mental hospital claimed to be the Grand Duchess Anastasia.

The hot planet When did global warming begin, and is there ever going to be a global cooling?

Human beings, *Homo sapiens sapiens*, evolved 200,000 years ago, a mere blink in the history of life on Earth, which dates back 3,800 million years. Throughout most of our time on Earth, the world has endured an Ice Age. Thick ice sheets and glaciers stretched down from the Arctic as far south as northern Europe and the Great Lakes of North America; global average temperatures were 10°C (50°F) colder than they are today. The ice caps contained so much of the Earth's water that, during the coldest periods, sea levels dropped to 120m (400ft) below their current levels, exposing land bridges that allowed human migrants to move into Australia from South-east Asia, and into North America from northeast Asia.

The one consistent rule of the Earth's climate is that it is never constant for long. About 11,000 years ago, the Earth warmed up and the ice retreated.

We entered the current epoch of geological history, the Holocene, which produced relatively warm global average temperatures of about 14°C (57°F). The warming coincided with the rapid development of human civilisation, with farming and urban culture. The Holocene climate is what we are used to. But is it 'normal'?

Between the Ice Ages

Snow traps air as it falls. By drilling out cores in polar ice sheets, scientists can analyse the air in layers of snow laid down as long as 800,000 years ago and trace climate fluctuations. The cores reveal a prolonged Ice Age, made up of long periods of cold known as 'glacials', punctuated every 40,000 to 100,000 years by relatively short periods of warming called 'interglacials', lasting about 10,000 to 12,000 years, and sometimes more. Our current period, the Holocene, is an interglacial.

In the 1970s this discovery caused some panic in the press and public imagination, if not so much among scientists. From 1940 to the mid-1970s, the global average temperature had fallen: winters were hard, notably in 1947 and 1962-3 in northern Europe. Now exceeding its 10,000th anniversary, was the current interglacial about to end and plunge the world into a new Ice Age?

The cause of the fluctuations between glacials and interglacials seems to be the slight irregularities in the way the Earth moves around the Sun. Over time, the Earth shifts between an elliptical (oval) orbit and a circular orbit. With an elliptical orbit, the Earth moves slightly further away from the Sun, leading to colder winters. The Earth also wobbles on its axis, which alters its tilt and affects the way its surface is exposed to the Sun. All these phenomena occur in

WINTERS ON THE THAMES During the 'Little Ice Age', the Thames in London froze so hard that people could walk, skate and even hold 'Frost Fairs' on it, as portrayed in this 17th-century painting.

A GREEN SAHARA A herd of giraffes engraved on rocks at Tassili des Ajjers, Algeria, reveal that the Sahara was a well-watered land in the Neolithic period, around 7,000 years ago.

cycles (called Milankovitch Cycles) of different lengths covering tens of thousands of years. Current thinking suggests that, under normal circumstances, the relatively warm temperatures of the Holocene might last some tens of thousands of years into the future, but estimates vary from 18,000 to 100,000 years.

Cold spells

Although the Holocene has produced a remarkably stable climate for more than 10,000 years, there have been fluctuations within it, of which the cold spell between 1940 and the mid-1970s was just one short example. The period from about AD 800 to 1300 is known as the Medieval Warm Period: global average temperatures appear to have been about as high as they are today, if not higher. Farming in Europe flourished and populations grew. The Greenland ice sheet withdrew, enabling Viking farmers to settle there after AD 985.

After 1300, winters became longer, the summer growing season shortened, and northern Europe suffered a 'Little Ice Age' from about 1560 until about 1870. Farming settlements in the mountains of Austria, Switzerland and Scandinavia were destroyed by advancing glaciers. During the coldest winters, the River Thames in London froze over for months, and 'Frost Fairs' were held on the ice, the last in 1814. Written accounts from Europe record the effects and distress of these times: it is not clear if the northern hemisphere alone was affected, but some evidence suggests that it was global.

Oscillations within an interglacial period are attributed to various phenomena, including cyclical variations in the Sun's surface activity and the cooling effect of massive volcanic

explosions that scatter millions of tonnes of sulphate particles high in the atmosphere, such as those that occurred in Iceland in 1783-84 and at Mount Tambora, Indonesia in 1815.

The great wipe-outs

These recent climatic fluctuations are shallow compared with some of the wilder swings of the more distant past. The Earth has been through much warmer phases, with global average temperatures as high as 22°C (72°F) and little or no ice at the poles. This was the case in the Triassic and Jurassic periods 251 to 145 million years ago, the era of the dinosaurs. Big shifts in climate and accompanying changes to habitat are thought to be the main causes of the seven periods of mass extinctions that have occurred in the Earth's past. One occurred at the end of the Permian era about 251 million years ago, when up to 90 per cent of animal species became extinct;

another at the end of the Cretaceous some 65 million years ago destroyed around half of the world's species, including the dinosaurs.

Theories about the causes of these climatic changes include collisions with large meteors that would have had the same catastrophic effect as the detonation of several million nuclear weapons. Nothing so spectacular is cited as the cause of the end of the last glacial period 11,000 years ago. A natural cycle of climatic change seems to have been enough to kill off the mammoths and numerous other large prehistoric mammals.

There is little talk these days about the threat of a new Ice Age. Since the mid-1970s, global average temperatures have followed an upward trend. The years since 1990 have included 10 of the hottest since records began in the 1850s. Is this just part of the normal cycle? It may be so: the global average temperature is roughly the same as it was in the Medieval Warm Period. But a new element has been causing concern: the effect of human activity, such as forest clearance, industrial pollution and, above all, the burning of fossil fuels (coal, petrol and natural gas). Is human activity aggravating a natural trend in global warming, an effect known as 'anthropogenic forcing'?

Global warming

In the early 19th century, the French mathematician and scientist Joseph Fourier proposed that the Earth's atmosphere played an essential role in keeping the world acceptably warm by trapping the Sun's heat, which would otherwise be bounced back into space.

Later, the Swedish chemist Svante Arrhenius elaborated on the theory, inventing the term 'greenhouse effect'. He also suggested that industrial pollution might complicate the greenhouse effect and cause a gradual warming. The main 'greenhouse gases' that retain the Sun's heat are water vapour (H_2O), carbon dioxide (CO_2), methane (CH_4), nitrous oxide (N_2O) and ozone (O_3). All occur naturally, but CO_2 in particular is produced by the burning of carbon-based fossil fuels. With increasing industrialisation,

especially since the 1970s, CO_2 emissions have risen to 380 parts per million (ppm) – higher than it has been in the past 800,000 years. And it is still rising, at a rate of nearly 2ppm every year.

This is a cause for concern because, historically, high levels of CO_2 have coincided with peaks in global temperature. If atmospheric CO_2 is now being pushed to an unprecedented level by human activity, then we run the risk of causing an unparalleled increase in world temperatures. The Earth is a highly complex 'climate machine' and there are numerous variables and areas of dispute. It is not even clear if CO_2 levels in the past have caused global temperatures to rise, or if natural increases in global temperatures have led to increases in CO_2 levels.

In 2007, the United Nations Intergovernmental Panel on Climate Change (IPCC) made the bold declaration – although tempered by some reservation – that 'most of the observed increase in globally averaged temperatures since the mid-20th century is very likely due to the observed increase in anthropogenic greenhouse gas concentrations'. Predictions suggest

that global average temperatures will continue to increase by as much as 6.4°C (43.5°F) by the year 2100, in the worst-case scenario. If that happens, polar glaciers and ice sheets will melt, causing sea levels to rise, threatening heavily populated coastal areas and cities. Melting glaciers might also disrupt the oceanic currents that dictate many of our weather patterns.

A warmer climate is likely to be more volatile, triggering an increase in storms, floods and droughts. Many species of plants and animals would not be able to adapt to the changes in habitat caused by a radical increase in temperature. Intense global warming would produce major climatic changes that would bring havoc to the world as we know it.

What is the time scale for such events? Computer projections suggest a vast range of possible outcomes, depending on the data used. But some scientists suggest that if carbon emissions rise to 450ppm by 2050, global average temperatures might reach a 'tipping point', after which recovery may be impossible. And then the natural – cooling – conclusion of our current interglacial period would be permanently postponed.

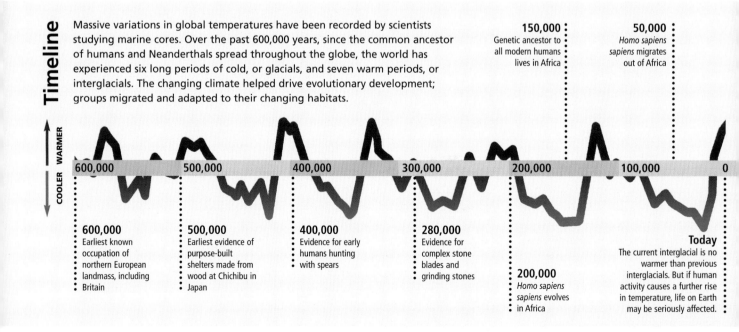

Timeline

Massive variations in global temperatures have been recorded by scientists studying marine cores. Over the past 600,000 years, since the common ancestor of humans and Neanderthals spread throughout the globe, the world has experienced six long periods of cold, or glacials, and seven warm periods, or interglacials. The changing climate helped drive evolutionary development; groups migrated and adapted to their changing habitats.

150,000
Genetic ancestor to all modern humans lives in Africa

50,000
Homo sapiens sapiens migrates out of Africa

WARMER / COOLER

600,000 500,000 400,000 300,000 200,000 100,000 0

600,000
Earliest known occupation of northern European landmass, including Britain

500,000
Earliest evidence of purpose-built shelters made from wood at Chichibu in Japan

400,000
Evidence for early humans hunting with spears

280,000
Evidence for complex stone blades and grinding stones

200,000
Homo sapiens sapiens evolves in Africa

Today
The current interglacial is no warmer than previous interglacials. But if human activity causes a further rise in temperature, life on Earth may be seriously affected.

When and why did the world's rainforests start to disappear?

It is hard to estimate how much of the world's surface was covered with woodland in the past. But what is certain is that our ancestors were burning and hacking down forests as soon as they learnt how to use fire and make sharp tools, at least 250,000 years ago. The process accelerated with the arrival of agriculture around 11,000 years ago. Forests were cleared to make arable land and pasture. Through the Bronze and Iron Ages, wood was used as a fuel to cook and to provide warmth, build houses, make weapons, furniture, boats and ships, and heat kilns and smelting furnaces.

Ancient expansion

Writing in the 4th century BC, Plato bemoaned the deforestation around Athens and the resulting soil erosion. Roman expansion devoured the forests around the Mediterranean before it turned to northern Europe. When European nations expanded globally in the 16th century, they took their hunger for timber with them. Plantation crops – sugar in the Caribbean, tea in India, cotton and tobacco in America – often demanded tree-clearance. From the late 18th century, the Industrial Revolution was even more voracious and after the 1850s was consuming timber from all the continents, bar Antarctica, at a faster rate than ever. The railways alone needed wood for 3,000 million sleepers worldwide.

Around 90 per cent of global deforestation probably took place before 1950. The rate of loss has continued unabated since then: the world's population has doubled in the last 40 years and continues to rise, putting increased pressure on forests and woodlands for all their uses.

In recent years, there has been a strong correlation made between destruction of the forests and an increase in global warming. Since

1970, over 600,000km² (232,000 sq miles) of Amazon rainforest have been destroyed, 150,000km² (58,000 sq miles), or 0.8 per cent of it between May 2000 and August 2006 alone. The Amazon holds the richest concentration of plants and animals on Earth and deforestation threatens this unique biodiversity and the potential for scientific discovery.

But it is a fine balancing act: the periods of heaviest forest clearance match those of Brazilian economic growth. It has also been argued that tax incentives that favour pastureland over natural forest ensure that forest

LAID BARE Clearance of rainforest in the Amazon Basin for oil exploration has a disastrous impact on the environment. It also encourages other forms of encroachment, such as agriculture, that in turn lead to impoverishment and erosion of the soil.

clearing is seen as a good hedge against inflation. These, combined with subsidised agriculture and programmes of colonisation, encourage the Amazon's destruction. Elsewhere, there is increased belief in the potentially calamitous consequences, but little agreement as to how it should be stopped.

LIVING AND WORKING 6

Time waits for no man
Who was it that decided our lives should be composed of seconds, minutes, hours, days, weeks, months and years?

'So what is time? If no one asks me, I know; if I seek to explain it, I do not know.' So stated the great church father St Augustine (AD 354-430).

The nature of time has fascinated philosophers and physicists alike. While formulating his laws of motion in the 17th century, Isaac Newton conceived the universe as a mechanism running, as it were, on a stream of time that moves at a constant rate for all observers. That clockwork notion remained the consensus for many generations of scientists and still seems intuitively true to most of us today. But in 1905, Albert Einstein's Special Theory of Relativity proposed a radically different view that appeared to defy all common sense. Using sophisticated mathematics, he

> ## 'So what is time? If no one asks me, I know; if I seek to explain it, I do not know.'
> St Augustine of Hippo

demonstrated that the rate at which time passes, as measured by a clock, is not the same for different observers in different frames of reference. Space and time are intimately connected, forming a four-dimensional continuum of length, breadth, depth – and time.

But for most of us, big conceptual questions do not much trouble our daily lives. Newton's clockwork laws remain accurate enough for us to synchronise our wristwatches and arrive at work, catch a train or meet for dinner at pretty much the same time.

The most primitive tribal societies evolved ways of measuring time,

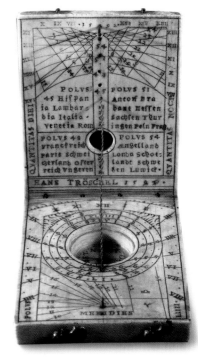

POCKET GADGET The 1592 German pocket sundial had a gazetteer of cities and their latitudes inscribed on its case, enabling travellers to orientate the dial and read the time from the correct scale.

sufficient for the needs of everyday life. Measurement started with reference to the Sun and Moon. The basic unit was the day – the time taken for the Earth to revolve on its axis around the Sun. The apparent

HERE COMES THE SUN The Samrat Yantra sundial in Delhi was built in the early 18th century to measure local time and the coordinates of the stars.

progress of the Sun through the heavens was measured by observing its position, or the length of its shadow. So it became possible to discern midday – the time when it was directly overhead and the shadow dwindled to its shortest length. A full natural day might then be reckoned from midday to midday. Any upright stick could be used to check the direction and length of the Sun's shadow; such sticks were used as early as 3500 BC.

In ancient civilisations more elaborate sundials were devised and served the western world for time-keeping for many centuries. In fact, anything that moved at a steady rate might be used for measurement. In ancient Egypt, short intervals were measured by the flow of water through a hole in the bottom of a vessel calibrated with a scale of hours. Anglo-Saxon monarch King Alfred is said to have used the burning of a candle to measure time. The draining of sand through an hourglass was employed from the Middle Ages – and is still used in the kitchen egg-timer.

Defining units of time

Where did the concept of the hour come from? The natural daily cycle is divided up into 24 hours according to a fairly arbitrary convention first established in ancient civilisations, such as Egypt, India and China. Their timekeepers subdivided the day either into one-twelfth of the time between Sunrise and Sunset; or one twenty-fourth of a full day. Both divisions reflected the widespread use of numbering in units of 12, the so-called duodecimal numbering system, which employs the dozen rather than 10 as its base (page 224).

Where 'day' meant the duration of daylight hours (rather than the full 24-hour cycle) some anomalies arose. Even in medieval Europe, before mechanical clocks came into use, an hour was one-twelfth of the period of daylight – so winter hours were shorter

Naming the days of the week

Where did the days of the week – and months of the year – get their names from? In pagan Britain the days of the week took their names from heavenly bodies or the gods associated with them. So, Sunday was the day of the Sun, and Monday that of the Moon. Tuesday seems to have been named for a warrior god named Tiw, Wednesday for Odin, chief of the gods. Thursday was named for Thor, the Teutonic god of thunder (above, with his hammer); Friday was the day of Frigg, wife of Odin; and Saturday was the day of Saturn, the planet and Roman god of agriculture. The names endured in Britain after its conversion to Christianity, though elsewhere in Europe, Church terminology sometimes triumphed over the pagan precedents. In France, for example, Sunday is Dimanche and in Portugal Domingo, both signifying the Lord's Day.

The months of the year are based on Roman models:
JANUARY: Janus, god of thresholds and beginnings
FEBRUARY: from *februum*, purification, a month of ritual cleansing
MARCH: from Mars, god of war
APRIL: from *aperire*, to open, a month when leaves open
MAY: Maia, goddess of growth
JUNE: Juno, goddess and wife of Jupiter
JULY: from Julius Caesar, who reorganised the calendar
AUGUST: from the emperor Augustus
SEPTEMBER: from *septem*, seven*
OCTOBER: from *octo*, eight*
NOVEMBER: from *novem*, nine*
DECEMBER: from *decem*, ten*
 * seventh, eighth, ninth and tenth months counting from March, the first month of the old Roman calendar.

Days of the week

English	French	German	Italian	Spanish
Monday	Lundi	Montag	Lunedi	Lunes
Tuesday	Mardi	Dienstag	Martedi	Martes
Wednesday	Mercredi	Mittwoch	Mercoledi	Miércoles
Thursday	Jeudi	Donnerstag	Giovedi	Jueves
Friday	Vendredi	Freitag	Venerdi	Viernes
Saturday	Samedi	Samstag	Sabato	Sábado
Sunday	Dimanche	Sonntag	Domenica	Domingo

than summer ones. The big clocks that appeared on cathedrals from the 14th century helped to spread the concept of fixed hours among ordinary people. The clocks did not have hands or a dial, but struck a bell every hour.

We have 60 minutes in an hour and 60 seconds in a minute because the Babylonians based their numbers on units of 60 (a multiple of 12). Around 2000 BC, they had a calendar with 360 days divided into 12 months of 30 days each. Their mathematicians chose a base number which divides up conveniently in a multitude of ways, so easing calculations with vulgar fractions.

While the Earth's relationship with the Sun gave us our notion of the day and of daylight hours, it also gave us the standard concept of the year. On average, our planet completes its orbit around the Sun every 365.24 days.

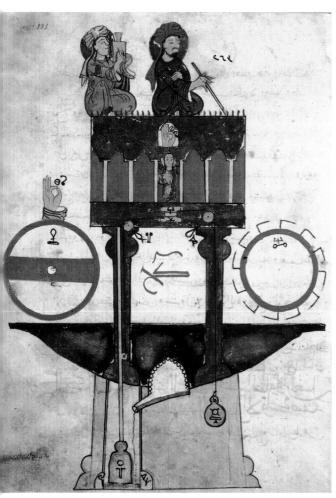

AUTOMATIC TIME A water-powered clock by 13th-century inventor Al-Jazari. A working model of the clock was constructed at London's Science Museum in 1976.

Unfortunately, this is not a round number and it gave calendar-makers headaches over the centuries. A calendar was an important grouping of days, which helped people to plan for agricultural activities as well as for business, religious festivals and domestic life.

Julius Caesar's leap year

To overcome the problem of a fractional day, the 'leap year' was devised. Julius Caesar introduced the system in 46 BC. Under his 'Julian Calendar', an extra day, 29 February, was added every four years. But this ingenious solution did leave a small discrepancy that added up over many years. In 1582 Pope Gregory XIII amended the Julian Calendar by adding a leap year only in 97 years out of every 400 (a closer approximation than 100 out of 400). The Gregorian Calendar was adopted in England in 1752, and is now used by most of the world.

Lunar calendars

In some cultures the annual calendar is built not around the Sun, but around the Moon's orbit of the Earth. The word 'month' comes from the Moon which takes about 29.5 days to travel round our planet and does it just over 12 times in a year. The Jewish calendar has 12 months of 29 or 30 days and an extra month is inserted seven times in a 19-year period. The Hindu calendar employs the concept of lunar days, which are precise thirtieths of a lunar month, and so do not match up with natural solar days. The standard western calendar is also based on the Moon's cycle. But because there are exactly 12 months in a year, the months do not quite keep in step with the Moon's phases.

As for the concept of the week, there is no special reason why it should consist of seven days – indeed the ancient Romans originally had an eight-day market cycle independent of months and years. The seven-

ETERNALLY ACCURATE A prototype clock conceived and built by the international cultural institution, the Long Now Foundation. It is designed to keep time for 10,000 years into the future.

In some cultures the calendar is built not around the Sun, but around the Moon's orbit of the Earth

day week was introduced in Rome in the first century AD, not by Christians or Jews but by believers in Persian astrology. A day was allocated to each of the five then-known planets, plus one each for the Sun and the Moon, making seven. When Christianity was declared the official religion of the Roman empire in the time of the Emperor Constantine (c.AD 325), the familiar biblical Hebrew-Christian week of seven days, starting on Sunday, became conflated with the pagan week and took its place in the Julian calendar.

Jigsaw of measurement

Creating a calendar with all its subdivisions involved fitting many different pieces of information into a jigsaw of time measurement. The

data included movements of the Sun, Moon and planets, as well as the need to anticipate the seasonal rhythms of ploughing, sowing and harvesting. Festive celebrations were also important. It was not until AD 336 that 25 December was declared the official date for celebrating Christmas (partly to replace the pagan winter solstice which celebrated the rebirth of the Sun).

Making time more precise

For thousands of years, when most people lived by farming the land, a few basic guidelines sufficed. Day began at cockcrow; livestock were penned as the Sun went down. At regular intervals communities were summoned to prayer by the tolling of church bells.

From about 1500, members of the gentry might carry a pocket watch powered by a mainspring, for private timekeeping. But it was the industrial age that created a more general need for precisely agreed time. Stage coaches, railway timetables, production schedules, the clocking in and out of factories and offices – all called for synchronisation – a tightening up of consensus about the time of day. Wristwatches started to become popular in France and Switzerland around 1900 and became increasingly indispensable for people in all industrialised nations.

Vital seconds

Modern science requires ever-greater precision in time measurement. Today, digital watches – and now mobile phones and computers – keep time with incredible accuracy, using quartz crystals and their natural vibrations at 100,000 times per second. The second itself has achieved a new status; it is no longer conceived as a mere subdivision of the minute, but the very basis of time measurement and defined by the frequency of radiation emitted in a specified transmission of an isotope of caesium.

When were time zones synchronised?

From the 19th century, railways and telegraph messages created a shrinking world and with it a need for practical thinking about time measurement. While pocket watches allowed the traveller to calculate time intervals with precision, there could be no time of day when people everywhere experienced a given time simultaneously. When it is midday in one spot, places to the east of that spot are already into their afternoon and it is still morning for those to the west.

While overland transport was confined to horse-drawn vehicles it had not mattered if Rome's midday, for example, was slightly later than Paris's. But trains travelling at a fixed number of miles per hour required a standard agreement on time, as did telegraphy, otherwise a message transmitted from east to west would appear to arrive before it had been sent.

Greenwich Mean Time

In 1880 the whole of Britain adopted the average local time at Greenwich, site of the Royal Observatory, as its standard, Greenwich Mean Time (GMT). Not long after, the systematisation of time measurement was introduced globally. At an international conference in 1884, the world was divided into 24 time zones, each about 15 degrees of longitude in width. Anomalies for the world traveller were reduced – though people sailing from Europe to the Americas, for example, had to get used to putting their watches back an hour for every time zone crossed.

STRAIGHT DOWN THE MIDDLE
0° longitude, the Prime Meridian, at Greenwich Royal Observatory, London.

Welcome to the working week
Most people today work a five-day week. But who decided that we should work all day – and that it was necessary to have a 'job'?

TOILING AWAY Medieval peasants rented small plots of agricultural land to grow crops for the landowners. They received any surplus for their own families.

Work is a fact of modern life. Children grow up knowing that one day they will have to earn a living. As adults we divide our waking hours into work and leisure, in the rueful knowledge that we have to submit to the former if we want to enjoy the latter. For most, work takes up five-sevenths of a week and about the same fraction of each lifetime. Our work is central to our sense of self, even at times when we are doing other things. Most, when asked who or what they are, will reply by stating their paid occupation: 'I am a teacher ... a doctor ... a farmer ...'

The first humans did not work in the way that we understand it today. Our distant ancestors spent much of their time searching for that day's food and shelter, a short-term and endlessly repeated process that was necessary for survival. Work today means consciously striving now in order to accrue a benefit in the future,

but is not as immediately urgent as hunter-gathering. The idea of the working day is a product of civilisation, and must have arisen at the same time as agriculture around 10,000 years ago in Mesopotamia. For most of history – well into the 20th century in Russia and China – the majority of people were peasants who subsisted by working the fields. They sowed and tilled, knowing that they would reap a crop to see them through the next winter. These people were by definition 'at work' in a sense that pre-civilised hunters weren't. So work is a consequence of a settled society – and so too is the more refined concept of a 'job'. Once a society reaches a certain level of sophistication, it finds it has need of specialists. Skilled people such

> **Our distant ancestors spent much of their time searching for that day's food and shelter**

as blacksmiths, carpenters, bakers, tailors, doctors and priests needed long years of training in order to perform their roles – and could not do that if they had to spend all their time growing vegetables and tilling fields. So civilised society allowed certain skilled individuals to opt out of the business of producing food. In exchange for the specialised services they provided, they were permitted to live off some of the surplus that the rest of the community produced.

Specialised professions
The more complex a society becomes and the more efficient it becomes at producing food, the greater the number of specialised professions it engenders. Eventually, a society becomes so complex and so efficient that most people are freed to do work that is far removed from the formerly all-consuming business of agriculture. This is the situation that society finds itself in today. The circumscribed livelihoods of people such as professional footballers, commercial airline pilots, estate agents, television presenters and management consultants can be accommodated – because we enjoy the luxury of a plentiful supply of food.

The same abundance made it possible for people not to work at all on some days. Over the course of the past 150 years, the working week of an average European or American has grown shorter and shorter. In 1849,

CREATING MORE BUYERS As well as introducing the first moving assembly line – a process copied by other companies like Chevrolet – in 1914 Henry Ford raised his workers' wages to $5 a day, reasoning that richer workers could afford to buy his cars.

when Britain's industrial might was at its peak, an English factory worker would be at his station for 12 hours and 15 minutes a day, six days a week; the working week for an unskilled person was 73 hours and 30 minutes. Shop assistants worked even longer, often 18 hours a day, six days a week – or 108 hours. It was in the retail sector in Britain that the idea of a 'short Saturday' took root. A religious organisation called the Metropolitan Early Closing Association proposed a half-day for Saturdays. The Association argued that shop workers were so tired on Sundays that they rarely went to church services. Give them Saturday afternoon off, and church attendance might go up. It was up to individual employers to decide for or against the short Saturday, and – perhaps surprisingly – many of them

found in favour of giving their hard-working employees more free time.

This was the first step towards the invention of the weekend. In 1850, the British Factory Act limited the working week for women and children to a 12-hour day on weekdays and a 2 p.m. finish on Saturdays. In 1878, the number of hours worked Monday to Saturday was cut to 56 for women and children. The six-day week was now a five-and-a-half-day week.

Incredible shrinking week

The half-day's work done on Saturdays was whittled down by changes in the law and by the lobbying of the trade unions. By the 1930s, the two-day weekend was standard in the United Kingdom. Elsewhere, including the United States, a full six-day week was still expected. In the USA, the

move to a short working Saturday, and then to a non-working Saturday, came about quite quickly before the Second World War. One of the first sectors to adopt the practice was the clothes-making industry, where a high proportion of the workforce was Jewish. A free day on Saturday made it possible for Jewish people to work alongside Gentiles and still observe the Saturday Sabbath. One American supporter of the two-day weekend was Henry Ford, an anti-unionist and unapologetic capitalist who might have been expected to try to squeeze every drop of sweat out of his employees. In fact he cut the working day in his plants from nine to eight hours as early as 1914, and in 1926 became one of the first American businessmen to close the factory gates on a Saturday. He backed the two-day weekend because he reckoned that people would use the extra leisure time to take to the roads and so the longer weekend would have the effect of raising demand for his automobiles.

In France, the five-and-a-half-day week was introduced in the 1920s, and was known as the *semaine anglaise*. The five-day week did not come until after the *événements* – the student protests and general strike

HIGH DAYS Workers from the north of England celebrate Wakes Week, the annual holiday for mill workers, at Blackpool in 1955. Special trains were laid on for them.

Where was the first factory?

It is reasonable to say that the first factory was in England – but its whereabouts depends on the definition of a factory. If it is a place where unfinished materials are turned into useable objects, one strong candidate is the ironworks at Coalbrookdale in Shropshire, sometimes called the 'birthplace of the Industrial Revolution'. Here, in 1709, Abraham Darby was the first to use coke to fuel a blast furnace for making iron pots. But at least 20 years before, a more primitive furnace at Coalbrookdale turned out balls for muskets and cannons.

If a factory is more narrowly defined as a building designed to house a mechanised manufacturing operation, then the first one was the Lombe Brothers' Silk Mill, on an island in the River Derwent in Derby. In production from 1719, the factory was powered by a water wheel that drove banks of weaving and spinning machines in the five-storey edifice.

The whole process, from raw material to finished product, was carried out under the same roof. It was a new and surprising way of making things, and not everybody was sure it was a good idea. The writer Daniel Defoe saw the Lombe factory in 1720, but failed to realise that he was looking at the future. 'Here is a curiosity in trade worth observing,' he wrote, 'as being the only one of its kind in England, namely, a throwster's [spinner's] mill, which performs by a wheel turn'd by the water … [It] performs the labour of many hands. Whether it answers the expence or not, that is not my business.'

COALBROOKDALE BY NIGHT, PAINTED BY PHILIP JAMES DE LOUTHERBOURG

of May 1968 that brought the whole country to a standstill. In workplaces across France, millions of irate employees downed tools to rally against harsh conditions and poor wages. In parts of Eastern Europe the weekend took even longer to arrive: free Saturdays were one of the demands of the Solidarity movement in Poland led by Lech Walesa that challenged the communist authorities in the 1980s over workers' rights.

Le weekend

In the Soviet Union the idea of a weekend was for many years so alien that there was no word for it. Even after the two-day weekend was introduced, Russians either had to say 'Saturday and Sunday' or else shoehorn the English term into the very different phonology of their native tongue: the word *ooikent*. Many other countries do the same: French for the weekend is 'le weekend'. The term, like the two consecutive lazy days it stands for, is one of England's gifts to the world.

Who invented the modern-day office?

Office work is, in a sense, as old as writing. Ancient Egyptian scribes, sitting cross-legged on the floor, were history's first pen-pushers. In medieval Europe, monks and priests, the only entirely literate section of society, carried out the business of keeping official records. The double meaning of the word 'cleric' – which denotes someone who does God's work on the one hand and paperwork on the other – dates back to the time when he was one and the same person.

By the 17th century, a class of laymen who did office work at a place outside the home had emerged. They were mostly civil servants working for government, but other organisations – large commercial companies, banks, law firms, warehouses and workshops – also had need of clerks and accountants to keep track of stock, workflow, orders and payments. The 19th century saw the rise of the 'black-coated workers' – armies of minimally educated young men who spent their days bent over ledgers in bleak counting houses.

The shift from the kind of bureau frequented by the underpaid heroes of Charles Dickens' novels to the modern office began in the 1880s, after the invention of the typewriter. It was the Trojan horse that gave women access to the all-male workplace, because operating the new machines was seen as a womanly accomplishment. 'Typewriting and shorthand are twin arts,' declared one London journal in 1891. 'Young ladies who aspire to succeed in one must make themselves proficient in the other. A typist who cannot write shorthand is very much like a pianist who cannot read music.'

The advent of the typewriter also marked the beginning of the mechanisation of the white-collar workplace. The first office buildings, like the first factories, came about because of the need to accommodate the cumbersome machinery involved: telephone switchboards, franking machines – then later photocopiers, fax machines, servers and computers.

Office buildings also required an internal layout that reflected the hierarchy and workflow of the administrative process: boardrooms, separate workspaces for managers with anterooms for their secretaries, executive bathrooms, typing pools and canteens. No single building exhibited all these features at once. The architecture of the modern office evolved gradually – like the bright, blinking computer terminal that now stands on every office-worker's desk.

EXERCISING SKILL Typists, such as these Italian women pictured in 1938, were tested for strength as well as speed – continuous banging of heavy keys was arduous work.

Past its sell-by date It is now often cheaper to buy a new item than to mend an old one. Who invented built-in obsolescence as an industrial strategy?

It is often supposed that planned obsolescence is a modern idea, a commercial strategy of the electronic age. It is also assumed that the practice is a by-product of a society in which consumers upgrade all the time because they can easily afford to do so, that it is a result of too much affluence. In fact, neither assumption is true: the term was coined at least 80 years ago; and the concept that it represented gained wide currency in the 1930s because it seemed to offer a way out of the Great Depression.

The term 'planned obsolescence' first appeared in print in a pamphlet that was published privately in 1932. Its author was a New York property developer named Bernard London. Looking back to the years before the Wall Street Crash, London wrote that: ' ... in the earlier period of prosperity, the American people did not wait until the last possible bit of use had been extracted from every commodity. They gave up old homes and old automobiles long before they were worn out, merely because they were obsolete ... They have now

gone to the other extreme and have become retrenchment-mad. People everywhere are today disobeying the law of obsolescence.'

Obsolescence by decree?

London went on to argue that citizens should be encouraged to junk their old stuff and buy new things – even though times were hard – because to do so would stimulate production in factories, get cash flowing through the retail sector, and so speed the recovery of the American economy. But the means he proposed to achieve this were decidedly authoritarian. He recommended that the US government 'assign a lease of life to shoes and homes and machines, to all products of manufacture'. When the time allotted to items such as a table and chairs was up, owners would be legally obliged to 'turn in their used and obsolete goods to certain governmental agencies'. In return, citizens would receive a voucher that they could put towards the cost of new goods. The

practical part of London's plan was, not surprisingly, ignored. But the paradoxical idea that there was money to be made from short-lived goods struck a chord with manufacturers. Since the lifespan of a product could not actually be fixed by law, as London proposed, then perhaps there was a technical means of achieving the same end.

One company known to have looked into the possibility was General Electric. In the early 1930s the firm conducted experiments to see if they could make their lightbulbs burn out more quickly. They looked at whether they could artificially engineer their products to have a shorter lifespan. 'If this were done,' ran a memo from the research department, 'we estimate that it would result in increasing our flashlight business approximately 60 per cent. We see no logical reason ... why such a change should not be made.' In the event, the company did not act on the proposal. What is more, no company has ever admitted to deliberately designing its products to break or fail sooner than they should. And in any case, 'death-dating', as this shadowy practice became known, can only work in a situation where one company has a monopoly of the market.

When there is open competition, consumers are likely to gravitate

> **Our whole economy is based on planned obsolescence**
>
> Clifford Brooks Stevens

OUT OF FAVOUR Gadgets such as these first generation Blackberry phones are often superseded by new models within a year or two of purchase.

towards the brand of lightbulb that seems to last longer. But after the Second World War, a new form of planned obsolescence came to the fore. And this time the consumer, far from being kept in the dark about it, willingly bought into it. The new twist on the idea was that manufacturers could use design to make people want to buy a product that they already owned. By constantly tweaking the appearance of an object, and by the clever use of branding and advertising, people could be persuaded to buy new versions of expensive and perfectly serviceable products, such as radios, TVs, even cars and houses. They would do this simply because they had come to believe that the old one looked out-of-date.

The lure of the new

The main proponent of this novel approach was a gifted industrial designer named Clifford Brooks Stevens. In 1954, he defined planned obsolescence as 'instilling in the buyer the desire to own something a little newer, a little better, a little sooner than is necessary'. Brooks Stevens claimed to have coined the term

'planned obsolescence' though in fact he had borrowed it from Bernard London – along with many of London's economic arguments.

'Our whole economy is based on planned obsolescence,' said Brooks Stevens in 1958. 'We make good products, we induce people to buy them, and then next year we deliberately introduce something that will make those products look old-fashioned, obsolete. We do that for the soundest reason: to make money.'

Brooks Stevens had a point: there would be no clothing industry, for example, if everyone waited until each shirt and jacket was threadbare before buying a new one. He also pointed out that the kind of psychologically induced planned obsolescence that he advocated was not as wasteful as it appeared, as many of the redundant goods – the two-year-old cars and last year's shoes – retained part of their value and were passed on down through the economy as second-hand items.

Brooks Stevens' ideas were controversial and widely challenged, but no one at the time countenanced that there could be serious ecological or environmental objections to

PERSONALITY MATCH A 1960s' magazine advertisement from the USA promoting Kelvinator fridges. It suggests an indelible link between the personality of the purchaser, their life and personal style, and the product they choose to buy.

design-led obsolescence. The notion that there were dangers to consigning hazardous items, such as unwanted mobile phones, computer monitors and refrigerators, to landfill sites was still in the future.

Electronics are the modern-day battleground of planned obsolescence. Computer technology is moving so fast that many users want to upgrade their hardware every two years – or less. Given that this is the case, there is no point in constructing digital cameras, MP3 players, laptops and flatscreens that will still be going strong when the machines are already technologically and psychologically obsolete. And so manufacturers use cheaper components that they know will break down in, say, five years or so. It is not exactly death-dating, but it looks a lot like it.

The book of knowledge Where did the idea of the encyclopedia as a great work of reference originally come from?

WORK OF ENLIGHTENMENT French writer-philosopher Denis Diderot's *Encyclopédie* was put together in the 18th century by 150 'men of letters and skilled workmen'. Its compilation took more than 30 years; on completion it comprised 35 volumes, including 12 volumes dedicated to engraved illustrations.

Long before the coming of writing, tribal knowledge and memories were preserved by oral tradition through storytelling. Myths and legends had a practical function, illustrating the people's engagement with their natural environment, recalling ancestry and illustrating morality, heroic themes and sacred truths. In prehistoric societies the repository of oral tradition might be a shamanic figure, bridging the gap between the natural and spirit worlds; later, castes of poets and scholars emerged, like the bards of European tradition, or the griot poets – the praise singers and musicians working in West Africa today.

The first encyclopedias were not books at all but sweeping epics that encompassed much of traditional knowledge in monumental and unified poetic visions. The Puranas of Hindu literature first appear in the 2nd century AD, expounding much earlier Indian lore relating to genealogies, law, the Earth and the cosmos and the exploits of gods and heroes. In the first books of knowledge everywhere, distinctions between human and divine affairs would long be blurred.

Greek and Roman influence

Composed in the 8th century BC, Homer's epic *Iliad* and *Odyssey* share the same mythological grandeur. But as knowledge became more specialised and differentiated, the Greeks invented the term *enkyklopaideia* to describe instruction in the whole circle of learning, or what we might today term

a 'general education.' They did not, at the time, imply an individual book, or books, of knowledge, though such philosophers as Aristotle (384-322 BC) did write on a wide range of subjects.

The Romans are credited with putting together the first systematised compendia that attempted to embrace all the sciences. Pliny the Elder's 37-volume *Historia naturalis* (c.AD 77) was a milestone, with material drawn from astrology, geography, agriculture, medicine, precious stones, botany and zoology. Though Pliny did not always discriminate fact from folklore, a respect for nature and a spirit of scientific curiosity mark his work. He writes that 'The largest land animal is the elephant, and it is the nearest to man in intelligence.' On the social life of bees, he notes: 'Their work is marvellously mapped out in the following manner. A guard is posted at the gates, after the manner of a camp. They sleep until dawn, until one bee wakes them up with a double or triple buzz as a sort of bugle call. Then they fly forth in a body.'

Widening horizons are revealed in Pliny's description of remote Iceland (which he calls Thule) 'in which as we have pointed out there are no nights at midsummer when the Sun is passing through the sign of the Crab, and on the other hand no days at midwinter; indeed some writers think this is the case for periods of six months at a time without a break'.

Pliny's nephew and heir, Pliny the Younger, wrote of him that 'He began to work long before daybreak … He read nothing without making extracts; he used even to say that there was no book so bad as not to contain something of value … When travelling, as though freed from every other care, he devoted himself to study alone. In short, he deemed all time wasted that was not employed in study.'

The passion for knowledge led indirectly to his demise. Pliny the Elder died in AD 79 while investigating the catastrophic eruption of the volcano Vesuvius – though it is thought more likely that he succumbed to a stroke or heart attack than that he was overcome by volcanic fumes.

The Cyclopaedia

Pliny's *Historia naturalis* remained a major source of scientific knowledge throughout the Middle Ages and beyond. And the idea that all information could be contained in one big book gained ground after the Renaissance. Scholars increasingly arranged articles alphabetically and chose to write them in everyday

language (rather than Latin) to make information more accessible. Published in 1728, Englishman Ephraim Chambers' two-volume *Cyclopaedia, or Universal Dictionary of Arts and Sciences*, was the first to use cross-references so that 'a chain may be carried on from one end of an article to the other'. This approach reflected Chambers' aim of presenting the sum of knowledge as a coherent whole. Chambers championed freedom of thought and his book's obvious hostility to religious dogma offended many men of the church, both Protestant and Catholic.

In the 18th century it was still possible to envisage individual readers possessing a comprehensive knowledge of just about all there was to know at that time. And every man or woman freed from ignorance would improve the future of humanity. The pioneering *Cyclopaedia* inspired a further landmark in the radical French *Encyclopédie* of the writer-philosopher Denis Diderot and the physicist-mathematician Jean le Rond d'Alembert. This began as a commissioned translation of Chambers' work but became a great compendium of original scholarship. Published in 35 volumes from 1751-80, it included more than 70,000 articles on subjects ranging from Asparagus to Zodiac. As work progressed, contributors came to number more than 150 scholars dedicated to the advancement of reason and science. They included such

> **Diderot was harassed by threats of police raids. His sight was damaged by hours of toil**

leading Enlightenment figures as Voltaire, Jean-Jacques Rousseau and Charles de Secondat, baron de Montesquieu, dubbed the *philosophes*, or philosophers. The whole project was imbued with radical philosophy, propounding a rational explanation of the universe and a secular morality. In promoting reason above religious faith, the so-called Encyclopédists presented a major intellectual challenge to the authority of church and state. Diderot was harassed by threats of police raids. His eyesight was damaged by the long hours of toil over manuscripts and proofs, and publication was twice suspended by the authorities. But because the critique of church and state was more implied than explicit, the *Encyclopédie* was eventually published in full.

Knowledge for political change

In 1770, the Crown official Antoine-Louis Séguier warned that 'The philosophers have with one hand sought to shake the throne, with the other to upset the altars. Their purpose was to change public opinion on civil and religious institutions, and the revolution has, so to speak, been effected. History and poetry, romances and even dictionaries, have been infected with the poison of incredulity. Their writings are hardly published in the capital before they inundate the provinces like a torrent. The contagion has spread into workshops and cottages.' The philosophers' great book of knowledge was among the major influences not only on the coming French Revolution, but in inspiring a radical, freethinking spirit that animated an age of revolutions across the face of a continent. As Voltaire himself remarked, France was becoming 'Encyclopédist' – and the whole of Europe too.

The ideological bias of the *Encyclopédie* resulted in omissions

ROMAN NATURE Pliny the Elder's only surviving work, *Historia naturalis,* describes in detail the making of papyrus, as well as chronicling Rome's vast art collection and gold mining in Spain.

How English was codified: Doctor Johnson's Dictionary

Writers in Shakespeare's day cared little for spelling rules, but needs changed with the spread of printing and rise of public literacy. Books became more widely available, requiring standard grammar, definitions and the spelling of words on the printed page.

The dictionary published by Samuel Johnson (1709-84) was not the first to come out in English, but the quality of definitions, based on meticulous research, made it stand out in its day, and it became a touchstone for all dictionaries that followed.

Johnson was a poet, essayist and critic who had left Oxford without taking a degree, and relied on hack journalism for making money. He was six feet tall, clumsy, partially blind and deaf. His biographer James Boswell reports that the painter William Hogarth thought Johnson an 'idiot' until he revealed his eloquence in speaking. Johnson's gruff aphorisms would become proverbial. His celebrated *A Dictionary of the English Language* appeared in 1755 after nine years' work. One feature was his use of quotations to illustrate usage. For Zed, for example, his definition read: 'Zed n.s The name of the letter z. Thou whoreson zed, thou unnecessary letter. Shakespeare.'

The dictionary also revealed many prejudices. Johnson was famously derogatory about the Scots, and his definition for 'Oats' was 'A grain, which in England is generally given to horses, but in Scotland supports the people.' In another entry he defined 'Patron' as 'Commonly a wretch who supports with insolence, and is paid with flattery'. His target was the fourth Earl of Chesterfield, who had agreed to be the dictionary's patron but then failed to come up with the necessary cash.

that the first *Encyclopaedia Britannica* sought to correct. Begun in Edinburgh, Scotland, in 1768, this 'Complete Dictionary of Arts and Sciences' was edited by a young scholar and scientist named William Smellie. Issued in 100 instalments, it was complete by 1771 and was graced by 160 copperplate engravings by Andrew Bell – an engraver of fine collars for gentlemen's dogs. His detailed anatomies of dissected female pelvises and wombs for the 40-page Midwifery entry so shocked George III that he ordered the pages to be ripped from every copy. Explicit as it was, the new encyclopedia was far from progressive by present-day standards. 'Woman' was flatly defined as 'the female of man', while 'Sex' was 'something in the body which distinguishes male from female'.

Many other encyclopedias first issued in the 19th century are still current today, including the German *Brockhaus* (1809), the *Encyclopedia Americana* (1833) and the French *Grand Dictionnaire Universel*, begun in 1866. This great work was initiated by lexicographer Pierre Athanase Larousse, but finished by his nephew Jules Hollier in 1876, after Larousse died from a stroke caused by overwork.

Not the last word

Such scholarly reference sets have not themselves proved flawlessly accurate. Owned by an American company since 1901, the *Encyclopaedia Britannica* is published today by the University of Chicago and readers have taken some mischievous delight in exposing the occasional howlers that have slowly crept into the text.

The most notorious was an entry describing the Salem Church Dam on the Rappahannock River, Virginia. For 20 years the *Encyclopaedia Britannica* carried an article on this feat of civil engineering. At 59m (194ft) high and 2,700m (8,850ft) long, the dam was said to be situated upstream from Fredericksburg, producing hydroelectric power and also serving for flood

The Christmas You've Dreamed of is Here Now

For Christmas and a Lifetime...

ENCYCLOPÆDIA BRITANNICA
Preferred for 185 Years

control. Unfortunately, no such dam existed. The Army Corps of Engineers drew up a proposal in 1944, but it was never built. Not until someone wrote to inform the editors of the error was the article removed. 'We are dealing with 44 million words, and we sometimes do make mistakes,' a spokesman for the *Encyclopaedia* acknowledged.

Knowledge goes online
Encyclopaedia Britannica published its first electronic version on CD-ROM in 1993, the same year that the Microsoft Corporation launched its multimedia encyclopedia *Encarta*. But with the development of the internet (page 184), knowledge began to shift online. The free online encyclopedia, *Wikipedia*, is one of the world's most popular websites, claiming in 2008 an astonishing 10 million entries in 253 languages. The word 'wiki' means

THE INFORMATION AGE The internet is now the major repository for the world's knowledge. In 2008 *Encyclopedia Britannica* had 120,000 articles online while the English language *Wikipedia* site had more than two million articles.

OLD TIMER Since its conception, the *Encyclopaedia Britannica* has been marketed as a trusty reference tool. *Time* magazine labelled it the 'patriarch of the library'.

'quick' in Hawaiian. And unlike the standard reference websites, it allows just about anyone in the world to create new entries or edit existing pages, providing their efforts survive vetting by a small group of volunteer administrators.

The website takes its name from its operating software, called a 'wiki', which is remarkably simple, amounting to little more than five lines of computer code. *Wikipedia* was conceived by Alabama-born internet entrepreneur Jimmy Wales in order to feed information into an earlier project called *Nupedia*. His original aim was to create a free online encyclopedia of a more conventional sort, using a team of highly qualified contributors. Revenue would be generated by a series of online advertisements. *Nupedia*'s writing was so slow that in 2001 a wiki was employed to open contributions up to the public at large. The idea caught on – and while *Wikipedia* proved a rip-roaring success, *Nupedia* quickly became

defunct, finally folding in 2003. *Wikipedia* is not without critics, who argue that its policy of open access makes its entries inaccurate and unaccountable. The site proved vulnerable from the outset to errors of fact and the deliberate posting of misinformation. Things came to a head in 2005 when a high-profile US journalist complained about an entry that falsely implicated him in the assassination of both US President John F. Kennedy and his brother Bobby Kennedy. *Wikipedia* subsequently required visitors to register before creating new entries.

Global learning
Whatever its limitations, *Wikipedia* meets a need in a fast-changing world where the urgency of keeping pace with technological innovation can scarcely be met by traditional publishing methods alone. And speed is not its only advantage. Behind the enterprise is a philosophy that *New Yorker* writer James Surowiecki proposed in his best-selling book *The Wisdom of Crowds*: large groups of people are inherently smarter than an elite few.

Somewhere between the traditional authority of the published book and the pooling of knowledge in cyberspace, a thrilling collaboration is taking place, creating a dynamic, global circle of learning.

Perfect ten Why do we sometimes count in multiples of 12 and not always 10?

Every healthy individual is born with a ready-made calculating machine. The human hand, with its four fingers and thumb, has probably served as a kind of abacus since the dawn of history, and from the two hands with their ten digits stemmed what is known today as the decimal system. A base number of 10 seems to have been used from around 3000 BC by the Elamite peoples of the Iranian plains and highlands east of Mesopotamia, where herding communities used it to count heads of sheep.

Counting in powers of 10 was also employed in ancient Egypt where the numbers 1 to 9 were represented by the relevant number of vertical strokes. The number 10 was shown by a hieroglyph of a yoke for cattle; 100 was represented by a coil of rope; and 1,000 by the drawing of a lotus plant. Decimal systems were later used in the Indus Valley, ancient China, ancient India and elsewhere.

The advantages of twelve

Why have people often used a base of 12 rather than 10? For most western cultures there are 12 months in a year, and 12 hours in the day. There are also 12 inches in the imperial foot; 12 ounces in a troy pound (the unit of measurement used for precious metals and gemstones); and 12 old British pence in a shilling. Comparable systems have been used in other cultures: Chinese clocks and calendars were traditionally based on the 12 Earthly Branches. Some experts have speculated that this system also began

with the human hand and the practice of counting by 3 x 4, by the three finger bones on each of the four fingers. This could be true; but there were other advantages. Twelve divides up more neatly than 10, making it better suited to many problems of division in everyday life.

ONE IN TWELVE An old UK penny, part of a monetary system using base 12. It was superseded in 1971 by a decimal system using base 10.

Yards, cubits, ells and metres

The term 'yardstick' is commonly used to describe anything that serves as a standard of measurement or judgement. It derives from a practical device used to establish lengths of up to three feet. The oldest surviving example is a silver rod made in 1445, which belongs to London's Merchant Taylors' Company.

The yard gets its name from the word for a wooden rod, although its exact origins are not definitely known. It may have come from the cubit used in ancient civilisations, which has often been identified as the length of a human stride or pace. From Egypt, Greece, Rome and elsewhere, research has identified eight ancient examples of the cubit, though their variety was bewildering, ranging in length from 44 to 64cm.

The length of a human stride may also have determined the yard. The Anglo Saxons reckoned the yard by the length of a man's girdle. Henry I of England apparently standardised it in the 12th century by measuring the distance from his nose to the thumb-tip of his outstretched arm.

Units of a similar length are found throughout human history. They can be seen as useful, medium-range human measurements inspired by walking, or using parts of the body as a guide – by contrast with the close-focus inch or the expansive, long-range mile. Another medium-range example was the ell, used for measuring cloth, equating to 45in (114cm) in England. This was a Saxon unit that was standardised by the time of Edward I, who demanded that there should be an exact copy of his ell-wand (measuring rod) in all the towns of his realm, although Scottish, Polish and Flemish ells were shorter.

When the metric system was introduced in 1799, the basic unit was yard-like in dimension. Different varieties of yard have survived, but the most commonly used is the international yard, at 0.9144 metres.

ANCIENT MEASURE The cubit rule used by Maya, finance minister to the pharaoh Tutankhamun c.1332-1322 BC. It is divided into 28 units of 1.86cm.

How did the metric system become the European standard?

International trade boomed in 18th-century Europe, but local systems of measures, like time differences, varied greatly, not only between countries, but also within them. For calculating everything from weights of potatoes to lengths of fabric, a simple, universal standard was badly needed. After the French Revolution of 1789, France's Academy of Sciences set up a committee to rationalise measures, headed by two eminent scientists, the chemist and economist Antoine Laurent Lavoisier and the mathematician Joseph Louis de Lagrange.

They decided that the system should be a decimal one, based on the unit of 10. The key measurement would be the metre, defined as one ten-millionth of the line running from the North Pole to the Equator. All other measurements were based on the metre; the gram, for example, was introduced as the unit of weight and comprised the weight of a cubic centimetre of distilled water. The decimal system became official in France in 1799, and as Napoleon's armies spread radical ideas across the face of Europe, more and more countries took it up.

Sadly, Lavoisier would never witness the success of his vision. Despite his services to science and France, he was denounced as a former farmer-general of taxes and was guillotined in 1794. Joseph-Louis Lagrange lamented, 'It took them only an instant to cut off that head, and a hundred years may not produce another like it.'

The number 12 has six factors (numbers that it can be divided by), which are 1, 2, 3, 4, 6 and 12. The decimal system has only four factors (1, 2, 5 and 10). If a man left his land to be divided equally between three or four sons, a base of 12 presented no problem. A base of 10 created the nuisance of fractions. There are present-day advocates of restoring the base of 12, especially for financial dealings where the 12 months of the year often enter into calculations.

Old but still useful

Ancient measures based on parts of the human body still live on. Mariners measured sea depths by the span of two outstretched arms. The unit was called a fathom and the word is still used, deriving from the Old English word *fæom* meaning 'a pair of outstretched arms'. In the equestrian world, hands are still used for

THE CORRECT QUANTITY An Italian draper, portrayed in a 15th-century fresco in the Castello di Issogne, uses a standardised stick to measure a piece of cloth.

calculating the height of horses – a hand refers to the palm, not including the fingers and is approximately 10cm (4in) – or four thumb widths long.

A ready-reckoning of the length of a human foot gave the ancient Greeks their measurement unit of the foot. The Roman version (*pes*) was slightly larger and subdivided into 12 inches (*uncia*), based on the width of a man's thumb. Meanwhile 'mile' comes from the Latin *mille passum*, literally 'thousand paces'. Each passus was five pes, so the mille passum had 5,000 pes. The distance was also known as a *milliarium*, literally 'milestone' and was reckoned to be 1,480m long, about 90 per cent of a modern mile.

The pleasure garden We are familiar with the idea of flowers that are beautiful but not useful, but when did humans start gardening for sheer visual delight rather than for food?

Some of the earliest prehistoric settlements show cleared patches of ground where fruit, vegetables and herbs were cultivated. The first kitchen gardens also included provision for medicinal herbs. But when did gardeners start to create decorative effects? Many of the earliest formal gardens are reported in dry, desert lands where trees signalled an oasis – the presence of water, shade and perhaps edible plant and animal life. So a verdant patch on the doorstep offered a pleasing visual reassurance both of nourishment and shade. Planned gardens, which included trees and ornamental ponds, were known in Egypt from as early as 2800 BC. Early on, flowers also acquired a cultural and religious significance. The lotus,

GARDEN OF EDEN 18th-century India's Mughal gardens were influenced by early Persian pleasure grounds. Mughal designs featured rectilinear planting, pools and fountains.

for example, possessed a practical use, as the flowers, young leaves and 'roots', or rhizomes, are all edible. But it was treasured by the Egyptians more for its symbolism and appears in hieroglyphs as emblematic of the Sun, of creation and rebirth (because the bloom closes at night and sinks below the water, rising and opening again at dawn).

Gardens in Persia reflected a special reverence for trees and for water, which in Zoroastrian tradition were subjects of deep veneration. Ancient Greek visitors found parks all over the Persian Empire, laid out both for hunting and to please the eye. Such pleasure grounds gave rise to the notion of Paradise. According to Xenophon, Socrates told his pupils that 'Everywhere, the Persian king is zealously cared for, so that he may find gardens wherever he goes; their name is Paradise, and they are full of all things fair and good'.

The Islamic influence
Islamic gardens were influenced by their Persian precursors. From the 9th century, Muslim Arabs spread gardening artistry from Spain across North Africa to India and Samarkand in Uzbekistan. Perhaps the most imaginative gardens were created by the ruthless Mughal emperor Shah Jahan in 17th-century India: the Shalimar Gardens in Lahore as well as those at the celebrated Taj Mahal at Agra.

Much of Europe's taste for ornamental gardening derived from the Muslim world. After the Crusades, plant-hunters went out to find rare specimens; men like the Frenchman Pierre Belon, who combed Egypt and the Holy Land in the 16th century, and Augier Ghislain de Busbecq, a writer, herbalist and diplomat in the employ of the Holy Roman Emperors, who found drifts of strange plants growing between Adrianople and Constantinople – and brought the first tulips back from Turkey.

During the 18th century, plants streamed into Europe. John Bartram was the first of the American-born plant-hunters; he roamed from Canada to Florida, discovering around 150 new varieties (including witch hazel), which he shipped to England. Sailing to South Africa with Captain Cook in 1772, Scottish botanist Francis Masson discovered more than 1,700 varieties, including belladonna lilies and red hot pokers.

Not all gardening traditions placed such emphasis on flowers. Donato Bramante in Renaissance Italy conceived grand gardens constructed with stone stairways, statues and water. His taste for architectural effects was continued by France's André Le Nôtre, creator of the immense symmetries of the 17th-century palace of Versailles, west of Paris, whose garden took 36,000 workmen to complete. In England, Lancelot 'Capability' Brown had a marked hostility to showy floral effects, preferring to weave his magic by evoking the natural landscape. Serpentine lakes, rolling lawns and scatterings of trees became the setting

Greek visitors found parks all over the Persian Empire

for the neo-classical villas of the 18th-century English aristocracy.

Yet the passion for flowers never died, and by the 19th century the stream of foreign exotics into Europe became a torrent. Plant-hunters sought rarities in some of the world's remotest regions, like the Sino-Himalayan mountains where the highest diversity of rhododendrons grew wild.

The English and their Edens
Perhaps nowhere did ordinary people become more passionate about gardening than in England. Through Victorian businessmen's propagation of seeds and bulbs, once-rare local species became commonplace features in the flower-beds of suburban villas and brick-built terraced houses. Legions of gardeners laboured to create colourful effects. As the English writer and poet Rudyard Kipling wrote:

Our England is a garden,
and such gardens are not made
By singing – 'Oh, how beautiful!' –
and sitting in the shade.

Were the Hanging Gardens of Babylon the first recorded gardens?

Greek historians considered Babylon's gardens a spectacular site. Their beauty was such that they were counted among the Seven Wonders of the Ancient World. The gardens rose up in terraces on which earth had been piled and were 'thickly planted with trees of every kind that, by their great size and other charm, gave pleasure to the beholder,' according to Diodorus Siculus.

Nebuchadnezzar's Eden
Though no conclusive evidence survives, sites in the valley of the Euphrates suggest they probably were a historical reality. The great stepped complex was 'hanging' in the sense that vines streamed down the tiered walls. (The name comes from a mistranslation of the Greek word *kremastos* or the Latin word *pensilis*, which mean 'overhanging' as well as 'hanging'.) The gardens were said to have been built by Nebuchadnezzar II around 600 BC, as a gift for his queen, Amytis. She had grown up among the wooded hills of western Iran and was homesick in the flatlands of what is now southern Iraq. So the king decided to create his towering marvel.

Babylon's fabled gardens were not the first horticultural wonders in the Middle East. More than 3,500 years ago the trading post of Dilmun (now Bahrain) gained a reputation as a lost garden of unearthly beauty. Dilmun's magnificence is thought to have influenced the Bible story of Eden.

I promise to pay the bearer
Who was the first person to convince a creditor that a humble piece of paper would represent a payment?

LUCKY MONEY Coins from ancient China were etched with auspicious characters. They often carried the name of the reigning emperor or the government of the time.

Before money was invented people traded by barter. But it was a system with clear limitations. If a tribesman wanted to swap a wooden canoe for meat, he needed first to find someone with meat – and carry his canoe with him. The idea of trading through tokens emerged in prehistory, independently in different parts of the world.

The idea of value
It was important that the token should be rare, or desirable, and so have inherent value. In the ancient world, monetary standards often started with units of livestock. Cattle have been called the world's 'first working capital asset': the English words 'capital', 'chattels' and 'cattle' all share a common root. As early as 9000-6000 BC cattle were currency and until well into the 20th century the Kirghiz of the Russian steppes used horses as their main monetary unit. Sheep served as a subsidiary unit and small change was given in lambskins.

Metals had intrinsic value, too. Around the 8th century BC, the first

> **Coins often contained holes so they could be strung together on a chain**

coinage began to appear in China. It was more portable than cattle and the metal coins often had holes so they could be strung together on a chain.

A paper promise
The first banknotes emerged in China from around AD 800 when the Tang Government started paying merchants with money certificates. The flimsy pieces of paper represented promises to pay, rather than having intrinsic value, but the bills were far lighter to carry than sacks of coins. They were known as 'flying cash', because of their tendency to blow away in the wind. They could be converted into hard cash on demand in the capital city.

Printed money was introduced under the Song dynasty (960-1279). By this time, the bills carried pictorial images as well as seals of the Currency Reserve Bank, founded in the Song capital, Kaifeng, in 1023. Red and black inks were used and confidential marks added to thwart would-be counterfeiters (a crime punishable by death). In 1154 a Bureau of Paper

Currency was set up in China, although mismanagement caused inflation to soar in the 12th century.

But paper money endured and by the time of the Mongolian Yuan dynasty (1206-1368), China depended exclusively on its circulation. The government tried to ban all transactions in or possession of silver or gold. Kublai Khan decreed that traders had to accept his paper money on pain of death. Inflation caused by unregulated printing of the paper currency was a problem. When Marco Polo visited the court of Kublai Khan he saw how the paper notes were made; wood was pulped, pressed into rectangles and cut to size. As he wrote in his *Travels*: 'All these pieces of paper are issued with as much solemnity and authority as if they were of pure gold or silver; and on every piece a variety of officials, whose duty it is, have to write their names and put their seals. And when all is prepared duly, the chief officer deputed

TRAINS OF BARTER Tuareg salt caravans are a familiar sight in Niger. Every autumn, camel trains wend their way across the desert, transporting barter foodstuffs on animals once used as barter themselves.

TRUSTING MOTTO The first US notes were cut by hand in 1907. It wasn't until 1955 that the law required the motto, 'In God We Trust', to be printed on all currency.

paper money had arrived – and would revolutionise commerce in the west.

In 1694, the Bank of England was founded to raise money for the war against France. Notes were issued in return for deposits of gold, with the promise to pay the bearer on demand. The system allowed for the note to be redeemed at the Bank by anyone presenting it for payment, not just the person making the deposit. The first notes were handwritten, and signed by one of the Bank's cashiers. They were made out for the exact sum deposited in pounds, shillings and pence. The decision was soon made to issue notes only for sums upward of £50. Since the average Englishman earned less than £20 a year, few had any use for them.

Notes for lower sums arrived in the 18th century, with £1, £2, £5 and £10 coming into circulation. Cashiers of the time still filled in the name of the payee, and signed each one individually. The Bank of Scotland came into being

by the Khan smears the seal entrusted to him with vermilion and impresses it on the paper, so that the form of the seal remains imprinted upon it in red; the money is then authentic.'

A commercial revolution

The first known use of paper as a form of currency in the west took place in the Dutch city of Leiden during the Spanish siege of 1574. The starving citizens were even forced to eat leather, at other times used as an emergency currency. So using paper from hymnals and other ecclesiastical missives, they created paper 'coins' known as planchets, using the same dies (moulds) used for minting coins.

The Leiden experiment was a reaction to extreme circumstances. The debasement of coinage in 16th-century Europe and knowledge of the Chinese use of paper money

NOTES OF OLD The first printed notes were produced by the Bank of England in 1855. Originally called 'White Notes', they were printed in black ink with a blank reverse.

may have influenced its adoption. Sweden was the first nation to formally issue the currency in the mid-17th century. In 1657 Johan Palmstruch founded the Stockholm Banco, a private company enjoying royal privileges in return for half of the bank's net profits. His first issue of banknotes followed in 1661. The venture over-reached itself, crashing catastrophically six years later, but

in 1695, the same year that banknotes were first issued in Norway (then a Danish colony). Louis XIV approved the printing of paper money in France in 1703; and in Germany, the town of Cologne issued banknotes two years later. In 1775, the United States of America and individual states issued 'Continental Currency' denominated both in Spanish dollars and the pounds sterling currencies used by the states. Like the paper currencies of the past, the continental currency was subject to 'printing press inflation' and was replaced by the silver dollar at a rate of 1 silver dollar to 1,000 continental dollars. Because of suspicion of paper money and problems finding a paper that was strong enough to last, many other European nations did not issue paper notes until the later 19th century.

The first fully printed notes were issued by the Bank of England in 1855 with the anonymous 'I promise to pay the bearer on demand the sum of … .' The formula is still the same today, even in the age of electronic money when vast sums are moved almost instantly by banks and investors worldwide.

Who first decided that gold was a more acceptable means of exchange than other rare commodities?

Sharks' teeth, metal bars, tobacco and cocoa beans have all served as hard cash. Pacific Islanders used feather money, consisting of coiled vegetable fibre decorated on one side with tiny red plumes. Native Americans used *wampum*, strings of beads made from clamshells ('wampum', meaning white, was the colour of the beads).

With the invention of metalworking, gold and silver were often used as money. The metals were scarce and likely to retain their value in the long term. They did not succumb to rust and could be polished or set with precious stones. In the Inca and Aztec cultures an association was made with the gold of the Sun and the silver of the Moon, conferring religious and ornamental values on the metals. Practical economics were not always the most important factors in determining what was used for money.

A valuable import

One of the earliest cultures to attach monetary significance to gold was that of ancient Egypt, where gold was imported from the southern kingdom of Nubia. Gold was also important in the southeast corner of the Black Sea where King Midas of Greek myth is thought to have been a historical ruler of Phrygia in the 8th century BC.

Medieval alchemists worked to produce gold from unlikely substances such as lead, laying the foundations for modern chemistry through their researches. Later, the European thirst for gold drove the Iberian conquests of the Aztecs and Incas, while the quest for a legendary El Dorado – a city of gold – led to epic voyages of discovery in Colombia and Amazonia.

For all the attraction of gold, its use as a monetary standard is more recent than might be imagined. The English pound was originally a quantity of silver weighing a pound (500g). The Spanish silver 'milled dollar' (also known as the piece of eight) was effectively the world currency in the 18th century. In 1819, following the inflation of paper money during the Napoleonic wars, Britain adopted the gold standard for the pound. From 1873, the Goldmark (or simply Mark) became the currency of the German Empire, reckoned at 1kg of gold. With two big imperial powers backing the system, other nations quickly followed, including France in 1878, Russia in 1897, Japan in 1897 and the United States in 1900. As well as the pound and the mark, gold became the stable unit of valuation for the dollar, rouble, yen and other currencies worldwide.

Though various countries broke with the gold standard during and after the First World War, the United States remained linked to it, and in time the gold-backed US dollar replaced the pound sterling as the leading global currency. In 1971, growing international inflation led the United States itself to abandon the gold standard.

VAULT OF GOLD Fort Knox is home to the United States Gold Bullion Depository. The vault, on Bullion Boulevard, has granite walls and a 22-tonne blast-proof door.

Tulips from Amsterdam
Why does Holland grow so many flowers?

FLASH OF COLOUR Tulips only bloom for 7-10 days before being harvested. This helps maintain the bulb's nutrients.

Tulips came to Europe from the Middle East. The first bulbs were planted in Holland in 1593, by Carolus Clusius, head of the botanical garden at the University of Leiden. He was stingy with his stock of bulbs and when he refused to give them up, a group of commercial growers stole part of his collection. The scarcity value of the rarities combined with the Dutch instinct for business to ginger up an already flourishing horticultural industry. The 1630s saw the emergence of professional tulip traders, lured by the potential profits from the rare blooms. But though demand rose fast, the supply of bulbs did not. Tulips take seven years to grow from seed and the resulting bulb only lasts a few years so demand far outstripped the available supply, driving up prices to extreme levels. Tulip mania lasted for three years, enhancing Holland's reputation as a centre of growing.

The importance of geography
Much of Holland is flat, lying below sea level and prone to flooding. Historically, the need to defend low-lying tracts known as polders with dykes (embankments) bred a particular ingenuity and spirit of cooperation among market gardeners. In some areas, the scarcity of land

meant that growing flowers and bulbs – though labour-intensive – brought higher returns than growing crops.

From the 1880s, horticulturalists set up cooperatives to protect themselves. Flower markets were held, at which the growers were also the owners. They set their own prices, also exchanging information about everything from market trends to new seeds and techniques of glasshouse building. Holland's powerful banking community supported initiatives and after the

Second World War, the growth of the floral industry was phenomenal.

Today, Aalsmeer Flower Auction near Amsterdam is the world's largest, housed under one roof in a building the size of nine football pitches. Holland annually exports some 10 billion blooms. Despite competition from new flower-growing centres, such as Ecuador, Ethiopia, Kenya and Colombia, the Netherlands still accounts for some two-thirds of the world's total floral production.

Holland's tulip mania

When the tulip craze broke out in Holland in the early 1630s, it was as if the whole nation had gone mad. A Dutch priest, Jodocus Cats, compared the craze to the bubonic plague also affecting Holland at the time. 'Another sickness has arisen,' he wrote. 'It is the sickness of the *blommisten* or *floristen*.' In 1636 William Crowne, an English politician and diplomat, noted that 'a Tulip-roote sold lately for 340 pounds'. A citizen would have cheerfully given a month's salary for a single bulb and a rare type could cost the price of a whole farm. Soon people were bartering their life savings or family jewels in exchange for the precious tulips.

A burst bubble
But the bubble soon burst on 'Tulip Mania'. Widespread panic ensued when investors realised that tulips weren't worth the money being paid for them. People frantically sold their bulbs, the market crashed and the once expensive bloom fell to the same price as an onion.

On the right side of the road Why do some countries keep to the left when most drive on the right?

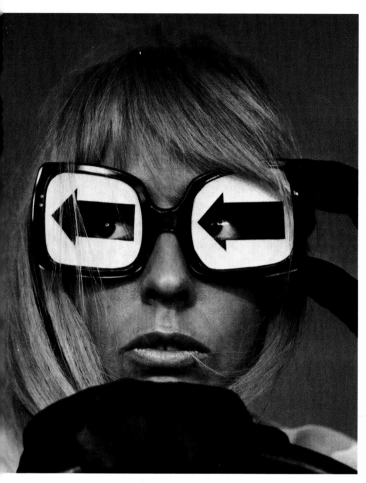

In February 2008, Donie Cassidy, the leader of Ireland's upper chamber, the Senate, suggested that Ireland should consider giving up driving on the left side of the road. He argued that Irish economic growth over the past decade had attracted many thousands of workers and tourists from Europe and America and that the move to the right would reduce road accidents caused by foreigners.

As Cassidy observed, most European nations now drive on the right, as does the USA, while in Britain and Ireland drivers still keep to the left. But left-hand driving is not so unusual – about a third of the world drives on the left – though many of the countries that do so are former British colonies. So how did the preference for driving on the left or right side of the road come about?

In the past almost everybody travelled in the centre of the road, shifting to the left when passing oncoming traffic. Foot soldiers and wheeled vehicles did so under the Roman Empire and the custom persisted throughout the Middle Ages. There was a practical reason for it. Swordsmen preferred to keep to the left of the road so their right arm was free to defend against potential enemies. The shift from left to right began with a change in transport technology. In the late 18th century, waggoners in America began using big carts pulled by several pairs of horses to haul their produce to market. The drivers sat on the left rear horse or on a separate horse on the left, so they could use their right arm to whip the team. Seated on the left, the drivers preferred oncoming traffic to pass on the same side so they could check they were clear of other vehicles' wheels. So, waggoners started driving on the right and, to avoid accidents, those travelling on foot did so, too.

Revolutionary shift

A more definitive switch to the right began with the French Revolution in 1789. Travelling on the left was associated with the old aristocracy. To keep a low profile, noblemen joined the lower classes on the right. In Paris in 1794, keeping to the right became an official traffic regulation. Afterwards, Napoleon's armies exported the new French rule across Europe: to the Low Countries, Switzerland, Germany, Poland, Russia and elsewhere. The change to the right was adopted, one by one, by the revolutionary American states. Britain stuck to the left-sided tradition and in 1835 the custom was enshrined in law, both at home and throughout the British Empire. Several other European states maintained the ancient preference for the left and the division between the left- and right-hand nations survived until after the First World War.

Switching sides

Spain presented an extraordinary case. For most of the interwar period the country had no national traffic regulations. In some cities, such as Barcelona, drivers were required to keep to the right; in others, including Madrid, they drove on the left (switching to the right only in 1924).

Over the years the general tendency in mainland Europe was to switch to the right as Spain had done. But some nations staved off the change for a

Traffic islands

The world's first traffic island was built in St James's Street, Piccadilly, London in 1864. It was funded by a gentleman named Colonel Pierpoint, who regularly braved the street's carriage traffic as he walked to his Pall Mall club. On completion, the Colonel crossed the street to inspect the island's construction – and was knocked down by a cab.

1928 in a change that also affected her colonies. Territories that bordered other left-driving countries were exempted. So it is that Macau and Mozambique kept the old system.

Left in Japan

Japan, the world's largest exporter of cars, also drives on the left. The habit dates back to the Edo period (1603-1867), when Samurai warriors, like European knights, preferred the left to keep their sword arm free for oncoming strangers. The first Japanese railway was built in 1872 with English technical aid and left-side platforms at stations. Later, electric tram cars were left-side running. If Japan had had American or French assistance in building the railway, the nation might be right-hand drive today.

long time. Sweden did not adopt right-hand drive until 1967. The change happened on 3 September when, at precisely 4.50 in the morning, all traffic was directed over to the right side of the road and halted. Everything stood absolutely still for 10 minutes. At 5.00am, when vehicles started moving again, they were already on the right side of the road – and they have remained there ever since.

Remnants of imperial rule

Britain stood resolute against change. Countries that were once part of the British Empire generally did the same. So, India, Australasia and most former British territories in Africa continue to drive on the left. The major exception is Canada, which adopted right-hand drive in the 1920s to harmonise with the United States. Burma also changed from left to right – but took the decision on the advice of a wizard who had the ear of former President Ne Win. However, their cars, mostly imported from Japan, remain right-hand drive. Left-sided Pakistan debated changing to the right in the 1950s, but decided against it chiefly because camel trains often travelled overnight while their drivers were

dozing. The authorities believed that old camels would not learn new tricks and follow a right-hand path.

Other left-hand driving anomalies date back to periods of imperial rule. Portugal switched to the right in the

Bringing light to city streets

The earliest street lamps were built in places controlled by the Arabic empire: Cordoba in Spain had street lighting as early as the 10th century AD. But even by the late 19th century most city streets were still lit by gas lamps, which required a lamplighter to patrol the city at dusk, igniting each one in turn (right). In 1876, Pavel Yablochkov, a Russian engineer, invented the arc lamp. It produced electric light by a voltaic arc, the result of the electrical breakdown of a gas, to produce a glowing discharge. The system, known as 'Russian lights', was exhibited during the Paris World's Fair of 1878, and later in London and Moscow. But the first place in the world to install electric streetlights was no such great metropolis; it was the small town of Godalming, Surrey, in 1881.

Going up in the world

We are now building skyscrapers with more than 100 storeys, but 130 years ago no building had more than 12 floors, the practical limit for traditional load-bearing construction. How did we reach so high?

AN ELEVATING EXPERIENCE Elisha Graves Otis first demonstrated his elevator brake before an audience In 1854. His device made modern skyscrapers viable.

Taiwan's Taipei 101 Tower, completed in 2003, is the world's tallest building. It soars to 508m (1,667ft) in height and weighs 700,000 tonnes, making it one of the world's heaviest man-made structures. The size of the 101-storey building is all the more remarkable since it stands in a country prone to earthquake and typhoon, and requires a colossal interior pendulum – a tuned mass damper – to counteract sway.

But Taipei is about to lose its record status to the Burj Dubai in the United Arab Emirates. Scheduled for completion in 2009, its projected height has not been officially disclosed, but figures suggest the spire of this glass, aluminium and steel tower will reach – or may even top – 818m (2,684ft).

How and why did the craze for skyscrapers begin? People have lived in modest multi-storey dwellings since ancient times; six-storey buildings were a familiar sight in imperial Rome. And the Yemeni town of Shibam is known as the 'Manhattan of the Desert'. The city has ancient origins, and many of the tall mud-brick houses date from the 16th century. Between five and ten storeys high, these elegant, close-packed dwellings owe their height to geology as much as to defence and prestige. For Shibam sits on a narrow land spur that rises above the flood plain. As the city prospered the only way to expand was upwards.

The Gothic cathedrals of medieval Europe used flying buttresses to stretch the limits of what was possible; but even these were limited in height. Like all previous buildings of any size, they were built with load-bearing walls – masonry or stone walls supporting most of the weight of the structure.

Elevators and frames of steel

Two 19th-century innovations paved the way for the skyscraper. The first was the development of a safe elevator. This was essential to the skyscraper, for the effort of climbing stairs placed a practical limit on buildings' height. Primitive lifts had been used for centuries to raise materials in mines and warehouses. But they were not reckoned safe for human use, because of fears a cable might break. In 1853, the American inventor Elisha Graves Otis promoted a safety device that prevented elevators from falling, using a mechanism to lock cars in place should ropes fail.

The following year he arranged with showman P.T. Barnum to demonstrate his device at the New York World's Fair. High up in an elevator cradled in an open-sided shaft, he called for the cable to be dramatically cut with an axe. The audience gasped, but the

brake kicked in and the platform held fast – elevators had arrived. Later in the century, electric motors made the elevator a practical solution to the problem of getting up and down the tallest buildings.

The second development took place in Chicago. In 1871, the city suffered a calamitous fire, but in the aftermath experienced such a building boom that developers had to build vertically, or not at all. A new construction method was devised, using cheap steel patented by the Englishman Henry Bessemer in 1855. Builders employed a grid of steel columns and beams to take the strain off the load-bearing walls. Chicago's now-vanished Tacoma Building, built by George Fuller in 1886-89, was the first true steel-frame skyscraper.

Racing skyward

The real race for the sky began in New York in 1929. As in Chicago, developers had to build vertically because there was no space to expand sideways. But the push for height was accelerated by other factors, too: floods of speculative capital spilling into commercial real estate and a mania for self-promotion among building barons.

Automobile tycoon Walter Chrysler vied to create the world's tallest building with George Ohrstrom of the Manhattan Trust Company, a 34-year-old banker building at 40 Wall Street. Dubbed 'the kid' because of his youth,

TOWERING PROBLEM Taipei 101 Tower is so high that the downward stress is believed to have reopened an old fault, triggering two significant earthquakes since its construction.

Ohrstrom appeared to be erecting the taller structure and to be completing a skyscraper in record time. In response, Chrysler came up with a plan. He had his architect William Van Alen add an arch to his own building's ornate steel dome, with a spike called a 'vertex' at the top. The Chrysler Building suddenly gained 186ft, and at 319m (1,046ft), surpassed its Wall Street rival to stand proud as world champion.

New York's tallest

Chrysler's building was a monument to himself and to American capitalism, an Art Deco fantasy embellished with American Eagle gargoyles and the shiny metal hubcaps of his own-brand automobiles. But it did not hold the world title for long. Even as the two tycoons were duelling, a third party entered the race. In December 1929, John Jakob Raskob, financier for General Motors, announced his plans for an Empire State Building that would dwarf even Chrysler's triumph. Completed in 1931, the 102-storey Empire State has 3,194,547 light bulbs, 113km (70 miles) of water pipe and 1,706km (1,060 miles) of telephone cable. Since the destruction of the Twin Towers in 2001, it survives as the tallest building in New York and the second tallest (after Chicago's Sears Tower) in the United States.

The pernicious weed Nature did not intend humans to smoke, yet it is a habit shared by billions across the globe. How did a weed from Virginia become so ubiquitous, creating huge fortunes while wreaking untold havoc on the world's population?

'*Tobacco is an Indian weed*' begins a popular ballad of the 19th century, exploring in allegory how smoking reflects human mortality. The clay pipe is easily broken, and its bowl stained black with sin is cleansed by fire. The smoke is likened to human vanity – gone in a puff – and in the last verse:

*The dust that from the pipe
 doth fall,
It shows we are nothing but dust
 after all,
For we came from dust, and return
 again we must,
Think of this when you're
 smoking tobacco.*

It was not known at the time the song was written quite how much tobacco-smoking would hasten mortality. Globally, tobacco consumption caused 100 million deaths in the last century. Figures for the 21st century may rise even further if current trends continue. How did the lethal habit so come to grip the world's population?
Tobacco is derived from leaves of plants in the genus *Nicotiana*, which had been used by native peoples of the Americas for calming effect long before the first European explorers arrived. Archaeologists date its first use to around the first century BC when the Maya of Central America smoked the leaf in sacred ceremonies. The habit was later known to the Aztecs. Nobles in the court of Montezuma smoked pipes with some ceremony after their evening meal, while lowlier citizens made crude cigars of rolled leaves. The Aguaruna aboriginals of Peru even appear to have used the herb to make hallucinogenic enemas. Cigars, pipes, snuff and chewing tobacco were all known to the

Native Americans, and Portuguese mariners were among the first Europeans to pick up the habit. They carried tobacco along their sea routes, raising crops at their trading posts for gifts and barter, as well as their own use. By the end of the 16th century, plantations were already thriving.

In 1561 the French ambassador to Portugal, Jean Nicot de Villemain (hence nicotine), wrote of tobacco's medicinal properties. The following year he sent snuff to Catherine de Médicis, to treat her son, Francis II's migraine headaches. Around 1565, tobacco was brought to England by the adventurer Sir John Hawkins. The courtier Sir Walter Raleigh later persuaded Elizabeth I to try smoking. By 1604 the custom had spread sufficiently widely

that James I condemned it as 'A custom loathsome to the eye, hateful to the nose, harmful to the brain, dangerous to the lungs ....'

Smoking in the streets
Tobacco reached Turkey at about the same time as it reached Europe. There, smoking quickly became widespread. The historian Ibrahim Peçevi wrote of people 'Puffing in each other's faces, they made the streets and markets stink'. In addition, Portuguese and Dutch trading vessels called at ports in Japan where the habit was spread by Buddhist monks, who used tobacco seeds to pay for lodgings along their pilgrimage routes. But the greatest

SMOKE AND CEREMONY
Pacal the Great, a 7th-century Mayan ruler, smokes a ceremonial pipe. Smoking was an elaborate, ritualised activity used on both state and religious occasions.

plantations grew up in North America, and the first permanent English colony probably owed its survival to the 'Indian weed'. Jamestown in Virginia, ravaged by famines, malaria and attacks by Native North Americans, was revived from 1612 when the English settler John Rolfe began growing a new strain of tobacco there. A year later the first shipment of his Virginia tobacco was sold in London, and plantations in North America were soon flourishing to such an extent that tobacco as well as money was used as a means of exchange in the colonies throughout the 17th and 18th centuries.

Opinion differed over the medicinal properties of tobacco. During the great plague that struck England in 1665, smoking was thought to have a protective effect; it was made compulsory for boys at Eton school to ward off infection. But already potential health hazards were being identified. In France it was reported that tobacco weakened young men and women and caused a 'withering of their nobler parts'; while in England the diarist Samuel Pepys reported a Royal Society experiment in which a cat quickly died when fed a drop of distilled tobacco oil. Various bans were instituted; in 17th-century Russia smoking briefly carried the death penalty, while in Switzerland the town council at Berne accorded the same penalties to smokers as to adulterers.

Habits and hazards of smoking

Snuff-taking was especially popular in the 18th century. The first American tobacco factories were small snuff mills established in Virginia in 1730, and Napoleon is said to have used 3kg (7lb) of snuff a month. Manufacture of pipe tobacco soon followed, while the cigar-smoking habit swept Europe in the 19th century. In 1826 England was importing a modest 12kg (26lb) a year. In 1830, the figure had rocketed to 100,000kg (220,460lb). Cuba would acquire a special reputation for the best cigars, as the microclimate to

CRAVEN "A"
THE GOOD, PURE CORK-TIPPED VIRGINIA CIGARETTES
Made Specially to
PREVENT SORE THROATS
CARRERAS LIMITED. 142 YEARS' REPUTATION FOR QUALITY

The instinct for the good things of life invariably calls for Craven 'A'

the west of the island specially favours the cultivation of high quality tobacco.

Cigarettes are said to have been invented by beggars in 18th-century Seville, who would pick up cigar ends discarded by wealthy young men and roll up the tobacco in paper. By 1845 their manufacture in Spain was sufficiently established for Prosper Mérimée to write his tale of Carmen, about a cigarette girl in an Andalusian factory. From the story, Bizet wrote his celebrated opera. A booming industry in the 19th century created tobacco barons and substantial government tax revenues. When cigarette manufacture was automated in the late 19th century they could be produced at low cost for a mass audience. The habit was seen as elegant and fashionable. During the First World War, cigarettes were issued to soldiers as part of their rations; rivalry between tobacco brands afterwards generated advertising gimmicks, including collectible cards featuring film and sporting stars. Cigarette brands spent millions of

> **Beggars ... would pick up cigar ends discarded by wealthy young men and roll up the tobacco in paper**

dollars on advertising, often focusing on the health and social advantages of their particular product.

After the Second World War, health concerns began to undermine smoking's glamorous image. Cigarettes were proven to be highly addictive in the early 1960s. The US National Institute on Drug Abuse calls the cigarette 'a very efficient and highly engineered drug delivery system', one that sends nicotine to the brain almost immediately. Nicotine increases levels of dopamine, a neurotransmitter that regulates feelings of pleasure. But because the effect is brief, the experience must be repeated for pleasure to continue – and so the smoker becomes addicted. Cigarettes were also shown to contribute to many types of cancer, particularly lung cancer – formerly considered a rare illness – heart disease, birth defects and other ailments. In 1970 the Public Health Cigarette Smoking Act in the United States banned cigarette advertising on television in an attempt to limit consumption.

While further, more stringent prohibitions have caused tobacco use to decrease in some countries, global consumption is attaining epidemic proportions. This is the case in many developing countries, whose people are now the primary targets of tobacco salesmen. Tobacco companies are currently manufacturing cigarettes at the rate of five and a half trillion a year – nearly 1,000 cigarettes for every man, woman and child on the planet.

Divided by a common language The British weren't the only Europeans to colonise the New World, so why do most Americans speak English?

Out of the 300 million people who live in the United States of America, around 215 million speak English. Yet only in June 2007 did English become the official language. The measure came as an amendment to an immigration bill, prompted by concerns about the number of Spanish-speakers who were coming across the Mexican border. Spanish is the second most common language in the US and its progress was reckoned by some to threaten America's heritage.

The new legislation, which was criticised by others as discriminatory, raised questions about the United States' sense of identity. The Spanish, not the English, were the first Europeans to colonise North America. And the Germans, rather than the English, comprise the United States' largest ancestry group. So why do most Americans speak English?

The answer begins in a historic clash of empires, when Europe's great powers sought control over the whole of North America. Spain took the lead, looking northward after the conquest of Aztec Mexico. Expeditions set out in the 1540s to the American Southwest, along the coast of California and into Florida. Saint Augustine, Florida, established in 1565 by Spanish explorers, became the first permanent European settlement in what is now the United States.

North American colonisation

The first English settlements came later, and to the north. The English adventurer Sir Walter Raleigh was unsuccessful in his attempts to found a colony in Virginia (now North Carolina) between 1584 and 1589. But a later English settlement at Jamestown prospered from about 1613 when the settlers started to grow tobacco. The date proved momentous both to Jamestown and to the spread of the English language. Without the wealth

JAMESTOWN GOVERNOR Captain John Smith was an early leader of the settlement of Jamestown, a key moment in establishing English in America.

that tobacco brought to the settlers and their later expansion south and west, vast tracts of the USA, south of New England, might have been Hispanic.

English immigration to North America, to the area that came to be known as New England, began with the arrival of the *Mayflower* pilgrims in Massachusetts Bay in 1620. The years from 1630 to the mid-1640s witnessed the 'Great Migration'. The population of Massachusetts was swollen with the arrival of more than 20,000 people fleeing persecution in England and seeking a 'Puritan Commonwealth' in the New World.

The Puritan immigrants were relatively prosperous, and travelled in family groups with their children and in roughly equal numbers of men and women. This was not so in other parts of North America, which were often populated by needy or ambitious young men, as well as African slaves imported to work on the plantations.

AMERICA'S HUB New York was first settled in 1626 by the Dutch. Other settlers soon arrived, lured by attractive offers of land and promises of a new life.

Ancestry with largest population in county

- African American
- American*
- American Indian
- Dutch
- English
- Finnish
- French
- German
- Hispanic/Spanish
- Irish
- Italian
- Mexican
- Norwegian
- Puerto Rican
- Other

* 7% reported their ancestry as American

Ancestral mosaic

Ancestry on continental America (not including Alaska) according to data acquired by the US Census Bureau in 2000. The country's diverse, multi-lingual heritage reflects the rippling effects of immigration from the East Coast and Latin America.

The New Englanders were skilled, with a high level of literacy, creating a remarkably heterogeneous population on the eastern seaboard.

Moving frontiers

From New England, settlement spread westwards to the Midwest and up and down the east and west coasts – the seaboards – before advancing across the continent in the later 19th century. Beyond New England, the American colonies attracted a colourful mixture of new émigrés from all over Europe. At first, Welsh and Germans settled in Pennsylvania and the Carolinas, which also witnessed an influx of Scots and Irish. South Carolina became a home to thousands of French Huguenots. There were Sephardic Jews from Holland and Portugal in Rhode Island, as well as Swedes and Finns in Delaware and later in Wisconsin and Minnesota.

New York was originally known as New Amsterdam – home to the Dutch colonists of 'New Netherland'. Visiting New Amsterdam in 1643, the French Jesuit missionary Isaac Jogues was amazed to discover that in a town of 8,000 people, 18 languages were spoken. In 1664, the city was captured

for the English by the Duke of York, promptly renamed, and destined to become English-speaking. France, too, had ambitions for a North American

Empire and cities such as Quebec and Montreal in Canada as well as Detroit, St Louis and New Orleans in the US all owe their origins to French

Why do Brazilians speak Portuguese when everyone else in South America speaks Spanish?

During Christopher Columbus's first two voyages to the Americas in 1492-96, mariners learnt how the Arawakan-speaking Taino people of the Greater Antilles lived in fear of their warlike neighbours who spoke Carib. The explorers had come to a place of linguistic diversity. Arawak and Carib were just two of a total 34 native language families that have been identified in South America, compared with only 21 in all of Africa, Asia and Europe combined.

The Iberian conquerors soon overran the continent, enforcing their own rule. In the late 16th century, around 200,000 Spaniards emigrated to South America, and set up plantations and estates. Spanish bureaucracy and government took

hold through the *encomiendas*, whereby conquerors employed native people in a form of legalised slavery. They also enforced their own tongue.

Spanish is today the official language of almost every country on the continent except Brazil, a colony of Portugal from 1500-1822. As a consequence, Brazilians today speak Portuguese rather than Spanish. Brazil's huge population means there are more Portuguese-speakers on the continent than Spanish-speakers.

Relics of empire survive in Suriname, where Dutch is spoken; and in Guyana where they speak English. But native tongues haven't died out. Quechua, for example, was the language of the Incas in the Andes and is still spoken in Peru and Bolivia.

forts and settlements. But France's defeat in the French and Indian War (1754-63) left French territory on the North American continent divided between the British and the Spanish.

The prowess of the British redcoats, allied with their American colonies, partly accounts for the spread of English. The cohesive New England culture had also prepared the ground for the Republic formed after the American Revolution. The US Constitution, adopted in 1787 as supreme law, was framed in English and reflected the English political precedent of mixed government with forces balanced against each other to prevent tyranny.

Meanwhile, Spanish settlements were founded in California at Los Angeles and San Francisco. Spanish dominion in the 18th century still encompassed much of present-day US territory, including the vast, former French colony of Louisiana. When the Spanish Empire fell into decline in the late 18th century, Napoleon Bonaparte recovered the state from Spain. Badly in need of war funds, he sold the land on to the US in 1803 for 60 million francs ($11,250,000). President Thomas Jefferson decided on the purchase, keen to secure access to the port of New Orleans. Acquiring the Louisiana Territory doubled the size of the United States at a cost of less than three cents per acre. And the inhabitants now found themselves under an English language government.

The US constitution, adopted in 1787, was framed in English

So it was that in the 19th century, when immigrants began to flood in from the Old World in their millions, the English tongue was waiting for them. From 1840 to 1900, Germans were the largest group of immigrants coming to the United States and became assimilated into the English-speaking community, although still retaining a strong cultural and even political identity in the 19th century. Germans remain the largest ancestry group in the country today.

Between 1892 and 1954, some 12 million immigrants entered America through Ellis Island, at the mouth of

New York harbour – an influx that peaked 1892-1924. The process of Anglicisation began almost at once but not usually at Ellis Island, as has often been claimed. Millions voluntarily changed their names or had a new name bestowed by a clerk or teacher who couldn't pronounce or spell children's names. Many chose an anglicised, shorter or simpler name to make them more employable. A Polish immigrant named Dzeckaeiar may have simplified the name to Decker, while an Italian named Giuseppe used the English translation, Joseph.

If the English language has triumphed in America, it has also changed almost organically there.

Thomas Jefferson himself predicted this development as the population increased in numbers and diversity. 'The new circumstances under which we are placed', he wrote in 1813, 'call for new words, new phrases, and for the transfer of old words to new objects. An American dialect will therefore be formed.'

Melting pot of words

'Bum', meaning tramp, is from the German immigrants' *bummler* ('loafer'). 'Glitzy' is Yiddish, from the German *glitzern* (to glitter). 'Chow' appears to come from the Chinese-American labourers' phrase *chow-chow* ('a mixture of foods'). To 'mosey along' was cowboy slang from archaic English meaning 'to walk with a slouch'. 'Jazz' probably comes from a Creole or

African word and was first used in the brothels of New Orleans where music and sex where on offer.

As for that supremely American invention 'OK,' its origins are tantalisingly mysterious. The term may come from the pidgin German *oll korrect*; from the Choctaw word *okeh* meaning 'it is so'; or from *waw-kay*, rooted in the West African languages of black slaves, *waw* meaning 'yes' and *-kay* adding emphasis. Whatever the truth, the term was unknown to the original English settlers and first appeared in print in 1839, in a March edition of the *Boston Morning Post*.

WARM WELCOME Immigrants on New York's Ellis island in 1912. The USA offered them not only a new life but the possibility of a whole new identity.

WHY DO THEY DO IT LIKE THAT? 7

What's in a name These days most people have a surname. When did we first start using them?

Everyone on the planet has a name to go by. It is almost as much a part of an individual's identity as the features of their face. And, like the human physiognomy, names come in an almost infinite variety. In some countries, such as Mongolia, a single name suffices for most purposes, and in China most names are only one syllable long, such as Chang, Li and Wu. In other places by contrast, names can be very long or complex, as is the case with the Indian singer Sripathi Panditaradhyula Balasubrahmanyam and the Spanish politician José María Álvarez del Manzano y López del Hierro.

Public and private names

However, there is a striking pattern within the diversity of names, a uniformity that hints at a universal function for names. People the world over tend to make do with two significant names (however many parts make up their 'full name'). One of the names is given at birth, and it is this by which they are known to their kin and their friends. The surname is inherited in some predetermined way from their family, tribe, or clan. It is as if there are two vital questions that a person's name needs to answer. The first is personal and individual: 'Who do you think yourself to be?'; the second is social and political: 'Which group do you belong to?'

In pre-industrial societies, the answer to the second question was nearly always self-evident or even common knowledge. Formal surnames were not necessary in an age when a person was personally acquainted with everyone that he or she was likely to come into contact with, and when few people travelled beyond their native village. If people with the same given name needed to be distinguished from one another, then this could be done informally by associating them with the job that they did ('Peter, who is the cartwright'); with a better-known relative ('Thomas, Adam's son.'); with the place where they lived (Margaret, who lives by the elm wood); or with some noteworthy characteristic (Elizabeth, who was such a fair child).

These four ways of characterising a person – by daily occupation, family connection, place of residence, or personal quirk – give rise to the vast majority of European surnames. The population of England, to take one

As surnames became more popular their literal meaning ceased to be relevant

example, began adopting surnames around the time of the Norman Conquest but they were not widespread until the late 13th century. This was a time when towns were growing bigger, and so it was no longer feasible to identify individuals by their Christian names alone. In the early stages of the process, descriptive by-names became permanently attached to individuals. Elizabeth, the fair child, became Elizabeth Fairchild; the phrase 'Peter the cartwright' shrank to Peter Cartwright; Thomas, Adam's son, was elided to make Thomas Adamson, and so on. And if Margaret Elmwood married Peter Cartwright, she would have left the elm wood and gone to live with her husband. Her old by-name would then no longer be correct or helpful, and people began to think of her as Margaret, wife of Peter Cartwright. Herein lies the origin of the long-standing custom whereby women change their surname on getting married.

Portable names

As surnames became more popular, their literal meaning quite swiftly ceased to be relevant. By the year 1500, no one expected a person with the surname Merivale actually to live in the 'pleasant valley' that his name memorialised. This detachment of surnames from their original meaning made it possible for them to be passed on unchanged from one generation to the next. Surnames had become markers of kinship rather than descriptive labels. So Peter Cartwright's son Thomas would be known as Thomas Cartwright, even after he grew up and began to earn his living as a cooper (barrel-maker) or a

THE UBIQUITOUS SMITH
A Roman relief of a blacksmith dating from the 1st century AD. The Latin name for a smith is *faber*, which is the root for names such as Fabbri and Ferrari.

fletcher (arrow-maker). By the same token, Thomas Adamson's descendants would bear the name Adamson – though the Adam in question was not their father or even their grandfather, and though some of them would be daughters, not sons.

Ancient inheritance

This phenomenon, whereby names coined for a specific person crystallise into inherited surnames, occurred sooner or later in most of the countries of Europe, and was then carried to countries that the Europeans colonised. So now, from the cities of San Francisco to St Petersburg, one finds people named after a forgotten village, an

BY THE WATERSIDE People with names such as Brook, Bourne, Burn, Beck and Beckett probably all had ancestors who lived beside a flowing stream.

obsolete profession, or a long-dead ancestor. What does the actress Scarlett Johannson have in common with the archaeologist Arthur John Evans, the Symbolist poet Vyacheslav Ivanov, the US president Andrew Johnson, the artists Paja Jovanovic and Robert McIan, and the playwright Eugène Ionesco? The answer is that they all have a surname that means 'son of John' – according to the languages and traditions of Denmark, Wales, Russia, England, Yugoslavia, Scotland and Romania, respectively.

Everywhere occupational surnames add up to a picture of the world of work at the time when names became fixed. The central importance of the blacksmith to village life is evidenced by the fact that Smith is a popular surname in most European languages, and is the most common surname of all in the English-speaking world. It is not that smithying was the most widely held job; it is that the person who mended everyone's plough and shod all the horses was likely to be known primarily for his trade, wherever he plied it. The French Lefèvres, the

Italian Ferraris, the Spanish Herreras, the Poles and Hungarians called Kowalski or Kovacs, as well as the Russian Kuznetsovs and the German Schmidts and Schmieds – all have someone in their past who knew how to strike an anvil with a hammer.

An ever-changing surname

In some parts of Europe, fixed surnames replaced a system based on 'patronyms', the use of a father's name as a surname. Well into the Middle Ages, a Spaniard named Martin, with a father called Fernando, would be known as Martin Fernandez. If Martin were to have a son named Ramiro, then the boy would be known as Ramiro Martinez. In other words, the family surname would change with every generation. An almost identical system operated in Scandinavia until the 19th century – a son of a Swede named Karl Erikkson would take the surname Karlsson – but in modern-day Scandinavia surnames are passed on in the usual European manner. The only country in Europe where patronymy persists is Iceland. Boys born to an Icelandic couple named Magnus and Helga will have the surname

NAMES IN COMMON All the people below have names with an identical meaning, 'son of John'.

SIR ARTHUR JOHN EVANS

EUGÈNE IONESCO

SCARLETT JOHANSSON

The Chinese system

China holds the distinction of having the world's oldest system of surnames, dating back to the third millennium BC. As in western countries, there are occupational surnames: Tao, for example, means 'potter'; and Wang, the most common name in the world, means 'king'. Many common Chinese names have meanings that are hard for foreigners to fathom. Chen (usually transcribed in Hong Kong as Chan) can mean 'arrange', 'explain', or 'old and stale'. The name He, meanwhile, can only be rendered colourlessly 'what', 'how', 'why', or 'which'. But more obscure still is Zhang; this, the third most frequently encountered surname on the planet, is an untranslatable word that denotes an unspecified quantity of flat objects, such as sheets of paper – hence 'chapter' or 'selection' in Mandarin.

NEW YORK YANKEES FANS HOLD UP A SIGN SUPPORTING PITCHER CHIEN-MING WANG.

Magnusson (or, more rarely, Helguson), while their baby girls will have the surname Magnúsdóttir (Magnus' daughter) or Helgadóttir (Helga's daughter). Iceland's geographical isolation, and its relatively small and immobile population, have made it possible for the Icelandic people to hang on to a method of naming that has remained unchanged since medieval times. An unusual feature of Icelandic nomenclature is that for most purposes surnames are not part of the polite form of address. In Iceland, it does not matter whether you are talking to the postman or the prime minister: it is usual and respectful to call them by their first name.

All these naming conventions came about organically over the course of several generations. But in many European countries there were ethnic minorities among which the use of surnames did not catch on so readily. This was a problem for governments: by the 18th century, the civil authorities were using surnames to identify individuals as a means of state control. Everybody had to have a surname so that records could be kept of taxes paid and so that young men could efficiently be called to serve in the army. At the same time, it was often in the interest of ambitious members of ethnic minorities to conform to the practices of the

dominant nation. So, through a mixture of cultural influence and political pressure, fixed surnames spread artificially to communities that had managed perfectly well without them previously.

This was the case in Wales and in the Gaelic-speaking highlands of Scotland. Here, on the Celtic fringe, surnames came into use only in the course of the 17th and 18th centuries. In the highlands, they showed a marked preponderance of patronymic forms. The Gaelic prefix 'Mac', meaning 'son of', was attached to many common given names – as in MacDonald or McAdam – but there were also many more fanciful names based on words that were never given names: McCaig (son of the poet), Macleod ('son of the ugly one'), and McIndeor ('son of the stranger'). In Wales, meanwhile, the Welsh patronymic prefix 'ap' was tacked onto given names, but it often eroded to leave just an initial 'p', and so yielded such distinctively Welsh names as Price ('ap Rhys', that is 'son of Rhys'), Pugh ('son of Hugh'), Pallister ('son of Alistair') and Parry ('son of Harry').

Imposed names

Perhaps the most striking instance of coercive surname-giving concerns the Jewish populations of central and eastern Europe. Jews were compelled to take surnames in Austria in 1787, in the many German states between 1807 and 1834, and in the Russian Empire between 1804 and 1835. The implementation of this law led to a frenzy of name-making, some of it with unpleasant overtones.

In Germany, Gentile customs officers were in charge of the assignment of names. An essential rule was that the names should look and sound German rather than Jewish, so Biblical or Hebrew words were not permitted. An easy way to implement this rule was simply to divide the Jewish population into four groups and arbitrarily assign them the surnames Big, Small, Black and White – Gross, Klein, Schwarz and Weiss – surnames which are still common among Jews of German origin.

Some wealthy Jews bribed German officials to allow them to take a redolent or ornamental name such as Rosenthal ('valley of roses), Mandelbaum ('almond tree'), or Goldberg ('golden mountain', a name which often also contained a concealed homage to a matriarch named Golda). Meanwhile, some anti-semitic officials amused themselves by saddling people with insulting or grimly comical surnames, such as Borgenicht ('Do not borrow'), Klutz ('clumsy'), or Verderber ('spoiler').

Buried meanings

Many German Jews outwitted the bureaucrats by taking surnames that looked German but had a hidden meaning for those in the know. Those belonging to the priestly caste of the *kohanim*, who elsewhere bore the surname Cohen or a variant of it, often opted for the name Katz, which looks like the German for cat but was understood by Jews as an acronym of the Hebrew phrase *kohan tsedek*: 'priest of justice'. Other kohanim took the obfuscation one stage further when they adopted the name Schiff – 'ship' – because there is a German word 'Kahn', meaning 'boat', that has the same consonants as the Hebrew, *kohan*.

By the end of the 19th century, practically everyone in Europe was equipped with a surname. But the coining of new names continued elsewhere in the world. In India, at the height of British influence, a rash of new and occupational names came into being: Contractor, Engineer, Doctor, Merchant. New English-language names continued to occur even after independence in 1947. The Indian government minister Rajesh Pilot took his surname in the 1970s after a stint in the Indian Air Force.

For a truly modern instance of surnaming, however, one must look to the Mongolian steppe. The nomadic people of Mongolia managed without surnames throughout the 20th century. In the 1990s, the new democratic government of Mongolia passed a bill that allowed people to choose surnames, but the law was largely ignored. It was not until the beginning of the 21st century that the government began to insist that all 2.5 million Mongolian citizens take a last name that would help to identify them on their ID cards.

Some Mongolians delved into the past and rediscovered forgotten family names that were known before the Communist takeover of the 1920s. Others invented names based on their own biography (Gürragcha, the first Mongolian in space, invented for himself the surname Sansar, which means 'cosmos'). But hundreds of thousands of Mongolians chose one name, Borjigin, which means 'wolf master' and was the clan name of Mongolia's most illustrious son – Genghis Khan.

GENGHIS AND SONS A 14th-century Persian manuscript of the warrior Temujin proclaiming himself Genghis Khan. His clan name is the most popular Mongolian surname.

What's in a kiss? When good-mannered people meet, they greet each other with a handshake, a kiss or, in more intimate circumstances, a hug. Why do we greet each other in the way we do?

The handshake is among the oldest and most universal of all social gestures, a symbol of trust from a more warlike age, since a hand offered in greeting is one that is unarmed. We shake with our right hand because this is the one with which a man would usually draw a weapon. Shaking hands might also dislodge a weapon concealed in a sleeve. The right hand is additionally favoured because in Arab and other cultures the left hand is considered 'unclean' and is never used for either eating or greeting.

In ancient Egypt and many other civilisations the handshake was more formal, signifying a binding contract, and has remained so to this day. In the Middle Ages the handshake also marked a pledge of allegiance.

By the 19th century handshaking had become both an honourable gesture and universal everyday greeting.

A firm handshake

The nature of the handshake is significant in forming a first impression. The 19th-century British caricaturist Thomas Tegg, in the treatise *A Present for an Apprentice*, instructed that one should 'take the hand of a stranger with more reserve than that of an acquaintance', and never 'receive the hand of a stranger with coldness or suspicion'. The hand of a well-known friend, however, 'can hardly be seized with too much affection, provided you sincerely feel it.'

In the following century, the American etiquette guru Emily Post

endorsed Tegg's condemnation of those who shake hands too vigorously, who wring your hand or who hold it limply like a wet fish. She concurred that a man should not take a lady's hand until she offers hers. A firm handshake is still interpreted to signify sincerity and strength of character.

In a handshake between people of different rank the subordinate, if male, would kneel on one knee. A woman would kneel, as she did before God, on both knees. From this full

KISSING THE AIR The theatrical air kiss became popular in celebrity circles in the late 20th century and has filtered down to the general population.

prostration the curtsy (from the word courtesy) developed and took on its most reverential form in 16th- and 17th-century France. A woman would be required to sink down, her right knee touching the ground and head lowered. In the medieval courts of Europe everyone, whatever their age or rank, was expected to bow (or if a woman to curtsy) when entering or leaving a room if people of higher rank were present.

The bow, which in Japan, China and Korea typically accompanies the handshake, began as a prostration before a superior and is still a means of emphasising status in a relationship. A hello to colleagues is a quick bend at a slight angle; a respectful greeting to customers or superiors is a deeper bow. The lowest bow, used to signal a formal apology, indicates vulnerability, most notably among samurai and other exponents of the martial arts.

The social kiss

The kiss is probably the oldest of all forms of intimate human bonding, since babies 'kiss' their mothers as they suckle. The Bible records that Esau greeted his brother Jacob with a kiss. The Greeks and Romans also greeted each other with kisses on the cheek and kissing is depicted on Indian artefacts dating to 1500 BC. The kiss was also a symbol of honour. The rules of the medieval courts of Europe demanded that a lord should kiss a newly invested knight on the cheek. In response the knight would kiss the lord's hand.

The kiss of greeting, delivered on the cheek and often accompanied by an embrace (hug), is still a demonstration of affection and good will. By the mid-17th century a Frenchman would 'salute' a lady on the cheek, and visitors to England commented on the prevalence of the practice of kissing. Diarist Samuel Pepys records how his friend Sir George Cartanet 'kissed me himself heartily'. But although it remained the custom on continental

---

Different countries, different gestures

The language of gesture, whether good manners or bad, has evolved very differently in various parts of the world. Signs that are perfectly acceptable in one place are the height of vulgarity – or even obscenity – in another. There is a huge difference between the vulgar two fingered V-sign, made with the palm facing inwards, and the V for victory sign, with the palm reversed, made famous by Winston Churchill in the Second World War.

Hands on hips
- Most countries - authority, self-assertion
- Malicious detachment or hostility - southern Italy
- Hostility - Mexico and other South American countries

Circle made with thumb and index finger
- A-OK - USA
- I'll kill you - Tunisia
- Money - Japan

Sitting with soles of feet or shoes exposed
- Relaxed posture - USA, Europe
- Sign of disrespect - Egypt, Malaysia and all Muslim nations

Palm upwards, fingers spread
- Give it to me - USA, UK
- You are stupid - Chile
- Obscene gesture - Greece

Sitting with legs crossed
- Generally disrespectful outside Europe and North America, especially in Saudi Arabia, Ghana and Turkey

Thumbs up
- Yes, OK, do it - USA, UK, most of Europe
- Vulgar sign of disapproval - throughout the Arab world, parts of Italy and Greece

Tapping the forehead
- I can't remember, my brain needs attention - UK
- You are stupid - Germany, Netherlands, Russia, Czech Republic and widely throughout Europe
- I'm sorry - India

Closed fist in the air
- Victory sign - UK, Europe
- Rude or vulgar gesture - Lebanon, Pakistan

Europe, the practice waned in Britain in the centuries that followed, the intimate kiss replaced by the handshake. A British kissing revival came only with the increased informality of the late 20th century, and the influence of celebrity culture. The air kiss, a purse-lipped gesture accompanied by a 'mwah, mwah' sound and in which no actual touching occurs, is a 20th-century invention of models and film stars, now widely imitated.

I can see clearly now ... When was it first realised that poor eyesight could be corrected by artificial means?

Throughout history, people have suffered from varying degrees of weak vision. Although this was undoubtedly an irritation for scholars and others who did close work for a living, it could be hazardous in any kind of vigorous activity, from military combat to harvesting crops. The workings of the eye were understood early in human history, but it was centuries before sight could be significantly improved through artificial means and in a form that could be made available to all.

Magnifying glasses

Transparent pebbles or semi-precious stones may have been used for magnification nearly 7,000 years ago. Around 54 AD, Pliny the Elder wrote that the Roman emperor Nero watched gladiatorial combat through a polished lens of beryl or emerald set on a ring. But he did this not so much to correct his vision as to cut out the glare of the Italian noonday sun: Nero's emerald was the first recorded use of something like sunglasses.

An early attempt to improve eyesight through the use of a lens is attributed to the philosopher Seneca the Younger, Nero's chief adviser. He is said to have read books by peering at them through a glass bowl of water, so as to magnify the letters on the page in front of him.

The Arab mathematician Alhazen wrote a long tract on optics – the science of vision and visual perception – at the beginning of the 11th century. He described the principle that created the effect of magnification. Alhazen was the first to prove that vision depends on light entering the eye (rather than on invisible rays emanating from the eyes, as many earlier Greek thinkers had believed), and he proved that light travels in straight lines. The principle of magnification is the key to correcting long-sightedness and bringing objects clearly back into focus. At around the same time as Alhazen was writing, 'reading stones' – thin, polished hemispheres of transparent crystals such as quartz or beryl – were being used for magnification. They could be moved along a line of text, magnifying a word at a time. They were not only efficient (being portable and adapted for use on a page), they were also based on sound science. By the end of the century, the stones were fitted into a frame with a handle to form an early kind of magnifying glass.

In 1268, the English philosopher Roger Bacon described how lenses might be used to change the point of focus on the retina, and in 1270 Marco Polo noted that elderly Chinese used convex lenses to help them read small print. The first rudimentary pair of spectacles, made by riveting two reading glasses together, was probably produced in Italy some time in the early 14th century.

By the 16th century, convex lenses to correct longsightedness had been joined by concave lenses, which could help shortsightedness or myopia. Innovations such as the spring bow, nose clips and straps made it easier for the wearer

> **Alhazen was the first to prove that vision depends on light entering the eye**

to keep their spectacles in place, although the side bars common today did not appear until the 18th century, and it was many years before glasses would stay on comfortably and effectively for longer periods. Many preferred monocles or lorgnettes, which were held in place by the wearer.

One solution for people who had poor close and far vision came in 1784 with Benjamin Franklin's invention of bifocals. In his original model, the distance and reading lenses were simply cut in half and set in the same frame, but by the early 20th century a version that combined both types of visual correction in a single lens had been developed.

While glass had long replaced semi-precious stones as the medium for lenses, it was in the late 19th century that Ernst Abbe and Otto Schott, in Jena, Germany, showed that

EARLY SPECS A 1352 portrait of Cardinal Hugo of Provence is the earliest representation of someone wearing glasses.

introducing elements such as lithium into optical glass gave a greater range of refraction and dispersion, leading to more accurate corrective lenses.

Early eyesight tests

The detailed eye tests that are carried out by an optician to determine what kind of glasses are required date from the 1860s and the work of Dutchman Franciscus Cornelis Donders. For much of the 19th and early 20th centuries, many people did not have access to such tests and bought their glasses from a market or shops such as Woolworths. The introduction of eye testing in schools was an important advance towards providing more

effective and accurate sight correction. In 1887, Adolf Fick made the first contact lenses. He originally devised them in order to correct astigmatism, the condition where the cornea is not uniformly curved, so that the eye focuses images at different distances. Early contact lenses covered the whole eye and were uncomfortable to wear for long periods of time. At first, the lenses could only be made by making an impression of the eye to form a cast for a mould. They remained relatively crude until a series of developments in the late 20th century, such as the introduction of gas

IN THE HAND An elegant gold and silver lorgnette made in the 1930s for an Italian count.

permeable and 'soft' lenses, as well as a reduction in the size of the lenses so that they scarcely covered the iris of the eye, made them far more comfortable and wearable.

Though spectacles and, later, contact lenses could deal with simple vision problems, some eye defects required medical solutions. During the Middle Ages, itinerant paramedics known as oculists treated most eye diseases. In 1583, the German doctor Georg Bartisch described and illustrated a number of diseases and their surgical remedies, including one for cataracts, in his *Ophthalmodouleia*. The first recorded surgical correction of 'strabismus', or lazy eye, was in 1738, while glaucoma was described in 1750 and astigmatism in 1801. The first academic course in ophthalmology was opened to students in 1803 at the University of Göttingen, Germany.

Modern trends

Developments in scientific knowledge now allow opthalmologists to re-shape the eyeball with lasers, and can eliminate the need for glasses, while cataract operations can swiftly restore eyesight even to those who have been unable to see for years.

Despite these advances, recent research has indicated that rates of myopia among young people have reached at an all-time high. It may be that modern lifestyles are to blame: we spend much of our time focusing on close objects, such as computer screens, while our ancestors would have scanned a wide horizon.

Why did men's watches move from pocket to wrist?

Until the 20th century, 'wristlet' watches were worn by women – and were considered an effeminate fad; 'real' men had pocket watches. When and why did the change occur?

Soldiers in complex battle situations found pocket watches clumsy to carry and operate in combat. So they were fitted onto leather straps with a 'cup' for the watch to rest in and worn on the wrist to free up the hands. The first men's wristwatches were issued to all officers in the German navy in 1880 and proved invaluable for synchronising naval attacks. Early military watches had leather straps and reinforced glass faces covered with a metal grille, often made of silver, to protect them from damage; from 1906 many watches were attached to expandable metal bracelets for adaptability.

By the First World War, the wristwatch had become a necessity for all troops and companies, such as Patek Philippe and Rolex, rushed to fulfil the demand. Hans Wilsdorf, one

WAR TIME a watch made for use by the US Signal Corps in the First World War

of the founders of Rolex, experimented doggedly to improve the accuracy and reliability of his watches. In 1926, he introduced the first waterproof watch, the Rolex Oyster. Although many soldiers had returned home from the front with souvenir 'trench watches', the wristwatch was still scorned by snobbish civilians. 'Real' men would still tell the time by their fob or pocket watch, and it was women who took to the wristwatch by the million.

MILITARY SHEARING Midshipmen at the US Naval Academy get a regulation haircut. The strict grooming standards are based on neatness, cleanliness and safety.

Short back and sides
Why do most men now have shorter hair than most women?

In 2004 Turkmenistan's 'President for Life' Saparmurat Niyazov banned the wearing by young men of long hair and beards. The ruling, primarily a move against individualism, rather than an Islamic diktat, evoked comparisons with similar laws passed in Albania in the 1970s when long hair, beards and moustaches were banned as unhygienic and insulting. As recently as the 1990s, long hair on men was outlawed in Singapore.

Post-war antagonism to long hair worn by men became vocal in the 1960s, when the heavy fringed haircuts of the Beatles appeared as a revolutionary alternative to the short back and sides that had been the acceptable style for men for most of the 20th century. In Russia during the Brezhnev era of the 60s and 70s, young people sporting Beatle 'mop tops' were arrested and taken to police stations to have their hair cut. Elsewhere in Europe and America the style was condemned by the older generation as 'degenerate'. Even more opprobrium was poured on the much longer 'hippie' hair sported by the group by the late 1960s, an era when long hair was synonymous with sex, drugs and rock 'n' roll and with protest against the Vietnam War.

The customs of hair length have their origins in practicality, sex and religion. Before the invention of cutting tools, hair was worn long by both sexes. Later, men in ancient Egypt shaved their heads to keep cool while women cut their hair short for the same reason, though they often wore wigs to cover their heads in public. In the 4th century BC Alexander the Great commanded his soldiers to wear their hair short and to shave off their beards so that enemies could not grab them during battle; the practical reasons for short hair in the military have ensured the durability of the custom throughout most of history.

The customs of hair length have their origins in practicality, sex and religion

Law and civilisation
In Roman society, most men wore their hair short and around the Empire the look became associated with law, discipline and civilised behaviour. From the start of the Christian era, St Paul's instruction to the Corinthians had an impact on fashion: 'Does not nature teach you that while long hair disgraces a man, it is a woman's glory?'

The short male haircut has persisted since then, although with interruptions. The Cavaliers, supporters of Charles I during the English Civil War (1642-51), wore their hair in ringlets below the shoulders. After the Restoration, men typically covered their shaved or cropped hair with extravagant wigs. In the 18th century the European fashion was for long hair braided into a pigtail or queue. In the East, the religious rule was reversed. Sikhs leave their hair uncut beneath a turban 'as God made them'. Obeying the dictum of Confucius that 'body, hair and skin are inherited from one's parents, do not dare damage them,' Han Chinese men also wore their hair long, knotted on the top of their heads. Only when the Manchus defeated the Han in 1644 were heads shaven and the hair at the back made into a queue – a mandatory style, harshly enforced. It became a symbol of subservience, but prevailed until the 20th century when a law was passed requiring plaits to be cropped.

Changing associations

While for women worldwide, long hair was a symbol of beauty and sexual allure – in China a girl with short hair was considered a poor marriage prospect and the bobbed haircuts of the 1920s generated outrage – the same has not been the case for men. Short hair has been worn through time primarily for practical reasons but remains a symbol of control and conformity.

Moustaches, beards and whiskers

Facial hair has been sculpted for as long as men have had sharp tools to shave with. Greeks and Romans tended to prefer a clean-shaven look, leaving luxuriant moustaches to the Celts and barbarians of the north. Roman coins, though, show emperors with a fine array of close-cropped sideburns, neat moustaches and narrow beards, displaying their personal take on the period's fashion.

In the 19th century, the moustache was so symbolic of strength that English soldiers were forbidden to shave their upper lips. The growing of moustaches had begun during the Napoleonic Wars, when French soldiers' moustaches were regarded as 'appurtenances of terror'. By 1914, when Lord Kitchener – duly sporting a bristling upper lip – pointed his recruiting finger, the moustache was synonymous with masculinity. No self-respecting officer would be clean shaven.

Beards, however, were impractical for infantry, since it was impossible to wear a gas mask over them. In the Royal Navy a 'full set' (beard and moustache worn together but not separately) was permitted for officers, as it is today. The custom dates to the 18th century, when water for washing and shaving was in short supply.

Big beards and power

In the 19th century, big beards merging into bushy sideburns were the height of fashion. It was no coincidence that, in aping the looks of prominent figures such as the statesmen Napoleon III, Benjamin Disraeli and Abraham Lincoln, men of all classes regarded facial hair as a sign of power and virility. French Romantics also set the fashion in whiskers while radicals such as Karl Marx and George Bernard Shaw sported big beards.

Locks of superhuman strength

The Biblical hero Samson was a Nazirite, belonging to a Hebrew sect whose vows included a promise to leave the hair uncut and the beard unshaved. Renowned as much for his womanising as for his physical superiority in his encounters with the Philistines, Samson's erotic liaison with the Philistine Delilah was destined to rob him of his strength.

Motivated by a bribe from her leaders, Delilah forced Samson to reveal his secret. The Book of Judges quotes him: 'If my head were shaved, then my strength would leave me ....' While he was asleep Delilah called a man to cut Samson's locks and delivered him to the Philistines, who gouged out his eyes.

In time, Samson's hair grew back. God then gave him the immense strength he needed to push against the pillars of the pagan temple and collapse it. He was killed, along with thousands of the Philistine enemy.

Long hair is associated with strength in many cultures. In medieval Japan, Samurai warriors wore their hair shaved at the front, with the rest of the hair long, oiled and wound into a topknot at the back. At the end of their career – or when defeated – their hair would be ceremonially cut. A variant of this twisted bun, called a *chonmage*, is worn by today's Sumo wrestlers. Hairdressers maintain the complex style, which varies according to the status of the sumo.

Among the Plains Indians of the Americas, long hair, decorated with beads and feathers, was a sign of virility. Their ritual scalping of captives was intended as an act of revenge and humiliation.

CAVALIER CURLS Flowing hair was fashionable in Royalist circles during the English Civil War. The king's cavalry commander Prince Rupert represented the cavalier ideal.

Here comes the bride We are used to the idea of traditional wedding ceremonies, but where did all the familiar features come from?

On 29 July 1981, a worldwide television audience of 750 million watched a classic example of a white wedding unfold when Prince Charles married Lady Diana Spencer at St Paul's Cathedral. For almost a decade thereafter her fairytale dress was a template for brides everywhere.

The bride wore white

White wedding gowns are a relatively recent phenomenon, before which almost any colour dress was acceptable, including black if the intended bridegroom was a widower. In early Celtic cultures, red was the bridal colour of choice, worn to invoke fertility; early Christians preferred blue, which was symbolic of truth and purity and used in depictions of the Virgin Mary, either for the whole dress or as a band around the hem. Right up until the late 19th century, most ordinary women were married in their 'Sunday best', which, adapted if necessary, could be worn again. Grey was much favoured as both modest and useful, and brown was not uncommon; white was usually just too impractical.

The white wedding dress as we recognise it today is a tradition started by Queen Victoria, who wore white to her own wedding to Albert of Saxe-Coburg in 1840. But white wedding gowns, worn as a token of the bride's purity and innocence, were worn by royalty and the wealthy long before then: Henry IV of England's daughter, Princess Philippa, is reported to have worn a tunic and mantle of white satin, edged with velvet and ermine, at her marriage to Eric of Pomerania (modern Scandinavia) in 1406;

ICONIC BRIDE Princess Diana wore a full-skirted dress of ivory silk taffeta designed by David and Elizabeth Emanuel. It was embroidered with 10,000 pearls and sequins and had a 7.5m (25ft) train that trailed down the aisle of St Paul's Cathedral.

VICTORIAN ROMANCE
Queen Victoria and her beloved Prince Albert. Her white satin and lace dress was an industry in itself. The lace kept more than 200 Devon lacemakers occupied from March to November of 1839.

Anne of Brittany, daughter of Francis II, Duke of Brittany, wore white at her third marriage in 1499 to Louis XII of France; while in 1572, Margaret of Valois is said to have married Henry of Navarre in a dress trimmed with white ermine, topped with a blue coat with a 1.5m (5ft) train. Mary, Queen of Scots wore white for her wedding with the Dauphin of France in 1558, flouting the French custom that white was only to be worn in mourning for French royalty. (Ironically, her husband died two years later.)

The bride's wedding veil has several different associations. It may have evolved as a symbolic protection from malign spirits, in particular the Evil Eye. It also implies a bride's submission to her future husband, the man to whom she allows the privilege of lifting the veil. It has also been seen as a representation or development of the Anglo-Saxon 'care cloth' that was held over the heads of both bride and groom. The Saxon cloth was itself related to the Jewish *chuppah*, a square vestment held over the heads of the couple, and to the linen canopy that is traditionally used in Catholic wedding ceremonies.

Flowers carried and worn are bridal essentials. A floral crown was once *de rigeur* for both bride and groom. The blooms were carefully chosen for their meanings – orange blossoms for fecundity and roses for love, and combined with herbs: rosemary for remembrance and sage for wisdom; garlic would be added to ward off evil spirits. The crowning of the bride with a coronet of gold or silver, sometimes entwined with flowers, is still observed in Eastern Orthodox weddings. The buttonhole worn by the groom is the remnant of his crown and also dates back to the custom of a knight wearing the colours of his lady to signify his love.

A legal union

It has been claimed that the earliest weddings, particularly in the countries of the Mediterranean, were little more than kidnappings, with the bride literally stolen from her family by her suitor. Today's best man, the bridegroom's supporter, and his wedding ushers are relics of northern Europe from the 5th to 10th centuries AD when the bridegroom had henchmen or 'bride knights' who would assist him in capturing his intended. The best man might also distract the bride's family while the bridegroom seized his prize. Bridesmaids were dressed alike to form a kind of protective shield against evil spirits. They also had the duty of warding off any vengeful suitors who approached the bride on her way to the wedding, or thieves who were intent on stealing her dowry. Gifts given to the bridesmaids by the groom are a relic of the ancient practice of marriage by capture: only by bribing her girlfriends with gifts would a man be able to carry off his bride. Bridesmaids today may well help prepare wedding flowers but in the past would have woven the bridal wreath and 'dressed' the bridal bed with flower petals.

In some early societies, such as Sumeria *c*.2000 BC, marriage laws did exist, but elsewhere many early marriages were informal, the fact of living together and producing children being sufficient for a union to be accepted. Marriage was also viewed as an economic arrangement by which two families were brought together. From this evolved the practice of marriage by purchase in which a bride was literally bought for a 'bride price', a custom featured by the English novelist Thomas Hardy in his 1886 novel, *The Mayor of Casterbridge*, based on a true story. As purchase ended, so began the reverse custom of a father providing the bridegroom and his family with both a daughter and a dowry. The giving of wedding presents, and the tradition that the bride's father gives her away and pays for the wedding, are the last remnants of these ancient customs.

> **Marriage was seen as an economic arrangement to bring two families together**

The dowry was – and in places such as India remains – a part of the arranged marriage. Throughout Europe arranged marriages were long commonplace for royalty and those of noble birth, often for political reasons. In 1254, the 15-year-old who was to become Edward I of England travelled to Spain for an arranged marriage to the nine-year-old Eleanor of Castile. As a wedding gift, Edward's father Henry III gave him several lands, including the Duchy of Gascony, a remnant of the French possessions once held by English kings. Many similar unions followed. A notorious example was the marriage of Caroline of Brunswick to George, Prince of Wales, later George IV of England. The marriage was a farce, partly because the two were incompatible, but mainly because 10 years earlier, in 1785, the Prince had secretly married his lover, Mrs Maria Fitzherbert.

Polygamy was often practised in early cultures: the Old Testament records Solomon as having 700 wives and 300 concubines. Legally binding, monogamous marriages were instituted by the ancient Greeks. Plato recorded that 'a man shall cohabit with a woman who has come into his house

DISPLAYING THE DOWRY Revellers from the Bulgarian mountain village of Ribnovo carry a bride's entire dowry through the streets. The bride's family would have started making the dowry items, including quilts and traditional costume, as soon as she was born.

with holy ceremonies'. In Imperial Rome it was customary to undertake a formal marriage in front of witnesses; the union could be legally dissolved with a similar ceremony. The consent of both bride and groom to the union dates to a statement made by Pope Nicholas I in AD 866. 'If this consent is lacking in a marriage,' he said, 'then all the other celebrations count for nothing, even if intercourse has occurred.'

With this ring

The church gradually became more involved in the law of marriage. In 1215, the Catholic church declared marriage to be a sacrament and it became a public institution involving a priest, witnesses and parental consent. After that time a couple could only marry privately by special licence.

The ring, an unbroken circle, is a symbol of betrothal and marriage. Some 10,000 years ago in Sumeria, a ring may have acted as a shackle to

BAND OF GOLD On her proxy marriage to James, Duke of York (later James II of England), in 1673, 15-year-old bride Mary of Modena wore this gold ring studded with rubies.

keep a captured wife in tow. A husband in ancient Egypt would place a gold ring (which was also a money token) on his wife's finger to indicate that he trusted her with his property. In ancient Rome the giving of the equivalent of today's engagement ring accompanied the delivery of the dowry. In the 16th century, the gimmal ring was popular. It consisted of two or three jewelled rings linked together

and signified the joining of two lives. The wedding ring, separate from the engagement ring, is usually a simple object today, but was once elaborately engraved and often encrusted with symbolic stones, either the birthstones of the bride or turquoise, the stone of Venus. Ornaments on the ring varied from intertwined hearts to a lover's knot or a pair of clasped hand, but the plain gold band has been the accepted style since the late 18th century.

In the Middle Ages, many brides would be chased by unmarried girls who would rip pieces off the wedding gown in the hope that it would act as a fertility charm. But as wedding dresses became more expensive, brides threw other objects, at first garters, then the wedding bouquet, to protect their investment and hasten the marriages of their girlfriends.

Emblems of fertility

The custom of throwing fertility objects over newlyweds dates to the ancient belief that the fruits of the Earth will bring about a fruitful marriage. Rice and grains have been used since ancient times and the ancient Greeks broke multi-seeded pomegranates over the heads of bride and groom. Figs were thrown in many countries for similar reasons and the Romans threw almonds. The first confetti comprised pink and white sugared almonds (known in Italian as *confetti*), which evolved into missiles made of plaster of Paris. Paper was safer and confetti cut in horseshoe shapes added further good fortune. Because evil spirits were believed to fear leather, shoes were thrown for luck or, as now, tied to the back of the couple's car as they departed.

In ancient times, feasting together was sometimes sufficient to declare a union of man and wife, though it was often accompanied by other actions, such as the joining of hands, and the accomplishment of shared tasks, such as sawing wood together. The bride cake – the forerunner of today's

The ring finger

It is believed that the ancient Greeks were the first to wear a wedding ring on the fourth finger of the left hand, from the romantic notion that a 'vein of love' ran from there to the heart. Until the 1700s in England, a wedding ring could be worn on any finger, and even the thumb. Thereafter, the left-hand ring finger became traditional.

The 16th-century Dutch author Levinus Lemnius maintained that a swooning woman could be revived by rubbing this finger to refresh 'the fountain of life unto which this finger is joined'. Physicians also used this one to stir their potions. The USA, France, Sweden, Brazil and many other countries follow the left-hand custom.

The Romans favoured the ring finger of the right hand because they considered the left unlucky (the Latin for 'left' is *sinister* which also means 'unfavourable'). This custom (though not belief) continues today in many countries, including India, Spain, Germany and Russia. In some, such as Belgium, the hand of choice even varies from region to region.

BESTOWING THE RING, FROM A 1443 SIENESE FRESCO BY DOMENICO DI BARTOLO

wedding cake – was broken over the bride's head to mark the end of her virginity and to ensure her fertility. The marzipan layer is said to represent the symbolic union of sweet and bitter, 'for better or worse'. The tiered cake dates from the 18th century, and was apparently inspired by the tiered tower of St Bride's Church in London's Fleet Street.

'Fertility foods', such as pomegranates and figs, were also part of the wedding feast. Drinking together was

also essential to the celebrations. Drinks ranged from wine to a soup eaten or drunk by both bride and groom from the same bowl. Honeyed wine (honey is a symbol of life, health and fertility) was popular as a toast, and is thought to have given rise, in the 16th century, to the word honeymoon. Now a secluded holiday, it was initially seen as the chance for the groom to escape with his newly captured bride from the wrath of her father.

I'm a Pisces Almost everyone in the western world knows their star sign, even if they think it is nonsense that being born at a certain time imparts particular characteristics. How did this notion become so prevalent?

In 1988, it was revealed that Nancy Reagan, the US First Lady, had regularly consulted an astrologer. This habit had been initiated by an assassination attempt on President Ronald Reagan in March 1981, whereupon Mrs Reagan invited astrologer Joan Quigley to advise her. Her aim was to plan the President's every move in order to minimise risk and utilise auspicious dates.

A storm erupted in the press. Barrett Seaman wrote in *Time* magazine: 'This was more than a charming eccentricity shared with the 50 million or so other Americans who, casually or in dead earnest, look to the alignment of the stars for guidance ... the First Lady's faith in the astrologer's pronouncements wreaked havoc with her husband's schedule. At times the most powerful man on earth was a virtual prisoner in the White House.'

The horoscopes most familiar today are daily, weekly, monthly, or annual predictions based on the Sun signs. As published in the media, these are derided by serious astrologers and although millions admit to reading them, very few – only five per cent in a recent British survey – admit to taking them seriously.

A true horoscope is a diagram showing the positions of the Sun, Moon, stars and planets placed as if the Earth were the centre of the Solar System. For an individual these positions relate to the exact moment and place of birth. The astrologer makes predictions based on the positions of the planets relative to the zodiac, a band in the sky divided into 12 sectors, each representing the passage of the Sun relative to a certain fixed constellation.

Ancient divining

Astrology is one of the oldest forms of divination. Ancient peoples used the positions of the stars, Sun, Moon and planets to predict such events as wars and famines. This was known as mundane astrology and ignored the fate of all except high-ranking persons like kings and warriors. The earliest astronomers were priests who were based at Chaldea in Babylonia, in present-day Iraq.

The oldest astrological texts date to the 18th century BC and contain such pronouncements as: 'If the sky is bright when the New Moon appears and it is greeted with shouts of joy, the year will be good.' Babylonian knowledge of the universe was limited. Each of the five planets

THE TURKISH VIEW Ottoman sultans regularly used astrology for guidance in politics and warfare. This illustration of the sign of Pisces is from a 16th-century Turkish treatise.

known to them – Jupiter, Venus, Saturn, Mercury and Mars – was connected with a deity and the movements of these planets denoted the activity of the god or goddess. The Babylonians initiated the concept of zodiac wheels – great bands of constellations seen in the night sky – which rise and set as the night progresses. These wheels form the basis of the more sophisticated idea of the signs of the zodiac.

The Egyptians, using detailed mathematical calculations, made their observations according to accurate calendars. The 13th-century BC Pharaoh Ramses II is credited with fixing the cardinal signs of Aries, Libra, Cancer and Capricorn as key points in the heavens. In ancient Greece, constellations became linked with four elements: earth, air, fire and water. This was one of the main principles laid out in the 2nd century BC by the Greek astronomer and geographer Ptolemy in his *Tetrabiblos*

BABYLONIAN BELIEF King Melishipak II presents his daughter to the moon deity, Nanna, c.1180 BC. In Babylonia, religious worship was tied to astrological belief.

(Four Books), the first astrological textbook. He defined three fire signs: Aries, Leo and Sagittarius; three Earth signs: Taurus, Virgo and Capricorn; three air signs: Gemini, Libra and Aquarius; and three water signs: Cancer, Scorpio and Pisces. Ptolemy's work remains the basis of western astrology, although much refined with the discovery of new planets (Uranus in 1781, Neptune in 1846 and Pluto in 1930) and with the work of later astrologers.

Professional astrologers were active in Imperial Rome and may have been responsible for refining the notion of 'house systems', as documented c.AD 20 by the Roman poet-astrologer, Marcus Manilius, in his *Astronomica*. Each of the 12 houses, which can be represented as sectors within the zodiac ring, is ruled by a sign of the zodiac. Each house represents an aspect of life. Since the zodiacal year begins on 21 March, the eve of the vernal (spring) equinox, the First House is the house of self, ruled by Aries (March 20 to April 19) and the planet Mars; the second is the house of possessions, ruled by Taurus and the planet Venus; and so on.

Chinese systems

In ancient China, astrology, astronomy and religion went hand in hand. Taoist priests were regarded as the most skilled diviners. In c.200 BC, the duties of the Imperial Astrologer were clearly defined: 'He makes prognostications according to the 12 years of the Jupiter cycle of good and evil of the terrestrial world' and 'from the colours of the five kinds of clouds he determines the coming of floods or drought, abundance or famine'.

There were links in early Chinese astronomy with Hellenistic teachings, but there were also significant differences. Chinese astrology focuses on a person's life path and the lucky and unlucky events that may befall them. It also sees a human life in terms of a balance between elements and signs and between yin and yang, the opposing forms of energy or 'chi'.

Chinese astrologers recognised five elements: metal, water, wood, fire and earth. The idea that each sign of the zodiac relates to an animal appears in many legends. One popular version is that Buddha invited all the animals to a New Year party but only 12 came: the rat, ox, tiger, rabbit, dragon, snake, horse, sheep, monkey, rooster, dog and pig. As a result, Buddha named a year after each of them, in the order of their arrival. Each year in this 12-year cycle now has a symbolic animal, whose characteristics are said to influence world events, as well as the personality and fate of everyone and everything born in that year.

Medicine and astrology

Astrology has always been associated with medicine, with each planet and star sign 'ruling' different body systems, organs and diseases. The Greek physician Hippocrates believed that a physician without a knowledge of astrology should 'call himself a fool rather than a physician'. The mid-17th century English herbalist Nicholas Culpeper thought that treatment without the use of astrology was like a 'lamp without oil'.

As astronomy developed during the Renaissance and the work of Galileo and Copernicus led to acceptance of the idea that the Earth revolved around the Sun, interest in astrology, at least among the educated, began to wane. But the Danish astronomer Tycho Brahe, who catalogued the stars and formulated laws of planetary motion, kept astrological diaries and consulted with royalty on astrological matters. 'Astrology,' he said, 'is not a

EGYPTIAN ZODIAC On the ceiling of the Temple of Hathor at Abu Simbel, Egypt, the four cardinal points of the zodiac are depicted as women in white.

delusive science when kept within bounds and not abused by ignorant people.' And his pupil, Johannes Kepler, who tracked and measured the orbits of the planets, saw the compilation of astrological predictions as a justified means of supplementing his income.

Your daily forecast

Through the centuries, astrology was routinely banned by the church and by the 18th century had become discredited as a cult of magic. Only in the 20th century was interest in astrology renewed.

In the years before the First World War, the English astrologer Walter Gorn Old wrote a regular column for *The Star* newspaper under the name 'Sepharial'. He predicted, often successfully, the price movements in the commodities market. But it was nearly 20 years before horoscopes truly entered the public consciousness.

On 21 August 1930, Princess Margaret was born and John Gordon,

CONSULTING THE ORACLE At a department store in Chinatown, Singapore City, people gather to read their horoscopes, set out under the 12 astrological years of the Chinese horoscope.

editor of the *Sunday Express*, asked for an astrological story on the new royal baby for his 24 August edition.

R.H. Naylor forecast that her life would be 'eventful' and predicted that 'events of tremendous importance to the Royal Family and the nation will come about near her seventh year' (the year of the abdication of Edward VIII). In 1933, in its column 'Plan with the Planets', *The People* published horoscopes by Edward Lyndoe. By 1940, every mass circulation Sunday paper and women's magazine had followed suit, with personal horoscopes syndicated worldwide.

Heavyweight support

Astrology also became the subject of more serious study throughout the century. The Swiss psychoanalyst Carl Gustav Jung, among others, gave credence to the significance of astrological symbols. He also conducted experiments on the mathematical aspects of horoscopes and how they affected successful relationships within marriage.

After comparing the birth signs of happily married couples and those who had divorced, Jung found that couples who were well matched in

astrological terms were most likely to find lasting happiness.

In the 1960s, Michel Gauquelin, a French mathematician, explored the accuracy of astrological predictions. He claimed to have found clear links between certain astrological signs and the professions of a large number of people for whom he had accurate times of birth.

The implied support for astrology from such high-profile figures helped to bring it into the mainstream. Besides consulting their newspaper horoscopes, a growing number of people had detailed astrological profiles compiled to predict how their life would turn out – or, like the Reagans, turned to astrology to organise their lives.

Despite its incredible popularity, however, astrology is still largely discredited by science. Its appeal, sceptics believe, lies in our acceptance of imprecise and broadly applicable statements that we willingly apply to our own situation. Our desire for simple explanations for why things are the way they are, why we do the jobs we do – and guidance as to the most suitable marriage partners – has fuelled a seemingly unstoppable industry.

People, personality and the planets

Can you really tell someone's star sign from their personality? Many believe you can. Obsessive neatness is often considered a Virgoan trait; obstinacy is thought typically Taurean; and flighty, inconsistent charm is characteristic of those born under the sign of Gemini. But whether people can be said to be typical of their particular star sign – known as their 'Sun sign' – is another question. Professional astrologers take the data from a person's entire birth chart into account in order to decode their client's character – a Piscean may turn out to have stronger Sagittarian traits, for example, depending on the planets' positions when they were born. Well-known people with strong characters are often cited as 'typical' examples of their sign. But they are often carefully selected, and it is equally possible to find atypical examples of their sign. Whether this bears out the professional view, or is more an indication of astrology's general worthlessness, depends on one's personal point of view.

Aries
21 March–19 April
Courageous, impetuous, energetic
• Thomas Jefferson, second US president (13 April 1743)
• Émile Zola, French author (2 April 1840)

Taurus
20 April–20 May
Patient, persistent, obstinate
• Ella Fitzgerald, US singer (25 April 1917)
• Salvador Dalí, Spanish Surrealist artist (11 May 1904)

Gemini
21 May–21 June
Progressive, clever, unstable
• Marilyn Monroe, US actress (1 June 1926)
• John F. Kennedy, US president (29 May 1917)

Cancer
22 June–22 July
Inspiring, sensitive, evasive
• Emmeline Pankhurst, campaigner for women's suffrage (14 July 1858)
• Rembrandt van Rijn, Dutch artist (15 July 1606)

Leo
23 July–22 August
Dignified, powerful, fearless
• Napoleon Bonaparte, general and emperor of France (15 August 1769)
• Henry Moore, British sculptor (30 July 1898)

Virgo
23 August–22 September
Creative, logical, pedantic
• Elizabeth I, English queen (7 September 1533)
• Agatha Christie, British crime novelist (15 September 1890)

Libra
23 September–23 October
Analytical, fair, gullible
• Mahatma Gandhi, Indian independence leader (2 October 1869);
• Oscar Wilde, Irish wit and writer (16 October 1854)

Scorpio
24 October–21 November
Magnetic, controlled, selfish
• Marie Antoinette, last queen of France (2 November 1755)
• Pablo Picasso, Spanish artist (25 October 1881)

Sagittarius
21 November–21 December
Just, profound, belligerent
• Winston Churchill, British prime minister (30 November 1874)
• Steven Spielberg, US film director (18 December 1946)

Capricorn
22 December–19 January
Independent, abstract, stubborn
• Marlene Dietrich, German actress (27 December 1901)
• Muhammad Ali, US boxer (17 January 1942)

Aquarius
20 January–18 February
Spiritual, perceptive, dispassionate
• Wolfgang Amadeus Mozart, Austrian composer (27 January 1756)
• Édouard Manet, French artist (23 January 1832)

Pisces
19 February–20 March
Kind, intelligent, restless
• Thomas Alva Edison, US inventor (11 February 1847)
• Samuel Pepys, English diarist (23 February 1633)

LEADER OF MEN Napoleon's 'Leo' qualities of leadership, self-belief and courage, and his gift for military strategy, made him utterly formidable on the battlefield.

GREAT VISIONARY Henry Moore blazed a Leonine trail into 20th-century art with his mighty and magnificent abstract sculptures.

Man's best friend – or favourite meal Why have dogs and cats become beloved pets, but other animals, like pigs and sheep, are eaten?

For most of their history, humans had an almost exclusively predatory relationship with the animals they hunted for food. Much later, probably as late as 10,000 to 15,000 years ago, the relationship between man and certain creatures changed radically as the process of domestication began. But why did some animals form a close bond with humans and not others? Why do we ride horses but not zebras? Why herd cattle but not bison or moose? And what was the defining difference between an animal raised for the benefit of humans, for its meat, hide and milk, and one that became a companion or pet?

The process of domestication

Domestication of animals and plants allowed humans to become more settled and their populations to grow. Animals kept for milk and dairy products were far more productive than those simply killed for meat. During their lifetime their manure could be used as fertiliser, and their

strength, in the case of cows and buffalo, could be harnessed to ploughs to allow cultivation of a far wider area. Horses, donkeys and camels were kept mainly to transport goods and people; they enabled the spread of human settlement more quickly, and over a wider area than would hitherto have been possible. The speed and agility of horses in particular gave their riders an advantage in warfare over peoples who lacked them.

But few animals – especially large ones – have become truly domesticated. The dog was probably the first, c.10,000 BC, in southwest Asia, China and North America. Of the herd animals, goats – hardy, sure-footed and omnivorous – were domesticated in the Zagros mountains of

THE USEFUL PIG Adaptable and happy to eat almost anything, pigs have lived alongside humans for millennia. This Chinese terracotta model of a pig in its sty is from the Eastern Han dynasty, c.AD25–220.

south-west Asia at least 10,000 years ago. Sheep and pigs – which were also found in a wide range of locations, including central Europe, Italy, northern India, China and Southeast Asia – followed not long after. Cows were domesticated around 6000 BC in south-west Asia, India and North Africa; and horses, donkeys and water buffalo by 4000 BC. Llamas and alpacas in South America, Bactrian and Arabian camels, reindeer, yak, gaur and banteng are the only other species considered to be genuinely domesticated, and it appears that the process of domestication of large animals was completed more than 4,500 years ago.

Other creatures, such as elephants, cheetahs and bears, though kept for hunting or other purposes, were tamed rather than domesticated. Both historically and more recently, there have been attempts to herd or farm other species, such as zebra, moose

What to eat, what not to eat?

In times of extreme hunger, any animal would have been 'fair game' and many still are in some parts of the world. In some countries cultural and religious taboos prevent the eating of certain species (such as cows in India, page 139); elsewhere they are a delicacy.

The eating of pork is prohibited in both Judaism and Islam. The ban comes from the book of Leviticus in the Old Testament, and is couched in a similar vein in the Koran. It states that pigs may not be eaten because although, like goats and sheep, they have cloven hooves, the fact that they do not chew the cud (and therefore do not eat grass) renders them unnatural. It may also be the case that their omnivorous scavenging diet is another reason why they are seen as unclean.

The taboo against eating horseflesh is rooted in the value of horses to human society, the close bond between man and horse and the association, by Christians, of horsemeat consumption and paganism. Archaeological evidence suggests that horses were used as food in prehistoric Europe and in Asia from c.4300 BC. A 15th-century English writer records a miserly lord saving money by serving horsemeat to his tenants. In France and elsewhere in Europe, eating horsemeat was legal by 1850.

In the forests of west and central Africa, there is a trade in so-called bushmeat, including the meat of the great apes: gorillas, chimpanzees and bonobos. Some are killed by local people for their own use; others to be sold on at a premium price. Unregulated, the trade may lead to the extinction of most of these species in the wild.

Whalemeat was a substitute for other meats during the Second World War in Europe but its oily texture made it unpopular. The Japanese, one of the few people who still hunt whales, regard it as a delicacy and are promoting it to a new generation.

A SIGN FOR A HORSEMEAT SHOP IN FRANCE

and bison, but they have not proved enduring or economically viable. Sub-Saharan Africa, with its host of magnificent wildlife, has never produced a domesticated native species. Why is this?

Three main factors influence the practicalities of animal domestication: the cost of rearing the animal, its rate of growth and its ability to reproduce in captivity. A large carnivore, such as a lion or tiger, would be prohibitively expensive to raise for meat, while an animal with a similar developmental and lifespan to humans – such as an elephant – would take too long to reach adulthood. And creatures with complicated courtship rituals or that require specialised circumstances to breed are unlikely to be successfully domesticated. The other requirements are a calm, non-violent disposition and a social or herd structure with a clear hierarchy. While many creatures have some of these characteristics, they usually have a fatal flaw – in antelope the tendency to panic, in zebra sheer irascibility – that makes them impossible to domesticate.

Food or friend?

Of all the animals that have formed bonds with humans, the dog and the pig share a number of characteristics. Both are intelligent and can be trained to obey commands. They are at home in the widest range of environments and are omnivorous. But one is regarded almost exclusively as a food animal whereas the other is eaten in only a few societies.

Recent research has shown that pigs were domesticated in a number of places around the world at much the same time. In all cases they derive from wild boars. The first steps in the process were probably initiated by the boars themselves. Bolder animals would venture close to settlements to seek food amid the human leavings. They tended to behave in a more friendly manner – possibly like that of curious juveniles – than most wild adults who were both aggressive and wary of humans. The tame scavengers got more food and could breed more easily. This kind of relationship between pig and human can still be seen today in villages throughout South America and Southeast Asia. Quick to grow, with a carcass that yields scarcely any waste and meat that was tasty even when long preserved, the worldwide popularity of the pig was assured.

Though the vast majority of pigs are still kept as livestock, a number of breeds have been promoted as pets in recent years and their playfulness and

> **Three main factors influence the practicalities of animal domestication**

Feathered friends

At least 3,000 years ago, Persian and Indian writers hailed the merits of caged birds. The mynah was sacred to the Indians while the Romans enjoyed talkative ravens. In the Middle Ages traders brought exotic birds, such as parrots, to Europe. A parrot that could recite the Lord's Prayer was reportedly bought by a Venetian cardinal for 100 pieces of silver, and in the early 15th century Pope Martin V appointed a Keeper of Parrots to serve in the Vatican. Marie Antoinette of France and Henry VIII of England are said to have owned African grey parrots, the arch mimics of the avian world.

When the Spanish colonised the Canary Islands in the 15th century they domesticated the songbirds that share the islands' name. Many were bought at high prices by Europe's wealthy and it became fashionable for a lady to receive visitors with a canary perched delicately on her finger.

The colourful budgerigar, native to Australia, was first brought to Britain in 1840 by the naturalist John Gould. In the 19th century, birdsong was particularly appreciated in rooms that would otherwise have been silent and the birdcage became an essential part of interior decor.

CARLOTA JOAQUINA OF SPAIN WITH A CANARY

intelligence extolled by breeders. These include the kune kune, a small breed from New Zealand, and the Vietnamese pot-bellied pig.

A unique relationship

In the history of domestication, the dog is a special case and has an exceptionally long-standing and close relationship with humans. All modern dogs are descended from the grey wolf, *Canis lupus*, but not, it seems, because the wolf was domesticated. It is possible that a kind of 'proto-dog' evolved, separately but in parallel to the wolf. These dogs chose to live near human settlements in much the same way as the 'village dogs' that are

found throughout Africa, Asia and South America. These ownerless dogs survive largely by scavenging, sometimes despised, but generally tolerated by the humans whose space they share. But at some point the relationship moved beyond toleration to become one of mutual benefit.

As early as 10,000 BC, dogs were being trained and bred to hunt and bring down prey and to guard camps: a piece of Mesopotamian pottery from that date shows a greyhound-like dog chasing a gazelle. By the first millennium BC, the Assyrians were breeding mastiffs for lion hunting and in battle the Romans used attack dogs in formations. The Romans distinguished between house or guard dogs, sheepdogs and dogs of the chase, which were subdivided into hunting and fighting dogs. By the

17th century, turning spits of roasting meat and tracking criminals were among the recorded jobs for dogs.

What separates dogs from other domesticated animals bred for their 'usefulness' is that they have also become pets. Most dogs have, as an element of their domestication, bonded with individual humans, whom they accepted as leaders of the pack. Ancient Egyptians kept small dogs with no discernible function apart from companionship, and went into mourning, shaving heads and eyebrows, when they died. An inscription read: 'The dog which was the guard of his Majesty. Abuwtiyuw is his name. His Majesty ordered that he be buried ceremonially and that he be given a coffin from the royal treasury, fine linen in great quantity.'

A number of smaller dogs such as the shih-tzu and Pekinese were held in esteem in China. Only members of the imperial family were allowed to own shih-tzus, which were cared for by eunuchs. In 2006, the amazingly well-preserved remains of 43 mummified dogs were found in a thousand-year-old pet cemetery in Peru. Some had their own graves and had been buried with blankets and food alongside

PAMPERED FRIEND The Persian artist Riza Abbasi painted this portrait of the affectionate relationship between a young foreigner – a Portuguese – and his dog in 1634.

tombs containing the mummified remains of the Chiribaya, predecessors of the Incas.

Like pigs, dogs' broad diet makes them unattractive as food in many societies and the close emotional bond with humans only enhances this. Those cultures that did raise dogs for meat – such as the Aztecs, ancient Polynesians and Chinese – tended to have no alternative except the pig.

In societies where other domesticated herbivores were available, dogs were simply not considered as a food animal. Though they are still bred as livestock in parts of east and Southeast Asia, the eating of dog meat worldwide remains an extremely rare event.

Cats have had a more chequered relationship with humans and have never been 'domesticated' in the strict sense that dogs were. But they were undoubtedly valued in ancient times. In 2004 in Cyprus, the 9,500-year-old grave of a cat was found close to that of a human interred with tools and jewels, suggesting that cats were kept as pets as well as for controlling mice in grain stores. In Ancient Egypt, they were even revered as gods: a huge cemetery of mummified cats was found at the temple of the cat-headed goddess Bastet in the city of Bubastis.

Cats probably reached Europe on trading ships but for centuries they were regarded as companions of witches and incarnations of the Devil. As late as the 17th century, it was considered sport to shoot at a cat hung in a basket at country fairs.

Felines in favour

By this time, however, the cat's reputation was recovering. Eminent figures such as the Archbishop of Canterbury, William Laud, who kept a tabby cat, and Cardinal Richelieu in France, who left provision in his will to care for his numerous felines, were among those who appreciated their companionship as well as their hunting skills. Cats abound in 19th-century painting – Manet, Renoir and Gauguin all painted them – while a cat called Tabby accompanied Abraham Lincoln to the White House.

TRAINING TOGETHER A Chinese soldier skips with his dog in an exercise designed to encourage bonding and keep both of them fit.

When Christmas became 'Christmassy'

Was Christmas as we know it invented in the 19th century or is it still an essentially medieval festival? When did all the traditions come together to form the festival we know today?

In London, switching on the lights in Oxford and Regent Street is an annual ritual performed by a media favourite of the moment. When it comes to decorating few can rival Dominic Luberto of Boston, USA. In 2007, he decked his home and garden with half a million lights, turning his doorstep into a holiday destination in its own right. But did today's gaudy Christmas start with Christianity – and when did the trappings we associate with it become so enshrined in western society?

Many familiar Christmas traditions have their roots in ancient pre-Christian ritual. A festival in which the Persians paid homage to Mithras, god of light and guardian against evil, was the inspiration for Christmas illuminations. Every year, on the eve of the winter solstice, his followers lit fires to celebrate the birthday of the unconquered Sun in the hope that, with the passage of the seasons, spring would soon be on its way.

Feasting and merry making

In the 4th century AD, the bawdy Roman festival of Saturnalia was celebrated with a week of feasting, gambling and merry making. Yule, a far older pagan Scandinavian celebration of the midwinter solstice, is the root of many other traditions including the burning of a Yule log – then in honour of the god, Thor – the decorating of fir and spruce trees and the hanging of holly and mistletoe.

To mark the birth of Christ, the early Church drew together elements of all these celebrations. The Venerable Bede wrote of Christian missionaries preaching to the Germanic peoples of northern Europe being instructed to superimpose Christian themes onto existing pagan holidays. The importance of Christmas grew following the adoption of Christianity

CHRISTMAS BLAZE The domestic light show is a recent Christmas 'tradition'. A source of pride and friendly competition, it is known in America as 'extreme decorating'.

by the emperor Constantine in 312 AD and the date ascribed to Christ's birth became increasingly prominent. Monarchs chose the date for their coronation and medieval chroniclers regularly recorded lavish celebrations held on Christmas Day by royalty.

The fall – and rise – of Christmas

In the years following the 16th-century Protestant Reformation in England, however, Christmas festivities came to be frowned on or suppressed. After the Civil War, the Puritan government ordered the observance of Christmas without feasting, and in 1647 Oliver Cromwell banned Christmas altogether by act of Parliament. Celebrating Christmas fell out of favour in America after the Revolution as it was considered to be an English custom.

By the 1820s, in a calmer, more secular atmosphere, writers such as William Winstanley, Charles Dickens and the American Washington Irving began to create a romanticised portrait of Christmases past and imagined. This revived the festival's popularity, and highlighted aspects of celebration and the coming together of family and friends. Some have claimed that Irving invented the traditions he described (page 293), but whatever their provenance, they were widely copied.

The symbols of Christmas

The legendary status of the Christmas tree dates from the 8th century AD, when St Boniface cut down an oak (a tree sacred to Thor), used it to build a chapel and a fir tree sprang up in its place. The fir was first taken indoors 'officially' in 1521 when Princess Hélène de Mecklenbourg took one to Paris after her marriage to the Duke of Orléans; Christmas trees were also popular with the Hanoverians.

Traditional Christmas fare

Late medieval diners enjoyed hearty Christmas feasts and dazzled their guests with luxurious sweetmeats made from ground almonds, sugar and crystallised fruits. By the 19th century, many of today's favourite Christmas foods were already well established. Others are much later arrivals.

A bird and all the trimmings

Until the 19th century, goose was the Christmas bird and, from the tradition of eating wild boar at Saturnalia and Yule, a pork or ham was as usual as poultry. The Spanish introduced turkey to Europe in 1519; Henry VIII of England is said to have eaten it at Christmas. Cranberries, the partner to the American Thanksgiving turkey (which doubled up for Christmas) since the time of the Pilgrim Fathers, have been widely available in Europe only since the 1950s.

Christmas cakes and puddings

The familiar dark, rich fruitcake is an evolution of the boiled plum cake of the 1700s, itself a refinement of the spiced plum porridge eaten in earlier centuries on Christmas Eve to line the stomach after a day's fasting. Only from the late 19th century was the cake served on Christmas Day. Before this it was saved until Twelfth Night on January 6th.

The *büche de Noël* or Yule log, popular from the 1870s, particularly in France, is a rolled sponge cake filled and coated with chocolate buttercream and decorated with a sprig of holly. It represents the luck-bringing log once burnt in the hearth.

German *stollen* is a rich fruit bread with a ridge down the centre that is believed to represent the swaddled infant Jesus. It has only been made with butter since 1650 when Prince Ernst von Sachsen, at the request of Dresden bakers, successfully petitioned Pope Urban VIII to lift the restrictions on the use of butter during Advent.

Like Christmas cake, Christmas pudding developed from plum pottage. The kind we eat today was a favourite of England's Prince Albert. Originally made with chopped beef and vegetables, dried fruit was added in the 16th century as well as chicken. Gradually, the meat in the pudding was dropped and suet added.

Mince pies

In the Middle Ages mince pies, or *chewettes*, were small shredded meat or fish pies made with sugar, spices and fruit, and by the 16th century were already popular at Christmas. By 1800 the pies grew smaller and the meat – the 'mince' – had disappeared. The idea that the first mince pie of the year is particularly lucky probably goes back to about the same time.

EDIBLE SYMBOL The *büche de Noël* is traditionally served in France after Mass on Christmas Eve.

Prince Albert is credited with their burgeoning popularity in England from the 1840s when he set up a tree at Windsor Castle, but in fact he made fashionable an existing tradition: by this time decorated trees had already been on public display for half a century and more.

Lights and legends

Christmas trees were decorated, often with tinsel, lights and baubles. Tinsel, originally made from beaten silver strips, was a German invention, arising from a legend that the spiders' webs on a poor woman's tree were turned to silver by the Christ child. Candles were initially the only source of light but in 1882, Edward Johnson, a colleague of the American inventor Thomas Edison, invented electric tree lights. These were an expensive luxury item until 1903, when they began to be mass-produced by the battery manufacturer Ever Ready.

Homes in the 19th century were also draped with boughs of evergreen holly and ivy, symbolic of renewal and everlasting life – a relic from the festival of Yule. Christianity took over the pagan symbolism and the red berries of the holly came to represent Christ's blood and its prickles the crown of thorns. Mistletoe was sacred

to the Druids and considered a fertility symbol by the Romans – who originated the custom of kissing under the mistletoe. The plant was also a token of peace and reconciliation and a kiss a symbol of pardon. Mistletoe's pagan associations are still recalled by many and it is widely thought inappropriate to use mistletoe for Church decorations.

So enduring was the evergreen symbolism that it even appeared on the first Christmas card in the form of delicate ivy tendrils. The card was designed by the English artist John Callcott Horsley in 1843, and depicts in its central panel a family sitting around the table with wine glasses in their hands, while side panels show a man and a woman giving alms to the poor. It is a romantic portrayal, but one that encapsulated the season's charitable and celebratory spirit.

Old customs revived

The 19th-century romanticisers of Christmas also highlighted customs such as the singing of carols, the setting up of a crib and the

performance of the pantomime. Carols were originally folk songs accompanied by a ring dance, and wassailing referred to carols sung outdoors at Christmas from medieval times. St Francis of Assisi introduced carols to church services in the 13th century but the revival of carols began in the early 19th century: 'Silent Night! Holy Night!' dates to 1818 and 'O Little Town of Bethlehem' to 1868.

St Francis is believed to have inaugurated the Christmas crib in 1223, in a cave near Greccio. The image of the baby Jesus was sculpted in stone, but the ox and ass were real. Mass was said around the manger and St Francis preached. His intention was to make Christ's birth come alive for people, and he was so successful that wooden nativity scenes were soon displayed all over Europe.

> St Francis is believed to have inaugurated the Christmas crib in 1223, in a cave. The animals were real and Mass was said around the manger

The Christmas pantomime, particularly the tradition whereby men and women swap roles to comic effect, began as a celebration of Saturnalia. Mummers, often masked, acted out their plays in the streets and mischief was rife, for this was the time when the Lord of Misrule held sway. The format was influenced by the Italian Commedia dell'arte, and fixed elements such as the lovers, father and servants are found today. But the 'father of modern pantomime' is considered to be August Harris, manager of the Drury Lane Theatre in London in the 1870s, where many of the strict conventions of modern pantomime found their final form.

The seductive story of Santa Claus and Rudolph

In 1812 the American writer Washington Irving wrote a story about the magical visits of St Nicholas – in the form of a rather wizened elf – to the Dutch houses in New York where he was known as Sinterklaas or Santa Claus. For good children he brought gifts, for the bad ones switches. The tale was based on the ancient legend of St Nicholas, an Anatolian bishop, the protector of sailors and children, whose feast day (the day of his death in 326 AD) is on 6 December. Until the Reformation in the 16th century, the feast of St Nicholas was widely celebrated throughout northern Europe, and even beyond this time the Dutch kept alive the tradition of a man dressed in red and white robes – a bishop's attire – riding a horse through the streets and giving gifts to children.

It was American cartoonist Thomas Nast who combined Irving's elf and the St Nicholas character into a jolly fat man with a beard. Nast's 1863 image of Santa climbing down the chimney sealed his identity, assisted by a series of Coca-Cola advertisements that began in 1931 featuring Santa in a red suit trimmed with white fur.

Sleigh bells glisten

In northern Europe, sleighs and reindeer feature in myth and legend. For Finns, Old Man Winter arrives on a sleigh pulled by reindeer. In Norse law Odin, with cloak and beard, held a hunting party every year on the midwinter feast of Yule and brought children gifts or punishments. For good luck, children would leave food for the god's trusty steed Sleipnir out on the hearth. The horse had eight legs and Santa's eight reindeer are thought to be a representation of this. The 1823 poem ' 'Twas the Night Before Christmas', attributed to the American writer Clement Clarke Moore, features both reindeer and the leaving of presents for children on Christmas Eve.

For all good children

Over 400 years ago, Dutch children put out wooden shoes for St Nicholas on the eve of December 6th, filling them with straw for his white horse. Shoes turned into Christmas stockings in the 19th century (thanks to Thomas Nast) when food was also left for the reindeer, but in France shoes are still left out on Christmas Eve for Santa to fill with gifts.

Santa's companion Rudolph the Red-nosed Reindeer was 'born' in 1939 when the Chicago department store Montgomery Ward asked copywriter Robert L. May, to write a Christmas story to give to shoppers as a promotion. Drawing on the Ugly Duckling tale and his childhood experiences, May settled on the idea of an underdog with a glowing red nose. Wanting to use alliteration, May rejected both Rollo and Reginald before choosing Rudolph as his hero.

ADVERTISING SANTA Coca-Cola's winter campaigns featuring a red-clad Santa started in 1931. Santa was already a well-known Christmas character; the publicity simply reinforced his image.

Superstitions and lucky charms All around the world, many people still believe that the supernatural intervenes in everyday life. Where do these ideas come from?

Worldwide, one in every 10 people is afflicted by triskaidekaphobia, the fear of the number 13. Estate agents find houses numbered 13 hard to sell and even a house numbered 12a may have a horseshoe hung at the threshold. This supposedly waylays evil because the Devil moves in a circle and the gap in the horseshoe will make him turn back.

Friday 13th is believed the unluckiest of all days. Although fewer people choose to drive their cars on that day, a 1993 study published in the *British Medical Journal* concluded that the number of car accidents on Friday 13th is higher than on other Fridays. The doom associated with 13 is a

superstition that probably stems from the Last Supper of Jesus with his 12 disciples, one of whom – Judas Iscariot – would betray him. The link with Friday comes from Christians remembering this event on Good Friday. From the same origin there arose the belief that if 13 people sit down at table, one of the assembly will die within the year. On Friday, 13 October 1307, King Philip IV of France had every member of the Knights Templar arrested on charges of heresy. He aimed to seize their wealth and therefore had them tortured to extract confessions of an extreme kind, including idolatry.

BURNED AT THE STAKE The Knights Templar were convicted of heresy and blasphemy. Their fate is depicted in the *Chronicle of France, c.*1308.

In the ancient world, numbers were the keys to understanding the universe and its magical forces. They were also culture-specific. In Babylon, where the numbering system was based on 60, the numbers from one to 60 were deemed blessed of the gods. In ancient China odd numbers, considered to be female, were believed to be luckier than even numbers, which were male.

One, the indivisible number of divine unity, two, the link between God and man and between a pair of humans, and three, the number of the Holy Trinity, have long been regarded as lucky. Four, especially in the form of a four-leaf clover, means perfection but is unlucky for the Chinese because it sounds like the word for death.

Both the Babylonians and ancient Egyptians thought seven (the sum of three and four, both propitious) to be lucky because it was the number of the sacred planets. In the Bible, it is significant that Noah led seven pairs of all clean animals, one pair of every unclean animal and seven pairs of birds into the ark. When the flood subsided, God, who had created the world in seven days, sent a redeeming rainbow with seven colours.

Worn for good fortune
The ancient Egyptians wore lucky charms or amulets as a protection against death and evil spirits. One of the oldest was the 'eye' of Horus, a sky god who took the shape of a falcon. His right eye represents a falcon's, including the 'teardrop' sometimes

BLESSINGS This life-size Hand of Power, raised in a gesture of benediction and adorned with charms, was believed to guard houses from evil in Roman times.

seen below it. Horus was called on by his mother Isis to destroy her wicked brother Set, and lost his eye after a series of battles with Set. When the eye was restored it was believed to have special powers. The eye symbol was also known as a 'wadjet', a deity with links to the Sun. Representations of the eye were made of precious metal and endowed its wearer with the strength of the life-giving Sun. Babies, and even valuable livestock, were given amulets for protection. Today's christening gifts are a remnant of this practice.

Amulets or talismans, worn as bracelets, necklaces, rings or even belts, are usually made of gold or silver, jewels or semi-precious stones. The five-pointed 'wizard's star' was

popular in medieval times. It was emblematic of the mysteries of the universe and believed to strengthen the soul. For the traveller, wearing an image of St Christopher, the patron saint of travellers, is lucky. According to legend, the saint once offered to carry a child, who then became heavier than any other burden. He later revealed himself as Jesus.

Talismans for the home
To propitiate spirits that protect the household, the skull of a human or animal – especially a horse – would be embedded in the walls when a house was built. Many ancient cultures believed it would ward off evil or illness, and its resistance to decay reflected a hope that the home would endure. Grotesque faces, still used in African countries and in Mexico, are also believed to ward off evil spirits.

The 'weak point' in a house is the keyhole, through which evil can enter or fairies steal a newborn baby, so keeping a key in the door is a safety precaution. This also explains why breaking or dropping a key is meant to be unlucky. Windows or 'wind eyes' are also vulnerable points. A multi-coloured glass ball might be hung up in a window to distract the evil gaze of a witch and absorb the impact of any venom that she might spit.

The ancient art of geomancy, or feng shui, decrees that, to avoid ill luck, the items within a home must be optimally placed relative to the lines of energy crossing the landscape.

JEWELLED PROTECTION A charm bracelet hung with tiny talismans is considered to be more effective made in gold and precious stones.

This derives from the links between ancient feng shui and astronomy. The Chinese used the study of astronomy to link humans with the universe and the pole stars, while the position in relation to the celestial poles determined the north-south axis of settlements.

Using these rules, a home should ideally be set with hills or tall trees to the north or back, and water flowing to the south or front, so that the favourable aspects of cosmic breath, or *chi,* are perfectly balanced with the unfavourable ones. Inside, screens will help to keep positive energy flowing out of the doors. A mirror should never be placed on the wall facing a bed because the spirit leaves the body at night and may be disturbed by its own reflection.

Staying lucky

All kinds of actions are supposed to influence luck. Crossing the fingers to avert bad luck or to induce a lucky event is thought to relate to the Crucifixion, as is the older and, for gamblers, even luckier action of crossing the legs. From Roman times, holding the thumb with the fingers of the same hand has been a way of keeping away ghosts. The same action was

a medieval way of keeping a witch from seeing you. Touching or knocking on wood for luck probably dates back to the ancient belief in tree spirits. But not just any wood will do. The ash and yew, trees of immortality, are luckiest while hornbeam was favoured as the wood of the sorcerer's wand. At sea, men believe that touching iron will confer the best protection against evil if someone should blaspheme.

Avoidance can be as important as action. Fear of walking under a ladder dates back to the old practice of hanging criminals after making them climb a ladder to their execution. Opening an umbrella indoors could bring ill fortune or even be an omen of death, particularly to the Chinese, who saw it as an insult to the Sun, their warmth-bringing deity.

The animals and people who cross your path may also affect - your fortunes. In Africa and Ancient Egypt, hares were symbols of both good and bad luck, symbolising mortality and renewal. They had many roles in Native American culture but in the most all-encompassing form

TEMPLE GUARDIAN A *yaksha* or mythical demi-god keeps evil spirits away from the Temple of the Emerald Buddha in Bangkok.

represented the life-giving power of the Sun. More recently they were thought to resemble covens of witches and were deemed unlucky. Cats, too, are both lucky and unlucky. They were revered as gods in Ancient Egypt but burned for their perceived links to witches in the Middle Ages and later. Their colour is significant. In Britain, black cats are lucky, but in most other places, white cats fill this role, in some instances bringing wealth. Sheep are lucky if you encounter them in a flock, but it is unlucky to count them – they, or you, may die as a result.

Theatre customs

Professions traditionally fraught with uncertainty, such as acting and fishing, have attracted many superstitions. In Greece and Rome, plays were performed to propitiate the gods and to help to assure every important event from the return of spring to fruitful harvests. Many customs still persist. An actor will keep a rabbit's foot, an ancient lucky charm, in a make-up box, and avoid knitting or whistling (which can summon evil) anywhere in the theatre at any time. A cat backstage is lucky, as are shoes that squeak on a first stage entrance. A visitor can bring good luck to the dressing room, but only if they enter right foot first.

'The Scottish Play' – actors will never call it *Macbeth* – has strong associations with ill luck. One theory is that the witches' speeches will curse the production. Another is that actors may be injured during the numerous scenes involving swordplay. Or it may simply be the case that the play was regularly staged as the repertory season came to an end and audiences were smaller than they had been.

To ensure good weather, safety at sea and a good catch, sailors and fishermen observe many superstitions. For a fisherman, meeting a woman in an apron is the height of bad luck and may even prompt an immediate return home. Launching a ship by breaking a bottle of wine over her bow dates

from the Greek practice of pouring wine over a ship as a gift to Poseidon, god of the sea. Because they are thought to embody witches, pins are never taken on board ship, but gold earrings offer protection from both shipwrecks and drowning. In the USA, May Day is auspicious for fishing, when, it is said, fish will 'bite almost a bare hook'.

Days and dates
It is an ancient belief that anything started on a Monday will not work out well – possibly because it was seen to be a day of reckoning after the events of the previous week. In France the name St Lundi was given to days when shoemakers would, for this reason, take a day off work. In the British Navy, 'Blue Monday' was the day when a sailor's misdeeds would be punished. But both nails and hair are best cut on Monday 'for health'.

Friday, the Roman 'day of Venus', was an auspicious day associated with love and beauty, but for Christians, who remember it as the day of the Crucifixion, it has many connections

with bad luck. The Christian tradition also underlies the belief that it was sinful (and unlucky) to work on a Sunday. In medieval times, many dates were considered unlucky. They were called 'dismal' or 'Egyptian' days from their links to bad luck or to events such as the 10 plagues of Egypt. One 15th-century calendar includes 32 such dates, beginning with 1 January and ending with 17 December.

Red, green and blue are the colours most associated with superstitions, as well as the 'non-colours' black and white. Red represents energy, life-giving blood and healing. As the colour of a talisman, it confers protection against both witches and the Devil. The custom of giving babies red coral teething rings reflects this ancient superstition. Green is a

GERMAN LORE A Green Man costume such as this, from a 17th-century German manuscript, would have been worn at the Nuremberg masked carnival.

symbol of life and its 'resurrection' in spring, and also of mischief. The two associations combine in the character of the Green Man or Jack in the Green. This figure is sometimes regarded as a fertility symbol, but at other times as malign, maybe even the Devil himself.

Blue, the colour of the sky, denotes truth and knowledge, and is thought to dispel the power of the Evil Eye. The association of blue clothes with good luck dates back to the time when the children of Israel fringed their clothes with 'blue ribands' for protection. Highly-regarded boy babies were given the same safeguard with blue clothing.

Black is bad, white good, mirroring dark and light, evil and purity. The two colours combine in magpies, birds feared on their own but welcome in pairs. The dual colouring relates to the bird's refusal to go into full mourning after the death of Christ.

Why do we go on pilgrimages? Over two million Muslims travel to Mecca each year, while Christians journey to Lourdes. How did the notion of making a pilgrimage to a sacred place arise? And why have some locations become such magnets for the faithful?

'Once more the bells tolled. Once more the victims' names were read. Once more New York and the nation harkened back to that terrible morning when terrorists in hijacked airliners struck and America shuddered. Only this time there were no blue skies to mock the mourners at Ground Zero.' So the New York *Daily News* described the most modern of pilgrimages to the site of the terror attacks of 9/11. For those who lost loved ones in the attack on the Twin Towers, their annual visit to the site of the tragedy is a personal journey. For others it is an attempt to come to terms with a global horror and one that may have a spiritual, as well as a personal and political, dimension.

Other locations of relatively recent traumatic events are also popular sites of pilgrimage. More people than ever now visit the First World War graveyards in France and Belgium and the remains of Auschwitz-Birkenau and other Nazi extermination camps. Ron Feinberg from Atlanta, Georgia, USA knew that, while visiting, he and his fellow travellers to Auschwitz 'would immerse ourselves briefly in the local culture and spend time wandering the cobblestone lanes and picturesque corners of these ancient and charming communities; [but] it was understood that there was a dark, melancholy side to all of this, that the trip would carry a hefty load of emotional baggage'.

Pilgrims from Australia and New Zealand travel to Turkey on 25 April, ANZAC day, in remembrance of more than 11,000 of their forebears who perished at Gallipoli in 1915. Visitors to the site today have many reasons for being there: for some it is simply part of their itinerary; for others it is a journey to a sacred place where they seek both a spiritual and an emotional connection to their ancestors and their country's past. David, a young Australian 'found one grave for G.P. Castle of the 2nd Battalion ... Private Castle was 25 and from New South Wales. I stood there looking at this man's grave and realised that I was 25 and from New South Wales'.

Early pilgrimage
From the earliest times, people have associated certain places with spiritual renewal and healing, and with their heroes or ancestors. Deities, saints or

holy figures were often believed to reside at places of pilgrimage and only by visiting them could their special blessing be conferred. When miracles have been witnessed at some sites, their magnetism is considerably increased.

Going on a pilgrimage was and is an opportunity for the pilgrim to travel beyond the boundaries of their normal life and to experience the world in a different way. They may have physical problems that they hope to heal or mental torments that they want to resolve. The idea of renewal and rebirth is particularly important in pilgrimage – leaving behind the old to embrace the new. At the same time, revisiting a place of trauma is now often recommended as a way of getting over a painful experience. And many look to make a new connection to their god,

CHAUCER'S PILGRIMS
Geoffrey Chaucer's
The Canterbury Tales –
24 in all – are told by
a motley group of
pilgrims to enliven
the journey from
Southwark in London
to Canterbury.

ancestors or those people who have endured similar experiences.

A pilgrimage can take place at any time of year, but spring, connected with the Judaeo-Christian rituals of Passover and Easter, has long been the most popular time. Geoffrey Chaucer, author of *The Canterbury Tales*, maintained that spring was the season when people become restless for both travel and renewal. Undergoing physical hardship in order to gain spiritual awakening and growth may be optional today but historically it was an inevitable consequence of long-distance travel. Many pilgrims could expect to endure anything from shipwreck to malaria. The custom of travelling as a group probably began to gain protection against brigands and natural hazards, as well as to combat loneliness.

Ancient sites

At least 10,000 years ago, Australian aborigines made pilgrimages to places such as Uluru (Ayers Rock) and still do so today. At these sacred sites, located on the Dreaming Trails that form an invisible network across the continent, they revisit their ancestors and play out ancient rituals that link past and present. By touching the rock they invoke the spirits of their ancestors, who confer a blessing in return. In the 19th century BC and undoubtedly for many centuries before, ancient Egyptian pilgrims were visiting Abydos, the place where Osiris, king of death and resurrection, died and was reborn.

By the first century BC, pilgrims from Greece and beyond were travelling to Delphi to consult the oracle, the priestess Pythia, installed there by the god Apollo after he killed the evil serpent Python. The oracle, consulted on everything from religion and marriage to money matters, could be questioned only after pilgrims had undergone purification in the waters of the nearby Castalian spring and a goat had been sacrificed. Questions were presented on stone tablets and a priest was on hand to interpret Pythia's babbled answers.

Elsewhere in Europe, pilgrims visited Neolithic monuments such as the stone circles at Avebury in Wiltshire, dating to 2600 BC. The stones themselves probably marked an earlier site of religious pilgrimage; the original ground plan represented the body of a serpent passing through a circle – a traditional alchemical symbol. As well as participating in religious rituals, pilgrims would expect to be enriched by sensing the energy accumulated and transmitted from the earth via the stones.

To Jerusalem

The Temple in Jerusalem, built by Solomon in 957 BC, was the spiritual centre of the Judaic world until its destruction in AD 70. All male Jews who could make the journey completed their pilgrimages to the Temple with sacrifices. The devout would make pilgrimages three times a year, at Passover, Shavuot (the reaping festival) and Sukkot (harvest). The Temple itself was a place of contemplation and prayer. Today, Jewish pilgrims visit the Western or Wailing Wall, whose base is the only remaining part of the outer wall that supported the Temple's structure. Many still insert pieces of paper bearing prayers of supplication into the cracks between the stones.

Christian pilgrims have visited the site of Christ's crucifixion, burial and resurrection since the 4th century, when Christianity was legalised in the Roman Empire. Even after the Muslims captured Jerusalem in AD 638, Christian pilgrims were permitted to visit the city. This changed in 1009, and especially after the Seljuk Turks took Jerusalem; apart from brief periods during the Crusades, it was not until the 14th century that Christians could once more visit Jerusalem. Most revered of Christian sites is the Church of the Holy Sepulchre, on the site where Joseph of Arimathea buried Jesus' body.

In the early years of Islam, Jerusalem, not Mecca, was the goal of Muslim pilgrims, specifically the rock that the Koran describes as the scene of the Prophet Mohammad's ascension into Paradise during his 'Night Journey'. Since it was completed in 691, the Dome of the Rock has marked this place. Within the mosque, lying exactly beneath the dome, lies the rock itself.

In search of the saints

Much Christian pilgrimage is focused on sites associated with the saints and apostles. Pilgrims can express appreciation for the sacrifices of the saints and in doing so find spiritual enlightenment. Places where saintly relics have been found are also thought to possess spiritual power. Historically, many had the advantage of being much more accessible than Jerusalem. Rome, where St Peter presided over the early Church and was crucified in around AD 64, has been a site of pilgrimage since Rome became the medieval centre of the Catholic Church. St Peter's Basilica, built over the grave of the saint, has been a goal for pilgrims since the 4th century.

In northwest Spain, Santiago de Compostela became a place of pilgrimage after Bishop Godescalc from Le Puy in Auvergne arrived with a group of followers: they were the site's first foreign pilgrims. The group hoped to gain spiritual enrichment from the place where the remains of the apostle James were thought to be buried. A witness to the transfiguration of Christ, James was martyred in Jerusalem in AD 44.

After his death, his body was, according to legend, put in a boat and taken to Spain. The burial place was identified in c.815 after a hermit named Pelagius was guided to a marble tomb by mysterious lights in the sky. King Alphonso II promptly declared James patron saint of the region. Following Godescalc's pilgrimage, the Way of St James – a merger of four routes from different parts of France – was established, with hospitals and priories dotted along the route. By the 12th century Santiago de Compostela was on a par with Jerusalem and Rome as a pilgrimage destination, as it is today.

Canterbury Cathedral was already sacred to those who venerated St Dunstan when Archbishop Thomas à Becket was murdered there, apparently on the orders of Henry II, in 1170. His killing was perceived as a martydom and several miracles were

TIBETAN PILGRIMAGE Thousands of pilgrims visit Potala Palace in Lhasa every day to walk a *kora* (clockwise circuit). This sacred site houses the tombs of past Dalai Lamas.

said to have occurred at his tomb. Becket was swiftly canonised and a wave of pilgrimage followed.

When the cathedral was rebuilt early in the 13th century and Becket's body moved to the Trinity Chapel, pilgrim numbers grew still further. In the 1380s, when Chaucer was writing *The Canterbury Tales*, even more people were flocking to Canterbury and continued to do so until 1538 when Henry VIII ordered Becket's shrine to be dismantled and its riches transferred to the royal coffers. Only in the 20th century was pilgrimage to Canterbury revived.

Muslim duty

Muslims must make the Hajj – a pilgrimage to Mecca – at least once in their lifetime. Numerically, the Hajj is without rival: more than two million make the journey each year, gathering in the sacred precincts of the Great Mosque to worship Allah. At the centre of the Mosque, pilgrims circle around the cube-shaped Ka'aba on whose southeast corner sits the Black Stone, formerly an object of pagan worship until it was cleansed by Mohammad in 630. Pilgrims are still required to circle and kiss the stone seven times.

Mecca is the city where Mohammad was born and died, but the Hajj commemorates events in the life of the Old Testament prophet Abraham, who lived in Mecca and endured a succession of trials of faith. In obedience to God's command, Abraham left his wife Hagar and their son Ishmael in Mecca, trusting that God would care for them. As she searched anxiously for water, a spring miraculously arose to quench the boy's thirst. It was at Mecca, too, that God ordered Abraham to build the Ka'aba on a site sacred to Adam. Later, paganism gradually took over and more than 300 idols were placed in the Ka'aba. Nudity and immorality became the hallmarks of its associated rituals. Only when Mohammad

Places of healing

The power of water is a recurring theme in pilgrimages to the world's most renowned places of healing.

Lourdes

In 1858, the Virgin Mary appeared to St Bernadette in a vision in the Grotto of Massabielle at Lourdes. Here the Blessed Virgin is said to have instructed Bernadette to drink from a previously undiscovered spring. The spring water is believed to possess healing powers. Since the vision, pilgrims, especially those in need of healing, have flocked to Lourdes by the million to immerse themselves in the grotto's 17 pools, six of them for men and 11 for women.

Walsingham

In 1061, Lady Richeldis, the wife of a Norman lord, had a vision of the Virgin Mary in which she was transported in spirit to the spot where the Angel Gabriel had appeared at the Annunciation. The Virgin commanded her to build a replica at Walsingham in Norfolk, eastern England, and the resulting shrine at Our Lady's Well became a popular place of pilgrimage attributed with healing powers. The shrine was destroyed during the

Reformation and rebuilt in 1931, since when it has remained a magnet for pilgrimages of healing.

The River Ganges

Hindus revere the River Ganges. They believe its water to be the embodiment of Ganga, the 'swift goer' and goddess of purification. Because the river is believed to have the power to purify and heal, the sick are carried to its banks and the ashes of the dead scattered in its sacred waters.

SOUVENIR PRINT FROM LOURDES, 1867

legitimised the Black Stone did Mecca become established as the holiest city in the Muslim world.

Places of enlightenment

In Buddhism, the earliest centres of pilgrimage were the places bound up with the life and teachings of the Master. They include Lumbini, now in Nepal, where Buddha was born, and Bodh Gaya in India where, under the Bo tree, Buddha was enlightened. Other sites are Sarnath, the scene of his first teaching, and Kushinara, where he died.

After Buddha's death, the remains of his body were collected from the

funeral pyre and divided into eight parts. A stupa or burial mound was erected over each one. Buddhist pilgrimage to honour Buddha and to experience rebirth in a divine location probably began as visits to these sacred locations. Although the act of pilgrimage is not a condition of being a devout Buddhist, many devotees of the faith have undertaken widespread wanderings across the globe to visit sacred shrines and to carry out good works for others. In doing so they have contributed significantly to the spread of Buddhism across the world.

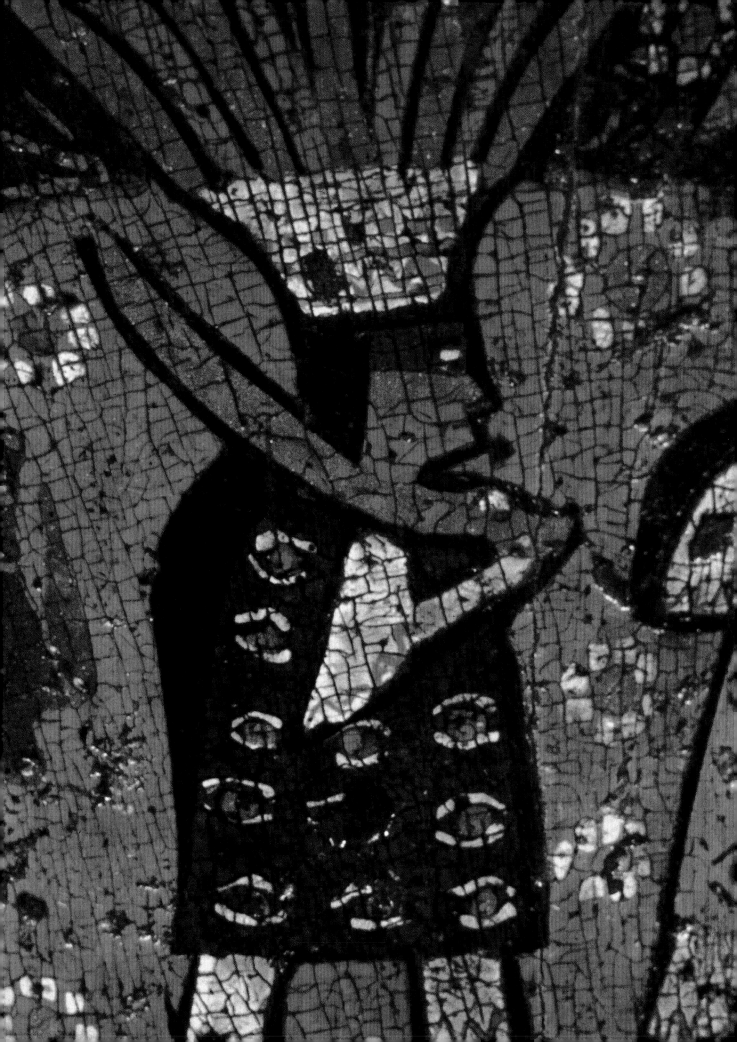

WAR AND PEACE 8

The nuclear club The desire to acquire nuclear weapons in some countries is matched only by the desire by other countries to prevent them. Who decided who could belong to the nuclear club?

SIGNED AND SEALED The 1963 Nuclear Test Ban Treaty was the first international agreement on nuclear weapons. Soviet Premier Nikita Khrushchev signed the treaty on behalf of the USSR.

Shortly after dawn on 16 July 1945, the USA became the world's first and sole nuclear power when a prototype atomic bomb was tested successfully in the New Mexico desert. The bomb's coming and its use against the Japanese – followed by development of the even more powerful hydrogen bomb – ushered humanity into a new, potentially disastrous era. Where the USA had led, other powers were determined to follow. The so-called nuclear club was the result.

The USA did not remain the world's sole nuclear power for long, despite its attempts to keep its new technology a secret. Probably thanks as much to its spies as its scientists, the USSR tested its own atomic bomb in 1949. Britain followed in 1952. France joined the nuclear club in 1960, China in 1964.

Today, the club probably has nine members. Of these, the USA, Britain, France, Russia and China are signatories of the 1968 Nuclear Non-Proliferation Pact, an agreement specifically devised to halt the spread of nuclear arms. It attempted to limit the number of countries permitted to have nuclear weapons to the five

nuclear nations. Currently, 189 other countries adhere to its terms. The remaining nuclear nations – India, Pakistan and Israel – were non-signatories. India carried out its first nuclear test in 1974. In 1998, it exploded five nuclear devices in succession. Pakistan's response was to test six of its own nuclear weapons the same year. Israel's position was more ambivalent. Enforcing strict secrecy the country refused to confirm whether or not it has developed its own nuclear arsenal. But most authorities believe that Israel possesses a stockpile of anywhere between 75 and 200 nuclear weapons, together

> 'We have genuflected before the god of science only to find that it has given us the atomic bomb, producing fears and anxieties that science can never mitigate.'
>
> Martin Luther King

with the ability to deliver them. A fourth authoritarian state, North Korea, tested its first bomb in 2006, though experts believe that the test was only partly successful.

Secrecy and subterfuge

Before the first bombs fell, keeping the workings of its nuclear weaponry secret had been US government policy. Even Britain, which had collaborated with the US in the so-called Manhattan Project to build the bomb and had been promised a share in the necessary nuclear technology, was completely left out in the cold when the McMahon Act became law in 1946. It forbade the release of such secrets to other powers – even to allies. The British response was immediate. Prime Minister Clement Attlee authorised work to develop a British bomb.

What perturbed the Americans most was the speed at which the USSR developed its own nuclear technology. US military intelligence had predicted that it would take the Russians a decade or more to build a nuclear bomb. They managed it in little more than three years. Senator Joseph McCarthy, leader of a strident anti-Communist witch-hunt in the USA, had no doubts that Soviet spies and US traitors were the reason why. President Harry Truman's response was to announce the launch of a crash programme to develop the even more powerful hydrogen bomb. As opposed to the atomic bomb, which relies purely on nuclear fission for its explosive effects, the hydrogen bomb is a fusion weapon, which uses a fission bomb as its trigger. The USA tested its first H-bomb in November 1952; the USSR followed with its own less than a year later.

Despite the wildness of McCarthy's allegations there were Soviet atomic spies who had managed to penetrate to the heart of the Manhattan Project. Among them was Klaus Fuchs, who was arrested in Britain in 1950. At his trial, Fuchs confessed to passing a detailed drawing of an atomic bomb to his KGB controllers. Spies in the USA included Ted Hall and George Koval. All in all, the atomic spies are believed to have saved the USSR two to eight years in the race to develop a nuclear device of its own.

A deadly arms race

The nuclear arms race was a key element in the Cold War (page 283). It became ever more competitive as the USA and the USSR feverishly stockpiled increasingly powerful warheads in their arsenals and other would-be nuclear powers entered the fray. Though France was a late starter, Charles de Gaulle, who became French President in 1958, was determined that his country should possess its own nuclear deterrent.

The Chinese looked to the USSR for aid. In 1955, the two countries had agreed that China would supply the USSR with uranium ore in return for Soviet help in producing nuclear weaponry. Though the deal did not survive the worsening of relations between the two countries later in the decade, the Chinese persevered. China conducted its first nuclear test in 1964, and tested its first hydrogen bomb three years later.

What happened next was a clear demonstration of the dangers of

TESTING TIME France's nuclear tests, such as this one carried out in 1970, took place in French Polynesia. The tests were strongly opposed because of their severe environmental impact.

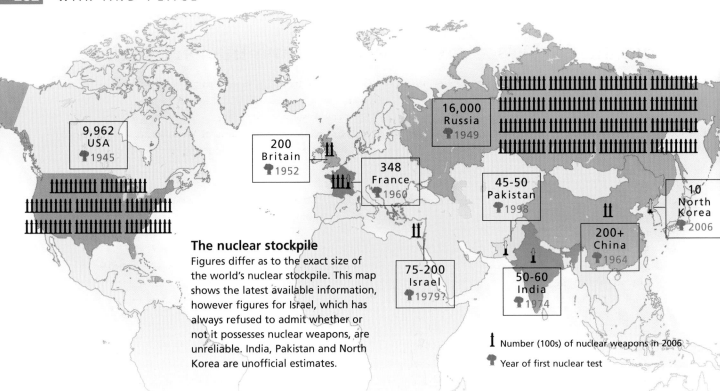

The nuclear stockpile

Figures differ as to the exact size of the world's nuclear stockpile. This map shows the latest available information, however figures for Israel, which has always refused to admit whether or not it possesses nuclear weapons, are unreliable. India, Pakistan and North Korea are unofficial estimates.

9,962 USA ♟1945

200 Britain ♟1952

348 France ♟1960

16,000 Russia ♟1949

45-50 Pakistan ♟1998

10 North Korea ♟2006

75-200 Israel ♟1979?

50-60 India ♟1974

200+ China ♟1964

♟ Number (100s) of nuclear weapons in 2006

♟ Year of first nuclear test

so-called dual-use technology – that is, technology that can be put to military as well as peaceful uses. Though originally designed for civilian purposes, many types of nuclear reactor produce fissile material, such as plutonium, as a by-product of their operation. What this means, at least in theory, is that any country with a nuclear power programme can decide to build its own nuclear weapons.

Nuclear states

India was the first to take advantage of this, when, in response to China's tests, it launched its own nuclear weapons programme. The Indians got the plutonium they needed from a nuclear reactor that had been gifted to them by Canada in 1960, on the understanding that the reactor should be used only for peaceful research. The USA had supplied other materials with a similar proviso. Both powers were outraged by subsequent developments, despite India's protests that it was testing what Prime Minister Indira Gandhi described as a 'peaceful nuclear device'. It was not until 2005 that the US finally classed India as 'a responsible state with

advanced nuclear technology' and agreed to full nuclear cooperation between the two nations.

India's fears of China's territorial ambitions were a powerful driver in the decision to develop nuclear weapons. Pakistan similarly feared Indian attack and determined to develop its own bomb. The question facing the Pakistanis was where to turn for the necessary technology.

In 1976, Pakistani scientist Abdul Qadeer Khan was appointed head of the country's nuclear programme. He arrived with a dossier of technical information, which it transpired he had stolen from a Dutch uranium plant where he had worked. His task was to set up a uranium enrichment capability – a process that was completed so rapidly as to fuel international suspicions that the Pakistanis had obtained outside help. China was the chief suspect.

Even more worrying, there was growing speculation that Pakistan was becoming the centre of a nuclear black market and that the country was ready to sell its technological know-how to other would-be nuclear powers. It is now known that the mastermind of the undercover

network behind this was none other than Khan himself.

In 2004, following Libya's revelation that Pakistani scientists had sold it clandestine weapons technology, Khan was put under house arrest in Pakistan. He then appeared on television to confess publicly that, between 1989 and 1991, he had sold nuclear weapons technology to Iran. From 1991 to 1997, he admitted, he had also had supplied nuclear technology secretly to Libya and North Korea. It is also claimed that, in 2001, just weeks before the 9/11 terrorist attacks on New York's Twin Towers, some of Khan's associates had met with Osama Bin Laden to discuss the possibility of providing al-Qaeda with a nuclear bomb.

The existence of a nuclear black market – in which Pakistan is not the only participant – and the political instability it promotes, concerns all responsible powers. True, Iraq's nuclear development programme, initiated by Saddam Hussein, was brought to an end as the result of Iraq's defeat in the 1991 Gulf War. But other states – notably Iran – are still thought to be actively pursuing their nuclear ambitions long after the end of the Cold War.

How did the Cold War start and what was the Truman Doctrine?

In 1946, when Winston Churchill warned the world that 'an iron curtain has descended across the continent [of Europe]', it was the signal for the start of an undeclared conflict. This was the so-called Cold War – a term coined by the American diplomat Bernard Baruch in a speech made to the US Congress in 1947. It was to last almost half a century, coming to an end with the collapse of Communism, first in Eastern Europe and then in the USSR itself.

Exactly why and when the conflict started is a matter of dispute but its roots lie in events that preceded the coming of peace in the Second World War. As the conflict drew towards its conclusion, the latent distrust between the USSR and its western allies started to develop and grow.

There were many reasons for the worsening of relations. Chief among them was the Soviet expansion west into Eastern Europe and the USSR's refusal to fulfil its pledge to allow democratic elections in what were instead to become Soviet puppet states. Then there was the failure to agree on the fate of defeated Germany. Here, just as it had been at the end of the First World War, the crucial issue was the question of reparations. The USSR was determined to strip Germany bare to rebuild its own economy, which was in a state of near collapse. The western powers would not accede to such demands. The Soviets grew distrustful of what they claimed was western intransigence, especially when faced with a point-blank refusal to let them in on the secrets of the atomic bomb.

Military muscle

By the beginning of 1946, American President Harry S. Truman had decided that he was 'tired of baby-sitting the Soviets'. The following year, in what became known as the Truman Doctrine (inspired by the writings of the US political scientist George Kennan), he stated bluntly that: 'It must be the policy of the United States to support free peoples who are resisting attempted subjugation by armed minorities or by outside pressures.' The Soviet response was immediate. As the USA, through the Marshall Plan, began to pump billions of dollars into Europe to fuel its economic recovery, the USSR and its satellites turned down the offer of such aid (although the Czechs would have liked to accept it). Instead, the blockade of West Berlin, a western enclave deep inside Soviet-occupied eastern Germany, was launched. A vast airlift ensured that the city remained under western control.

It was clear to Truman that military as well as financial muscle was needed. In 1949, the North Atlantic Treaty Organisation (NATO) was formed. The USA was now committed militarily to defending Europe against any act of aggression. As the US National Security Council put it a year later, the USA sought, 'by all means short of war, to block further expansion of Soviet power … and, in general, so to foster the seeds of destruction within the Soviet system that the Kremlin is brought at least to the point of modifying its behaviour to conform to generally accepted international standards'. It was to take many long years for this second hope to be fulfilled.

AID FROM THE AIR
The arrival of supplies at Tempelhof Airport during the 1948–9 Berlin Blockade, a Cold War confrontation decisively won by the west.

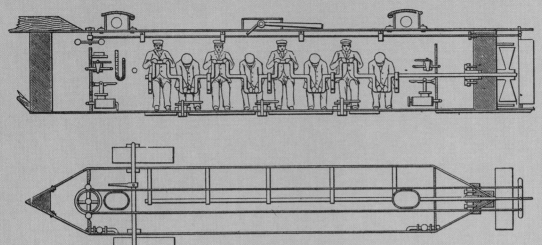

SUBMERGED MEN The CSS *H. L. Hunley* was the first successful military submarine. To power it, eight men sat on the port side and cranked the propeller; a commander steered and deployed the weapons system.

Deep threat
Today's nuclear-powered and nuclear-armed submarine is the ultimate deterrent, with the capability to annihilate any hostile country. How did the improbable notion of enclosing men and weapons in a submersible tube first come about?

In 1870 the French novelist Jules Verne published his science fiction masterpiece, *Twenty Thousand Leagues Under the Sea*, the story of the mysterious submarine *Nautilus* and of Captain Nemo, its enigmatic commander. In real life, the submarine did not come of age until the 20th century – and even then it had to overcome the opposition of determined naval diehards. Speaking in 1901, Admiral Sir Arthur Wilson, later Britain's First Sea Lord, declared

that the submarine was 'underhand, unfair and damned unEnglish'. The government, he said, should 'treat all submarines as pirates in wartime and hang their crews'. Grand Admiral Alfred von Tirpitz, architect of Germany's new Imperial High Seas Fleet, was initially just as unreceptive to the idea. 'The submarine', he wrote in 1902, 'is at present of no great value in war at sea'.

Admiral Sir John 'Jacky' Fisher, the man behind HMS *Dreadnought*, the

first of Britain's huge new battleships, revolutionary in conception, thought differently. 'It is astounding to me', he opined, 'how the very best amongst us fail to realise the vast impending revolution in naval warfare and naval strategy that the submarine will accomplish.' Fisher was to be proved right, though he never dreamed just how deadly a weapon the submarine would become.

The first known description of a submarine dates from centuries before

NUCLEAR SUB The US Navy's attack submarine USS *Hampton* surfaces through ice at the North Pole. The submarine is powered by an SG6 nuclear reactor and equipped with 12 Tomahawk Land Attack Missiles.

to around 1580. It was the work of William Bourne, an English naval gunner turned innkeeper who was also something of a scientific dilettante. He devised a plan for 'a Ship or Boate that may goe under the water unto the bottome and so to come up again at your pleasure'. The vessel he proposed, so he claimed, would 'swimme when you would and sinke when you list'. Though ingenious, the idea never got off the drawing board.

Cornelius Drebbel, a Dutch savant who was James I of England's 'court inventor', was luckier. In 1623, he launched the world's first working submarine. It was a completely enclosed rowing boat topped with a watertight web of greased leather. Floating almost awash, it was driven beneath the surface by its 12 stout rowers, their oars protruding through seals cut into the hull. When the oarsmen stopped rowing, the boat rose slowly back to the surface again. An ingenious system of float-supported air tubes ensured that, in theory, the vessel could stay submerged safely for several hours. The submarine journeyed down a

> '**I must confess that my imagination refuses to see any sort of submarine doing anything but suffocating its crew and foundering at sea**'
>
> H.G. Wells

stretch of the River Thames at a depth of about 15 feet – a feat reportedly witnessed by the king himself.

Underwater attack

David Bushnell, a patriotic American engineer, built the first submarine ever to mount an attack on an enemy warship. His craft was christened the *Turtle* because of its resemblance to a sea turtle floating in the ocean. On 7 September 1776, it was towed down the Hudson River near New York to attack HMS *Eagle*, the flagship of the British squadron blockading the city. The plan was for Sergeant Ezra Lee, the vessel's sole crew member, to submerge and then move under his target by cranking two propellers – one to drive the *Turtle* forwards and the other to force it up and down. Once in position, Lee was to drill into the British ship's hull, attach a keg of gunpowder with a time fuse to it, and then crank the *Turtle* away, surfacing once he was safely out of range. It sounded fine in theory, but things turned out differently. Lee's drill failed to penetrate the hull and he became disoriented. With his air supply running out – the *Turtle* could stay submerged for just 30 minutes – he was left with no choice but to surface, when he was spotted by a British lookout. Luckily for him, he managed to get away.

Just over 20 years later, Robert Fulton, another American inventor, met with similar lack of success when he offered to build Revolutionary France a submarine for use against Britain. Such was his confidence that he was prepared to construct and operate his invention – his *Nautilus* – at his own expense, provided that the French paid him a bounty for every vessel he destroyed. Fulton made several attempts to sink British ships, but with no success. Eventually, the French lost faith in what they had hoped would prove a wonder weapon. Fulton broke up the *Nautilus* and sold the remains for scrap. Nevertheless, the United States, a new great power, was now at the centre of events.

Ironically it was during the American Civil War that for the first time a submarine attacked a surface warship successfully. On 17 February 1864, a Confederate submarine, the CSS *H.L. Hunley*, sank the Federal steam sloop USS *Housatonic* off Charleston harbour. Its triumph was short lived, since the *Hunley* never returned to its base, vanishing with all hands. It was finally located in 1995, having sunk less than a mile away from the scene of the action.

Without a reliable system of propulsion that would work under water as well as on the surface, it was impossible for any such vessel to realise its potential, since human endurance limited size, speed and range. Lack of vision when submerged was another problem, as was the lack of a specialised weapon to fire at targets. The torpedo, first produced in the 1860s, proved to be the weapon that was needed, but the other problems defied solution until the early 20th century.

Rechargeable batteries and electric motors solved the underwater part of the problem. For surface propulsion, steam was tried, but the heat generated made such submarines literally too hot for their crews. Petrol and kerosene power was just as problematic. The solution was the diesel engine. At the same time, the introduction of the periscope gave submariners sight.

Underwater power

Germany was first to realise the military potential of submarines. Its U-boat fleet, though small at the start of the First World War, was the most up-to-date in the world and it soon began sinking British merchant ships faster than they could be replaced. This entailed abandoning the accepted rules of naval war.

An international outcry – especially after the sinking of the passenger liner *Lusitania* with the loss of 1,198 civilian lives in May 1915 – led to the Germans' decision to suspend the campaign. In early 1917, they restarted it, gambling that the U-boats would starve Britain into submission. They were even prepared to run the risk of the USA declaring war, arguing

JUMPING SHIP US Navy submarines sank most of Japan's merchant fleet in the later years of the Second World War. A sinking ship is seen through the periscope of the USS *Wahoo* in April 1943.

that Britain would be forced to surrender before American participation could prove effective. Though the Germans came close to success, the gamble failed when the British introduced escorted armed convoys. Shipping losses fell dramatically as a result.

German aims in the Second World War were identical. By then, German tactics were more sophisticated. Rather than working alone, U-boats now operated in wolf packs – groups of several U-boats attacking convoys on the surface at night. They then submerged to track their targets, resurfacing to resume their attacks the following evening.

The first wolf pack went into action in September 1940, shortly after Hitler proclaimed a total blockade of Britain. The Battle of the Atlantic followed. At its height, merchant ships were being sunk so fast that Allied defeat looked inevitable. But an all-out shipbuilding effort, secret naval intelligence and the introduction of improved anti-submarine weapons and tactics, turned the tide. By May 1943, the Germans had lost the battle – in that month alone, 41 U-boats were sunk.

One difficulty the Germans solved was the problem of recharging the

BATTERY POWER Early French designs included the battery-powered *Gustave Zédé* of 1893.

L'intérieur du « Gustave-Zédé » pendant sa marche sous l'eau.

batteries powering a submarine's electric motors. To do this, the submarine had to surface so that it could start up its air-breathing diesels. The answer was the snorkel. Originally a Dutch invention, its introduction allowed submarines to use their main engines while running just below the waves.

The overall appearance of submarines remained much as it had been since the early years of the century, with the addition of deck guns to sink ships on the surface and to provide some anti-aircraft protection. Then the Americans decided to develop a novel design, created in 1940 by German scientist Helmuth Walter. They used his ideas for a streamlined hull that would increase underwater speed and range, but did not adopt his notion of a hydrogen-peroxide fuelled power plant. Instead, the US Navy looked to nuclear power. Its advantages were obvious. A nuclear reactor did not need air in order to operate. It did away with the need for banks of batteries, and it had almost limitless

fuel endurance. With air-scrubbing systems to keep the air inside pure, a nuclear-powered submarine could remain submerged almost indefinitely. It would also be faster on the surface and much faster under the water. US Navy engineers, led by Admiral Hyman G. Rickover, 'Father of the Nuclear Navy', began working with the Atomic Energy Commission on a prototype nuclear power plant in 1951. In 1954, the USS *Nautilus*, the first of an entirely new breed of submarines, came into service. Her surface speed was 18 knots, but she could manage an astounding 23 knots when submerged.

The submarine had a new power source. It would soon be equipped with a devastating new weapon. Experiments with submarine-launched missiles began in the USA in 1948, with a

> **'Of all the branches of men in the Forces, there is none which shows more devotion and faces grimmer perils than the submariner.'**
>
> Winston Churchill

copy of the German V1 Flying Bomb. However, the submarine had to surface to erect a launching ramp and ready the missile, making it vulnerable. This changed in 1960, when the USS *George Washington* launched a Polaris intercontinental ballistic missile while underwater. Poseidon and later Trident missiles, with multiple nuclear warheads, succeeded Polaris. Such is Trident's range that it can hit any likely target from a US harbour.

Submarines had long been ship-killers. Now, hard to detect and almost impossible to track, they became the lynchpins of the nuclear deterrent itself. Though the world has changed, this is the position they still enjoy.

FIRST OF A KIND The first nuclear-powered submarine, the USS *Nautilus*, takes to the water in 1954 at Groton, Connecticut.

The cockpit of Europe
From Roman times through to the Second World War and the near present, Belgium – particularly Flanders – has been the cockpit of Europe. Why is it so strategically important?

It was an accident of geography: its plains make it a natural invasion route for armies on the march east and west. The phrase 'cockpit of Europe' was in widespread use by the end of the 19th century, when E. Cobham Brewer defined it in his *Dictionary of Phrase and Fable*.

Later, General Charles de Gaulle of France christened the region the 'fatal avenue'. Undoubtedly, it has been a fatal location for millions, since more bloody battles have been fought there than in any other region in Europe. As a result, it has suffered far more than its fair share of death, destruction and human misery.

Romans, Belgae and Franks
The flatness and accessibility of the area made it a natural corridor for armies on the march. Only the hills of the Ardennes in the southeast offer a major barrier to an army on the move. Even the largest rivers, the Meuse and the Scheldt, are navigable over most of their length, and relatively easy to cross. Control of Flanders has been crucial to any power seeking access to the British Isles, the Netherlands, Germany and France.

The Romans were the region's first invaders. In 57 BC, Julius Caesar pushed his legions northwards as part of a plan to conquer Gaul (France). As his men advanced, they encountered a group of tribes of mixed Celtic and Germanic origins whom Caesar referred to collectively as the Belgae. He found them fearsome opponents. Rising after rising was savagely repressed until the region was finally pacified.

Roman rule lasted until the collapse of the empire in the west in the 5th century AD, after which there were further invasions – this time, from the east – by the Huns and the Franks. The Franks eventually took control, thanks largely to Charlemagne. He carved out a vast new empire at the start of the 9th century. In 862, one of Charlemagne's successors, Charles the Bald, agreed to the marriage of his daughter Judith, to Baldwin I, one of his nobles. When, in 864, the king appointed his son-in-law Count of Flanders, Baldwin became the ruler of a new, semi-independent principality in the northwest of present-day Belgium.

An age of constant war
Under Baldwin and his successors, the wealth and importance of Flanders grew. But the region became a focal point for continuing conflict between France and England. As was to be the case in the future, the inhabitants – the Flemish – were caught between rival ambitions. In 1384, the area came under the control of the Dukes of Burgundy and then, as a result of dynastic intermarriage, the Habsburg rulers of the Holy Roman Empire and Spain. In 1556, the Spanish branch of the family took over. Flanders, together with Holland, became known as the Spanish Netherlands. From 1568 to 1697, Flanders was a seething crucible of seemingly perpetual conflict. No fewer than seven major wars were fought there, all interconnected and some overlapping. Various factors lay

THE FINAL BATTLE Napoleon's defeat at the Battle of Waterloo brought to a close 23 years of war.

behind them. They included Spain's decline as the pre-eminent European power, the rapid rise of Louis XIV's France to replace it, continual conflict between Catholics and Protestants, the emergence of the Dutch as a major force and the eventual British recognition that France, not Spain, was now the nation's main enemy.

The first of these wars started when the Protestant Dutch rose against Spanish Catholic rule. The conflict lasted on and off for 80 years. There followed the Thirty Years' War, the Franco-Spanish War, the so-called War of Devolution, the Franco-Dutch War, the Anglo-Dutch War and, finally, the Nine Years' War, which broke out in 1688.

A brief period of peace ended with the outbreak of the War of the Spanish Succession in 1701. Again, Flanders was a major battleground, with France, allied to Spain and Bavaria, lining up against Britain, the Dutch Republic, Austria and the other member states of the Holy Roman Empire. Under the powerful Louis XIV, France's aim was European dominance. His opponents were determined to check his ambitions, and to preserve what diplomats termed the 'balance of power'.

Harsh defeat

The Battle of Ramillies, on 23 May 1706, was the turning point of the war. The Duke of Marlborough, one of Britain's most brilliant generals, led the coalition forces against the French and their Bavarian allies. In less than four hours, the Franco-Bavarian army was defeated and forced into headlong retreat. From a total of 60,000 men, an estimated 20,000 were lost.

Under the terms of the Treaty of Utrecht, Flanders passed to the Dutch, who quickly agreed to cede it to Austria. The Spanish Netherlands were renamed the Austrian Netherlands. The area remained as part of Austria up until the end of the 18th century because, despite a

Europe's battleground

Fought in and fought over, the land known today as Belgium has been the site of more battles than any other country in Europe. Bloody conflicts – including some of the most decisive in history – have sullied its plains from the 14th century to the Second World War.

successful French invasion during the War of the Austrian Succession in 1744, the peace treaty agreed at Aix-La-Chapelle in 1748 confirmed the pre-war status quo.

The French revolutionary army succeeded where the Bourbon kings had failed. In 1792, the French armies swept in. They gained control of the entire region by their victory over the Austrians at the Battle of Fleurus in June 1794. The French held the area until Napoleon was first deposed in 1814. The next year, the area saw Napoleon's final defeat when he clashed with the Duke of Wellington's army at Waterloo, south of Brussels.

The battle was fought on 18 June 1815. Napoleon was desperate for a quick victory over Wellington before the rest of his enemies could mobilise against him. After the battle, Wellington described his victory as 'the nearest-run thing', but ultimately leadership errors led to the complete rout of the French. By the terms of the settlement subsequently agreed at the Congress of Vienna, Flanders and the other southern provinces of the region became part of the Netherlands. In 1830 they broke away from Dutch

rule to become independent and the kingdom of Belgium was born.

What happened shortly afterwards was unusual. For once, the great powers were in accord. By the Treaty of London, signed in 1839, Britain, Austria, France, Prussia, Russia and the Netherlands all guaranteed Belgian independence and the country's permanent neutrality. Any future invasion would provoke armed intervention by the other signatory powers against the aggressor.

The Schlieffen plan

Peace was broken in 1870, when France and Prussia went to war, but both sides were careful to respect Belgian neutrality. On the outbreak of the First World War in 1914 the outcome was very different. Thanks to the alliance between France and Russia, Germany now faced war on two fronts – one in the west and the other in the east.

In 1905 Count Alfred von Schlieffen, Chief of the German General Staff, believed that he had the answer. In the event of war, the bulk of the German forces would be thrown against the French. Once they had forced

France's surrender, they would be moved rapidly to the east to take on the Russians. Schlieffen gave himself six weeks to win victory in the west. The question was how this could be done. Any attempt to advance across the Franco-German frontier was likely to be checked by its formidable defences. In addition, the French planned to concentrate their army there, ready to launch their own thrust into Germany. Schlieffen's answer was crude, but simple. The bulk of his armies would advance through Belgium and on into northern France, eventually swinging around Paris from the west. The French, Schlieffen reckoned, would be forced to fight a decisive battle or run the risk of envelopment.

In the event, Count Helmuth von Moltke, Schlieffen's successor, tinkered with the plan by sending reinforcements to the east, where the Russians were attacking ahead of schedule. The planned swing around Paris had to be curtailed, giving the French and their British allies the chance to regroup and counterattack the exposed German flank.

The Germans hesitated, fell back and dug in. The Allies found it impossible to break through their defences. Four years of stalemate followed, as bitter trench warfare raged along a front stretching from the English Channel to the Swiss border.

Flanders saw some of the most savage fighting of these sad years. Three major battles were fought around the town of Ypres alone. In the second, in April 1915, the Germans unleashed poison gas for the first time. The Allies were quick to copy them. The bloodiest

> ## Mud and rain and wretchedness and blood. Why should jolly soldier-boys complain?
>
> Siegfried Sassoon

DEATH AND DESECRATION Constant artillery barrages left the landscape of Belgium ravaged during the Third Battle of Ypres in 1917.

encounter was the Third Battle of Ypres – or Passchendaele – fought between July and November 1917. Repeated British attacks failed as torrential rain – and the effects of continual artillery bombardments – turned the Ypres lowlands into a practically impassable swamp. By the time the offensive came to an end, the British had 310,000 dead and wounded and the Germans 260,000.

Birth of the blitzkrieg

To avoid another surprise attack, from the 1930s the French constructed a line of fortifications known as the Maginot line along its borders with Germany and Italy. But the line failed in its purpose. Flanders became a major European battleground again during the Second World War, when, in May 1940, Adolf Hitler launched his long-expected blitzkrieg on the Western Front.

The plan was more or less the Schlieffen plan in reverse. While the Allies rushed their troops forwards into Belgium to meet what they believed to be the main German thrust, Hitler's crack panzer divisions were worming their way undetected through the hilly Ardennes, ready to take the French by surprise at Sedan. The breakthrough was immediate and total. The German panzers headed towards the English Channel to encircle and cut off the bulk of the Allied forces which, now stranded at Dunkirk, had to be evacuated. France surrendered quickly when new German attacks followed. The entire campaign lasted a bare eight weeks.

The war that wasn't

In the post-war era, the area of Flanders was still a potential battleground. NATO planners believed that, if the Cold War ever turned hot, the numerically superior Soviet and Warsaw Pact forces facing them were bound to take the traditional invasion route west. Recently discovered documents reveal that Soviet intentions were dramatically different. While diversionary attacks were being launched in the north, a massive strike force of at least 70 armoured divisions would sweep west from Czechoslovakia into neutral Austria, then Switzerland. From here they would break out into France's Rhône valley around Grenoble and Lyon. They would then drive on to envelop Paris from the south and west. It would be a surgical strike into NATO's underbelly and might well have been successful, had it ever been put into practice.

Why has the country of Poland been invaded so frequently?

Few countries have been invaded so frequently as Poland. Today, the country stretches across a broad, flat plain that is easily reached from both west and east. Because of its vulnerability and importance, Poland's boundaries have shifted hundreds of miles east and back again over the centuries as surrounding powers have fought for control.

From the late 1700s until the end of the First World War, Poland vanished from the map. A once proud, fiercely independent nation fell victim to the ambitions of its neighbours. In three successive partitions in 1772, 1793 and 1795, Poland was divided between Prussia, Russia and Austria.

Polish independence, proclaimed anew in 1918, was to last for just 21 years. In September 1939, German and Soviet troops invaded the country.

As agreed in the secret clauses of the Soviet-German Non-Aggression Pact of the previous month, Poland was again partitioned. Both Germany and the USSR treated the Poles barbarously. By the end of the war, more than six million – 22 per cent of the population – had perished.

After the war, Poland's borders moved again, this time to the west, but the country remained firmly under Communist control. Communism was to last until its general collapse at the end of the 1980s and the return of democracy to a country that had been promised it more than 40 years before.

MELTING POT The ethnic mix of Poland's population has added to its troubles. German citizens of Danzig fill the streets to greet Hitler's army in 1939.

BUNGLED BATTLE The 1476 Battle of Grandson was disastrous for the hapless Duke of Burgundy. While fighting the Swiss, his men took fright and retreated, leaving his riches strewn across the battlefield.

Citizen soldiers Every Swiss citizen is required to do military service and those in the reserves keep their guns under their beds. Why, since Switzerland has been strictly neutral for hundreds of years?

Switzerland has a longer history of neutrality than any other country in Europe. A 15th-century Swiss saint, Nicholas of Flüe, advised his countrymen, 'Don't get involved in other people's affairs' and 500 years later a poster for a 2001 referendum on the future role of Swiss troops in international conflict asked, 'Are Swiss sons to be sacrificed in other people's affairs?' The belief in non-involvement is long-held.

In 1516, following the Swiss defeat at the Battle of Marignano, 'the everlasting peace' was concluded between the Swiss cantons and neighbouring France. This was one of the founding acts of Swiss neutrality.

But a country's neutrality does not stop its citizens being prepared to fight to defend their freedom. Switzerland is typical. Although the country has been neutral for centuries – formal international recognition of Swiss neutrality came about as a result of the Congress of Vienna in 1815 after Switzerland was occupied by the French during the Napoleonic Wars – the Swiss do not rely solely on this status to protect themselves against potential aggressors.

Hague Convention

The other officially neutral states of Europe in the 21st century – Sweden, Ireland, Finland, Iceland and Austria – share the Swiss position. All of them are mindful of 'the rights and duties of neutral powers … in case of war on land' set out in the 1907 Hague Convention. Its signatories agreed that the territory of a neutral power was inviolable. They recognised, too, that 'the fact of a neutral power resisting, even by force, attempts to violate its neutrality cannot be regarded as a hostile act'. These and the other articles of the Convention governing neutrality are accepted in international law.

The Swiss have not always been a peaceful people. In medieval times, they fought for independence from their Habsburg overlords, inspired by the legendary exploits of William Tell. He is still a national hero, even though he probably never existed. Such was the reputation Swiss troops won on the battlefield that, for a time, they were the most sought-after mercenaries in the whole of Europe. Armed with fearsome pikes and halberds (a metal axe blade mounted on a long shaft), they carried out ferocious close-formation mass attacks against their foes.

Many Swiss fought for France. In the early 16th century, Francis I enlisted some 120,000 of them to take part in his wars and Swiss soldiers continued in French service up to the time of the French Revolution. In 1793, the Swiss Guard fought to the death to defend the Tuileries Palace in Paris against the revolutionaries, even though Louis XVI, the king they were defending, had already fled.

The Swiss served the Popes bravely as well. In 1506, Pope Julius II sanctioned the formation of his own Swiss Guard in Rome. In 1527, it fought practically to the last man to defend the city against attack by Emperor Charles V. Later reformed, it still mounts guard outside the Vatican.

Threats to neutrality

In 1874, Swiss law was changed to ban all military recruitment of Swiss citizens by foreign powers. In 1927, it was made illegal to volunteer to fight in a foreign army. But little more than a decade later, Swiss neutrality was to face its sternest test.

Between 1914 and 1918 all the belligerent powers had respected Swiss neutrality. During the Second World War, the country came perilously close to facing German attack. Detailed invasion plans were drawn up on several occasions.

The invasion never materialised. It is thought that Adolf Hitler did not see Switzerland as an immediate threat, while it was clear that the Swiss militia aimed to put up determined resistance. The Swiss plan was to block the tunnels through the Alps, which the Germans were allowed to use, and to fight a protracted war of attrition from fortified positions high up in the Alps. The aim was to make it clear to the Third Reich that the

overall cost of an attempt at invasion would far outweigh any potential benefits.

One further factor may well have contributed to the German decision to leave Switzerland in peace. The Swiss franc was by then the only freely convertible major currency in the world. Between 1940 and 1945, the German Reichsbank sold 1.3 billion francs' (US$440 million) worth of gold to Swiss banks in exchange for Swiss francs and other foreign currency. Much of this gold was plundered from the occupied countries or seized from victims of the Holocaust.

After the war, Switzerland continued to safeguard its neutrality. It did not even become a member of the United Nations until 2002. The country remained absolutely determined to preserve its independence, as was demonstrated in the late 1960s, when a group of Swiss Army officers in civilian clothes was arrested by Austrian officials for spying on its fortifications on the Czech border. The reason was dramatically simple. The Cold War was then at its height and Swiss military intelligence had learned of a daring Soviet plan to outflank NATO defences by launching a massive attack from Czechoslovakia into Austria, on into Switzerland and so into France. The Swiss Army had 600,000 tough soldiers at the ready – again prepared, if necessary, to fight the invaders from the mountain fortress redoubts. Fortunately, they were not to be put to the test.

Armed neutrality once again proved successful. It remains a core principle of Switzerland's democracy today and the strategy looks likely to survive for many years to come.

During the Second World War, Switzerland came perilously close to facing German attack

TROOPS OF COLOUR Swiss Guards protect the gates of the Vatican City. Each year in May they renew their vows, promising to serve the Pope 'to the death'.

Political suicide Where did the idea of killing others by killing yourself come from? What kind of people are suicide bombers and how do they justify their actions?

Suicide attacks are not a recent phenomenon. The first recorded attack took place in Biblical times. In the Old Testament, the Book of Judges tells how the Hebrew hero Samson, blinded and a prisoner of the Philistines, used his superhuman strength to pull down the central pillars of a Philistine temple, bringing destruction on his enemies, though perishing himself in the process.

In the 11th and 12th centuries, the Assassins, a Shiite sect, were active in

Syria and present-day Iran (page 145). In late 1944, Japan's *kamikaze* pilots launched waves of suicide attacks against their foes, crashing their bomb-laden aircraft onto enemy warships and other shipping in a desperate attempt to sabotage the Allied advance across the Pacific towards the Japanese islands.

During the Vietnam War, Vietcong sympathisers blew themselves up together with US soldiers. Similar tactics have characterised the Tamil

resistance in Sri Lanka. Over the years, many other people have shown their willingness to die while carrying out attacks in pursuit of political goals and they are becoming more common.

Since the attacks of 11 September 2001 in the USA, suicide bombers have struck in many places around the world, from Indonesia and India through Iraq and Palestine to Russia and Morocco. In 2005, the deadly bombings on the London Underground marked the first time that suicide bombers had successfully mounted an attack in western Europe. The following year, Afghanistan saw its first suicide bomb attacks, as Taliban rebels stepped up their struggle to undermine the government and drive out the NATO forces that had come to its support.

The pace of such attacks has also quickened dramatically. The Rand Corporation, a Californian think tank, estimates that around three-quarters of all suicide bombings have taken place since the 11 September attacks. In Iraq alone the numbers are staggering. Since the US-led invasion in 2003, hundreds of bombings have taken place. It is estimated that two out of every three attacks are suicide bombings. In May 2005, 90 such bombings took place, nearly as many as the Israeli government says have been carried out in Israel and the Occupied Territories since 1993.

The Hezbollah tactic

Suicide bombing became a favoured *modus operandi* in the 1980s among militant Palestinians, and was used in Lebanon from 1983 at the instigation of Hezbollah, a Shiite organisation with influence in Palestine and much of the Middle East. Two Hezbollah operatives drove trucks laden with explosive into a Beirut barracks housing US and French soldiers, who were serving as part of an international peacekeeping force. The explosions killed 241 US Marines and 58 French paratroopers.

Four months later, the USA withdrew its forces from the country. Many believe that this decision was a direct result of the attacks. Certainly, that was what Hezbollah thought. Buoyed by its apparent success, the organisation went on to carry out several dozen more suicide attacks.

Where Hezbollah led, others followed. The phenomenon spread from the Middle East to Sri Lanka. There, the Liberation Tigers of Tamil Eelam, or Tamil Tigers, a separatist group fighting for independence for

Dying for their emperor

In Japanese, the word *kamikaze* means 'divine wind'. Legend records that a sudden typhoon destroyed the armada of 4,400 ships that the Mongol warlord Kublai Khan had launched against Japan, and saved it from invasion.

More recently, kamikazes were Japanese pilots, who launched wave after wave of suicide attacks against Allied shipping during the closing stages of the Pacific campaign of the Second World War. They tried to crash their explosive-laden aircraft into their targets, acting as manned guided missiles. The planes were flown by dedicated aircrew, most of whom were volunteers who believed that it was an honour to die for Japan and its emperor.

In effect, it was a logical extension of the notion of *seppuku* ('ritual suicide'). This formed an integral part of the feudal code of *bushido*, the laws by which Japan's warrior samurai class had traditionally conducted their lives.

Rear Admiral Masafumi Arima is the man credited with the first kamikaze attack. He led a force of 100 dive-bombers in an attempt to sink the aircraft carrier USS *Franklin* near Leyte Gulf in October 1944. Though unsuccessful, Anma was posthumously promoted to the rank of admiral. The attacks reached their peak between April and June 1945 during the battle for Okinawa.

The policy had its critics. In March 1945, one Japanese officer commented, 'The right way is to attack the enemy with skill and return to the base with good results. A plane should be utilised over and over again. That's the way to fight a war … There will be no progress if flyers continue to die.' The last official kamikaze attack took place on 15 August 1945, shortly before Japan's unconditional surrender.

A JAPANESE KAMIKAZE PILOT TIES THE NAVAL ENSIGN AROUND HIS HEAD BEFORE A MISSION

the country's Tamil ethnic minority, carried out scores of suicide bombings from the late 1980s onwards. The Tamil Tigers were responsible for almost a quarter of the 315 suicide attacks carried out around the world from 1980 to 2003.

The first bombing took place in 1987, when a Tamil Tiger captain blew himself up along with 18 government troops at an army camp in the northern part of the island. Four years later, in May 1991, Thenmuli Rajaratnam assassinated Rajiv Gandhi, the former Indian prime minister, and 16 bystanders when she blew herself up with a suicide belt. Two years after that, another suicide bomber killed the Sri Lankan president Ranasinghe Premadasa and 22 others in an attack in Colombo, the Sri Lankan capital. The Tamil Tigers also staged devastating attacks on the country's central bank, its holiest Buddhist shrine and its international airport.

Terrorists or martyrs?

The reason why suicide bombing is a tactic favoured by many terrorist groups is simple: it offers a substantial advantage. There is no need to plan for remote or delayed detonation of the explosives involved. Nor do escape plans have to be devised or rescue teams organised. One bomber in a confined and crowded space can inflict heavy casualties.

Suicide bombing is also a highly effective psychological weapon, spreading anxiety and suspicion even among those not directly affected by it. Fear of death is a potent force, and the willingness to embrace it a graphic demonstration of serious intent.

Almost all suicide attackers are volunteers. Overall, the main motivation is intense frustration over a territorial or political grievance. In the case of Islam, many attackers are

buttressed by the notion of martyrdom, sacrificing their lives for their cause in the expectation that they will be rewarded in the afterlife.

In his 1996 *fatwa* attacking the USA and its allies, Osama bin Laden, the al-Qaeda leader, stated that 'these youths love death as you love life'. In common with other Islamic fundamentalist organisations, al-Qaeda interprets the Koran in a way that suits its political and operational needs.

It is also linked to the notion of *jihad*, or holy war. Faisal Bodi, a leading Muslim commentator, stated bluntly that: 'In the Muslim world, we celebrate what we call the martyr-bombers. To us, they are heroes, defending the things we hold sacred.'

In contrast, Ihsanic Intelligence, a prominent Islamic think tank based

The main motivation is intense frustration over a territorial or political grievance

in London, condemned such acts as 'anathema, antithetical and abhorrent to Islam'. It seems that the theological and moral position is as polarised as the reasoning used by some Muslims to justify committing such acts in the first place.

MONUMENT TO PROTEST
Czech philosophy student, Jan Palach, died in 1969 after setting himself on fire in central Prague in protest against the Soviet invasion of his country. Tens of thousands of mourners followed his coffin.

The politics of death by starvation

Suicide – or its threat – has been used as a means of non-violent political protest many times. In early 20th-century Britain, militant suffragettes, fighting for the right of women to vote, used the threat of suicide as a weapon by going on hunger strike when held in prison. The government's response was to force-feed the prisoners but, when the brutality of this procedure proved unpopular, it passed the so-called 'Cat and Mouse Act' (1913) through Parliament. Suffragette hunger strikers were then released if they became too weak, but once recovered, were re-arrested and taken back to prison to finish their sentences.

Irish republicans employed the same tactics in their battle for independence from Britain after the First World War. This time, the outcome was tragic. In 1920, Terence MacSwiney, the Lord Mayor of Cork, died while on hunger strike in London's Brixton Prison. So, too, did Joe Murphy and Michael Fitzgerald, two Cork IRA men who died in Cork Jail.

History repeated itself 60 years later, when, in 1980, republican prisoners – most of whom were members of the Provisional IRA – launched a mass hunger strike in the Maze prison as a protest against the British Government's decision to revoke the special status previously granted to paramilitary prisoners in Northern Ireland. Bobby Sands was the first of seven IRA prisoners to die while on hunger strike the following year.

Probably the most celebrated hunger striker of all was Mahatma Gandhi. He and many of his followers put themselves at considerable risk to effect political change. He went on hunger strike on several occasions as part of his protest against continued British rule in India. The strikes won Gandhi public support, both in his own country and abroad. For their part, the British could not afford to let him die, realising that his death would provoke a powerful enough backlash across India to threaten their rule.

The last time that Gandhi went on hunger strike was for a different reason. It was his attempt to halt the bloody conflict that had broken out between Hindus and Muslims during the lead-up to independence and continued after the sub-continent's partition into India and Pakistan.

When Gandhi saw the extent of the violence, he announced that he would not eat until the clashes stopped and India had disgorged the 550 million rupees (about £40 million) that it was withholding from Pakistan. It was his last political success before his death at the hands of a Hindu fanatic.

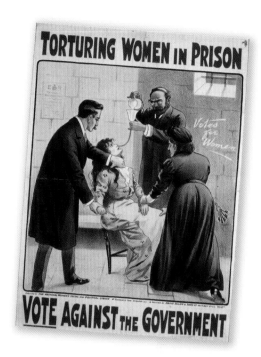

STARK STATEMENT A suffragette poster of feeding by force in prison. The procedure has been used in recent times at the US Guantánamo Bay prison camp.

NON-VIOLENT PROTEST The hallmark of Mahatma Gandhi's political career was a steadfast belief in peaceful protest.

A sense of uniformity
Combat uniforms are very different from ceremonial ones. When did soldiers first start wearing uniforms? And why did they change from bright to drab?

It was only when armies started to get bigger and more organised that they began to adopt a standard uniform for all their troops. Though there are some notable examples in ancient times – in classical Greece the scarlet cloaks worn by the Spartan *hoplites* identified them as warriors of Sparta, while Roman centurions wore the crests of their helmets perpendicular to the front – it was not until the 17th century that the wearing of standardised uniforms became more commonplace.

The process began in the mid-17th century during the Thirty Years' War, when Gustavus Adolphus, the ruler of Sweden and one of the great reforming military commanders of history, ordered his infantry into standard yellow or blue regimental dress. In Britain, the soldiers of Oliver Cromwell's New Model Army, raised in 1645 to fight for the Parliamentarian cause in the Civil War, followed suit. Then, across the English Channel, the French adopted the concept. France was the leading nation in Europe and possessed the best and most prestigious army of the time, so other countries soon followed its example.

Choosing which colour

At first, what soldiers wore did not differ greatly from standard civilian dress. Early uniforms usually consisted of a tricorn hat, a long-skirted coat, a waistcoat and breeches. The feature that distinguished soldiers from civilians was their canvas gaiters, which came up to the mid-thigh and had multiple buttons. They were designed to protect the breeches and stockings when on the march.

Army dress was surprisingly quick to become standardised in both its cut and its general outline. What made the difference was colour. The British and the Danes favoured red. The French, Spanish and Austrian infantry started off in light grey and then changed to white. As part of his policy of reform, Peter the Great ordered Russian

In January 2008, the Russian government inspected a new couture collection of military uniforms. As *The Times* reported: 'Chisel-jawed servicemen and leggy female models stood to attention in chic fur collars, stylish peaked caps and gold embroidered tunics as Mr Putin, the Commander-in-Chief, examined the dashing new look on Monday ... Fashion commentators said that the uniforms revived some of the glamour of Russia's imperial tradition in

PARADE-GROUND PERFECTION Soldiers of the army of the People's Republic of China in an exactly ordered formation. Military service in China is compulsory.

combination with its recent Soviet history. *Izvestia* newspaper said that the designs recalled the Hussar style of 19th-century Russia ... The defence ministry spent £2 million to commission the designs of new uniforms.' The updating may cost Russia at least £300 million in all.

POTSDAM GRENADIERS King Frederick William I of Prussia, himself only 1.5m (5ft) tall, recruited specially tall soldiers to serve in a ceremonial regiment.

troops into dark green uniforms in 1700, while, from the time of Frederick William I, the Prussian soldiers were dressed in dark blue.

Why armies adopted the colours they did is not clear. The popular belief that the British infantry was ordered into red to conceal bloodstains is a fallacy. It is far more likely that red was selected because it was generally regarded as a national colour, or because red madder, the dye that was employed, was widely available and cheap to purchase.

Officers and men

While uniform became standardised for rank and file soldiery, officers were relatively slow to take to it. During the late 1600s, they often dressed in individual styles and colours according to their own tastes and means, and it was accepted practice for them to have to pay for their own clothing. Nor did they wear insignia to denote specific ranks until well into the following century, when epaulettes (worn singly or in pairs on the shoulders) were introduced.

By this time, military dress was starting to become more and more colourful and ornate, even at the expense of practicality. After the Napoleonic Wars, uniforms became even showier and less comfortable to wear, particularly for the cavalry, generally reckoned to be the elite branch of every army at this time. Cavalry regiments across Europe copied the flamboyant clothing of the Hungarian hussars and the Polish lancers. Their closely fitting uniforms, as well as being colourful, were liberally adorned with intricate braiding across the body of the jacket, 'Austrian knots' on the sleeves, elaborate systems of cords and other accoutrements.

Designer dandies

In 1826, the British commander Lord Bingham commissioned his fashionable tailor to produce uniforms that he himself had designed for his regiment, the 17th Lancers. Their smart dress earned them the nickname 'Bingham's Dandies'. Only the Earl of Cardigan's 11th Hussars could match the Lancers in sartorial splendour. Cardigan's troops were nicknamed the 'cherry bums' because of the tightness of the scarlet trousers they wore. Cardigan was so proud of the effect that he would pay his smartest troopers to stand in St James's at the height of the London season, come to attention and salute him as he sauntered along the street.

Bright and distinctive attire on the battlefield had made military sense when opposing armies met one another face-to-face, and each side wished to be visually overwhelming. From the middle of the 19th century, with changes in the way war was waged, the adoption of more covert tactics and the development of modern weaponry, colourful uniforms

BRITISH GRENADIERS An officer of the 1st Foot Guards in 1798. The regiment gained its Grenadier title at Waterloo.

DASHING HUSSARS An officer of the British Army's 11th Hussars in the mid-19th century. He wears a type of fur cap, known as a kolbak, and a dolman jacket.

were destined to become relics, at least on the battlefield. Instead of standing out, troops needed to blend in with the landscape for safety.

The British army introduced khaki drill for wear in India and Africa in 1848. The drab colouring provided better camouflage and was adopted as standard service wear throughout the army in 1902, the same year that the US Army also adopted khaki for all but full-dress ceremonial occasions. The German and Austro-Hungarian armies selected different shades of grey – field and pike grey, respectively – while, in 1908, following their defeat in the Russo-Japanese War, the Russians changed to a grey shade of khaki.

> **Military dress was more colourful ... even at the expense of practicality**

Some armies held out against change for longer. While most other nations had by then adopted khaki or grey for their uniforms, when France entered the First World War in 1914, its soldiers at first were still clad in what proved to be a near suicidal uniform for the modern battlefield. Their dress – that had changed little since the time of Napoleon – consisted of bright red trousers and a blue double-breasted overcoat, complete with flapping tails and shiny brass buttons. A smart, rakish *képi* was standard headgear. But from 1915, a more practical, horizon blue battledress took over, with the *képi* being replaced by a stout steel helmet. Gorgeous uniforms disappeared from combat forever.

The eccentricities of military headgear

At various times in history, certain units have adopted specific items of headgear for ceremonial and practical. reasons. Bearskins are tall fur caps that form part of the ceremonial uniform of several regiments in the British Army. The privilege of wearing them was granted to the Grenadier Guards after the Napoleonic Wars in recognition of the role they played in

routing Napoleon's Imperial Guard at Waterloo in 1815.

The wide-brimmed hats of Italy's elite *Bersaglieri* are festooned with plumes of capercaillie feathers. Today, the *Bersaglieri* keep up the tradition by decorating their combat helmets the same way. For their part, soldiers in the Australian army still wear the felt slouch hat, turned up on one side.

Other types of headgear have vanished from the scene. The German *Pickelhaube* had royal origins. Made of

hardened leather reinforced with metal trim – the insignia at the front denoted the regiment's state – with a metal spike at its crown, it was devised by King Frederick William IV of Prussia in 1842 and intended to create an impression of military force and aggression. But in trench warfare, it offered little defence against shell splinters, and enemy snipers could easily spot the spike. The American 1912/1921 Soft Service Cap suffered from the same defects. Resembling a cowboy hat, it too provided little protection in the trenches.

BEARSKIN

PICKELHAUBE

BERSAGLIERI HAT

How did the rules of drilling and marching in step evolve?

Formal military drill originated with the Greeks and the Egyptians. The Roman Flavius Vegetius Renatus wrote the first surviving military manual, compiling a three-volume treatise on the imperial army around AD 390. He emphasised how new recruits should practise marching together: 'Nor is anything of more consequence either on the march or in the line than that they should keep their ranks with the greatest exactness ... For troops who march in an irregular or disorderly manner are always in great danger of being defeated.'

Little has altered in more than 2,000 years. The Drill Book of the modern British Army asserts that 'the foundation of discipline in battle is based on drill.' The writer Robert Graves, who fought in the First World War, concurred. He said there were 'three types of troops: those who could not drill; those good at drill, but with no guts; and those who had guts and could drill well ... these last fought best of all.' What did change was the speed at which soldiers marched when moving in combat.

A Roman legion is thought to have marched at a pace of 100 steps a minute. In the American Revolutionary War, British forces marched at 60 steps a minute, though probably with longer strides than the Romans. George Washington's Continental Army were faster, at 74 steps a minute. Today, the US Army marches at 106 steps a minute.

The goosestep, in which marching troops swing each leg in turn up into a practically horizontal position before crashing it back down again, is one of the most celebrated marching steps of all time. Some military historians believe it was introduced into the Prussian infantry in 1726, others that it was brought back to

KEEPING IN STEP Soliders from Turkey perform a ceremonial goosestep during the changing of the guard ceremony, Atatürk Mausoleum, Ankara.

Germany from Italy by Hessian troops, who had learned the step from their Italian allies. Whatever its origins, the goosestep became indelibly associated with the German militarism that helped cause both the First and the Second World War.

Its supporters claimed that the step was a perfect physical demonstration of the virtues of military discipline and a sign of fighting efficiency. Though mainly associated with the German Army, other nations adopted it too. Catherine the Great (who was of German birth) introduced it into the Russian Army as part of her military reforms. In present-day Russia, the step still features on formal military occasions, as it does in China, North Korea, Vietnam and Cuba. The Chilean Army

employs the goosestep on ceremonial occasions, as does the army of Iran.

In Italy, the fascist dictator Benito Mussolini introduced the goosestep into his army in 1938 and it became known as the *Passo Romano*, or Roman step. Curiously, just as Mussolini was remonstrating with his generals because his forces could not perform the step properly, the Germans were restricting its use. After 1940, recruits were no longer taught how to perform it. The step took weeks of practice to get right and to march without injury, troops had to be incredibly fit, as it required enormous physical exertion and stamina to goosestep correctly.

> 'those who had guts and could drill well ... these last fought best of all'
>
> Robert Graves

Who sets the limits on war? Wars are supposed to be fought according to rules set out in the Geneva and Hague Conventions, but whose rules are they – and how are they enforced?

The laws of war have three purposes. They are intended to mitigate the effects of war by protecting combatants and non-combatants from unnecessary suffering; to safeguard the human rights of those who fall into the hands of an enemy; and to restore peace more quickly.

In the 6th century BC, Sun Tzu, the celebrated Chinese author of *The Art of War*, argued that limits should be put on the ways in which wars were conducted. The Roman writer Cicero was one of the earliest exponents of the idea of a just war. In medieval Europe, knights had a code of battlefield chivalry, while in 1625 the Dutch jurist Hugo Grotius wrote *On the Law of War and Peace*, in which he argued for the humane treatment of civilians in times of war. Until the

UNDER FIRE Goya's depiction of Spain's brutal, unregulated Peninsular War. Impromptu fighting, or *guerrilla*, was common. The word has been used ever since to define these 'little wars'.

mid-19th century, such conventions as existed were neither internationally recognised nor universally binding. Instead, they varied according to which code the parties decided to accept and could be amended, ignored or even discarded, depending on circumstances.

Protecting the soldiers

In 1864, the first steps were taken towards agreeing a universal set of rules of war. Thirteen countries signed the first Geneva Convention. It laid out rules to protect wounded soldiers on the battlefield and the doctors and nurses tending them. The Convention was organised by the International Committee for Relief of the Wounded

– now the Red Cross – the brainchild of Henri Dunant, the Swiss humanitarian who headed the committee. He had been horrified by the way in which the wounded had been left to die untreated at Solferino, a bloody battle fought in Italy in 1859.

In *A Memory of Solferino*, Dunant recalled the scene and the 38,000 casualties on both sides who lay there untended: 'When the sun came up … it disclosed the most dreadful sights imaginable. Bodies of men and horses covered the battlefield; corpses were strewn over roads, ditches, ravines, thickets and fields … The poor wounded men that were being picked up all day long were ghastly pale and exhausted … Some who had gaping wounds already beginning to show infection were almost crazed with suffering. They begged to be put out of their misery and writhed with faces distorted in the grip of a death-struggle.'

EMERGENCY CARE Surgeons from the Japanese Red Cross tend the wounded after a battle in the Russo-Japanese War of 1904-05.

Later conventions built on the work of the first. All of them were chiefly concerned with the treatment of civilian non-combatants and prisoners of war. They did not tackle the question of battlefield conduct and permissible weapons. This was the task of the Hague Conventions of 1899, 1907 and 1954 and the Geneva Protocol of 1925. The latter banned poison gas and bacteriological warfare. A further convention in 1972 reiterated the prohibition, outlawing the development, production and stockpiling of such weapons and calling for the destruction of any already in existence.

Three international peace conferences at The Hague produced numerous rules of war that became binding on all signatory states. They set out how war should be conducted, which weapons are strictly illegal, and how the rights and property of individuals caught up in such conflicts should be protected.

The conventions also set out procedures for the peaceful settlement of disputes, all of which should be followed through before it is legal to go to war. If war becomes inevitable, it has to be formally declared before any attack is made. When, in 1941, Japan launched a surprise attack on the US naval base at Pearl Harbor, it was acting illegally – but more by accident than design. To keep within the rules of war they had intended their ultimatum to be delivered to Washington just before the onslaught started. But because it took so long to decode, their ambassador reached the White House hours after the event.

The combatants' responsibilities

Most of the rules governing battlefield conduct are simple. It is illegal to abuse a white flag, the accepted sign of surrender or truce. It is a crime to kill or injure a person who has surrendered, or to attack a defenceless person or place. Troops may not use an enemy flag, uniform, or insignia – or the Red Cross – for any military

Where did the idea of war crimes come from and why were some trials criticised?

The Hague Conventions defined war crimes. The definition was established as binding international law by the Nuremberg and Tokyo war crimes trials, held in 1945 and 1946. In them, prominent members of the German and Japanese leaderships were indicted and tried before international tribunals.

Nuremberg trials

At Nuremberg, the defendants stood accused of four major crimes. First came the crimes against peace – the planning and waging of a war of aggression. The second charge was war crimes, which covered all violations of the accepted laws of war, including ill treatment of prisoners of war. The third charge was crimes against humanity. This was designed to bring the perpetrators of the Holocaust to justice. All those indicted at Nuremberg were also subject to a fourth, rather vague charge of conspiracy in any aspect of the first three charges.

Though the trials were criticised by some, largely because the victors were judging the defeated, they set a precedent that has been followed ever since. Similar tribunals include the International Criminal Tribunal for the Former Yugoslavia and the International Criminal Tribunal for Rwanda. The status of the International Criminal Court, set up in The Hague in 2002, is controversial, since some nations – notably the USA and Israel – refuse to recognise its jurisdiction. When former Iraqi President Saddam Hussein was found guilty of committing war crimes and sentenced to death in 2006, an Iraqi court heard the case instead.

BEHIND BARS Slobodan Milosevic represented himself at the UN War Crimes Tribunal in 2001. He would become the first former president to be prosecuted in The Hague.

purpose. Nor can enemy public property be taken or destroyed unless this is essential for military operations.

Sick or wounded soldiers must always be treated humanely. It is illegal to kill, mutilate, torture, or perform any kind of medical experiment on a wounded or sick person. It is also illegal to treat such a person in a degrading or humiliating way or to hold them hostage. For civilians, the aim is to give them the same protection as wounded troops, prisoners of war and others not active in the conflict. It is illegal to attack civilians or use them as 'human shields' to protect a position. Nor are troops allowed to confiscate personal property unless it is in some way being used against them.

If a territory is occupied, the occupying force has extra legal responsibilities. It has to cater for the basic needs of the people under its control, providing them with food, clothing, shelter and medical attention. It also has to maintain law and order. Civilians may be ordered to work, but they must be paid for their efforts and cannot be forced to undertake anything in a military capacity. Nor can they be treated as slave labour.

As with the sick or wounded, the Hague and Geneva Conventions protect prisoners of war from violence, indignity and medical experimentation. All they can be asked to provide when questioned are their names, ranks, military identification numbers and dates of birth. Other interrogation tactics and techniques, such as torture, are illegal. Prisoners are subject to the laws of the armed forces that are holding them, so a recaptured escapee, for example, can be legally punished.

Prisoners of war cannot be held in prison cells, unless it is for their own protection. They have to be sent to special internment camps, where they should enjoy the same rights as their captors grant to their own armed forces: food, water, shelter, clothing, the ability to exercise and other basic

> ## 'There was never a good war or a bad peace.'
>
> Benjamin Franklin

WHITE FLAGS FLYING A group of Bavarian civilians surrender their village to US Army forces in April 1945 in the final weeks of the Second World War.

BAD TREATMENT Russian prisoners of war taken by the Germans in 1941 crowd a makeshift camp. Both the Germans and the Soviets made little attempt to treat enemy prisoners properly and many died.

human needs. Representatives of a so-called protecting power – usually a neutral state – should be allowed to inspect such camps regularly.

With such rules in place, dealing with their violation should be straightforward, but this is not always the case. Part of the problem, especially in recent times, lies in defining who is and who is not a soldier from an officially recognised army, and so subject to the rules of war. Anyone accused of violating them is entitled to a fair trial. But it can take years to reach agreement as to whether international law has been violated and then to bring the case before an appropriate tribunal.

International input

The International Court of Justice – also known as the World Court – in The Hague is now widely accepted as the forum for hearing international disputes. It is more concerned with disputes between states than in trying cases involving individuals. For this reason, the International Criminal Tribunal for Yugoslavia was set up by the United Nations in 1991 to try the leaders of the former Yugoslavia for violating international humanitarian law. More than 100 people have been brought before it to face charges including genocide, crimes against humanity and war crimes.

Why is the use of biological and chemical weapons banned by the laws of war?

Biowarfare had been around for centuries before the Biological Weapons Convention finally banned it in 1975. Its history is grisly: in 1346, the Tatars catapulted the corpses of diseased soldiers into the besieged city of Kaffa in the Crimea, in a bid to infect its inhabitants.

During the Seven Years' War in the 18th century, Sir Jeffrey Amherst, commander of British forces in North America, presented blankets and handkerchiefs contaminated with smallpox to some Native American chiefs who had been invited to confer at Fort Pitt. The plan was to 'reduce', as he put it, the size of the tribes hostile to the British crown.

In modern times, despite the billions poured into bacteriological research by all the major powers, only one nation has resorted to biowarfare. During the Second World War, Japan attacked 11 Chinese cities with biological weapons, including the dropping of plague-infested fleas, causing epidemics that lasted for years afterwards. Viruses and other such weapons were so uncontrollable in their effects that their further use was seen as being too risky to contemplate.

This was not the case with poison gas. Building on the experience gained in the First World War, when both sides employed gas widely on the battlefield, all major nations in the Second World War stockpiled gas weapons, but they were never used. The shared knowledge that both sides possessed such a deadly weapon may have had a deterrent effect. The last European nation to use gas in war – in direct contravention of the 1925 Geneva Protocol – was Italy in its war against Ethiopia in 1935-6.

The USA employed herbicides and defoliants – notably Agent Orange – on a large scale in the Vietnam War. They were later shown to have long-term human side effects. And, in Iraq, Ali Hassan al-Majid, one of Saddam Hussein's most notorious henchmen, won the nickname of 'Chemical Ali' for the gas attacks he launched against Kurdish nationalists in the northern part of the country in 1988. Like his master, he was eventually tried and found guilty of genocide in 2007.

Giving peace a chance Today it is impossible to imagine war breaking out between France, Germany and Britain, yet 70 years ago Western Europe was in the midst of horrifying conflict. How did we get to this state of apparently perpetual peace?

KEEPING WARM German citizens collecting wood for the winter. A country brought to its knees by total war had to survive by any means necessary.

'What is Europe now? A rubble heap, a charnel house, a breeding ground for pestilence and hate.' The year was 1947, the speaker was Winston Churchill, and there was little exaggeration in his claims.

The Second World War had killed almost 10 million citizens of the western European lands and put two-thirds of their factories out of commission. Agricultural production had plummeted by 50 per cent. The worst hit country was Germany, which was divided into four zones of occupation, controlled by the USA, Britain, France and the Soviet Union. By the war's end it had lost 40 per cent of all its buildings to bombing and street fighting. Most of the major cities had been rendered almost uninhabitable and only one serviceable bridge still spanned the Rhine.

The fate of the civilians was just as grim. Many were surviving on just 700 calories a day, less than half the minimum specified in pre-war League of Nations guidelines and just a sixth of the daily ration allocated to US soldiers in the American zone. In August 1945, 4,000 Berliners were reckoned to be dying of malnutrition each day. The Germans have a phrase for the time: *Stunde Null* (Zero Hour). It was the nation's lowest point since the dark days of the Thirty Years War three centuries earlier.

Fast-forward to the present day, and the picture that Churchill described seems hard to imagine. Germany and Western Europe have experienced more than 50 years of steady growth, interrupted only by the oil shocks of the 1970s. Once bitter enemies, the states of Western Europe are now firmly allied as partners within the European Union. When Churchill spoke, France and Germany had fought three brutal wars in less than eight decades. Today, the borders between the two countries are open and thousands of schoolchildren cross them yearly on student exchanges to stay as guests in family homes.

So what brought about the transformation? Radical changes in mindsets were needed, yet there was no inevitability to the process. Peace only came as a result of a turnabout in attitudes. It was a revolution that occurred almost unnoticed, for few people at the time were aware that a historic watershed had been crossed.

A strategy for control
In 1945, Allied aims were punitive rather than conciliatory. Their main concern was not to build a community of nations but to ensure that Germany

would never be in a position to threaten Europe and the world again. Strategists drew up plans aimed at crippling all German industries whose products could have military potential.

Jean Monnet, an economist and a future architect of European union, proposed a scheme for France to annex the Ruhr and Saar basins, heartlands of German heavy industry. Production throughout the country was to be reduced to half pre-war levels, and ordinary Germans were expected to be satisfied with the living standards they had known at the height of the Great Depression. The occupying powers set about putting the plan into effect.

Factories were closed and plant was dismantled, crushing any hope of German recovery. While in Britain, manufacturing production was already back to pre-war levels by 1946, and France reached the same position in 1948, Germany remained mired in

poverty and hunger. The Allies ended up footing the bill to feed the hungry civilian population.

The turning point
What happened to change attitudes was the sight – and the cost – of so much misery. Faced with a growing humanitarian crisis, it became clear to the occupiers that something had to be done. To make matters worse, Stalin's Soviet Union was tightening its grip on Eastern Europe, and political observers feared that unless the economic situation improved, Germany – and perhaps other western lands – might choose to ally with the Soviets. In May 1947 William L. Clayton, Assistant US Secretary of State for Economic Affairs, reported: 'Europe is steadily deteriorating. The political position reflects the economic. One political crisis after another merely denotes the existence of economic distress. Millions of people in the cities are slowly starving.'

A massive injection of capital was needed to jump-start the process of renewal and Clayton's memorandum helped to secure it. A month later US Secretary of State George Marshall announced the European Recovery Plan, better known as the Marshall

> Strategists drew up plans aimed at crippling all German industries

PHOENIX FROM THE ASHES
The futuristic dome of the new Reichstag soars above Berlin; Norman Foster's design symbolises a move towards a united Germany.

Plan. Over the next four years an extra US$13 billion was pumped into war-torn national economies that were already showing signs of new life.

Germany was a particular beneficiary of the US largesse. It was by no means the largest recipient, getting only two-thirds the sum that France received and less than half the amount that reached Britain. But the new policy also signalled a change of attitude. The emphasis was now on helping Germany to recover so that it could look after itself. The end of factory dismantling and the removal of restraints on growth had a dramatic effect, the more so after the Deutschmark replaced the worthless Reichsmark in 1948, providing the nation with the hard currency it needed for economic lift-off.

The impact of the Marshall Plan

The results of the change of policy were dramatic. Coming to power in 1949 as the first Chancellor of the Federal Republic of Germany, Konrad Adenauer and his finance minister, the corpulent, cigar-smoking Ludwig Erhard, presided over a prolonged period of sustained growth. By 1950 people were already starting to talk of a Wirtschaftswunder – the 'economic miracle' that in time would transform a prostrate nation into the economic powerhouse of post-war Europe.

And, as optimists had hoped, the benefits of German recovery were not limited to Germany. By the end of 1950, industrial output across Western Europe as a whole was one-third higher than its pre-war level. In just three years, steel production had increased by 70 per cent, and vehicle production by 150 per cent, while exports had nearly doubled.

The message was clear enough. At the end of the First World War, the victorious Allies had pursued punitive policies, imposing harsh reparations on Germany. The result had been hyperinflation and, ultimately, the rise of Hitler. Now far-sighted statesmen reckoned that the opposite approach might achieve better results. By burying the hatchet and seeking joint prosperity, everyone might benefit.

The idea of European cooperation was not new. Victor Hugo had argued for a United States of Europe in the mid-19th century. In 1946, Churchill picked up the idea, calling for the creation of 'a kind of United States of Europe' based on a partnership between France and Germany, with Britain and the USA looking on. 'In this way only,' he urged, 'will hundreds of millions of toilers be able to regain the simple joys and hopes which make life worth living.'

The hope of Europa

Continental intellectuals had another term to describe the dream of a united Europe – 'Europa'. In 1943, as a member of the French Resistance, Albert Camus had written in his Letters to a German Friend: 'I must make a confession. During the entire time we were stubbornly and silently serving our country, an idea and a hope were ever present within us, namely the idea of Europa, the hope of Europa.'

The growing prosperity of the Marshall Plan years provided a seedbed in which such ideas could bloom. But the first fruit of the post-war idealism was not the Common Market. Rather it was an institution that Churchill proposed in his Zurich speech: the Council of Europe. Founded in 1949, the Council exists to this day, with 47 member states in contrast to the European Union's 27. It was the Council, not the EU, that was responsible for establishing the Convention for the Protection of Human Rights, as well as for introducing the familiar European flag. Even Beethoven's 'Ode to Joy', which now provides obligatory background music for all major EU functions, was first used as a pan-European anthem under the auspices of the Council of Europe.

The Schuman Declaration

The EU's own origins stretch back to a Franco-German initiative of the type that Churchill had foreseen. In May 1950, in response to approaches from Konrad Adenauer, France's Foreign Minister, Robert Schuman, issued the

BEETLE BOOM In 1955, the one-millionth Volkswagen Beetle rolled off the assembly line in Germany.

CEMENTING TIES Chancellor Adenauer celebrates with President Charles de Gaulle after signing the Friendship Treaty.

move towards further economic integration. The 1957 Treaty of Rome established the European Economic Community (EEC), the precursor first of the European Community (EC) and then of today's European Union (EU). Besides changing names, the European family grew dramatically over the next half century, with the original six nations expanding to today's 27.

With prosperity came growing cordiality. France's President Charles de Gaulle struck up a close relationship with Chancellor Adenauer, and the cooperation pact the two men signed in 1963 is known to this day as the Friendship Treaty. Since that time the EU has had downs as well as ups, and many people have complained of the strangling effect of Brussels bureaucracy. But the basic idea of cooperation between member nations has never been seriously challenged. Peace, it seems, has broken out at last.

Schuman Declaration. It proposed the establishment of a joint administration to run Western Europe's coal and steel industries, centred on the disputed Ruhr and Saar regions. Schuman stated, 'This is no longer a moment for empty words. For peace to have a real chance, there must first be a Europe'.

Robert Schuman was himself a product of both France and Germany. His father came from the disputed area of Lorraine at a time when it was part of the Kaiser's German Empire, and Robert always spoke French with a German accent. Even though he was born in Luxembourg, he served in a civilian capacity on the German side in World War One. He only became French in 1919 when Alsace-Lorraine was given back to France as part of the post-war settlement.

The idea behind the Schuman Declaration came in part from the economist Jean Monnet, who had had a change of heart since the days of the Monnet Plan to annex the Ruhr. From 1950, he threw himself enthusiastically behind the cause of European union, earning in time the honorary title of 'Father of Europe'.

Chancellor Adenauer reacted enthusiastically to the Schuman Declaration, telling a colleague, 'That's our breakthrough!' The result was the foundation of the European Coal and Steel Community (ECSC), bringing the two industries under joint control. The agreement was signed in 1951 not just by France and Germany but also by Italy, led by the pro-European Alcide de Gasperi, and by Belgium, the Netherlands and Luxembourg – which had already established a customs union of their own three years earlier.

The ECSC proved such a success at creating jobs and boosting trade that the member states were soon happy to

The European Union

European integration and accession can be traced back to 1957 and the advent of the European Economic Community (EEC). A total of 27 countries have now joined the EU.

1957 Signature of the Treaty of Rome (*6 members*)

1973 EEC members joined (*9 members*)

1981 Greece joined (*10 members*)

1986 EEC members joined (*12 members*)

1990 Part of the EEC after unification of Germany

1995 EEC members joined (*15 members*)

2004 EEC members joined (*25 members*)

2007 EEC members joined (*27 members*)

Membership pending

Everything but the truth We
are inured to governments and big businesses promoting their side of the story and spinning news to suit their own purposes. Who invented propaganda in the first place and how did it grow to become an all-pervading feature of everyday life?

REVOLUTIONARY PROPAGANDIST
Writer Tom Paine's 1776 pamphlet 'Common Sense' helped spread the idea of American independence.

Many people assume that propaganda is a modern phenomenon, but examples have been recorded from much earlier eras. The word comes from the Latin *propagare*, meaning 'to propagate', and was first used in 1622, when Pope Gregory XV set up a committee of cardinals to oversee the spreading of Catholicism in pagan lands. He named the new committee the Congregation for the Propagation of the Faith.

Greeks and Romans

The ancient Greeks were the world's first true propagandists. Classical philosophers – notably Plato and Aristotle – advocated the use of rhetoric as a means of influencing their fellow citizens and laid down strict rules to govern its practice. These were not always obeyed, as Themistocles, a leading Athenian soldier and statesman, demonstrated. In common with his contemporaries, he realised how easy it was to manufacture rumours and use them to influence events. When he found himself confronting the vastly superior army of the Persian Emperor Xerxes in 480 BC, he circulated a report that many of his outnumbered troops were about to flee rather than face battle. Xerxes promptly detached half his navy to trap the supposedly deserting Greeks. In the resulting battle, the Persian fleet was decimated and, unable to supply his troops, Xerxes was forced into humiliating retreat.

The Roman emperors used propaganda to depict themselves and their achievements to advantage. Through literature, architecture, art and elaborate public ceremonial, they hammered home to their subjects that imperial Rome stood for peace, good government and the rule of law.

In contrast, any society that the Romans were in conflict with was caricatured as barbaric, lawless and a threat to the stability and prosperity that the emperors were determined to preserve. The systematic demonisation of the Egyptian Queen Cleopatra was typical. To her own people, she was a capable, popular leader. To the Romans, she was a dangerous immoral menace. Octavius Caesar (who later appointed himself the Emperor Augustus) launched the first attacks on her reputation during the queen's lifetime, and these continued for more than a century after her death. The poet Horace, writing in the late 1st century BC,

HIGH SEA SPIN The Armada's humiliating defeat in 1588 was reported across Europe as a great victory by the Spanish.

described her as 'a crazy queen … plotting to demolish the Capitol and topple the empire'. Lucan, another Roman poet, later unkindly labelled her 'the shame of Egypt, the lascivious fury who was to become the bane of Rome'.

Printing and propaganda

Around 1,600 years later, another powerful woman, Elizabeth I of England, used propaganda to her own ends. Her reputation was enhanced by the 'Cult of Elizabeth' in which she was portrayed as the 'Virgin Queen', totally devoted to her country and its people. Shakespeare's history plays, which vilified the Tudors' opponents (most notably Richard III) and glorified their supporters, also helped to cement the 16th-century Tudor dynasty's right to rule.

The coming of printing at the end of the Middle Ages helped to disseminate this Elizabethan mythmaking. It changed the ways that propaganda could be used and distributed, once ordinary people became more literate and could be influenced by it. Elizabeth's enemies exploited the power of the printed word as much as she did: when his Armada fleet was utterly defeated by the English navy in 1588, Philip II of Spain instigated a multi-lingual, Europe-wide printed propaganda campaign claiming the exact opposite.

By the end of the 1700s, both the instigators and

> **'Make the lie big, make it simple, keep saying it and eventually people will come to believe it.'**
>
> Adolf Hitler

targets of propaganda were changing. In France, the writings of philosophers Voltaire and Jean-Jacques Rousseau inflamed opposition to royal absolutism. In Britain's North American colonies, John Adams and Tom Paine roused American feelings against George III and the alleged tyranny of British rule. What they realised, in common with other notable thinkers, statesmen and politicians of the time, was that popular opinion was now a force that it was impossible to ignore. Accordingly, they began to devise new ways of shaping and moulding it. Friedrich von Gentz, a German political journalist who won fame for his attacks on the French Revolution and Napoleon, noted that, 'Public opinion ought not to be neglected or disdained for a single moment.'

Like the Caesars before him, Napoleon Bonaparte was a deft manipulator of propaganda. 'Government', he declared, 'is nothing unless supported by opinion.' In January 1800, he suppressed 60 of the 73 newspapers published in France. 'Three hostile newspapers', he said, 'are more to be feared than a thousand bayonets.' Manipulating the news for his own advantage became his forte. 'Truth', he once commented, 'is not half as important as what people think to be true.' It was a precept that Adolf Hitler was to share just over a century later.

Telling the big lie

During the First World War, all the warring powers used propaganda to bolster morale at home and as a psychological weapon against their enemies. The British, with a specially designated Department of Propaganda masterminded by Lord Northcliffe, the most powerful press baron of the day, proved particularly effective. So did the Americans, with their Committee on Public Information. As he admitted in the treatise of his beliefs, *Mein Kampf*, Adolf Hitler learned much from their example.

Hitler also realised that, to win over his audience, it had to believe – or want to believe – what it was being told. Nazi propaganda was so effective because most Germans wanted to believe that they had not

MASTER PROPAGANDIST Joseph Goebbels addresses a Nazi meeting. Carefully staged mass rallies were just one of the methods he used to demonstrate Nazi power and communicate their ideology.

DIRECT MESSAGE Soviet leaders kept communication simple. This 1919 dragon poster reads 'Death to World Imperialism'.

common denominator. 'All propaganda,' he wrote, 'must be popular and its intellectual level must be adjusted to the most limited intelligence among those to whom it is addressed. Consequently, the greater the mass it is intended to reach, the lower its purely intellectual level will have to be.'

Rewriting history

When the Nazis came to power, the task of producing propaganda for Hitler's regime was given to the newly created Ministry for Public Enlightenment and Propaganda and its minister, Joseph Goebbels. A propagandist of genius, he swiftly brought all Germany's newspapers, magazines, books, art, music, movies and radio firmly under Nazi control. Propaganda became integral to daily life. Film-makers like Leni Riefenstahl created powerful documentaries, such as *Triumph of the Will*, to glorify the Führer and celebrate the regime's triumphs. In her film of the 1936 Berlin Olympics, she portrayed German athletes as perfect examples of the Aryan master race. The government sponsored the production of cheap radios, which quickly found their way into almost every home in the country. They were designed to be incapable of receiving foreign programmes, and it was soon made a crime to listen to radio stations broadcasting from outside the Reich.

Soviet propaganda was equally powerful. From the start of their

regime, the Bolsheviks exploited every means at their disposal to spread revolutionary ideas and an understanding of the main tenets of Marxism. After Joseph Stalin assumed supreme power this was combined with an all-pervading cult of personality. All Soviet citizens had a duty to dedicate themselves to the service of their leader and to help him in the revolutionary transformation of Russian society.

To this end, accounts of the past and of current affairs were frequently and ruthlessly distorted. The Bolsheviks became rewriters of history, retelling past events so that they emerged from them favourably. Photographs were doctored, and former comrades like Leon Trotsky, who had fallen foul of the regime, literally vanished from the visual record. Even the history of the revolution itself was amended to make it appear that Stalin was closer to Lenin than he actually had been.

During the Second World War, three types of propaganda were used: black, white and grey. Black propaganda was designed to mislead the enemy by disseminating false information, undermining morale and spreading doubt, disquiet and depression. The British set up a powerful radio station called Soldatensender Calais, purporting to be a German station broadcasting jazz, sports results and news bulletins to the German forces in France. Its subversive broadcasts could be picked up deep inside Germany, and included 'situation reports' on the D-Day landings that were transmitted to confuse and disorientate the German commanders on the beaches.

White propaganda was more or less factual. Generally, it told the truth, though sometimes the facts might be biased in the propagandists' favour.

> '*Propaganda is to a democracy what the bludgeon is to a totalitarian state.*'
>
> Noam Chomsky

lost the First World War. It was preferable to be told that they had been stabbed in the back on the Home Front by defeatists and Jews. So the Nazis told them repeatedly that the people responsible for Germany's humiliation were the 'November criminals', who had negotiated the armistice with the Allies and then accepted the Treaty of Versailles.

Hitler and his cronies quickly realised what a powerful weapon the Allies had unwittingly handed over to them through the harsh terms of the treaty. 'In the oppression of the treaty and the shamelessness of its demands, there lies the greatest propaganda weapon for the reawakening of the nation's spirit,' he said.

Scapegoat for suffering

Hitler never let truth get in the way of his ambitions. He gave the people a scapegoat for the privations they were suffering. The Jews, he proclaimed, were responsible for all the nation's ills. His rabid anti-Semitism found a ready audience and was carefully tailored to appeal to the lowest

So-called grey propaganda was a blend of the other two approaches. William Joyce, a leading British fascist who fled to Germany just before the outbreak of war, was a master at this. His broadcasts to Britain from a Hamburg studio – signalled by the words 'Germany calling, Germany calling' – contained nuggets of fact embedded in the Nazi message, all delivered in the unmistakable style that earned him the nickname, Lord Haw Haw.

Propaganda in the Cold War

Both the US and Europe, and the USSR and its allies, used propaganda extensively during the Cold War. Their aim was to influence their own peoples, each other and other nations, usually non-aligned or those in the developing world.

Both sides reflected the prevailing climate, as the Cold War blew hotter and colder. In the early 1950s, Senator Joseph McCarthy was the USA's leading anti-Communist propagandist. For four years, he kept up a stream of accusations against supposed Communists and Communist sympathisers relying on false information, rumour and hearsay. His spell was broken only when his witch hunts were exposed as baseless. Thirty years later, President Ronald Reagan coined the phrase 'the evil empire' to describe the Soviet bloc. It was his justification for launching a massive new anti-missile defence programme, which he named Star Wars.

Today, propaganda is more pervasive than ever before. Global television and the internet produce a barrage of information, which may be true or false. In their book, *The Age of Propaganda*, the social commentators Anthony Pratkanis and Elliott Aronson wrote: 'Every day we are bombarded with one persuasive communication after another. These appeals persuade not through the give-and-take of argument, but through the manipulation of symbols and of our most basic human emotions.'

The hidden arsenal

The events leading to the invasion of Iraq in 2003 appeared to demonstrate how far governments were prepared to go to manipulate public opinion. The UK and US governments claimed to have uncovered evidence that, in defiance of United Nations resolutions

LEAFLET WARNINGS Propaganda from the US psychological warfare unit was dropped on Iraq in the 1991 Gulf War. The red leaflet reads: 'Flee and save your life or remain and meet your death!' The black leaflet warns: 'We shall bomb your position again ... You will never be safe!'

and the peace terms agreed after the Gulf War in 1991, Saddam Hussein's regime still possessed an arsenal of weapons of mass destruction. Both nations argued that this, in itself, was sufficient justification for military intervention. After the invasion, no such weapons were found. A 2008 report by The Center for Public Integrity revealed that President George W. Bush and members of his administration had made at least 935 false statements in the two years following the 9/11 terrorist attacks in the USA, regarding the threat posed by Iraq. Whether these were the result of poor intelligence or deliberate attempts at misinformation remains a matter for debate.

HORROR IN VIETNAM Children flee the burning village of Trang Bang in southeastern Vietnam, after a napalm attack in June 1972, closely followed by a group of news photographers. Such instant and widespread reportage made it hard for the US to hide atrocities.

INDEX

PICTURE CREDITS

AA The Art Archive. BAL Bridgeman Art Library.
GI Getty Images. MEPL Mary Evans Picture Library.
SPL Science Picture Library. V&A Victoria and Albert Museum.

Front cover: ImageState/Heritage-Images/© the Board of Trustees of the Armouries (background); GI/Proehl Studios/The Image Bank, TL; GI/Gary Yeowell/The Image Bank, TM; PunchStock/DigitalVision, TR; GI /Blake Little/Stone, B.

Back cover: Courtesy Ronald Grant Archive/©Paramount Pictures.

Spine: GI/Proehl Studios/The Image Bank, T; GI/Gary Yeowell/The Image Bank, TM; PunchStock/DigitalVision, TM; GI/Blake Little/Stone, B.

1 GI/Proehl Studios/The Image Bank, TL; GI/Gary Yeowell/The Image Bank, TM; PunchStock/DigitalVision, TR; GI/Blake Little/Stone, B. **2** GI/Proehl Studios/The Image Bank, TL; **2-3** GI /Blake Little/Stone, B**. 3** GI/Gary Yeowell/The Image Bank, TL; PunchStock/DigitalVision, TR. **4** *Laps on Skis, illustration from 'Historia de Gentibus Septentrionalibus' by Olaus Magnus (1490-1558), published in Rome, 1555 (woodcut) (b/w photo), Italian School, (16th century).* British Library, London, UK/ BAL, TL. **4-5** *'Here Begynneth the Knightes Tale', illustration from 'The Canterbury Tales' by Geoffrey Chaucer (c.1345-1400) printed by William Caxton (c.1422-91) 1434 (woodcut) (b/w photo), English School, (15th century).* Private Collection/BAL. **6-7** AA/Liberty Leading the People July 28, 1830 painting by Eugene Delacroix/ Musée du Louvre Paris/Gianni Dagli Orti. **8** AA/ Museum of the City of New York/ 29.100.709. **9** GI/National Geographic/Michael S.Yamashita. **10-11** Corbis/ Robert Harding World Imagery/Gavin Hellier. **12** SPL/NASA, TL; PA Photos/ AP/Francois Mori, TR.**14** GI/David Silverman. **15** GI/ National Science Foundation/Rob Jones, B; Corbis/Kit Kittle, ML. **16** Corbis/ Philip Gould, T; *Trappers Starting for the Beaver Hunt, 1837 (w/c & gouache on paper), Miller, Alfred Jacob (1810-74).* © Walters Art Museum, Baltimore, USA/BAL, B. **17** *A View of the Taking of Quebec, September 13th 1759 (colour engraving), English School (18th century).* Private Collection/BAL. **18** Corbis Sygma/Alain Nogues. **19** Corbis/Earl & Nazima Kowall. **20-21** akg-images. **22** AA/ Musée du Château de Versailles/ Gianni Dagli Orti. **23** akg-images. **25** *The Tower of Skulls (photo), Turkish School, (19th century).* Nis, Serbia/BAL, T; GI/Time & Life Pictures, B. **26** Roy Williams, MR; PA Photos/ AP/Greg Marinovich, B. **27** GI/AFP/ Dimitar Dilkoff. **28** GI/AFP/ DARDE. **29** *The Battle of the Boyne on 12th July 1690, 1690 (oil on canvas) by Jan Wyck (1640-1700).* National Army Museum, London, UK/BAL, T; *Portrait of Toussaint L'Ouverture (1743-1803) from the 'Universal History of the 19th Century' engraved by Joseph Julien Guillaume Dulompre (b.1789) (engraving) (b/w photo) by Duc, (18th century) (after).* Bibliothèque Nationale, Paris, France/ Giraudon/ BAL, B. **30** GI. **31** GI/AFP/Paul Faith. **32** Alamy/Wild Places Photography/ Chris Howes. **33** National Geographic Image Collection/The Living Tongues Institute for Endangered Language. **34** GI/AFP/Fayez Nureldine. **35** akg-images/Erich Lessing, T; *Fr 22495 f.43 Battle between Crusaders and Moslems, from Le Roman de Godefroi de Bouillon (vellum), French School, (14th century).* Bibliothèque Nationale, Paris, France/BAL, B. **36-37** GI/AFP/Moshe Milner. **37** akg-images/ Bildarchiv Pisarek. **38** *The building of the Fatehpur Sikri Palace, from the 'Akbarnama', c.1590, Mughal, (illustrated text).*V&A, London, UK/ BAL. **38-39** Topfoto. **40** Corbis/ Reuters/Kamal Kishore. **41** Corbis/Reuters/Ajay Verma. **42** Corbis/ Tibor Bognár. **43** *Blue and white kraak pomegranate ewer painted with birds and flowers, Wanli, 1580-1600 (porcelain), Chinese School.* Private Collection, Paul Freeman/ BAL, L; *Manufacture of Porcelain: Hand Modelling & Moulding (w/c and gouache on paper), Chinese School, (19th century).* © Peabody Essex Museum, Salem, Massachusetts, USA/ BAL, R. **44** Corbis/Ric Ergenbright. **45** Photoshot/UPPA/ Newscom, L; Topfoto/The Image Works/Rob Crandall, R. **46-47** National Geographic Image Collection/Albert Moldvay. **48** SPL/GeoEye. **49** AA/ Museo Correr Venice/Gianni Dagli Orti. **50** *The Virgin of Vladimir Church in St. Petersburg, c.1840 (colour litho) by Perrot, Ferdinand Victor (1808-41).* Pushkin Museum, Moscow, Russia/BAL. **51** Corbis/Eye Ubiquitous/Julia Waterlow. **52** AA/ Ca Rezzonico Museum Venice/Alfredo Dagli Orti. **53** Alamy/ Eye Ubiquitous. **54** AA/Winchester Cathedral/ Gianni Dagli Orti. **55** Alamy/Philip Scalia. **56** AA/Museum der Stadt Wien/ Gianni Dagli Orti. **57** AA/Victoria and Albert Museum London/ Eileen Tweedy. **58** AA/Private Collection. **59** National Geographic Image Collection/James L.Stanfield. **60** Photolibrary Group/ Anthony Blake/Fresh Food Images. **61** Corbis/Sandro Vannini, T; *Solanum Pomiferum from 'Hortus Eystettensis' by Basil Besler (1561-1629) pub 1613 (hand coloured engraving), German School, (17th century).* Private Collection. The Stapleton Collection/BAL, B. **62-63** Cephas Picture Library Ltd./Nigel Blythe. **64** Chateau Perron, TM, Maven Wines, TR. **65** Roy Knipe, www.thorogood.net. **66** AA/ Archaeological Museum Thebes Greece/Gianni Dagli Orti, T; Still Pictures/ M.Rutkiewicz, B. **67** laif, Camera Press London/ Kruell. **68** Franck Prignet/LeFigaro, Camera Press London. **69** AA/ Montecassino Abbey Archives/Gianni Dagli Orti. **70** *Plate IV from 'Beeton's Everyday Cookery and Housekeeping Book', edited by Mrs Isabella Beeton, 1888 (colour litho), English School, (19th century).* British Library, London, UK, © British Library Board. All Rights Reserved/BAL. **71** Photolibrary Group/Anthony Blake/ Fresh Food Images. **72** Piggly Wiggly, LLC. Keene, NH, USA. **72-73** GI. **75** GI/Abid Katib. **76** GI. **77** MEPL. **78** Robert Opie. **79** MEPL, L; Rex Features/Roger-Viollet, R. **80** White Castle. **81** Corbis/Lynsey Addario, T; Shutterstock/ Vincent Giordano, B. **82** AA/Museo della Civilta, Romana Rome/Gianni Dagli Orti. **83** Reuters/ Dylan Martinez. **84** GI/AFP/STF. **85** GI/Popperfoto. **86** *A Game of Polo, from the Large Clive Album, Indian School, (17th century).* V&A, London, UK, The Stapleton Collection/BAL. **87** GI/Matthew Stockman. **88** GI/Shaun Botterill, T; *The Grand Jubilee Match between the North and South of England, to commemorate the 50th anniversary of the M.C.C. 10th July 1837 (colour litho), English School, (19th century).* © Marylebone Cricket Club, London, UK/ BAL, B. **89** Arsenal Football Club. **90** GI/ Bongarts/Gunnar Berning. **91** AA/Gianni Dagli Orti, T; AA/Musée d'Art et d'Histoire Metz/Gianni Dagli Orti, B. **92** AA/ Museo Nazionale Terme Rome/Gianni Dagli Orti, T; GI/Jamie Squire, B. **93** GI/Popperfoto/ Bob Thomas. **94** GI/ Allsport/Chris Cole, T; GI, B. **95** AA/Private Collection/ Gianni Dagli Orti. **96-97** GI. **97** AA/Musée du Louvre Paris/ Gianni Dagli Orti T. **98** *The Claque in action, c.1830-40 (litho), French School, (19th century)/ Bibliothèque des Arts Decoratifs, Paris, France.* Archives Charmet/BAL. **99** *King, Queen and Jack playing cards (coloured wood engraving), French School, (17th century).* Bibliothèque Nationale, Paris, France, Lauros /Giraudon/BAL. **100** ©Lebrecht Music & Arts/DS RA, T; © Lebrecht Music & Arts/C.Osborne, B. **101** ©Lebrecht/ Royal Academy of Music. **103** ©Lebrecht Music & Arts. **104** GI, L; 'The Young Ones' by Cliff Richard & The Shadows, released 11th August1961. Licensed courtesy of EMI Records Ltd. The Columbia trademark courtesy of SONY BMG Music Entertainment, M. **105** GI/Time & Life Pictures/Charles Trainor. **106** *Astley's Amphitheatre from Ackermann's "Microcosm of London", Rowlandson, T. (1756-1827) & Pugin, A.C.(1762-1832).* Private Collection/BAL. **107** AA/Museo della Civilta Romana Rome/Gianni Dagli Orti, T; MEPL, B. **108** AA. **109** ArenaPAL/ Marilyn Kingwill. **110** *Camera obscura, Optics Chapter, plate V, illustration from the 'Encyclopedie' by Denis Diderot (1713-84) (engraving) (b/w photo), Goussier, Louis-Jacques (1722-99) (after).* Private Collection, Archives Charmet/BAL, R; John Meek, L. **111** *Photography on the Common, from 'Street Life of London', 1877 (b/w photo), Thomson, John (1837-1921).* © Museum of London, UK/BAL, T; *Kodak Brownie camera with original box, c.1902 (wood & cardboard), English School, (20th century).* NMPFT, Bradford, West Yorkshire/ BAL, B. **112** *Party of French and English Troops in the Camp of the 4th Dragoon Guards, from an album of 52 photographs associated with the Crimean War, 1855 (b/w photo), Fenton, Roger (1819-69).* National Army Museum, London /BAL. **113** MEPL. **114** Corbis/Eadweard Muybridge, T; GI/Time & Life Pictures/Hansel Mieth, B. **115** The Kobal Collection/Limot. **116-117** Courtesy Ronald Grant Archive/© Paramount Pictures. **118** Courtesy Ronald Grant Archive, T; Los Angeles Public Library/Security Pacific Collection, B. **119** Courtesy Ronald Grant Archive. **120** Courtesy Ronald Grant Archive/© Warner Bros. **121** Courtesy Ronald Grant Archive/© Notice Peliculas Rodriguez. **122** *Number 6, 1948 (oil on paper laid down on canvas), Pollock, Jackson (1912-56).* Private Collection/James Goodman Gallery, New York, USA/BAL, © ARS, NY and DACS, London 2008. **124** *Nocturne in Black and Gold, the Falling Rocket, c.1875 (oil on panel), Whistler, James Abbott McNeill (1834-1903).* The Detroit Institute of Arts, USA, Gift of Dexter M. Ferry Jr./BAL, BL. **124-125** *Fountain, 1917/64 (ceramic), Duchamp, Marcel (1887-1968).* The Israel Museum, Jerusalem, Israel/ Vera & Arturo Schwarz Collection of Dada and Surrealist Art/BAL, © Succession Marcel Duchamp/ ADAGP, Paris and DACS, London 2008. **125** *The Physical Impossibility of Death in the Mind of Someone Living, 1991 Glass, steel, silicon, formaldehyde solution and shark 2170 x 5420 x 1800 mm.* © Damien Hirst. All rights reserved, DACS 2008/Photo: Prudence Cuming Associates, TR. **126** AA/ Institute of Slavonic Studies/Marc Charmet. **127** Reuters/ Desmond Boylan. **128** *Adam and Eve (oil on panel), Cranach, Lucas, the Elder (1472-1553).* Koninklijk Museum voor Schone Kunsten, Antwerp, Belgium, Giraudon/BAL. **129** Photolibrary Group/ Stockbyte/Stockdisc, T; *Hands of an Apostle, 1508 (brush drawing), Dürer, Albrecht (1471-1528).* Graphische Sammlung Albertina, Vienna, Austria /BAL, B. **130** *Central panel of Triptych with Adoration of the Trinity, 1523 (oil on panel) Oostsanen, Jacob Cornelisz van (1470-1533).* Gemaeldegalerie Alte Meister, Kassel, Germany, © Museumslandschaft Hessen Kassel / BAL. **131** *Ms H 7 f.111r Jonah and the Whale, from the Bible of Jean XXII (vellum), French School, (15th century).* Bibliothèque de la Faculté de Medecine, Paris, France,/ BAL. **132-133** GI/AFP/ OSSERVATORE ROMANO. **133** *Title page from the Luther Bible, c.1530 (coloured woodcut), German School, (16th century).* Bible Society, London, UK/BAL, TL. **134** Corbis/Gregor M.Schmid. **135** *Auto de Fe in the Plaza Mayor, Madrid, 30 June 1680 (detail), Rizi, Francisco (1608-85).* Prado, Madrid, Spain, Index/ BAL. **136** akg-images/British Library. **137** Corbis/ David Lees, TL; Reuters/Oleg Popov, TR, BR; Bradbury & Williams, BL; Sonia Halliday Photographs, M. **138** AA/Alfredo Dagli Orti. **139** Alamy/Louise Batalla Duran. **140** Corbis/epa/Hassan Ali. **141** Corbis/ Kazuyoshi Nomachi. **142** AA/Hazem Palace Damascus/Gianni Dagli Orti. **143** Corbis/epa/Warren Clarke. **144** MEPL. **145** akg-images. **146** Rex Features/Sipa Press, T; Topfoto/AP, B. **147** Corbis/Reuters/Handout/MNFI. **148** Corbis Sygma/Mike Stewart, T; Topfoto/ The Image Works/Chet Gordon, B. **149** PA Photos/AP/Suzanne Plunkett. **150** Campaign for Nuclear Disarmament, M. **150-151** Corbis/Louie Psihoyos. **151** SPL/Louise Murray, T. **152** GI/Time & Life Pictures, T; **153** © Bryan & Cherry Alexander, B. **154** PA Photos/AP/Pablo Martinez Monsivais. **155** AA/Agora Museum, Athens/Gianni Dagli Orti, T; Photoshot/World Illustrated/ Classic-Image, B. **156** AA/Musée Carnavalet Paris/Marc Charmet. **157** The British Museum. **158** PA Photos/AP. **159** Corbis/Peter Turnley, T; *Allegory of Freemasonry and the Paris Commune, 1871 (colour litho), Moloch (Colomb B.) (1849-1909).* Private Collection, Archives Charmet/BAL, B. **160** Rex Features/Sipa Press. **162** *Cotton Claudius E.IV fol.201 Richard of Wallingford (1326-55) Abbot of St. Albans in 'History of the abbots of St. Albans' by Thomas of Walsingham (d.c.1422) (vellum), English School, (14th century.* British Library, London, UK, © British Library Board. All Rights Reserved/BAL, T; *The Human Foetus in the Womb, facsimile copy (pen & ink on paper), Vinci, Leonardo da (1452-1519) (after), facsimile.* Bibliothèque des Arts Decoratifs, Paris, France, Archives Charmet/BAL, B. **163** Corbis/Bettmann. **164** AA/Saint Stephen's Cathedral Vienna/Alfredo Dagli Orti, L; MEPL, R. **165** GI/Time & Life Pictures. **166** The Kobal Collection/Selznick/United Artists. **167** Reproduced with permission of Punch Ltd, www.punch.co.uk, T; PA Photos/AP/ Sigmund Freud Museum, B. **168** Corbis/epa/Nic Bothma, T; The University Library, University of Sussex, Brighton, B. **169** AA/Musée du Louvre Paris/Gianni Dagli Orti. **170** John Meek, T; Camera Press/ Gamma/Eric Vandeville, B. **171** MEPL. **172** AA/Musée du Louvre Paris/Gianni Dagli Orti. **173** Camera Press/Alessandro Della Valle/ Keystone. **174** © Discovery Channel/ photo by John Spaulding. **175** Corbis/Jim Craigmyle. **176** Corbis/Staffan Widstrand, T. **176-177** Panos/Sven Torfinn. **178** AA/Alfredo Dagli Orti. **179** Bradbury & Williams, T, AA/Private Collection/ Gianni Dagli Orti, BR. **180** akg-images/ Erich Lessing, T; Bradbury & Williams, B. **181** AA/Biblioteca Comunale Palermo/Gianni Dagli Orti, T; AA/ Archaeological Museum Florence/Gianni Dagli Orti, B. **182** AA/ Marc Charmet. **183** AA/Private Collection/Marc Charmet. **184** Panos/Ami Vitale. **185** Rex Features/Sipa Press. **186** Science & Society Picture Library/Science Museum, MR; Vint Cerf, BR. **187** ©CERN, BL; SPL/David Parker, MR; Google logo ©2008, Reprinted with permission, BR. **188** Still Pictures/ Biosphoto/ Michel Gunther, BL; GI, TR. **189** Still Pictures/ K.Thomas. **190** Douglas Engelbart/ Bootstrap Alliance. **191** Mat Allen/ Courtesy Commodore International Corporation. **192** Reuters/ Kimberly White. **193** PA Photos, T; SPL/NIBSC, B. **194** Map: The World Health Organisation. **195** Panos/ Penny Tweedie. **196** AA/Egyptian Museum Cairo/Gianni Dagli Orti, BL; GI, BM. **197** AA/Musée Guimet, Paris/Gianni Dagli Orti, T; AA /Anti-Vaccine Society/ Eileen Tweedy, B. **198** Corbis/Bettmann. **199** SPL/Will & Deni McIntyre. **200** GI/Time & Life Pictures. **201** SPL. **202** SPL/ Philippe Psaila. **203** Reuters/Str Old, T; GI, BL, BR. **204** *Frost Fair on the Thames, with Old London Bridge in the Distance, painting formerly attributed to Jan Wyck (1640-1700), c.1685 (oil on canvas), English School, (17th century).* Yale Center for British Art, Paul Mellon Collection, USA/ BAL. **205** Photoshot/ World Illustrated. **206** Natural History Museum/ Ancient Human Occupation of Britain. **207** SPL/Peter Bowater. **208** AA/British Library. **209** SPL/AGSTOCKUSA/N.Warren Winter. **210** AA/ Musée de la Renaissance (Château) Ecouen/ Gianni Dagli Orti, T; AA/Eileen Tweedy, B. **211** Werner Forman Archive/ Thjodminjasafn, Reykjavik, Iceland (National Museum). **212** AA/Topkapi Museum, Istanbul/Gianni Dagli Orti, T; The Long Now Foundation/Rolfe Horn, B. **213** © Angelo Hornak. **214** AA/Torre Aquila Trento/Gianni Dagli Orti. **215** Topfoto/ HIP/National Motor Museum, T; Topfoto, MR. **216** GI, T; *Coalbrookdale by Night, 1801 (oil on canvas), Loutherbourg, Philip James (Jacques) de (1740-1812).* Science Museum, London, UK/BAL, B. **217** Rex Features/Alinari/A.Bruni. **218** Reuters/Lucas Jackson. **219** Image courtesy of the Advertising Archives/ Electrolux Home Products, Inc. **220** AA/ Private Collection/Gianni Dagli Orti. **221** akg-images/ British Library. **222** AA/Courage Breweries/Eileen Tweedy. **223** Image courtesy of the Advertising Archive/Encyclopedia Britannica, Inc., T; Corbis/ Gideon Mendel, B. **224-225** AA/ Musée du Louvre Paris/Gianni Dagli Orti. **224** Royal Mint, T. **225** *A Cloth Merchant Measuring Cloth (fresco), Italian School, (15th century).* Castello di Issogne, Val d'Aosta, Italy, Giraudon/BAL, T. **226** *A Mughal Princess in her Garden (gouache on paper), Indian School, (18th century).* Free Library, Philadelphia, PA, USA/BAL. **228** AA/Alfredo Dagli Orti, T. Still Pictures/Das Fotoarchiv/ Markus Matzel, B. **229** AA/ National Archive Washington DC, T; Copyright Bank of England, B. **230** GI/Time & Life Pictures. **231** Corbis/Robert Harding World Imagery/Gary Cook, T; *Tulipa Octaviani del pont, and Tulipa Elegant, from 'Hortus Floridus', published 1614-15 (coloured engraving), Passe, Crispin I de (c.1565-1637).* Private Collection, The Stapleton Collection/BAL, B. **232** Corbis/ Hulton-Deutsch Collection. **233** *Stage Waggon, engraved by J. Baily, pub. by J. Watson, 1820 (engraving), English School, (19th century).* Private Collection/BAL, T; *The Lamplighter, from 'Les Femmes de Paris', 1841-42 (colour litho), Geniole, Alfred Andre (1813-61).* Musée de la Ville de Paris, Musee Carnavalet, Paris, France, Lauros/ Giraudon/BAL, B. **234** Corbis/Bettmann. **234-235** Alamy/

Jon Arnold Images Ltd. **236** AA/Palenque Site Museum Chiapas/ Gianni Dagli Orti. **237** MEPL/ILN Pictures. **238** *Captain John Smith (1580-1631), 1st Governor of Virginia, c.1616 (oil on canvas), English School, (17th century).* Private Collection/BAL, T; *View of New York (oil on canvas), Dutch School, (17th century).* Private Collection/BAL, B. **239** Map: US Census Bureau **240-241** Corbis. **242** Library of Congress Prints and Photographs Division. **243** GI/ChinaFotoPress. **244** AA/Museo della Civilta Romana, Rome/Gianni Dagli Orti. **245** *The Brook, 1874 (oil on canvas), Foster, Myles Birket (1825-99).* © Manchester Art Gallery, UK/BAL, T, GI, BL; GI/Roger Viollet/ Lipnitzki, BM; GI/Sean Gallup, BR. **246** PA Photos/ AP/Ed Betz. **247** *Ms.Supp.Pers. 1113. fol.44v Temujin has himself proclaimed Genghis Khan, his sons Ogodei and Jochi to the right, from a book by Rashid al-Din (ink and gouache on vellum), Persian School, (14th century).* Bibliothèque Nationale, Paris, France/BAL. **248** GI/ AFP/Adrian Dennis. **249** Roy Knipe, www.thorogood.net. **250** akg-images. **251** AA/Alfredo Dagli Orti, T; Courtesy of the National Watch & Clock Museum, Columbia, Pennsylvania USA, B. **252** Corbis/ Anna Clopet. **253** *Portrait of Prince Rupert (1619-82) (oil on canvas), English School, (17th century).* Private Collection/BAL, B. **254** Corbis Sygma. **255** *Marriage of Queen Victoria (1819-1901) and Prince Albert (1819-61) at St. James's Palace on 10th February 1840, engraved by Charles Eden Wagstaff, 1840 (etching) (b/w photo), English School, (19th century).* The Illustrated London News Picture Library, London, UK/ BAL. **256** *Mary of Modena's wedding ring, 1674 (gold & ruby), Italian School, (17th century).* His Grace The Duke of Norfolk, Arundel Castle/BAL, T; Reuters/ Stoyan Nenov, B. **257** AA/Santa Maria della Scala Hospital Siena/Alfredo Dagli Orti. **258** AA/ Bibliothèque Nationale, Paris, T; akg-images/ Erich Lessing, B. **259** AA/Ragab Papyrus Institute Cairo/Gianni Dagli Orti. **260** Rex Features/Chris Martin Bahr. **261** AA/Malmaison Musée du Château/Gianni Dagli Orti, T; Reproduced by permission of the Henry Moore Foundation/ GI/Time & Life Pictures, B. **262** AA/British Museum/Alfredo Dagli Orti, T; AA/Musée Cernuschi Paris/Gianni Dagli Orti, B. **263** Corbis/ Edifice/Graham Miller. **264** AA/Museo del Prado Madrid/ Gianni Dagli Orti, T; *Young Portuguese, Persian, 1634 (w/c, gold and ink on paper), Abbasi, Riza-i (c.1565-1635).* The Detroit Institute of Arts, USA, Gift of Robert H. Tannahill in memory of Dr W.R. Valentiner/BAL, B. **265** Corbis/Reuters/ China Daily. **266** Alamy/Chad Ehlers. **267** Photolibrary Group/ Foodpix/ Brian Hagiwara. **268** MEPL. **269** The Coca-Cola Company. **270** MEPL, T; *Roy 20 C VII f.44v Burning of the Templars, c.1308 (vellum), French School, (14th century).* British Library, London, UK, © British Library Board. All Rights Reserved/BAL, B. **271** *Hand in the attitude of benediction embellished with charms to increase its power, late Roman period (bronze).* British Museum, London, UK/BAL, T; *Bracelets and good luck charms, 19th and 20th centuries (gold and semiprecious stones).* Private Collection, Archives Charmet/ BAL, B. **272** AA/Mireille Vautier. **273** GI, T; AA/Bodleian Library Oxford, B. **274** GI/National Geographic/Martin Gray. **275** *Roy 18 D II f.148 Lydgate and the Canterbury Pilgrims Leaving Canterbury from the 'Troy Book and the Siege of Thebes' by John Lydgate (c.1370-c.1451) 1412-22 (vellum) (detail of 8063), English School, (15th century).* British Library, London, UK, © British Library Board. All Rights Reserved/BAL. **276** GI/Guang Niu. **277** *Souvenir of the Pilgrimage to Lourdes, made for the International Exhibition in Paris, 1867 (colour litho), French School, (19th century).* Private Collection, Archives Charmet/ BAL. **278** AA/University Museum Cuzco/Mireille Vautier. **279** PA Photos/AP/Toronto Star/Rick Madonik. **280** PA Photos/ AP. **281** GI/AFP. **283** Topfoto/Roger-Viollet. **284** MEPL, T. **284-285** PA Photos/AP/Kevin Elliott. **286** Corbis, T; *The Interior of the 'Gustave-Zedei' while Underwater, 1899 (colour engraving), French School, (19th century).* Private Collection, Archives Charmet/BAL, B. **287** GI/ Popperfoto. **288** AA/Victoria and Albert Museum London/ Eileen Tweedy. **290** AA/Australian War Memorial. **291** Topfoto/ullsteinbild. **292** AA/Burgerbibliothek Bern/Eileen Tweedy. **293** GI/Christopher Furlong. **294** PA Photos/ AP. **295** GI. **296** GI/AFP/Gerard Leroux. **297** MEPL/The Women's Library, T; Topfoto/AP, B. **298** Reuters/Jason Lee. **299** akg-images, L; AA, R. **300** *11th or the Prince Albert's Own Regiment of Hussars, from the Historical Records of the British Army, c.1843.* British Museum, London, UK/BAL, T; Corbis/Vittoriano Rastelli, BL; akg-images, BM, BR. **301** Reuters/Umit Bektas. **302** *Barbarians!, plate 38 of 'The Disasters of War', 1810-14, pub. 1863 (etching), Goya y Lucientes, Francisco Jose de (1746-1828).* Private Collection, Index/BAL, T; *Surgeons from the Japanese Red Cross, from 'Le Petit Journal', 1905 (colour litho), French School, (20th century).* Bibliothèque Nationale, Paris, France, Archives Charmet/BAL, B. **303** GI/AFP/Jerry Lampen. **304** akg-images. **305** GI. **306** Topfoto. **306-307** GI/Travelpix Ltd, B. **308** akg-images. **309** akg-images/ ullstein bild. **310** *'Wha Wants Me', cartoon showing Tom Paine and the Rights of Man by Isaac Cruikshank (1756-1811/16).* British Library, London, UK, © British Library Board. All Rights Reserved/BAL, T; AA/Society of Apothecaries/Eileen Tweedy, B. **311** akg-images/ullstein bild. **312** David King. **313** Reuters/HO Old, T; Corbis/Bettmann, B.

How It All Started was published by The Reader's Digest Association Ltd, London. It was created and produced for Reader's Digest by Toucan Books Ltd, London.

First edition copyright © 2008

The Reader's Digest Association Limited
11 Westferry Circus, Canary Wharf
London E14 4HE
www.readersdigest.co.uk

We are committed both to the quality of our products and the service we provide to our customers. We value your comments, so do contact us on 08705 113366 or via our website at **www.readersdigest.co.uk**

If you have any comments or suggestions about the content of our books, you can email us at **gbeditorial@readersdigest.co.uk**

CONSULTANT Asa Briggs

WRITERS Tony Allen, Jonathan Bastable, Ruth Binney, Jeremy Harwood, Tim Healey and Antony Mason

FOR TOUCAN BOOKS
Editors Jo Bourne with Alice Peebles, Natasha Kahn, Donald Sommerville
Picture researchers Caroline Wood with Angela Anderson, Jane Lambert, Mia Stewart-Wilson, Sharon Southren
Picture manager Christine Vincent
Proofreader Marion Dent
Indexer Michael Dent
Editorial assistant Tom Pocklington
Fact checker Jacob Field
Design Bradbury and Williams
Maps Red Lion Mapping

FOR READER'S DIGEST
Editor Lisa Thomas
Art editor Julie Bennett
Pre-press account manager Dean Russell
Product production manager Claudette Bramble
Production controller Katherine Bunn

READER'S DIGEST, GENERAL BOOKS, UK
Editorial director Julian Browne
Art director Anne-Marie Bulat
Head of book development Sarah Bloxham
Managing editor Nina Hathway
Picture resource manager Sarah Stewart-Richardson

Colour origination Colour Systems Ltd, London
Printed and bound by Ajanta Offset, India

The publishers would like to thank Stephen Oppenheimer for his assistance with the feature 'Under the skin', and for permission to base artwork on the original map from his book *Out of Eden: The peopling of the world*, Constable, 2004. Thanks are also due to Sir Alan Munro for advice on the Middle East and to Sheena Meredith for help with the AIDs feature.

Pictures in chapter introductions

1 Nations and Cities *pages 8-9*
Plan of New Amsterdam (later New York), 1660; a view of skyscrapers along Wall Street, Lower Manhattan, c.2006

2 Eating and drinking *pages 52-53*
A banquet for a visiting archbishop in Venice, 1755; sushi circulating at a Japanese restaurant, Bluewater shopping mall, UK

3 Greatest show on Earth *pages 82-83*
A charioteer receiving his trophy after winning a race in Rome, 1st century AD; Liverpool captain Steven Gerrard and team triumphant after the Champions League final, Istanbul, Turkey, 2005

4 Religion and ideas *pages 126-127*
Soviet poster celebrating the power of Communism, c.1920; Tibetan monks in Kathmandu protesting peacefully against the Chinese crackdown in Tibet, 2008

5 Discovery and change *pages 172-173*
Relief of an ancient Egyptian scribe, Saqqara, c.2500 BC; young woman at her laptop in the Gardens of Turia, Valencia, Spain, 2007

6 Living and working *pages 208-209*
Planting herbs in a walled garden in 15th-century France; growing tobacco without soil in a commercial greenhouse, Kansas, USA

7 Why do they do it like that? *pages 242-243*
A 17th-century samurai in elaborate regalia; rock fans at the Midi Music festival in Beijing, 2006

8 War and peace *pages 278-279*
Inca warrior on a painted wooden vase, Cuzco, c.1200; a Canadian soldier on foot patrol in Afghanistan, scanning through his gun sight, 2006

Concept code:	UK2268/G
Book code:	400-338 UP0000-1
ISBN:	978 0 276 44338 1
Oracle code:	250011783H.00.24